Inclusion

Inclusion
A Guide for Educators

edited by

Susan Stainback, Ed.D.
and
William Stainback, Ed.D.

University of Northern Iowa

·P·A·U·L·H·
BROOKES
PUBLISHING Co.

Baltimore • London • Toronto • Sydney

Paul H. Brookes Publishing Co.
Post Office Box 10624
Baltimore, Maryland 21285-0624

Typeset by Signature Typesetting & Design, Baltimore, Maryland.
Manufactured in the United States of America by
The Maple Press Company, York, Pennsylvania.

Library of Congress Cataloging-in-Publication Data
Inclusion: a guide for educators / edited by Susan Stainback and William Stainback
   p.   cm.
   Includes bibliographical references and index.
   ISBN 1-55766-231-2
   1. Mainstreaming in education—United States.   2. Classroom management—United
States. 3. Special education—United States.   4. Problem children—Education—United
States.   I. Stainback, Susan Bray.   II. Stainback, William C.
LC3981.I637   1996
371.9′046′0973—dc20   95-42607
                                                                     CIP

British Library Cataloguing-in-Publication data are available from the British Library.

Contents

I BACKGROUND

II BASIC STRATEGIES

III COLLABORATION

IV CURRICULUM CONSIDERATIONS

V BEHAVIORAL CONSIDERATIONS

VI OTHER CONSIDERATIONS

Contributors

Sandy Alper, Ph.D.
Chair
Department of Special Education
University of Northern Iowa
Cedar Falls, IA 50613-0601

Jennifer Asmus, Ed.S.
Intern
Pediatric Psychology
University of Iowa
251 University Hospital School
Iowa City, IA 52242-1011

Wendy K. Berg, M.S.
Senior Research Assistant
University of Iowa
251 University Hospital School
Iowa City, IA 52242-1011

Kathryn D. Bishop, Ph.D.
Associate Professor
University of San Diego
School of Education
5998 Alcala Park
San Diego, CA 92110

Barbara E. Buswell
Co-Director
PEAK Parent Center
6055 Lehman Drive, Suite 101
Colorado Springs, CO 80918

Katheryn East, Ed.D.
Instructor
Department of Educational Psychology
University of Northern Iowa
Cedar Falls, IA 50614

Mary A. Falvey, Ph.D.
Professor
School of Education
California State University
5151 State University Drive
Los Angeles, CA 90032

Marsha Forest, Ed.D.
Centre for Integrated Education and
   Community
Inclusion Press International
24 Thome Crescent
Toronto, Ontario M6H 2S5
CANADA

Michael F. Giangreco, Ph.D.
Research Assistant Professor
University of Vermont
College of Education and Social Services
University Affiliated Program of Vermont
499C Waterman Building
Burlington, VT 05405-0160

Christine C. Givner, Ph.D.
Associate Professor
School of Education
Division of Special Education
California State University
5151 State University Drive
Los Angeles, CA 90032

Jay Harding, Ed.S.
Project Coordinator
University of Iowa
251 University Hospital School
Iowa City, IA 52242-1011

Wade Hitzing, Ph.D.
Director
Society for Community Support
1045 Wittman Drive
Fort Meyers, FL 33919

Annette Iverson, Ph.D., NCSP
Associate Professor
Department of Educational Psychology and
  Foundations
University of Northern Iowa
Cedar Falls, IA 50614

Cheryl M. Jorgensen, Ph.D.
Institute on Disability/University Affiliated
  Program
University of New Hampshire
312 Morrill Hall
Durham, NH 03824

Kimberlee A. Jubala, M.Ed.
Educator
San Diego Unified School District
851 Chalcedony
San Diego, CA 92109

Anastasios Karagiannis, Ph.D.
Assistant Professor
Department of Educational and Counselling
  Psychology
Faculty of Education
3700 McTavish
McGill University
Montreal, Quebec QC H3A 1Y2
CANADA

Christina Kimm, Ph.D.
Associate Professor
California State University
5151 State University Drive
Los Angeles, CA 90032

Herbert Lovett, Ph.D.
76 G Street
Boston, MA 02127-2919

Connie Lyle O'Brien
Responsive Systems Associated
58 Willowwick Drive
Lithonia, GA 30038-1722

John O'Brien
Responsive Systems Associated
58 Willowwick Drive
Lithonia, GA 30038-1722

Jack Pearpoint, Ph.D.
President
Inclusion Press International
24 Thome Crescent
Toronto, Ontario M6H 2S5
CANADA

Michael Peterson, Ph.D.
Professor
Special Education and Rehabilitation
Division of Teacher Education
College of Education
Wayne State University
217 Education Building
Detroit, MI 48202

Diane Lea Ryndak, Ph.D.
Assistant Professor
Department of Special Education
G315 Norman Hall
University of Florida at Gainesville
Gainesville, FL 32611-7050

Daniel D. Sage, Ed.D.
Professor Emeritus
Syracuse University
Editor
Inclusion Times
208 Breakspear Road
Syracuse, NY 13219

Mara Sapon-Shevin, Ed.D.
Professor
Teaching and Leadership Program
Syracuse University
150 Huntington Hall
Syracuse, NY 13244-2340

C. Beth Schaffner
Coordinator of Inclusive Schooling
PEAK Parent Center
6055 Lehman Drive
Suite 101
Colorado Springs, CO 80918

Maureen Smith, Ph.D.
Assistant Professor
Department of Exceptional Education
State University College of Buffalo
1300 Elmwood
Buffalo, NY 14222

Lynne C. Sommerstein, M.Ed.
Co-Chair, New York Schools Are For
  Everyone (SAFE)
15 Shadow Wood Drive, East
Amhurst, NY 14051

Susan Stainback, Ed.D.
Professor
College of Education
University of Northern Iowa
Cedar Falls, IA 50614

William Stainback, Ed.D.
Professor
College of Education
University of Northern Iowa
Cedar Falls, IA 50614

Greg Stefanich, Ed.D.
Professor
Department of Curriculum and Instruction
University of Northern Iowa
Cedar Falls, IA 50614

Cindy Strully, M.A.
Jay Nolan Community Services
25006 Avenue Kearny
Valencia, CA 91355

Jeffrey L. Strully, Ed.D.
Jay Nolan Community Services
25006 Avenue Kearny
Valencia, CA 91355

Jacqueline S. Thousand, Ph.D.
Research Associate Professor
University of Vermont
College of Education and Social Services
499C Waterman Building
Burlington, VT 05405

Richard A. Villa, Ed.D.
President
Bayridge Educational Consortium
6 Bay Ridge Estates
41 Lakeshore Drive
Colchester, VT 05446

David P. Wacker, Ph.D.
Professor of Pediatric Psychology
University of Iowa
251 University Hospital School
Iowa City, IA 52242-1011

Marilyn R. Wessels
Co-Chair, New York Schools Are For
  Everyone (SAFE)
Gatehouse
1365 VanAntwerp Apartments
Schenectady, NY 12309

Preface

Inclusive classrooms start with a philosophy that all children can learn and belong in the main-stream of school and community life. Diversity is valued; it is believed that diversity strengthens the class and offers all of its members greater opportunities for learning.

Robert Barth (1990), a Harvard professor, described the value of diversity as follows:

I would prefer my children to be in a school in which differences are looked for, attended to, and celebrated as good news, as opportunities for learning. The question with which so many school people are preoccupied is, "What are the limits of diversi-ty beyond which behavior is unacceptable?"… But the question I would like to see asked more often is, "How can we make conscious, deliberate use of differences in social class, gender, age, ability, race, and interest as resources for learning?"… Differ-ences hold great opportunities for learning. Differences offer a free, abundant, and renewable resource. I would like to see our compulsion for eliminating differences replaced by an equally compelling focus on making use of these differences to improve schools. What is important about people—and about schools—is what is dif-ferent, not what is the same. (pp. 514–515)

The editors and contributing authors of *Inclusion: A Guide for Educators* strongly believe that diversity should be valued. But what are some basic, practical strategies for making use of differences in race, ability, gender, and social class to enhance learning for *all* students? While maintaining a steadfast, positive philosophy and attitude regarding inclusion is the *key* to achiev-ing success, teachers and other personnel also need to be aware of practical strategies they can utilize on a daily basis in the classroom, school, and community to enhance successful inclusion.

The terms *inclusive school* and *restructuring* or *school renewal* are often used in this book. Thus, it might be helpful to review here what is meant by these terms. An *inclusive school* is one that educates all students in the mainstream. Educating all students in the mainstream means that every student is in general education and general classes. It also means that all students are pro-vided with appropriate educational opportunities within the mainstream that are challenging yet geared to their capabilities and needs; they are likewise provided with any support and assistance they or their teachers may need to be successful in the mainstream. But an inclusive school also goes beyond this. An inclusive school is a place where everyone belongs, is accepted, supports, and is supported by his or her peers and other members of the school community in the course of having his or her educational needs met.

The terms *school renewal* and *restructuring* also are used throughout the professional liter-ature of the 1990s in education and in this book. These terms mean different things to different people, but essentially the terms are used to describe the need to transform the public schools into caring and sensitive institutions capable of responding in humane and effective ways to the unique needs and capabilities of all students. This involves more than the renegotiation and reor-ganization of the boundaries and structures of special and general education, the placement of students with disabilities in general education classes, the way we assess the needs and capabilities of students and instruct them, or how we organize the school day. It also means, and perhaps much more important, the rethinking of our attitudes and beliefs about children, education, and the atmosphere and culture(s) of schools throughout the United States and other countries.

The primary focus of this book is on practical strategies that capitalize on differences among students and school personnel to enhance social success and educational achievement for all students. The book is composed of 26 chapters divided into six sections. The authors briefly review in Section I the rationale for and historical overview of inclusive schooling as well as outline why inclusion can be a force for school renewal. Basic, fundamental practical strategies for achieving successful inclusion are outlined and discussed in Section II. In Section III, attention is turned to the question of "How can students, teachers, and a variety of other school personnel collaborate together to design and implement specific strategies for achieving social and educational success for all students?" Presented in Section IV are numerous procedures for and examples of how the curriculum in general education classrooms can be designed and adapted to meet all students' needs. The topic of Section V is behavioral concerns in inclusive classrooms and specific practical strategies for facilitating positive behaviors and reducing inappropriate ones. In Section VI, the authors address the concern of how all students can maintain a positive self-identity and concept in inclusive classrooms. Also discussed in Section VI is how families and school personnel can work closely together to promote inclusive schooling for all students. In the final chapter in this section, the authors address the major concerns some people have about full inclusion of all students into the mainstream of the public schools.

The compilation of this text could not have been possible without the contributions of many people. The editors would like to take this opportunity to laud the outstanding contribution of each of the contributing authors. In addition, the contributions of the many students, parents, educators, and other community members who offered their ideas, concerns, and moral support throughout the development of this book are acknowledged. We also are grateful to Dr. Sandy Alper, who has provided encouragement and support for all our scholarly endeavors, including this book. Finally, we would like to heartily thank our colleagues at Paul H. Brookes Publishing Co., who have encouraged and contributed significantly to the sharing of the ideas and concepts of the many authors in this book.

REFERENCE

Barth, R. (1990). A personal vision of a good school. *Phi Delta Kappan, 71,* 512–571.

Inclusion

I

BACKGROUND

1

Rationale for Inclusive Schooling

Anastasios Karagiannis,
William Stainback, and Susan Stainback

EXCLUSION IN SCHOOLS sows the seeds of social discontent and discrimination. Education is a human rights issue and persons with disabilities should be part of schools, which should modify their operations to include all students. This is the message that was clearly articulated at the 1994 UNESCO World Conference on Special Educational Needs (International League of Societies for Persons with Mental Handicap, 1994). In a wider sense, inclusive schooling is the practice of including everyone—irrespective of talent, disability, socioeconomic background, or cultural origin—in supportive mainstream schools and classrooms where all student needs are met. This chapter discusses the reasons for inclusive schooling in terms of benefits to students, teachers, and society. By educating all students together, persons with disabilities have the opportunity to prepare for life in the community, teachers improve their professional skills, and society makes the conscious decision to operate according to the social value of equality for all people with the consequent results of enhanced social peace. To achieve inclusive schooling, general and special educators and resources must come together in a unified, consistent effort.

There are three interdependent practical components in inclusive schooling. First, support networking, the organizational component, involves the coordination of teams and individuals who support each other by formal and informal connections (Stainback & Stainback, 1990a, 1990b, 1990c; Villa & Thousand, 1990). Stone and Collicott (1994) have described a successful three-layered system of networking: school-based service teams, district-based service teams, and partnerships with community agencies. All of these teams function in a mutually supportive way to empower staff and

3

students. Second, collaborative consultation and teaming, the procedural component, involves individuals with a variety of expertise who work together to plan and implement programs for diverse students in mainstream environments (Harris, 1990; Porter, Wilson, Kelly, & den Otter, 1991; Pugach & Johnson, 1990; Thousand & Villa, 1990). Third, cooperative learning, the instructional component, relates to the creation of a classroom learning atmosphere in which students of varying abilities and interests can achieve their potential (Johnson & Johnson, 1986; Sapon-Shevin, 1990). Heterogeneous grouping (Slavin, 1987), peer tutoring in various forms (Delquadri, Greenwood, Whorton, Carta, & Hall, 1986; Jenkins & Jenkins, 1981; Osguthorpe & Scruggs, 1986; Stainback, Stainback, & Hatcher, 1983), and learning groups for instructional and recreational activities (Aronson, 1978; DeVries & Slavin, 1978) are some of the elements of cooperative learning. More recently, multilevel instruction (Collicott, 1991; Stone & Moore, 1994) has synthesized the elements of cooperative learning into a cohesive approach.

The benefits of inclusive arrangements are multiple for everyone involved in schools—all students, teachers, and society as a whole. Programmatic and supportive facilitation of inclusion in the organization and processes of schools and classrooms is a decisive factor in success.

BENEFITS TO ALL STUDENTS

In the words of Vandercook, Fleetham, Sinclair, and Tetlie (1988), "in integrated classrooms all children are enriched by having the opportunity to learn from one another, grow to care for one another, and gain the attitudes, skills, and values necessary for our communities to support the inclusion of all citizens" (p. 19). However, simply including students with disabilities into general education classrooms may not result in learning benefits (e.g., Marston, 1987–1988). It has consistently been found that students with a variety and various levels of disability learn more in integrated settings when appropriate educational experiences and support are provided than they do in segregated settings (Brinker & Thorpe, 1983, 1984; Epps & Tindal, 1987). When proper arrangements are present, inclusion works for all students with and without disabilities in terms of mutually held positive attitudes, gains in academic and social skills, and preparation for living in the community.

Positive Attitudes

Positive attitudes toward students with disabilities develop when appropriate guidance and direction from adults are provided in integrated settings (Forest, 1987a, 1987b; Johnson & Johnson, 1984; Karagiannis, 1988; Karagiannis & Cartwright, 1990; Stainback & Stainback, 1988; Strully, 1986, 1987). Facilitated interaction and communication aid in the development of friendships and peer work. Students learn to be sensitive to, understand, respect, and grow comfortable with individual differences and similarities among their peers.

Gains in Academic and Social Skills

Apart from positive attitudes, research since the early 1970s has repeatedly shown the tremendous benefits that children gain from socialization with their peers during the school years (see Johnson & Johnson, 1987, for a review). Children learn many academic skills (Madden & Slavin, 1983) as well as daily life, communication, and social skills (Cullinan, Sabornie, & Crossland, 1992) through sustained interactions with their peers. All students, including those with disabilities, need both teacher–student and student–student interactions that model academic and social skills.

For students with significant cognitive disabilities, it is a good idea not to be preoccupied with academic skills. Strain (1983) has supported that "it is quite reasonable to question the predominant and pervasive segregation of autistic-like children into 'handicapped' only groups" (p. 23). For these students, the opportunity to acquire social skills by being included is what matters. In a dispute over placement in El Paso, Texas, the United States Court of Appeals for the Fifth Circuit stated that "although a handicapped child may not be able to absorb all of the regular education curriculum, he may benefit from nonacademic experiences in the regular education environment" (*Daniel, R.R. v. State Board of Education*). Persons with disabilities become ready for community living when they are included in schools and classrooms.

Preparation for Community Living

In general, the more time students with disabilities spend in inclusive settings, the better they do educationally, socially, and occupationally (Ferguson & Asch, 1989; Wehman, 1990). Some parents intuitively know that inclusive schooling increases their child's opportunities for adjustment in life:

> When she's finished with school, she'll be able to be in some sort of integrated situation. She'll have social skills she wouldn't have had and an ability to function in more complex situations than she would've been able to do if she'd stayed segregated. (Hanline & Halvorsen, 1989, p. 490)

Professionals who have the opportunity for close contact with children in schools understand the importance of schools in preparing students with disabilities for community life. Two teacher aides in an inclusion project expressed this understanding quite clearly:

> Because they're with their peers, to keep up... they want to do what the other children are doing. It's encouragement for them, they see what is going on around them, they're being stimulated all the time.... It's as simple as that....
>
> I can see it every day... when I first dealt with [Tia] a few years ago... she was very quiet.... Now I can see her in the schoolyard or waiting for the bus talking... [and] getting involved with the other children....
>
> Tia said one day to me that she'd like to be a teacher.... [Y]ears ago, if she had told me that, I would have said "there's no way that this child can"... and now I have to sit here and say "yes, some day she will be able to teach children how to read." (Karagiannis, 1988, pp. 146–147)

Avoiding the Harmful Effects of Exclusion

When these positive effects are contrasted with the negative effects of exclusion, the benefits of inclusive schools become even more pronounced. Academically, socially, and occupationally segregated placements are damaging to students. After conducting a series of studies, Wehman (1990) concluded that "[s]egregated classes do not lead to independence and competence, but instead foster an unrealistic sense of insulation" (p. 43). *Brown v. Board of Education* (1954), clearly stated that separate education can

> generate a feeling of inferiority as to [children's] status in the community that may affect their hearts and minds.... This sense of inferiority... affects the motivation of the child to learn... [and] has a tendency to retard... educational and mental development. (p. 493)

This concern is reflected in the experiences of individuals with disabilities who have been placed in segregated environments. A student who attended separate special classes throughout his school years stated that

> The only contact we had with the "normal" children was visual. We stared at each other. On those occasions, I can report my own feelings: embarrassment.... I can also report their feelings: Yech! We, the children in the "handicapped" class, were internalizing the "yech" message—plus a couple of others. We were in school because children go to school, but we were outcasts with no future and no expectation of one. (Massachusetts Advocacy Center, 1987, pp. 4–5)

Another person with disabilities who was segregated in her school years reported:

> I graduated... completely unprepared for the real world. So I just stayed in the house all day, a shut-in, believing a job was out of the question.... Believe me, a segregated environment will not do as preparation for an integrated life.... (Massachusetts Advocacy Center, 1987, p. 4)

In general, segregated placements are harmful because they alienate students. Students with disabilities ultimately receive little useful education for real life, and students without disabilities ultimately experience an education that places little value on diversity, cooperation, and respect for others who are different. In contrast, inclusive schooling provides persons with disabilities the opportunity to acquire skills for the workplace and the community. Students with disabilities learn how to function and interact with their peers in the "real" world. Equally important, their peers as well as teachers learn how to function and interact with them.

BENEFITS TO TEACHERS

What is at issue in inclusive schooling is not whether students should receive appropriate educational experiences and specialized tools and techniques they need from qualified school personnel and specialists. The issue is that students should receive these services in integrated settings and that teachers should be assisted in updating their skills. The face of schools in our evolving society is changing, and teachers "must acquire new skills in working with students who are academically and socially disadvantaged" (Schloss, 1992, p. 242). In this transformation of the teaching profession, teachers have the opportunity to develop their professional skills in an atmosphere of collegiality, collaboration, and peer support. The benefits are several.

Collaborative Support and Improvement of Professional Skills

The first benefit to teachers is the opportunity to plan and conduct the business of education as part of a team. Many teachers feel alienated in schools because the ethic of teaching by one's self provides few or no chances for supportive peer interaction. Collaboration allows teachers to consult with each other and to provide psychological support.

Second, peer collaboration and consultation help teachers to better their professional capabilities. In a summary of research regarding the important features and outcomes of the consultation and teaming process, Elliott and Sheridan (1992) concluded that teachers "exposed to consultation services believe that their professional skills have improved" (p. 319). In addition, the authors concluded that the number of children referred for special education services decreased significantly after 4–5 years of consultation services and that children with special needs tended to do better in school. The implications of the research are clear: When there is supportive school collaboration, teachers improve their skills with visible effects on student learning.

Participation and Empowerment

The third benefit to teachers is that they become aware of developments in education, are able to anticipate changes, and take part in shaping daily school life. In the words of Sindelar, Griffin, Smith, and Watanabe (1992), teachers "are empowered by elevating their status, keeping themselves informed of changes occurring in their fields, and ensuring that they participate in decision making" (p. 249). Research has indicated that the majority of general educators are willing to join special educators in making general education classes more flexible and conducive to learning by students with disabilities if they are involved in the planning process and have choices about the design and types of support and assistance they will receive (Giangreco, Dennis, Cloninger, Edelman, & Schattman, 1993; Myles & Simpson, 1989) and receive in-service training.

The transformational experiences of many teachers who participate in inclusive arrangements are striking, even when initial reactions are negative:

> I made the full swing of fighting against having Bobbi Sue placed in my room to fighting for her to be in a mainstream classroom working with kids in the way that she had worked with them all year long. I'm a perfect example of how you have to have an open mind. (Giangreco et al., 1993, p. 365)

For some teachers, adapting their teaching to include students with disabilities is an easy transition, almost anticlimactic after the initial anticipation has worn off:

> Having Ellen right there, you have to deal with it; and I found out that I can do it. There is nothing here that is very different than getting along with a whole lot of other people in life. (Giangreco et al., 1993, p. 365)

Assisting teachers to become better professionals in the context of inclusion makes them aware that instructional challenges will eventually benefit all students:

I've used a lot of the ideas that I started out using last year because I spent a lot of time thinking about them to incorporate Katie. I've used them again this year even though I don't have a special needs kid because I found them successful with the regular ed kids.... (Giangreco et al., 1993, p. 370)

BENEFITS TO SOCIETY

By far the most important reason for inclusive schooling is the social value of equality. We teach students by example that, despite differences, we all have equal rights. In contrast to the past experiences of segregation, inclusion reinforces the practice of the idea that differences are accepted and respected. Because our societies are in a critical phase of evolving from industrial to informational and from national to international, it is important that we avoid the mistakes of the past. We need schools that promote wider social acceptance, peace, and cooperation.

The Social Value of Equality

The *Brown v. Board of Education* decision made clear that separate is *not* equal. It is simply discriminatory that students labeled disabled must earn the right or become ready to be in the educational mainstream. It is nonsensical to wait for educational researchers to prove that they can profit from the mainstream education while other students are allowed unrestricted access simply because they have no such label. No student should have to pass a test or wait for favorable research results to live and learn in the mainstream of school and community life. Inclusive schooling makes sense and is a basic right—not something one has to earn.

When schools include all students, then equality is respected and promoted as a value in society, with the visible results of social peace and cooperation. Following are the statements of three parents whose children attended an elementary school that included students with disabilities:

I think that this integration has broadened and deepened my child's understanding of the diversity of the human condition. It has, to some extent, extended the degree to which he can empathize with others, and brought forth a sense of responsibility to be humane and helpful....

He knows there is a difference between himself and the handicapped child—but he accepts it as a difference and not as something to be afraid of or make fun of, a part of life....

My child is not really familiar with the difference between a regular and a mentally handicapped child. When I tried to explain the difference, he said he would not mind being in the same class as mentally handicapped students. (Karagiannis, 1988, p. 179)

When schools exclude some students, prejudice is entrenched in the consciousness of many students when they become adults, with the results of increased social conflict and dehumanizing competition. This is reflected in the feelings of a student who was moved from an integrated elementary school class to a segregated class in junior high school:

I felt good when I was with my [elementary] class, but when they went and separated us that changed us. That changed our ideas, the way we thought about each other, and turned us to enemies toward each other because they said I was dumb and they were smart. (Schafer & Olexa, 1971, p. 96)

To maximize acceptance and social peace, all children should be given the opportunity to become part of the educational and social mainstream. The past experience of segregation speaks of what is to be transcended: inequality and control.

Overcoming Past Experience and Patterns

The unfortunate arrangements in the past for people with disabilities were summarized on the floor of the U.S. Senate by then-Senator Lowell Weicker:

The history of society's formal methods of dealing with people with disabilities can be summed up in two words: SEGREGATION and INEQUALITY.... As a society, we have treated people with disabilities as inferiors and made them unwelcome in many activities and opportunities generally available to other Americans. (D.C. Update, 1988, p. 1)

In the past, it was decided that some children or adults should be excluded from our regular lives, classrooms, and communities because they were perceived to be a threat to society. The motives for this exclusion were twofold: to help students and to control students. In the past, the motive of control took precedence over the desire to help (Karagiannis, 1992, 1994).

The desire to control students in segregated institutions has been particularly strong during times of sweeping change. During the 19th and early 20th centuries, when the economic basis of the United States was changing from agriculture to industry, schools were central to the creation of a literate and disciplined work force. Students with disabilities were viewed as obstacles to the smooth operation of schools and classrooms because they lacked the skills to meet academic and disciplinary demands. It was thought that their presence would harm other students' learning or even have a corrupting moral influence. Special schools and institutions were set up to help the learning needs of students with disabilities and to ensure that these corrupting influences would be contained. The structure and organization of these separate settings were heavily based on control. During the 20th century, institutions consolidated in numbers, and control was their major outcome, *not* assistance. The view that persons with disabilities had little economic potential for society contributed to this outcome (Karagiannis, 1992).

International Information Society and Equality

Societies are undergoing fundamental changes. They are being transformed from industrial to informational and from national to international societies. The terms *electronic highway, information highway,* and *home office* are not just buzzwords but are indications of the emerging new world of work. More people will be making a living by processing information and servicing clients, either in person or electronically, than by factory work as was the case in industrial society. At the same time, societies are becoming multicultural, and inclusion is one of the fundamental principles on which to base the transformation of society (Karagiannis, 1994).

The social value of equality is consistent with the motive of assisting others and the practice of inclusive schooling. We have to ensure that students with disabilities are supported to become participants and contributors in the shaping and well-being of this new kind of society. We have to avoid the mistakes of the past when students with disabilities were left to live in the margins of society.

In light of this knowledge, we cannot continue to ignore the effects of segregation. In an increasingly diverse society, inclusive schooling of students with disabilities socializes other students to be accepting of individuals who are different. Placing students with disabilities into segregated schools or special classes prevents this beneficial socialization and sends a destructive message of intolerance.

If we truly want a fair, egalitarian society in which all people are considered to have equal worth and equal rights, we need to reevaluate how we operate our schools in order to give students with disabilities the opportunities and skills to participate in the emerging new society. If we want nurturance and equality for all people in our society, segregation in schools cannot be justified. In the words of Forest (1988), "If we really want someone to be part of our lives, we will do what it takes to welcome that person and accommodate his or her needs" (p. 3). Appropriate educational experiences and related services can and should be provided in the mainstream.

PARADIGM SHIFT IN EDUCATION

The change in how and what special education services should be provided comes from a paradigm shift that has been under way since the 1970s. According to Hahn (1989), there are two perspective on disabilities. The *functional limitations* perspective has been prevalent in the past and has many followers even today. From this viewpoint, the task of educators is to fix, improve, or make ready students who are unsuccessful without any concerted efforts to adapt the schools to the students' particular needs, interests, or capabilities. Those students who do not fit into the existing programs are relegated to separate settings.

The functional limitations standpoint is gradually being replaced by the *minority group* perspective, which calls on educational organizations and environments to be adapted, improved, or made ready to address the needs of all students. Segregation and practices such as identification and labeling, which usually absorb a large amount of resources, are seen as social discrimination and a denial of the provision of skills for participatory citizenship (Cummins, 1987; Snow, 1984; Stainton, 1994).

Although not focused directly on educational issues, passage of the Americans with Disabilities Act of 1990 (ADA) (PL 101-336) is an indication of the influence of the minority group paradigm. This act aims "to provide a clear and comprehensive national mandate to end discrimination against individuals with disabilities giving them the same protection in our society available to other individuals protected by civil rights laws" (*TASH Newsletter,* 1989, p. 1). The minority group paradigm and the ADA articulate a different world view for the future with regard to disability. According to Daniels (1990), the ADA expresses the conviction that "the way to promote productivity and independence of people with disabilities is to remove the barriers that our society has created and restore the rights of citizens with disabilities to partake of the opportunities available to Americans" (p. 3).

Accordingly, all students, including those with disabilities, should be able to attend their neighborhood school, which should live up to its responsibility to adapt to a diversity of student needs. This is certainly the demand expressed by many self-advocates and parents of children with disabilities (Biklen, 1992; Ferguson & Asch, 1989; Snow, 1989; Strully, 1986, 1987; Worth, 1988). If our societies and communities are going to be ethically, morally, and legally just, inclusion is a must.

CONCLUSION

Only a few years ago, it was considered unrealistic by most people to even discuss the possibility of educating all students, including those with significant disabilities, in mainstream schools and classes. Now this is being done successfully in a small but growing number of schools in Australia, Canada, Italy, the United States, and other countries (Berrigan, 1988, 1989; Biklen, 1988; Blackman & Peterson, 1989; Buswell & Shaffner, 1990; Forest, 1987a; Hunter & Grove, 1994; People First Association of Lethbridge, 1990; Perner, Dingwall, & Keilty, 1994; Porter & Richler, 1991; Schattman, 1988; Thousand & Villa, 1994; Villa & Thousand, 1988).

In the expected expansion of inclusion, it will be necessary to monitor the effects of the financial constraint that is becoming a mark of our times. Inclusion is not, nor should it become, a convenient way to justify budgetary cuts that may jeopardize the provision of essential services. Genuine inclusion does not mean dumping students with disabilities into general education classes without support for teachers or students. In other words, the primary goal of inclusive schooling is not to save money: It is to adequately serve all students.

People with disabilities sometimes need specialized instructions, tools, techniques, and equipment. All of these supports for students and teachers are to be integrated into and *coupled with* a restructuring of schools and classes. Supports should be *central*, not peripheral, to the mainstream of education. In this manner, the benefits of inclusive schooling reach all students, teachers, and society in general. According to Skrtic (1994), inclusion is more than a model for special education service delivery. It is a new paradigm for thinking and acting in ways that include all persons in a society where diversity is becoming the norm rather than the exception.

The challenge, therefore, is to extend the foothold of inclusion to more schools and communities, while at the same time keeping in mind that the primary purpose is to *facilitate* and *assist* the learning and adjustment of all students, the citizens of tomorrow. Our schools and communities will become as good as we decide to make them.

REFERENCES

Americans with Disabilities Act of 1990 (ADA), PL 101-336. (July 26, 1990). Title 42, U.S.C. 12101 et seq: *U.S. Statutes at Large, 104,* 327–378.

Aronson, E. (1978). *The jigsaw classroom.* Beverly Hills, CA: Sage Publications.

Berrigan, C. (1988). Integration in Italy: A dynamic movement. *TASH Newsletter,* 6–7.

Berrigan, C. (1989). All students belong in the classroom: Johnson City Central Schools, Johnson City, New York. *TASH Newsletter, 15*(1), 6.

Biklen, D. (Producer). (1988). *Regular lives* [Video]. (Available from WETA, P.O. Box 2226, Washington, DC 20013.)

Biklen, D. (1992). *Schooling without labels: Parents, educators, and inclusive education.* Philadelphia: Temple University Press.

Blackman, H., & Peterson, D. (1989). *Total integration neighborhood schools.* La Grange, IL: La Grange Department of Special Education.

Brinker, R., & Thorpe, M. (1983). *Evaluation of integration of severely handicapped students in regular classrooms and community settings.* Princeton, NJ: Educational Testing Service.

Brinker, R., & Thorpe, M. (1984). Integration of severely handicapped students and the proportion of IEP objectives achieved. *Exceptional Children, 51,* 168–175.

Brown v. Board of Education, 347 US 483 (1954), p. 493.

Buswell, B., & Shaffner, B. (1990). Families supporting inclusive schooling. In W. Stainback & S. Stainback (Eds.), *Support networks for inclusive schooling: Interdependent integrated education* (pp. 219–229). Baltimore: Paul H. Brookes Publishing Co.

Collicott, J. (1991). Implementing multi-level instruction: Strategies for classroom teachers. In G.L. Porter & D. Richler (Eds.), *Changing Canadian schools: Perspectives on disability and inclusion* (pp. 191–218). Downsview, Ontario, Canada: G. Allan Roeher Institute.

Cullinan, D., Sabornie, E.J., & Crossland, C.L. (1992). Social mainstreaming of mildly handicapped students. *The Elementary School Journal, 92*(3), 339–351.

Cummins, J. (1987). Psychoeducational assessment in multicultural school systems. *Canadian Journal for Exceptional Children, 3*(4), 115–117.

Daniel, R.R., v. State Board of Education, 874 F.2d 1036 (5th Circuit, June 12, 1989).

Daniels, S. (1990). Disability in America: An evolving concept, a new paradigm. *Policy Network Newsletter, 3,* 1–3.

D.C. Update. (1988, July). Senator Lowell Weicker on the Americans with Disabilities Act, p. 1.

Delquadri, J., Greenwood, C.R., Whorton, D., Carta, J.J., & Hall, V.R. (1986). Classwide peer tutoring. *Exceptional Children, 52,* 535–542.

DeVries, D.L., & Slavin, R.E. (1978). Team games tournament: A research review. *Journal of Research and Development in Education, 12,* 28–38.

Elliott, S.N., & Sheridan, S.M. (1992). Consultation and teaming: Problem solving among educators, parents, and support personnel. *The Elementary School Journal, 92*(3), 315–338.

Epps, S., & Tindal, G. (1987). The effectiveness of differential programming in serving students with mild handicaps: Placement options and instructional programming. In M.C. Wang, M.C. Reynolds, & H.J. Walberg (Eds.), *Handbook of special education: Research and practice: Vol. 1. Learner characteristics and adaptive education* (pp. 213–248). New York: Pergamon Press.

Ferguson, P., & Asch, A. (1989). Lessons from life: Personal and parental perspectives on school, childhood, and disability. In D. Biklen, A. Ford, & D. Ferguson (Eds.), *Disability and society* (pp. 108–140). Chicago: National Society for the Study of Education.

Forest, M. (1987a). *More education integration.* Downsview, Ontario: G. Allan Roeher Institute.

Forest, M. (1987b). Start with the right attitude. *Entourage, 2,* 11–13.

Forest, M. (1988). Full inclusion is possible. *IMPACT, 1,* 3–4.

Giangreco, M.F., Dennis, R., Cloninger, C., Edelman, S., & Schattman, R. (1993). "I've counted Jon": Transformational experiences of teachers educating students with disabilities. *Exceptional Children, 59*(4), 359–372.

Hahn, H. (1989). The politics of special education. In D.K. Lipsky & A. Gartner (Eds.), *Beyond separate education: Quality education for all* (pp. 225–242). Baltimore: Paul H. Brookes Publishing Co.

Hanline, M., & Halvorsen, A. (1989). Parent perceptions of the integration transition process: Overcoming artificial barriers. *Exceptional Children, 55,* 487–493.

Harris, K.C. (1990). Meeting diverse needs through collaborative consultation. In W. Stainback & S. Stainback (Eds.), *Support networks for inclusive schooling: Interdependent integrated education* (pp. 139–150). Baltimore: Paul H. Brookes Publishing Co.

Hunter, M., & Grove, M. (1994, August). *Queensland-Australia: Policy and practices.* Paper presented at the Excellence and Equity in Education International Conference, Toronto.

International League of Societies for Persons with Mental Handicap. (1994, June). The Inclusion Charter. UNESCO World Conference on Special Educational Needs: Access and Quality, Salamanca, Spain.

Jenkins, J.R., & Jenkins, L.M. (1981). *Cross age and peer tutoring: Help for children with learning problems.* Reston, VA: Council for Exceptional Children.

Johnson, D., & Johnson, R. (1984). Classroom learning structure and attitudes toward handicapped students in mainstream settings: A theoretical model and research evidence. In R. Jones (Ed.), *Attitudes and attitude change in special education* (pp. 118–142). Reston, VA: Council for Exceptional Children.

Johnson, D.W., & Johnson, R.T. (1986). Mainstreaming and cooperative learning strategies. *Exceptional Children, 52,* 553–561.

Johnson, D., & Johnson, R. (1987). *Learning together and alone.* Englewood Cliffs, NJ: Prentice Hall.

Karagiannis, A. (1988). *Three children with Down syndrome integrated into the regular classroom: Attitudes of a school community.* Unpublished master's thesis, McGill University, Montreal.

Karagiannis, A. (1992). *The social-historical context of special education and mainstreaming in the United States from independence to 1990.* Unpublished doctoral dissertation, McGill University, Montreal.

Karagiannis, A. (1994, August). *The waves of special education over the last two hundred years: Significance and implications for inclusive schools.* Paper presented at the Excellence and Equity in Education International Conference, Toronto.

Karagiannis, A., & Cartwright, G.F. (1990). Attitudinal research issues in integration of children with mental handicaps. *McGill Journal of Education, 25*(3), 369–382.

Madden, N., & Slavin, R. (1983). Mainstreaming students with mild academic handicaps: Academic and social outcomes. *Review of Educational Research, 53,* 519–569.

Marston, D. (1987–1988, Winter). The effectiveness of special education. *Journal of Special Education, 21,* 13–27.

Massachusetts Advocacy Center. (1987). *Out of the mainstream.* Boston: Author.

Myles, B., & Simpson, R. (1989). Regular educators' modification preferences for mainstreaming mildly handicapped children. *Journal of Special Education, 22,* 479–489.

Osguthorpe, R.T., & Scruggs, T.E. (1986). Special education students as tutors: A review and analysis. *Remedial and Special Education, 7*(4), 15–26.

People First Association of Lethbridge. (1990). *Kids belong together* [Video]. (Available from Expectations Unlimited, P.O. Box 655, Niwot, CO 80544.)

Perner, D., Dingwall, A., & Keilty, G.C. (1994, August). *Province-wide implementation of inclusion—Strategies and reflections.* Paper presented at the Excellence and Equity in Education International Conference, Toronto.

Porter, G. (Producer). (1988). *A chance to belong* [Video]. Downsview, Ontario (Canadian Association for Community Living, 4700 Keele St., Downsview, Ontario).

Porter, G.L., & Richler, D. (Eds.). (1991). *Changing Canadian schools*. Downsview, Ontario, Canada: G. Allan Roeher Institute.

Porter, G.L., Wilson, M., Kelly, B., & den Otter, J. (1991). Problem solving teams: A thirty minute peer-helping model. In G.L. Porter & D. Richler (Eds.), *Changing Canadian schools: Perspectives on disability and inclusion*. Downsview, Ontario, Canada: G. Allan Roeher Institute.

Pugach, M.C., & Johnson, L.J. (1990). Meeting diverse needs through professional peer collaboration. In W. Stainback & S. Stainback (Eds.), *Support networks for inclusive schooling: Interdependent integrated education* (pp. 123–137). Baltimore: Paul H. Brookes Publishing Co.

Sapon-Shevin, M. (1990). Student support through cooperative learning. In W. Stainback & S. Stainback (Eds.), *Support networks for inclusive schooling: Interdependent integrated education* (pp. 65–79). Baltimore: Paul H. Brookes Publishing Co.

Schafer, W., & Olexa, C. (1971). *Tracking and opportunity*. Scranton, PA: Chandler.

Schattman, R. (1988). Integrated education and organization change. *IMPACT, 1*, 8–9.

Schloss, P.J. (1992). Mainstreaming revisited. *The Elementary School Journal, 92*(3), 233–244.

Sindelar, P.T., Griffin, C.C., Smith, S.W., & Watanabe, A.K. (1992). Prereferral intervention: Encouraging notes on preliminary findings. *The Elementary School Journal, 92*(3), 245–259.

Skrtic, T. (1994, August). *Changing paradigms in special education*. Paper presented at the Excellence and Equity in Education International Conference, Toronto.

Slavin, R.E. (1987). Ability grouping and student achievement in elementary school: A best-evidence synthesis. *Review of Educational Research, 57*, 293–336.

Snow, J. (1989). Systems of support: A new vision. In S. Stainback, W. Stainback, & M. Forest (Eds.), *Educating all students in the mainstream of regular education* (pp. 221–231). Baltimore: Paul H. Brookes Publishing Co.

Snow, R.E. (1984). Placing children in special education: Some comments. *Educational Researcher, 13*(3), 12–14.

Stainback, S., & Stainback, W. (1988). Educating students with severe disabilities in regular classes. *Teaching Exceptional Children, 21*, 16–19.

Stainback, S., & Stainback, W. (1990a). Facilitating support networks. In W. Stainback & S. Stainback (Eds.), *Support networks for inclusive schooling: Interdependent integrated education* (pp. 25–36). Baltimore: Paul H. Brookes Publishing Co.

Stainback, S., & Stainback, W. (1990b). Inclusive schooling. In W. Stainback & S. Stainback (Eds.), *Support networks for inclusive schooling: Interdependent integrated education* (pp. 3–23). Baltimore: Paul H. Brookes Publishing Co.

Stainback, W., & Stainback, S. (1990c). The support facilitator at work. In W. Stainback & S. Stainback (Eds.), *Support networks for inclusive schooling: Interdependent integrated education* (pp. 37–48). Baltimore: Paul H. Brookes Publishing Co.

Stainback, S., Stainback, W., & Hatcher, L. (1983). Handicapped peers' involvement in the education of severely handicapped students. *Journal of The Association for Persons with Severe Handicaps, 8*(1), 39–42.

Stainton, T. (1994, August). *Tools for participatory citizenship: The necessity of inclusive education*. Paper presented at the Excellence and Equity in Education International Conference, Toronto.

Stone, J., & Collicott, J. (1994, August). *Supportive inclusive education: Creating layers of support*. Paper presented at the Excellence and Equity in Education International Conference, Toronto.

Stone, J., & Moore, M. (1994, August). *Multilevel instruction and enrichment*. Paper presented at the Excellence and Equity in Education International Conference, Toronto.

Strain, P. (1983). Generalization of autistic children's social behavior change: Effects of developmentally integrated and segregated settings. *Analysis and Intervention in Developmental Disabilities, 3,* 23–24.

Strully, J. (1986, November). *Our children and the regular education classroom: Or why settle for anything less than the best?* Paper presented at the 13th annual conference of The Association for Persons with Severe Handicaps, San Francisco.

Strully, J. (1987, October). *What's really important in life anyway? Parents sharing the vision.* Paper presented at the 14th annual conference of The Association for Persons with Severe Handicaps, Chicago.

TASH Newsletter. (1989). Senate overwhelmingly approves Americans with Disabilities Act, *4,* 1–2.

Thousand, J.S., & Villa, R.A. (1990). Sharing expertise and responsibilities through teaching teams. In W. Stainback & S. Stainback (Eds.), *Support networks for inclusive schooling: Interdependent integrated education* (pp. 151–166). Baltimore: Paul H. Brookes Publishing Co.

Thousand, J.S., & Villa, R.A. (1994, August). *Strategies to create inclusive schools and classrooms.* Paper presented at the Excellence and Equity in Education International Conference, Toronto.

Vandercook, T., Fleetham, D., Sinclair, S., & Tetlie, R. (1988). Cath, Jess, Jules, and Ames...A story of friendship. *IMPACT, 2,* 18–19.

Villa, R., & Thousand, J. (1988). Enhancing success in heterogeneous classrooms and schools: The power of partnership. *Teacher Education and Special Education, 11,* 144–153.

Villa, R.A., & Thousand, J.S. (1990). Administrative supports to promote inclusive schooling. In W. Stainback & S. Stainback (Eds.), *Support networks for inclusive schooling: Interdependent integrated education* (pp. 201–218). Baltimore: Paul H. Brookes Publishing Co.

Wehman, P. (1990). School to work: Elements of successful programs. *Teaching Exceptional Children, 23,* 40–43.

Worth, P. (1988, December). *Empowerment: Choices and change.* Paper presented at the annual conference of The Association for Persons with Severe Handicaps, Washington, DC.

2

Historical Overview of Inclusion

*Anastasios Karagiannis,
Susan Stainback, and William Stainback*

> *Educate him [the African American] and you have added little to his happiness...you have not...and cannot procure for him any admission in to the society and sympathy of white men.* (An Address to the Public by the Managers of the Colonization Society of Connecticut, 1828, p. 5)

> *An authority should exist... to dispose of lads who... are... known to be profane, intemperate, dishonest and as far as they may be at their age, abandoned to crime.* (Reverend Joseph Tuckerman, as minister to the poor in the city of Boston in the 1820s, cited in Hawes, 1971, p. 80)

> *Now that we are able to discover in the early years of the elementary school... through the use of... [intelligence] tests, which is the pure silk and which the sow's ear... we as educators shall so... apply the educational process... [so] that the silk shall be made into a silk purse and the sow's ear into a pigskin purse....* (John L. Tilsdley, 1921, p. 54, district superintendent of New York City high schools, in the Fifth Yearbook of the National Association of Secondary School Principals)

> *The heart of this commitment is the search for ways to serve as many... children [with disabilities] as possible in the regular classroom by encouraging special education and other special programs to form a partnership with regular education.* (Madeleine Will, 1986, p. 20,

Assistant Secretary of the Office of Special Education and Rehabilitative Services, launching the Regular Education Initiative)

THE TENSION BETWEEN exclusion and inclusion has been a shaping force in U.S. society and education. Public schools, in particular, have experienced stages of incorporating a larger number of children with disabilities into classrooms. In the United States until approximately 1800, the great majority of students considered to be learners with disabilities were not deemed worthy of formal education, even though they were perceived as brothers and sisters who were part of the community. After independence, the call for separating all dependents and deviants (Hawes, 1991; Rothman, 1971) affected people with disabilities for many years to come. During the 19th and much of the 20th centuries, there was a lengthy period of institutional segregated education for persons with disabilities.

Many previously segregated learners have benefitted from the social movement toward inclusive education. This movement has been sometimes slow and hesitant, but the overall result has been progress. As we approach the 21st century, the goal of universal inclusive education is within our reach. This chapter reviews the path of this movement in the United States from the late colonial period and beginning of the nation, the formation of public schools and separate institutions, and the "menace scare" of the early 20th century to the civil rights movement of the 1960s, the enactment of the Education for All Handicapped Children Act of 1975 (PL 94-142), and the recent development of support for merging general and special education systems and the impact of this on current schools.

THE BEGINNING YEARS

For most students in the United States who were poor, were from a minority group, or had disabilities, the first hurdle was merely to receive an education. As early as 1779, a plan for the first state-supported school system was proposed by Thomas Jefferson to help provide poor people in Virginia with an education. At the time, the plan was rejected because of "the refusal of well-to-do citizens to pay taxes for the education of the poor" (Rippa, cited in Sigmon, 1983). The situation was similar in most of the other states (Cremin, 1980).

Benjamin Rush, a physician in the late 1700s, was one of the first Americans to introduce the concept of educating persons with disabilities. It was not until 1817 that one of the first special programs of education was established by Thomas Gallaudet at the American Asylum for the Education and Instruction of the Deaf and Dumb in Connecticut. Other programs for educating students with various disabilities were established soon afterward. For example, the New England Asylum for the Education of the Blind was founded in 1829 in Watertown, Massachusetts, and the Experiential School for Teaching and Training Idiotic Children was founded in 1846 in Barre, Massachusetts. The establishment of these institutions was part of the larger picture of the transformation of colonial society into a national one at the end of the 18th century and the beginning of the 19th century.

At the conclusion of the American War of Independence in 1783, affluent groups and private citizens established a number of philanthropic societies whose main concern was to ensure that marginal societal groups would not threaten the republic and the mainstream American values of the time. These philanthropic organizations played a leading role in the establishment of public schools and segregated rehabilitative institutions, including training institutions and schools for people with disabilities (Davies, 1930; Hawes, 1971; Kanner, 1964; Mennel, 1973; Pickett, 1969; Richards, 1935; Rothman, 1971; Schlossman, 1977; Schwartz, 1956). Most of the individuals placed in rehabilitative institutions were judged to be members of a number of overlapping groups: paupers, deviants, persons with visible disabilities, minorities, and many newly arrived immigrants.

The motives of social assistance and control were intermixed in the workings of such institutions. Some leaders of special education at the time, such as Samuel Gridley Howe (Schwartz, 1956), made remarkable efforts to promote the idea that all children, including those with disabilities, deserved schooling. However, the fact that training schools for persons with disabilities were organized like asylums, with a militaristic structure, doomed them as places where children were controlled rather than taught. This trend toward segregation, for controlling the "undesirables," would reach its high point during the 20th century.

THE CREATION OF PUBLIC SCHOOLS

Institutions for individuals with disabilities continued to grow in numbers and size during the late 19th century until the 1950s. Concurrently, another trend was developing: the creation of public "common schools" where most children were educated. Between 1842 and 1918 all states legislated compulsory schooling, and public schools drew enormous amounts of funding for growth (Rury, 1985; U.S. Bureau of the Census, 1975; U.S. Department of Education, National Center for Education Statistics, 1991).

However, various groups of children were excluded from the mainstream of public schools. African Americans and Native Americans were largely educated in separate school systems. Similarly, students with visible and significant disabilities continued, for the most part, to be segregated. Residential institutions and special schools remained the norm for educating students who were blind or deaf or had physical disabilities. Students with significant developmental disabilities were generally denied educational services of any type and resided primarily in the back wards of large state institutions. According to Sigmon (1983), "almost all children who were wheelchair-bound, not toilet trained, or considered ineducable were excluded because of the problems that schooling them would entail" (p. 3).

THE MENACE SCARE, TRACKING, AND SPECIAL CLASSES

At the turn of the 20th century, the eugenics movement helped to entrench the dehumanization of persons with disabilities. Between 1900 and 1930, there was widespread public perception that people with disabilities had criminal tendencies and were the most serious menace to civilization because of their genetic makeup. This perception added to the willingness of many educators and the public to allow segregation and other practices such as sterilization (Davies, 1930; Goddard, 1914, 1915; Gosney, 1929; Laughlin, 1926; Worthington, 1925) and encouraged tracking and the expansion of special classes in public schools.

Tracking by academic ability was routinely used to relegate poor and disadvantaged children to lower, nonacademic streams (Chapman, 1988). Exceptions to compulsory education, primarily affecting children from the lower socioeconomic groups, were made. Special classes at the low end of tracking became one of the defining characteristics of public schools. According to Chaves (1977), special classes "came about, not for humanitarian reasons, but because such children were unwanted in the regular public school classroom" (p. 30). This is not meant to imply that many individuals who have worked in special classes and special education throughout these periods have not had humanitarian motives.

Teachers in general education classrooms perceived educators working in special education classes as having special preparation and a special capacity for the work. They were a breed apart, and it was seen as inappropriate to expect teachers lacking such preparation and inclination to participate in educating students in wheelchairs and students with learning difficulties. This type of defensive and rejective reasoning led to the creation of what might be termed "little red schoolhouses for students considered exceptional" within regular school buildings. Students with disabilities and special educators were in a regular school, but in many ways were not *part* of it. As special classes increased in number, attitudes among general and special educators and evolving administrative models for segregated education ensured that general and special education developed on parallel, rather than converging, lines.

The magnitude of the separation between general and special education was reflected in the increase in the numbers of students identified as having disabilities. Between 1932 and 1969–1970, general elementary and secondary school enrollments increased by 73%, from 26,275,000 to 45,550,000 students (U.S. Department of Education, National Center for Education Statistics, 1990, 1993); in comparison, enrollment in special programs increased by 1,552%, from 162,000 to 2,677,000 students (U.S. Bureau of the Census, 1975).

By the 1950s and 1960s, the use of special classes in public schools was the preferred educational delivery system for most students with disabilities. It was during this period, however, that public attitudes about the place of individuals with disabilities in schools and in the community began to change.

IMPACT OF THE CIVIL RIGHTS MOVEMENT

In 1954, *Brown v. Board of Education,* in which it was ruled that separate is not equal, provided a powerful push away from segregated options for educating minority students. Apart from challenging exclusionary educational policies for African Americans, this ruling also led the way toward increased scrutiny of the segregation of students with disabilities.

During the 1950s and 1960s, parents of students with disabilities founded organizations such as the National Association for Retarded Citizens and initiated advocacy actions for educating their children. A group of special education leaders, including Blatt (1969), Dunn (1968), Dybwad (1964), Goldberg (Goldberg & Cruickshank, 1958), Hobbs (1966), Lilly (1970), Reynolds (1962), and Wolfensberger (1972), began advocating for the rights of students with disabilities to learn in more normalized school environments with their peers. For the first time, and on a fairly wide basis, the restrictions imposed by segregated institutions, special schools, and special classes were presented as problematic. The wheel of change had been set in motion.

EDUCATION IN THE LEAST RESTRICTIVE ENVIRONMENT

The natural sequel to *Brown v. Board of Education* (1954) for students with disabilities followed in the 1970s. Court decisions in Pennsylvania (*Pennsylvania Association for Retarded Children v. Commonwealth of Pennsylvania,* 1971, 1972,) and the District of Columbia (*Mills v. D.C. Board of Education,* 1972) established the right of all children labeled as mentally retarded to a free and appropriate education. In 1973, the Rehabilitation Act of 1973 (PL 93-112), particularly Section 504, and later amendments (Rehabilitation Act Amendments of 1986 [PL 99-506]; Rehabilitation Act Amendments of 1992 [PL 102-569]) guaranteed the rights of individuals with disabilities in employment and in educational institutions that receive federal funding. Further pressure by parents, courts, and legislators resulted in the Education for All Handicapped Children Act of 1975 (PL 94-142), which was enacted in 1978. This law, reauthorized as the Individuals with Disabilities Education Act of 1990 (IDEA) (PL 101-476), extended the right to a free public education to all children, regardless of disability, in the least restrictive environment possible. Spurred by the passage of PL 94-142 (the Education for All Handicapped Children Act of 1975), by 1976 all states had passed laws subsidizing public school programs for students with disabilities. In addition, several national associations of general educators passed resolutions in support of mainstreaming. Many states began requiring general education teachers to take relevant preparatory coursework.

At about this time, a number of people, most notably Norris Haring, Lou Brown, Wayne Sailor, Doug Guess, and William and Diane Bricker, began advocating the education of students with significant disabilities in neighborhood schools. In 1979, The Association for Persons with Severe Handicaps (TASH) and, a few years later, the Society for Children and Adults with Autism adopted similar resolutions calling for the termination of segregated placements. However, it was not until the mid-1980s that the current dual systems of general and special education were directly challenged (Stainback & Stainback, 1984).

INCLUSION OF ALL STUDENTS
IN THE MAINSTREAM OF EDUCATION

By the late 1970s and early 1980s, many students with disabilities began to be integrated into regular classrooms on at least a part-time basis. Even many students with significant disabilities, who had not been served in the past, started to receive educational services in regular neighborhood school environments (Certo, Haring, & York, 1984; Knoblock, 1982; Lusthaus, 1988; Strully & Strully, 1985; Villa & Thousand, 1988).

In 1986, the U.S. Department of Education Office of Special Education and Rehabilitative Services issued the Regular Education Initiative (REI) (Will, 1986), which incorporated some of the ideas proposed by Stainback and Stainback (1984) for merging special and general education. The purpose of the REI was to develop ways to serve students with disabilities in general classrooms by encouraging special education programs to develop a partnership with general education. Wang, Birch, and Reynolds, among others, have been strong supporters of the initiative (Reynolds & Birch, 1988; Wang, Reynolds, & Walberg, 1987).

By the late 1980s, attention to the need to educate students with significant disabilities in the mainstream of education intensified. In 1988, a resolution adopted by The Association for Persons with Severe Handicaps, calling for the integration of special and general education, heightened the debate concerning a unified system of education (Lipsky & Gartner, 1989; W. Stainback & S. Stainback, 1992; Stainback, Stainback, & Forest, 1989; York & Vandercook, 1988). There was advocacy for and experimentation with integrating students with significant disabilities into general education classrooms part or full time (Forest, 1987; Gartner & Lipsky, 1987; Karagiannis, 1988; Karagiannis & Cartwright, 1990; Sapon-Shevin, Pugach, & Lilly, 1987; W. Stainback & S. Stainback, 1987, 1992; S. Stainback and W. Stainback, 1988, 1990; Strully, 1986; Thousand & Villa, 1988, 1991; Villa & Thousand, 1992). Despite a steady trend toward inclusion, there have also been attempts to slow, stop, and even reverse inclusive schooling.

RESISTANCE TO INCLUSION

Such attempts to resist inclusive schooling are still evident. Some scholars and researchers have argued against the inclusion movement (Fuchs & Fuchs, 1994; Kauffman, 1993; Kauffman, Gerber, & Semmel, 1988; Lieberman, 1988). A number of states have made teacher certification based on disability categorization more rigid, and some organizations and states have proposed the reinstitution of segregated schools for students with disabilities (see Stainback & Stainback, 1992a). In addition, some interagency collaboration efforts may also work more for control and stigmatization rather than for successful inclusion of disadvantaged students, including students with disabilities (Karagiannis, 1992).

Perhaps the most revealing indicator of resistance to inclusion is contained in the statistics concerning students with disabilities. There have been sharp increases in numbers of children identified as having disabilities since 1970, but only minimal overall improvement toward more inclusive placements since the enactment of PL 94-142 (the Education for All Handicapped Children Act of 1975).

Between 1969–1970 and 1990–1991, elementary and secondary public school enrollment in the United States decreased by 11%, from 45,550,000 to 41,217,000 students (U.S. Department of Education, National Center for Education Statistics, 1993). Special education enrollment, however, increased by 78%, from 2,677,000 students in 1970 to 4,771,000 students in 1990–1991. Apparently, the increases in the Learning Disability (LD) category are largely responsible for the overall increase in the identified special population (U.S. Bureau of the Census, 1975; U.S. Department of Education, National Center for Education Statistics, 1993).

In the period between 1977–1978 and 1989–1990, there was little or no change in placements of students with disabilities as a group at the national level. In 1977–1978, 68% of students with disabilities were in general education class and resource room environments compared with 69.2% in 1989–1990. Placement of students with disabilities in separate classes was 25.3% in 1977–1978 and 24.8% in 1989–1990. Separate public school facilities and other separate environments educated 6.7% of students with disabilities in 1977–1978 and 5.4% of students with disabilities in 1989–1990 (U.S. Department of Education, Office of Special Education and Rehabilitative Services, 1980; U.S. Department of Education, National Center for Education Statistics, 1993). With respect to the LD category, which comprises approximately half of the special student population, McLeskey and Pacchiano (1994) reported that there was little progress in educating more students with LD in general education classrooms and resource rooms between 1979 and 1989.

Despite this overall national picture, the pattern of placement of students with disabilities is not the same across states. There are states such as Iowa, New Hampshire, Rhode Island, South Dakota, and Texas in which contradictory practices promoting both exclusion and inclusion exist at the same time. There are also a number of states that have made substantial progress toward inclusion, such as Idaho, North Dakota, Oregon, and Vermont (Karagiannis, 1992). Scholars and practitioners in these latter states have accomplished much in terms of widely disseminating the innovative, successful organizational and instructional arrangements for achieving inclusion.

MOMENTUM FOR INCLUSION

The inclusion movement has gained unparalleled momentum in the early 1990s. There is a growing international organization (Schools Are For Everyone), with thousands of members throughout the United States and other countries, with the sole purpose of promoting inclusion. The influence of the inclusion movement is now felt outside the field of special education and in the courts and is part and parcel of general education reform efforts.

Leading general education journals such as *The Elementary School Journal* and *Educational Leadership* have published articles (Alper & Ryndak, 1992; Villa & Thousand, 1992, respectively) on how inclusion might be accomplished. Newspaper articles, for example in *USA Today* ("Full inclusion," 1993; "School 'tracking,'" 1994) and the *Wall Street Journal* ("More schools," 1994), have reported related stories.

The courts are increasingly being called upon to render judgments regarding inclusion. In an important case, *Oberti v. Clementon* (1993), a U.S. circuit court ordered the inclusion of a student with severe disabilities: "We construe IDEA's mainstreaming requirement to prohibit a school from placing a child with disabilities outside of a regular classroom if education of the child in the regular classroom, with supplementary aid and support services, can be achieved satisfactorily." Perhaps the public has yet to see the last chapter of the history begun by *Brown v. Board of Education* in the 1950s. The U.S. Justice Department Assistant Attorney General for Civil Rights made known the department's intentions to challenge school tracking as "the segregating tool of the '90s" ("School 'tracking,'" 1994). The challenge is clearly based on the laws and rulings that have found segregation in schools illegal.

In the 1990s, one important accomplishment is the linking of the inclusion movement with general education reform. School restructuring for all learners is seen as a primary goal by major professional associations including the Association for Supervision and Curriculum Development (ASCD) (1992) and the National Association of State Boards of Education (NASBE) (1992). One of the ASCD's six resolutions (1992) was for the inclusion of special programs through instructional environments that eliminate tracking and segregation. The resolution supported services that focus on the prevention of learning problems rather than on after-the-fact labeling. Also, the ASCD strongly advised minimal restrictive regulations and the flexible use of funding to promote success for all children. The NASBE Study Group on Special Education (1992), after 2 years of study of special education and the general education school reform movement, urged in its report *Winners All: A Call for Inclusive Schools* (1992) the creation of a unified educational system. This group recommended major changes in organizational and instructional practices, preservice and in-service personnel preparation, licensure, and funding.

The number of schools attempting to actualize the ASCD's and NASBE's vision of inclusive education has grown rapidly. Literature has appeared describing some of these schools and the methods they employed to adapt curriculum and instruction and to alter the traditional schooling paradigm (S. Stainback & W. Stainback, 1990, 1992; Stainback, Stainback, & Forest, 1989; Thousand & Villa, 1994; Thousand, Villa, & Nevin, 1994; Villa, Thousand, Paolucci-Whitcomb, & Nevin, 1990; Villa, Thousand, Stainback, & Stainback, 1992). The momentum that has been created certainly has the potential to expand the practices of inclusion to an even larger number of schools.

CONCLUSION

Segregationist philosophy and practices of the past have had detrimental effects on persons with disabilities, schools, and society in general. For persons with disabilities, the idea that they could be helped in separate settings cut off from the rest of society strengthened social stigmas and rejection. For mainstream schools, rejection of children with disabilities contributed to rigidity and homogenization of teaching to fit the myth that, once classes had only normal students, instruction would need no further modification or adaptation. For U.S. society in general, rejection reinforced the "us against them" mentality that contributed to a widespread inability to appreciate social and cultural diversity and to celebrate the meaningful things that unite us. Going beyond educational exclusion means dismantling the "last bastion of segregation" (Kennedy, 1986, p. 6). The gradual departure from the exclusionary educational practices of the past provides all students an equal opportunity to have their educational needs met within the mainstream of general education. This move away from segregation is facilitated by efforts to unify general and special education into a single system. Despite obstacles, the expansion of the inclusion movement into the wider educational reform effort is a telling signal that schools and society will continue to shift toward increasingly inclusive practices.

REFERENCES

Alper, S., & Ryndak, D. (1992). Educating students with severe handicaps in regular classes. *The Elementary School Journal, 92,* 373–387.

An Address to the Public by the Managers of the Colonization Society of Connecticut. (1828). New Haven: Treadway & Adams.

Association for Supervision and Curriculum Development. (1992). *Resolutions 1992.* Alexandria, VA: Author.

Blatt, B. (1969). *Exodus from pandemonium.* Boston: Allyn & Bacon.

Brown v. Board of Education, 347 US 483 (1954).

Certo, N. Haring, N., & York, R. (Eds.). (1984). *Public school integration of severely handicapped students: Rational issues and progressive alternatives.* Baltimore: Paul H. Brookes Publishing Co.

Chapman, P.D. (1988). *Schools as sorters.* New York: New York University Press.

Chaves, I.M. (1977). Historical overview of special education in the United States. In P. Bates, T.L. West, & R.B. Schmerl (Eds.), *Mainstreaming: Problems, potentials and perspectives* (pp. 25–41). Minneapolis: National Support Systems Project.

Cremin, L.A. (1980). *American education: The national experience, 1783–1876.* New York: Harper & Row.

Davies, S.P. (1930). *Social control of the mentally deficient.* New York: Thomas Y. Crowell Co.

Dunn, L.M. (1968). Special education for the mildly retarded—Is much of it justifiable? *Exceptional Children, 35,* 5–22.

Dybwad, G. (1964). *Challenges in mental retardation.* New York: Columbia University Press.

Education for All Handicapped Children Act of 1975, PL 94-142. (August 23, 1975). Title 20, U.S.C. 1400 et seq: *U.S. Statutes at Large, 89,* 773–796.

Forest, M. (1987). Start with the right attitude. *Entourage, 2,* 11–13.

Fuchs, D., & Fuchs, L. (1994). Inclusive schools movement and the radicalization of special education reform. *Exceptional Children, 60,* 294–309.

Full inclusion for the disabled in public schools. (1993, April 21). *USA Today.*

Gartner, A., & Lipsky, D. (1987). Beyond special education. *Harvard Educational Review, 57,* 367–395.

Goddard, H.H. (1914). *Feeblemindedness: Its causes and consequences.* New York: Macmillan.

Goddard, H.H. (1915). *The criminal imbecile: An analysis of three remarkable murder cases.* New York: Macmillan.

Goldberg, I., & Cruickshank, W.M. (1958). The trainable but noneducable: Whose responsibility? *National Education Association Journal, 47,* 622.

Gosney, E.S. (1929). *Sterilization for human betterment.* New York: Macmillan.

Hawes, J.M. (1971). *Children in urban society: Juvenile delinquency in nineteenth century America.* New York: Oxford University Press.

Hawes, J.M. (1991). *The children's rights movement: A history of advocacy and protection.* Boston: Twayne Publishers.

Hobbs, N. (1966). Helping the disturbed child: Psychological and ecological strategies. *American Psychologist, 21,* 1105–1115.

Individuals with Disabilities Education Act of 1990 (IDEA), PL 101-476. (October 30, 1990). Title 20, U.S.C. 1400 et seq: *U.S. Statutes at Large, 104* (Part 2), 1103–1151.

Kanner, L. (1964). *A history of the care and study of the mentally retarded.* Springfield, IL: Charles C Thomas.

Karagiannis, A. (1988). *Three children with Down syndrome integrated into the regular classroom: Attitudes of a school community.* Unpublished master's thesis, McGill University, Montreal.

Karagiannis, A. (1992). *The social-historical context of special education and mainstreaming in the United States from independence to 1990.* Unpublished doctoral dissertation, McGill University, Montreal.

Karagiannis, A., & Cartwright, G.F. (1990). Attitudinal research issues in integration of children with mental handicaps. *McGill Journal of Education, 25*(3), 369–382.

Kauffman, J. (1993). How we might achieve the radical reform of special education. *Exceptional Children, 60,* 294–309.

Kauffman, J., Gerber, M., & Semmel, M. (1988). Arguable assumptions underlying the regular education initiative. *Journal of Learning Disabilities, 21*(1), 6–11.

Kennedy, T., Jr. (1986, November 23). Our right to independence. *Parade Magazine,* 4–7.

Knoblock, P. (1982). *Teaching and mainstreaming autistic children.* Denver: Love Publishing Co.

Laughlin, H.H. (1926). The eugenical sterilization of the feebleminded. *Journal of Psychoasthenics, 31,* 210–218.

Lieberman, L. (1988). *Preserving special education for those who need it.* Newtonville, MA: GloWorm Publications.

Lilly, S. (1970). Special education: A tempest in a teapot. *Exceptional Children, 32,* 43–49.

Lipsky, D.K., & Gartner, A. (Eds.). (1989). *Beyond separate education: Quality education for all.* Baltimore: Paul H. Brookes Publishing Co.

Lusthaus, E. (1988). Education integration…Letting our children go. *TASH Newsletter, 14,* 6–7.

McLeskey, J., & Pacchiano, D. (1994). Mainstreaming students with learning disabilities: Are we making progress? *Exceptional Children, 60*(6), 508–517.

Mennel, R.M. (1973). *Thorns and thistles: Juvenile delinquents in the United States, 1825–1940.* Hanover, NH: The University Press of New England.

Mills v. D.C. Board of Education, 348 F. Supp. 866 (D.D.C. 1972).

More schools embrace full inclusion of the disabled. (1994, April 13). *Wall Street Journal,* p. B1.

National Association of State Boards of Education Study Group on Special Education. (1992, October). *Winners all: A call for inclusive schools.* Alexandria, VA: Author.

Oberti v. Board of Education of The Borough of Clementon School District, 995 F.2d 1204 (3rd Cir., 1993).

Pennsylvania Association for Retarded Children v. Commonwealth of Pennsylvania, 334 F. Supp. 1257 (E.D.Pa. 1971) and 343 F. Supp. 279 (E.D.Pa. 1972).

Pickett, R.S. (1969). *House of refuge: Origins of juvenile reform in New York state, 1815–1857.* Syracuse, NY: Syracuse University Press.

Rehabilitation Act of 1973, PL 93-112. (September 26, 1973). Title 29, U.S.C. 701 et seq: *U.S. Statutes at Large, 87,* 355–394.

Rehabilitation Act Amendments of 1986, PL 99-506. (October 21, 1986). Title 29, U.S.C. 701 et seq: *U.S. Statutes at Large, 100,* 1807–1846.

Rehabilitation Act Amendments of 1992, PL 102-569. (October 29, 1992). Title 29, U.S.C. 701 et seq: *U.S. Statutes at Large, 100,* 4344–4488.

Reynolds, M. (1962). Framework for considering some issues in special education. *Exceptional Children, 28,* 367–370.

Reynolds, M.C., & Birch, J.W. (1988). *Adaptive mainstreaming.* New York: Longman.

Richards, L.E. (1935). *Samuel Gridley Howe.* New York: D. Appleton-Century.

Rothman, D.J. (1971). *The discovery of the asylum: Social order and disorder in the new republic.* Boston: Little, Brown & Co.

Rury, J.L. (1985). American school enrollment in the progressive era: An interpretive inquiry. *History of Education, 14,* 49–67.

Sapon-Shevin, M., Pugach, M., & Lilly, S. (1987, November). *Moving toward merger: Implications for general and special education.* Paper presented at the Tenth Annual TED Conference, Arlington, VA.

School "tracking" to be challenged as biased. (1994, May 4). *USA Today,* p. 3a.

Schlossman, S.L. (1977). *Love and the American delinquent: The theory and practice of "progressive" juvenile justice, 1825–1920.* Chicago: University of Chicago Press.

Schwartz, H. (1956). *Samuel Gridley Howe: Social reformer, 1801–1876.* Cambridge, MA: Harvard University Press.

Sigmon, S. (1983). The history and future of educational segregation. *Journal for Special Educators, 19,* 1–13.

Stainback, S., & Stainback, W. (1988). Educating students with severe disabilities in regular classes. *Teaching Exceptional Children, 21,* 16–19.

Stainback, S., & Stainback, W. (Eds.). (1990). *Support networks for inclusive schooling: Interdependent integrated education.* Baltimore: Paul H. Brookes Publishing Co.

Stainback, S., & Stainback, W. (Eds.). (1992). *Curriculum considerations for inclusive classrooms: Facilitating learning for all students.* Baltimore: Paul H. Brookes Publishing Co.

Stainback, S., Stainback, W., & Forest, M. (Eds.). (1989). *Educating all students in the mainstream of regular education.* Baltimore: Paul H. Brookes Publishing Co.

Stainback, W., & Stainback, S. (1984). A rationale for the merger of special and regular education. *Exceptional Children, 51,* 102–111.

Stainback, W., & Stainback, S. (1987). Educating all students in regular education. *TASH Newsletter, 13*(4), 1, 7.

Stainback, W., & Stainback, S. (1992). *Controversial issues confronting special education.* Boston: Allyn & Bacon.

Strully, J. (1986, November). *Our children and the regular education classroom: Or why settle for anything less than the best?* Paper presented at the annual conference of The Association for Persons with Severe Handicaps, San Francisco.

Strully, J., & Strully, C. (1985). Teach your children. *Canadian Journal on Mental Retardation, 35*(4), 3–11.

Thousand, J., & Villa, R. (1988). Enhancing educational success through collaboration. *IMPACT, 1,* 14.

Thousand, J., & Villa, R. (1991). A futuristic view of the REI: A response to Jenkins, Pious, and Jewell. *Exceptional Children, 57,* 556–562.

Thousand, J., & Villa, R. (1994, August). *Strategies to create inclusive schools and classrooms.* Paper presented at the Excellence and Equity in Education International Conference, Toronto.

Thousand, J.S., Villa, R.A., & Nevin, A.I. (Eds.). (1994). *Creativity and collaborative learning: A practical guide to empowering students and teachers.* Baltimore: Paul H. Brookes Publishing Co.

Tilsdley, J.L. (1921). Some possibilities arising from the use of intelligence tests. *Fifth Yearbook of the National Association of Secondary School Principals,* 45–54.

U.S. Bureau of the Census. (1975). *Historical statistics of the United States, colonial times to 1970* (Vols. 1 & 2). Washington, DC: Government Printing Office.

U.S. Department of Education, National Center for Education Statistics. (1990). *Digest of education statistics, 1990.* Washington, DC: Government Printing Office.

U.S. Department of Education, National Center for Education Statistics. (1991). *Digest of education statistics, 1991.* Washington, DC: Government Printing Office.

U.S. Department of Education, National Center for Education Statistics. (1993). *Digest of education statistics, 1993.* Washington, DC: Government Printing Office.

U.S. Department of Education, Office of Special Education and Rehabilitative Services. (1980). *Second annual report to Congress on the implementation of Public Law 94-142: The Education for All Handicapped Children Act.* Washington, DC: Author.

Villa, R., & Thousand, J. (1988). Enhancing success in heterogeneous classrooms and schools: The power of partnership. *Teacher Education and Special Education, 11,* 144–154.

Villa, R., & Thousand, J. (1992). How one district integrated special and regular education. *Educational Leadership, 50*(2), 39–41.

Villa, R., Thousand, J., Paolucci-Whitcomb, P., & Nevin, A. (1990). In search of new paradigms for collaborative consultation. *Journal of Educational and Psychological Consultation, 1,* 279–292.

Villa, R.A., Thousand, J.S., Stainback, W., & Stainback, S. (Eds.). (1992). *Restructuring for caring and effective education: An administrative guide to creating heterogeneous schools.* Baltimore: Paul H. Brookes Publishing Co.

Wang, M., Reynolds, M., & Walberg, H.J. (1987). *Handbook of special education research and practice.* Oxford: Pergamon Press.

Will, M. (1986). *Educating students with learning problems—A shared responsibility.* Washington, DC: U.S. Department of Education, Office of Special Education and Rehabilitative Services.

Wolfensberger, W. (1972). *The principle of normalization in human services.* Toronto: National Institute on Mental Retardation.

Worthington, G.E. (1925). Compulsory sterilization laws. *Journal of Social Hygiene, 11,* 257–271.

York, J., & Vandercook, T. (1988). Feature issue on integrated education. *IMPACT, 1,* 1–3.

3

Inclusion as a Force for School Renewal

John O'Brien and Connie Lyle O'Brien

INCLUDING STUDENTS WITH significant disabilities in general education class-rooms heightens the awareness of each interrelated aspect of the school as a community: its boundaries, its benefits to members, its internal relationships, its relationships with the outside environment, and its history (Taylor, 1992). As most people who have faced the possibility of inclusion know viscerally, this heightened awareness usually comes in the form of fear and defensiveness, expressed in terms that sound similar from both sides of the boundary separating students on the basis of disability. The feelings of both special and general education teachers could be summed up as follows: "Students like that have always been educated with others like themselves. Both they and their teachers work in fundamentally different ways than we do, and, what's more, their teachers have different affiliations, different sources of funds, and different accountabilities than we do. Having those students here with us will distract us from our real purpose and disrupt our routines. Besides, we don't know how to teach students like that. Both groups of students will be disadvantaged; those students' parents would never allow it to happen and neither would our students' parents."

The art of facilitating inclusion involves working creatively with this state of heightened awareness to redirect the energy bound up in fear toward problem solving

Preparation of this chapter was supported through a subcontract from The Center on Human Policy, Syracuse University, for the Research and Training Center on Community Living. The Research and Training Center on Community Living is supported through a cooperative agreement (No. H133B80048) between the National Institute on Disability and Rehabilitation Research (NIDRR) and the University of Minnesota Institute on Community Integration. Members of the Center are encouraged to express their opinions; these do not necessarily represent the official position of NIDRR.

that promotes reconsideration of boundaries, relationships, structures, and benefits. When this redirection fails, students with disabilities remain on the outside of education, or they drift with their individualized education programs (IEPs) and their aides the way Peter did (Schnorr, 1990). When this redirection succeeds, the life of a classroom shifts, in surprisingly quiet ways, to make room for new relationships, new structures, and new learning, as it did for Katie (Logan et al., 1994). Table 1 outlines some of the contrasts between Peter's and Katie's experiences in first grade.

Differences between the two children do not explain the difference in their experiences—in fact, as described, Katie's disabilities were more significant than Peter's. What made the difference was the guiding idea that directed the behavior of the adults involved with the two children. Peter received a professionally prescribed dose of mainstreaming as a part of his special education; whatever his experience of it was, he was only visiting schoolmates in their classroom, whose boundaries, relationships and structures were, by adult design, minimally influenced by his presence. Katie belonged

Table 1. Contrasting experiences of Peter and Katie in first grade

Peter	Katie
Boundaries	
Joins a class of 23 students for one period in the morning and during special period after lunch for art, music, PE, & library. "He's not in our class… He comes in the morning when we have seat work. Then he leaves to go back to his room." (Schnorr, 1990, p. 235)	Full-time member of regular class of 22 students. "I like Katie bekos I like to pla weth her. I like to help her weth her work. I like to count weth her…." (Logan et al., 1994, p. 43)
Adult relationships	
General class teacher has no instructional responsibility; Peter brings his work with him. Peter comes to art and music with two other special education students and a special education teaching assistant.	General education teacher has instructional responsibility with assistance in designing instruction and 2 hours daily support from special educator or teaching assistant, who acts as a co-teacher for the entire class.
Structures	
When Peter is with them, other students work at their seats on individual work sheets. "We do math and he colors" (Schnorr, 1990, p. 236). Peter leaves art, music, PE, and library 15 minutes before other students.	Cooperative learning groups, peer tutoring, and the buddy system are used. Learning activities are adapted to promote integration (e.g., Katie picks out two flashcards [learning to count], and her partner adds the numerals and states the sum [learning to add]).
Benefits	
Goals for Peter in the regular classroom are all social (even though all activities when he is there are either individual or conducted in a subgroup of special students).	Goals for all children are cognitive and developmental. An interdisciplinary unit, "How can I make a change in my community," focused on disability issues including accessibility and inclusion. "…Me and Katie like to rede together. She holds the other side of the book and repete after me…" (Logan et al., 1994, p. 43).

Note: PE, physical education.

to her class, and, because special educators and general educators collaborated to give educational meaning to her membership, the adaptations her presence stimulated benefitted her, her classmates, and her teachers.

INCLUSION IS A CULTURAL FORCE FOR SCHOOL RENEWAL

Across the political spectrum, people concerned about schooling call for reform, restructuring, and renewal. The students, parents, teachers, and administrators who are actively engaged in the day-to-day work of including students with significant disabilities represent a powerful cultural force for school renewal, a force that Fullen (1993), a long-time student of change in schools, described this way:

> In most restructuring reforms, new structures are supposed to result in new behaviors and cultures, but mostly fail to do so. There is no doubt a reciprocal relationship between structural and cultural change, but it is much more powerful when teachers and administrators begin working in new ways only to discover that school structures are ill-fitted to the new orientations and must be altered.... (p. 68)

Based on this understanding, positive effects of inclusion on school renewal come only when the people engaged 1) notice discrepancies between what they want to do and what current boundaries, relationships, and structures allow; and 2) adapt those boundaries, relationships, and structures to make the next steps to inclusion possible. For example, most teachers and administrators working for inclusion find that their work calls for a far more collaborative relationship between special education teachers and general education teachers than existing structures can support. As they work to collaborate, they may find themselves reconsidering the tradition that has separated them, renegotiating the physical and temporal boundaries of the classroom, reallocating responsibilities, and finding new ways to share the benefits of working collaboratively. In turn, these changes can lead them to negotiate for changes in job descriptions, supervisory arrangements, and conditions of employment.

Inclusion as a potential force for school renewal is easily thwarted. Involved people may breathe a sigh of relief if a student with a disability simply manages to be present in class without precipitating any of the anticipated disasters, and they may then raise no further questions about the school's practice. The weight of a school's history—customary labor demarcations, jealousies over resource allocations, rivalries for control, habitual animosities, cynicism, and overcommitment to too many reform programs at once—can overwhelm a school's capacity to adapt to the possibilities that inclusion presents. Ironically, people may be distracted from the sustained work of reshaping boundaries, relationships, and structures by the growing visibility of inclusion as a concept. Administrative directives may impose inclusion in an attempt at structural change, thus reversing the less dramatic but potentially more powerful process of generating cultural shifts that lead to adaptations in structure. Thereby, the chances are increased that inclusion will join the long list of disappointing reforms we tried in the 1990s. Practitioners eager to reflect recommended practice may simply relabel their current activities as inclusive rather than transform their practice, and competing interest groups may raise inclusion as a banner or as a target in their campaigns on other school-related issues.

FOR INCLUSION TO THRIVE, SCHOOLS MUST BE CONSCIOUS COMMUNITIES

Sergiovanni (1994) described the importance of community to schooling this way:

Community is the tie that binds students and teachers together in special ways, to something more significant than themselves: shared values and ideals. It lifts both teachers and students to higher levels of self-understanding, commitment and performance—beyond the reaches of the shortcomings and difficulties they face in their everyday lives. Community can help teachers and students be transformed from a collection of "I's" to a collective "we," thus providing them with a unique sense of identity, belonging, and place. (p. xiii)

Without this sense of community, Sergiovanni argued, efforts to achieve superior academic results or even to maintain discipline are fundamentally hindered. If it is to be achieved at all, community in school must be a conscious effort. Building community requires thoughtful and sustained work in responding to at least three influential social trends. First, most public schools bring together students and staff from diverse backgrounds and circumstances; and, often, intergroup conflicts, unsolved outside of school because no effective civic mechanisms support resolution, create chronic tensions, which occasionally erupt and shatter the uneasy truces that allow everyday school life. Second, more and more children and their families have to discover how to create a decent, satisfying life in the face of the many powerful forces that strain family and neighborhood ties (this is as true of teachers and their families as it is of any other family) (Martin, 1992). Third, our experience has showed that there is a growing number of children and adults who do not defer to authority without question; they expect to be sold rather than told and, without a negotiated sense of shared purpose, they will ask, "What's in it for me, right now?"

No one who is actually working to build community confuses community with utopia. Communities can be stratified and justify terrible inequalities in access to resources. Community members can shame and bully one another into claustrophobically narrow roles. A community can feed its sense of unity with hatred of difference, with manipulated fear of enemies, and with scapegoating. Guiding a school's development is not about invoking community as a magic panacea. It is about the courageous and thoughtful struggle for respectful relationships, equal opportunity for individual initiatives, mutual support with life's troubles, the sharing and celebration of each member's unique gifts, fair resolutions of conflicts, and the need to confront threats with integrity. Building community is helpful as a guiding idea for a school because it can provide a way to understand these fundamentally human issues in a way that organizes sustained action.

The full promise of inclusion lies in the kind of school community that can develop as students with significant disabilities raise the awareness of the unspoken dimensions of school life and provide opportunities for everyone who shares that life to learn more rewarding ways to be together. Students with significant disabilities are, of course, neither the only teachers of these lessons of community nor are they the only beneficiaries of schools that are willing to learn from them. Students with academic and artistic gifts also have much to teach about the costs of separating and grouping children on the basis of a single dimension of their lives and about the benefits of carefully building community (Sapon-Shevin, 1994); so too can the many students pushed to the margins of school life by the consequences of poverty, racism, sexism, and differences in learning style, which are all too often exacerbated by the many separate programs intended to remediate them (Wang, Reynolds, & Walberg, 1994); so too can teachers who feel the lack of collegiality and mutual support and who dislike being treated as poorly milled parts of a malfunctioning machine (Sarason, 1990).

Students with significant disabilities, however, can make a particular contribution to building community in school precisely because their presence in general education classrooms, vocational education programs, and student activities has been, to most people, unthinkable. If neighborhood schools are places where students can successfully learn together despite obvious and extreme differences in ability, they must be very different sorts of places than many people have thought.

Three themes emerge from observing classrooms working to include students with significant disabilities and from listening to students and teachers reflect on their experience (O'Brien, 1994; O'Brien, 1992, 1993). First, adults make more of inclusion than students do, both in that they fear greater problems and in that they are more excited by the outcomes. Many students in inclusive schools are puzzled when adults from other districts visit to see them doing everyday things alongside students with disabilities. Second, although some students are indifferent and a few say that they would prefer not to have classmates with significant disabilities, a great number of students report enjoying getting to know, doing things with, and helping students with significant disabilities. Third, contrary to common and persistent worries, the inclusion of students with significant disabilities does not seem to result in the decline of overall student achievement. In fact, the impression that students with significant disabilities make a positive difference to achievement is common, although schools supported this impression only occasionally through systematic study (Cooper, 1993).

Among the benefits that students in inclusive schools from kindergarten to high school commonly report are discovering commonalities with people who superficially look and act very different; taking pride in helping someone make important gains who seems less able; having opportunities to care about others; acting consistently with important values, such as promoting equality, overcoming segregation, or defending someone who is treated unjustly; developing skills in collaborative problem solving, communicating, instructing, and providing personal assistance; learning directly about difficult things, including overcoming a fear of differences; problem solving around classroom relationship problems; dealing with difficult, violent, or self-injurious behavior; dealing with the effects of family issues on a classmate's life; and facing and supporting one another through the serious illness, and sometimes the death, of someone their own age (O'Brien, 1994; O'Brien, 1992, 1993).

These are not necessarily ideal relationships. A student with a disability can sometimes seem more like a class project than a full and equal class member. Not only are the relationships of a student with a disability as volatile and occasionally painful as those of students without disabilities, but some students without disabilities can assume a quasiprofessional or maternalistic role. In our experience, many more girls and young women are involved in close relationships with students of both sexes with disabilities than are boys and young men (O'Brien, 1994; O'Brien, 1992, 1993). A number of parents of older students with disabilities have said that their hopes for close, equal, and enduring friendships that extended spontaneously into life after 3:00 P.M. faded as their child's classmates began to date, drive, and work after school. Even given these limitations, however, many students in inclusive classrooms act capably and resourcefully in situations that adults often find daunting. What seems most important for this resourcefulness is that teachers encourage students to face real problems that occur in the common life of their classrooms, with the clear expectation that they make a significant contribution to resolving them.

The guiding idea of building conscious community offers the best direction for the work of deepening and strengthening students as resources for each other's education. Building community does not lessen the importance of academic work or vocational preparation; it simply recognizes that, without continual effort to build an environment of respectful relationships and of caring about people, ideas, and things, the achievement of academic and vocational goals will be very limited indeed (Noddings, 1992).

LEARNING TO BUILD COMMUNITY MEANS LINKING PERSON-TO-PERSON LEARNING TO SOCIAL ARCHITECTURE

The way to build community begins in the learning that happens when people who have been separated meet face to face, discover one another, and begin to adapt to one another. A conscious community develops when people use cycles of person-to-person learning to develop a social architecture—the set of tools, systems, and structures that as norms define the school as an organization—that expresses and supports that learning (Figure 1). (See American Management Association, 1994, and Senge, 1994, for discussion about the work of a learning organization.) The person-to-person learning cycle incorporates expanded awareness, new personal skills and capabilities, and a deeper sense of purpose (Figure 2). When teachers who are anxious about including

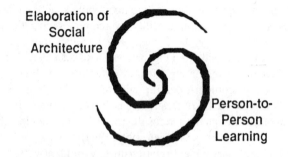

Elaboration of
Social
Architecture

Person-to-
Person
Learning

Figure 1. The process of building conscious community.

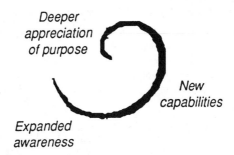

Figure 2. The person-to-person learning cycle.

students with significant disabilities identify their fears of inadequacy in teaching them, an awareness emerges of the need for new capabilities in designing instruction and dealing constructively with differences. As discussion, problem solving, and practice expand their capabilities, teachers come to see their classrooms and their teaching in new ways that deepen their appreciation of the purpose of their work. In turn, a deeper sense of purpose can set the scene for further expansion of awareness and further development of capabilities.

In competent school communities, person-to-person learning shapes the social architecture, which are the boundaries, relationships, and structures that organize space, time, talents, and money. Clearer guidelines create new tools, and new tools shape new systems (Figure 3). Through planning with and for the whole school, shared exploration of a deepened sense of personal purpose among teachers and students can clarify the guiding ideas that organize the school's daily life. Through systematic reflection on effective practice, new capabilities take form in new tools and procedures. Through an expanding awareness from day-to-day problem solving and conflict resolution, the school system can be adapted to make the work people want to do easier. Table 2 includes some examples of tools (ways of dealing with particular problems) and systems that developed from inclusion of children with significant disabilities.

In turn, shifts in social architecture can stimulate person-to-person learning. Public commitment to building community can generate important questions and

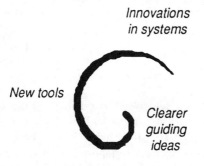

Figure 3. The process of elaborating social architecture.

Table 2.   Tools and innovations developed in response to inclusion

GUIDING IDEA

The school is a place where...
...all are welcome to contribute to the work of the school
...each belongs as a valued member
...all students and adults support one another as active learners

Tools	Systems
MAPs (O'Brien & Forest, 1989): A way to engage students, parents, and teachers in developing a shared understanding of a student and a common vision of that student as an active learner who enjoys the benefits of class membership and contributes his or her gifts to other members of the class.	Cooperative Learning (Johnson & Johnson, 1994; Sapon-Shevin, Ayres, & Duncan, 1994): Structures 1) interdependent performance on common curricular tasks, 2) individual accountability for achieving instructional objectives and personal responsibility for contributing to group effectiveness, 3) purposeful face-to-face cooperation in small groups, 4) systematic development of interpersonal and group skills, and 5) continual improvement of learning group functioning through systematic evaluation.
Creative Problem Solving (CPS) (Giangreco, Cloninger, Dennis, & Edelman, 1994): A systematic approach to creative problem solving that taps student and teacher creativity by orchestrating divergent and convergent thinking to specify 1) objectives, 2) relevant facts, 3) effective problem definition, 4) potential ideas for solution, 5) good solutions, and 6) acceptance of a plan of action.	Circles of friends (Pearpoint & Forest, 1993): A way of inviting and sustaining people's expressions of their care for one another through the exchange of practical help, problem solving, advice, and personal support in day-to-day activities of interest to circle members.
Membership Stories (Ferguson, 1994): A way to guide reflection and learning about the ways in which groups of students create shared definitions that incorporate students with disabilities and the ways in which groups of students include one another in shared activity.	Partner Learning (Thousand, Villa, & Nevin, 1994): Structures student–student partnerships in which one student exercises responsibility for assisting another student's learning through coaching academic learning, mentoring, participation in school activities, or mediating the resolution of conflicts.
PATH (Pearpoint, O'Brien, & Forest, 1993): A way to organize people with diverse points of view and differing gifts to search for explicit and scheduled patterns of shared action that will move them toward a shared vision of common values.	Inclusion Facilitators (Tashie et al., 1993): Redefines the job of the special education teacher as a collaborator with all teachers, related service providers, and parents with the mission "to facilitate, however necessary, the full inclusion of students who have disabilities as active, participating learners in regular age-appropriate classes and neighborhood schools" (p. 7).

Note: MAPs, Making Action Plans; PATH, Planning Alternative Tomorrows with Hope.

conflicts among teachers and students. These situations can create occasions to expand awareness and clarify personal purpose. Tools, such as MAPs (Making Action Plans) (O'Brien & Forest, 1989) or Membership Stories (Ferguson, 1994), can provide occasions for expanding capabilities. Innovations in systems, such as the adoption of collaborative learning approaches or the redefinition of the role of special educators to be collaborating teachers, can provide an environment conducive to creating new tools and a new sense of shared purpose.

The following provides a glimpse of the tools and systems that developed in one fifth grade classroom. The first-year teacher, Cristina, worked with her mentor, Ann, who taught the class next door, and a special education teacher, Julie, who planned and taught with both of them.

Students are working in groups, designing fire-safety posters as part of a performance assessment for their health unit. John, Helen, Connie, and Jeff use the first three minutes of their work time in a creative problem-solving process. Julie, John's inclusion teacher, sits with the group and asks them to think of ways to give John, their classmate with Down syndrome, practice with his IEP goals—answering "what" questions, staying on task, and performing fine motor skills like tracing letters and pictures. She then asks the group to recap the last group project they did with John: the parts they thought went well and the parts they thought could have gone better.... After one minute of fact-finding, Julie asks the group to think of ideas to solve the problems they have identified. Julie writes down everything the group says: "Ask John questions"; "Give John time to answer"; "Give John choices"; "Take turns helping John while the rest of us work on project"; "Give John a buddy." After brainstorming for one minute, Julie reads out the ideas and asks the group to say which ones they think might help. After another one-minute discussion, Julie and the group pick their "best" solutions to try during the group's work on the the the fire-safety project.

Only three minutes have elapsed since the class began their group projects. John's group has a "game plan" to make the most of their allotted time.... John, Connie, Helen, and Jeff take a few more minutes to agree on major topics and details to include in their poster. They also decide who will be responsible for each part. Helen is working with John today, and looks through a book with him to get ideas for illustrations for their poster. John says, "Let's draw a door with a peephole to see the fire." Helen makes a dotted-line door for John to trace. Helen then turns to Connie and discusses the fire-safety rules that will go beside the door. Helen writes the first two rules in yellow highlighter so John can trace them. While John works on his tracing, Jeff illustrates another part of the poster; and Helen and Connie outline the next set of details. Helen periodically looks up from her work with Connie and encourages John. Connie and Jeff also look up from their work to encourage John and give him opportunities to respond to "what" questions: "What are you drawing?" "What color is that?" "What am I drawing?" Julie and Cristina are circulating through the classroom, giving help as needed. From time to time, Julie drifts back over to check on John and his group. This time she reminds John to take his time tracing and gives Helen a "thumbs up" for the good coaching she is giving John. Cristina is recording individual grades for cooperative work skills as she circulates. Everyone in John's group gets highest marks today. (Rankin, 1994, p. 23)

The kind of learning that this example illustrates can only come by choice. School leaders can invite the kind of sustained dialogue necessary to clarify important guiding ideas, or they can simply issue a command: "As of now, this school is an inclusive community." Teachers can thoughtfully incorporate new tools into their practice and develop their capabilities, or they can mindlessly run techniques, complain about their lack of effect, and proclaim inclusion a failure. School board members can guide a process of systems adaptation that will strengthen the entire school community, or they can reactively impose a reform on the school system.

BUILDING COMMUNITY IS CREATIVE WORK

One determinant of the scope and depth of person-to-person learning and the effectiveness of adaptations of social architecture is the shared creativity of the people involved. Ackoff (1991) described creativity as a three-step process: 1) identify fundamental assumptions that appear to be self-evident that guide ordinary behavior in ways that significantly reduce the range of available choices, 2) deny the validity of the identified assumptions, and 3) explore the consequences of denying these assumptions.

The inclusion of students with significant disabilities offers rich opportunities to expose and challenge some of the fundamental assumptions that may constrain school effectiveness. The surest road to uncovering these fundamental assumptions begins with a careful exploration of the conflicts that polarize people around the issue. A conflict of this type presents two key features: It is framed as an either/or choice, and it generates strong emotions that pull people to one side or another and keep them there. Table 3 identifies three common conflicts in efforts to create more inclusive school communities.

Emotions attached to these conflicts often generate one of three responses that frustrate creativity and limit inclusion as a force in school renewal. First, people may try to ignore the conflict. Second, they may focus their energy on fighting those who hold the opposite view, often appealing to outside allies such as unions or judges and thus shifting the conflict to more distant and familiar ground such as contract negotiations or adjudication of rights. Third, they may decide to compromise—that is, locate a point somewhere on the line between the poles that reflects the balance of power between the two groups.

A better response is to move into the conflict by carefully considering what is at stake and what the possibilities are. An assumption that promotes these conflicts is that the only possible resolution is a win/lose outcome: If we have more classroom practices that support friendships, then we must pay for this in declines in skills or academic attainment; if we have more inclusion, then we must have fewer of the specialized services students require; if we have greater benefits for students with disabilities, then students without disabilities must suffer.

Gharajedaghi (1985) provided a useful conceptual tool to guide this work. He suggested discrediting the assumption that these win/lose trade-offs are necessary conditions of inclusion by substituting "and" for "or" in the formulation of the conflict (see Table 3) and by considering what shared action has the potential to integrate the conflicting views. Dialogue about how the people involved in the conflict understand both camps is essential to crafting an organizing theme for action—a common goal to which people in conflict can commit their energies and a direction to stimulate problem finding and problem solving. Sarason (1990) also appealed to this kind of thinking in asking, "How can we liberate the human mind to use its capacities in ways that are

Table 3. Recurring conflicts concerning inclusive schools

Inclusion	or	Specialized services
Classroom activities that support social experiences and friendships	or	Classroom activities that support acquisition of academic or vocational skills
Students with disabilities benefit	or	Students without disabilities benefit

productively expressive of those capacities at the same time that they strengthen a sense of community" (p. 1). Figure 4 illustrates the shift in thinking that Gharajedaghi (1985) formulated and Sarason (1990) confirmed. Shifting attention from a win/lose contest between inclusion and specialized services to a search for ways to ensure that each child in a school receives individualized support for successful learning can help people to explore ways to modify current boundaries, relationships, and structures. Professionals may reconsider the time and role demarcations that have led to the routine administration of specialized services in brief separate meetings between a therapist and a child or a small group of children and take a collaborative approach to using their skills in concert with classroom teachers; this work will probably bring them some stress as they reconsider their beliefs about their separate professions (York, Giangreco, Vandercook, & Macdonald, 1992). They may explore ways in which classroom and school activities can be adapted to serve educationally important purposes, as when one speech therapist decided that the natural interactions among children during story time provided her with the best setting to work on improving a student's communication, or when another shifted her priorities in order to assist a student to get better word recognition software for his laptop computer so that he could participate more independently in English class (O'Brien, 1994).

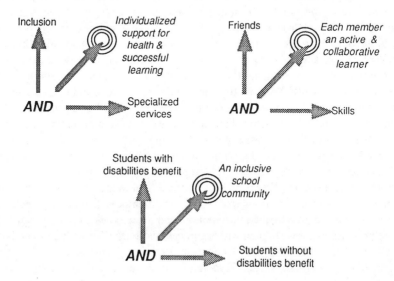

Figure 4. Reframing common conflicts.

Some changes call for a new context. A classroom organized in straight rows to promote student–teacher relationships aimed narrowly at either individualistic pursuit of teacher-controlled activities or competition that ranks students from best to worst shrinks the space available for developing opportunities and supports almost to the vanishing point. A classroom organized to promote cooperative learning and partner learning can promote positive social relationships and the practice, challenge, and support necessary for all students to develop relevant academic skills. This kind of school is a demanding place to be as an adult because each member of the school, including the teachers, administrators, custodians, and cafeteria workers, must accept personal responsibility for being an active and collaborative learner.

INCLUSION IS NOT COMPETITION

The perceived competition between children with significant disabilities and children without disabilities offers many possibilities for reflection. The source of this conflict are two assumptions that can deeply constrain building an inclusive school community: 1) that students are best understood as either passive consumers of adult-designed programs or noncompliant subverters of adult-designed programs, and 2) that schooling, totally controlled by adults, provides the necessary education that develops full citizens. These assumptions posit the school as an education factory in which students are the raw materials transformed into willing workers and good citizens through standardized procedures. They conflict with the idea of school as a conscious community of learners in which students find the personal models, disciplines, skills, and information necessary to their education.

The experience of students and teachers engaged in the work of inclusion provides reasons to question both of the above assumptions. Given the opportunity, students of all ages and diverse abilities demonstrate resourcefulness as collaborators in the design of and active contributors to classrooms and schools that work a little better for everyone. Students whose presence has been unthinkable because of their obvious disabilities can make as much of a contribution to building a community of active learners as anyone else. Working together, students, teachers, and parents can create school communities that contribute more to everyone's education exactly because they openly engage in some of the real human difficulties and significant uncertainties that are easily hidden in the busy order of school routine.

Students with significant disabilities, as outsiders, can stir strong human emotions and energies. Some students, teachers, and parents welcome the difficult lessons that arise from their presence. Others react to fear and fight to maintain control by sanitizing the schoolroom and cleansing it of significant differences. In order to work with the messiness, the uncontrollability, the emotion, and the darkness stirred in many adults by the presence of a few children with significant disabilities, those who want to make inclusive communities need to reflect on what education means, how it can be supported, and how it can be subverted. Stopping to reflect on an old story might teach us about education.

EDUCATION IS THE WAY OF BECOMING A HUMAN BEING

The following is an old story about how people become human beings that is useful for exploring the conflicts that emerge on the road to inclusive education.

Once there was a powerful king whose beloved queen died within days of giving birth to their long-awaited son. The king loved his son fiercely and determined to do all that was necessary to prepare the prince to be a great king after him. He gave his son the finest tutors to strengthen and discipline his body and his reason. He gave his son loving attendants and playmates to share the palace with him. Most important of all, the king protected his son from contact with old age, poverty, pain, and suffering.

The prince studied hard and played hard so that he would become a king worthy of his father's respect and love. He grew straight, strong, and smart, but was more and more troubled that he knew too little of life. And so he asked his riding companion, whom he loved and trusted, to take him to see how people lived outside the walls of the palace.

When the companion asked permission for the trip, the king told him exactly what route and schedule to follow, and the king sent guards ahead to see that everything was cleaned and tidy and that the aged, the infirm, and the poor were hidden from sight. "Make sure," he commanded, "that my son is edified only by the sight of those who are able and successful and handsome."

The prince and his companion had perfect weather for their trip, and everywhere the prince went he met healthy, happy people. He was thinking to himself that he was foolish to be anxious about his knowledge of life because everyone he met seemed much like himself. But suddenly a very old ragged woman, twisted with the burden of her years and confused by a cloud over her memory, tottered into the prince's path and shattered his complacency with her babbling.

The prince had never seen anything like this old woman, and he demanded to know if this was indeed a person or if it were some other kind of creature. Reluctantly, his companion told the prince that he had glimpsed old age, which comes to all creatures, even to the king himself. Upset, the prince returned quickly to the palace and spent a sleepless night trying to assimilate this new experience.

The king was furious. Not only had the prince been troubled by the sight of old age, but he had resolved to take even more trips outside the palace walls to learn more about life.

In the coming days, despite the frantic efforts of tutors and guards terrified into more and more careful preparation by the king's wrath, the prince met people who were poor, and people who were sick, and people who were broken by failure, and people who were mourning the death of a friend. And, considering these troubling aspects of his humanity, the prince left his distraught father's palace to find his own life's path.

We sketched the story of Prince Siddhartha from his father's point of view because we feel within us, and we hear all around us, the urgency of people who fervently want their children to grow up strong and able to take their places. Although we are not powerful kings and queens, we want to defend our children against anxiety and distraction and see them grow up smart and happy, and we feel an urgency to build secure walls around their childhood in order to strengthen their bodies and focus their minds on the demands of adulthood. Because we do not live in palaces, but in a world where economic uncertainty, random violence, inexplicable diseases, and dangerous drugs undermine even our highest walls, our fervor easily turns to a frantic search for control of every detail of our children's contacts and routines. Because our children are not material princes and princesses, we fear that they will too soon face an adult world whose impersonal demands will overpower them and disappoint their dreams, and so we teeter between indulgence to compensate them for the hurt that will come and harshness to harden them to face it stolidly.

Siddhartha, whose story is much more richly told by Martin (1990), followed his life's path out of the palace walls and toward a world filled with pain and suffering, and thereby he traced out the lessons that became Buddhism. The beginning of his ancient story can speak to our predicaments in the education of children and young people. No matter how we try to buffer them, our children face the human realities of poverty, pain, sickness, disability, injustice, aging, and death. Indeed, they yearn to confront these realities so strongly that denial of them stunts their growth as human beings. Parental love and protection and provision of opportunity, discipline, information, and skills offer the young person some resources for transforming revulsion, fear, or morbid fascination into important knowledge. Young people, respectful of parental anxiety for their happiness and of the desire that they follow parental plans, are likely to find the best way through these hard realities with the guidance of a trustworthy mentor who truthfully responds to spoken and unspoken but real questions. Being a worthy mentor means courageously entering a conflict between the parent's desire to protect the child from difficulties by exercising control and the young person's desire to learn by directly engaging difficulties and exploring shadows. The journey of human growth may include periods of traveling alone, as Siddhartha's did, but his journey, like every human journey, begins and ends and progresses, through personal relationships whose quality determines the depth of education.

COMMANDS ARE FUTILE AS A WAY TO BETTER EDUCATION

We raise these considerations because we believe that the voice of the king dominates most current debates over schooling in general and inclusion in particular. When politicians promise to discipline teachers so that schools will be as reliable, efficient, and clean as microchip factories and as morally upright as Sunday school picnics, the king speaks loudly through them. When parents contest bitterly with one another to dominate school boards so that their children will be protected from the difficulties of accommodating people with diverse cultures, beliefs, and ideas, the king speaks loudly through them. When the president of a teachers' union asserts that the rush toward inclusion of children with disabilities is the contemporary trend that will have "the profoundest and most destructive effect on schooling" (Shanker, 1994), the king speaks loudly through him.

In each case, the king's command is the same: Keep awful things away from my children, guard the gates, keep out what threatens, purge the enemies within our walls, and control every detail of daily life so that my children will grow up and take my place. In each case, the king's command may be motivated by love and concern and could lead to his children having some of the resources they need to become responsible adults. In each case, the king's voice grows louder and louder because his commands become futile when his voice drowns out the other voices that are necessary in the drama of human development.

Authoritatively demanding that schools assume responsibility for education that is both effective in real life as well as safe and sure because it controls all the details of children's lives is futile for at least five closely connected reasons. First, the command contradicts itself because human growth requires both boundaries and challenges to boundaries, both time within the walls and time to travel outside the walls. Second, the command assigns too much of the wrong sort of responsibility to schools by making schooling equivalent to education. Much contemporary debate assumes that variations in standardized test scores reveal the educational results of public investment rather than simply provide a quantitative check on some of the effects of schooling. While administrators seek to drive up test scores, the human work of education goes on, sometimes in school, sometimes at home, sometimes in the community. Third, while no sensible person would allow a school to become an unwelcoming or a dangerous place, growing up as a human being in a complex and conflict-ridden world involves dealing with substantial risks from an early age. The educational costs of ignoring all painful experience within the conscious life of schools are very great. Fourth, the culture of commands and the fear of disobedience lead to peculiar distortions of truth that make everyday life in schools unnecessarily difficult. Inclusion of students with significant disabilities, which has been said by some to be destroying our schools, has seen only 5 in 100 children with mental retardation, only 5 in 100 children with autistic disorder, and only 6 in 100 children with multiple disabilities enroll full time in general education classes (U.S. Department of Education, 1994). Despite many expert proclamations that ordinary teachers cannot, will not, be supported adequately in managing a classroom that includes children with significant disabilities, a small but steadily growing number of teachers are, in fact, receiving such support (Rankin et al., 1994). Fifth, the high volume of talk and activity around the school reform might lead citizens to conclude that 1) there are highly effective methods for changing schools, and 2) classroom behavior has been changed repeatedly and radically through high-visibility educational reforms. However, Fullen (1993) reviewed research on systematic efforts to change schools and concluded that 1) no reliable means of implementing mandated school change exists, and 2) even when administrators and teachers work systematically and with substantial extra resources to stimulate change they are far more likely to change structures or written curricula than they are to change actual classroom behavior. Sarason (1990) considered different studies and came to similar conclusions, noting that the overall performance of schools continues to deteriorate relative to social expectations and that schools remain intractable to reform efforts.

CONCLUSION: BUILDING INCLUSIVE
COMMUNITY LINKS SCHOOLING WITH EDUCATION

Education leads children and adults out of comfortable routines to the challenges and the pleasures of drawing on the lessons in human experience to face life's realities. Education occurs through being with others, and the gifts and fallibilities of others shape the extent and the texture of each member's growth. Schooling offers people more resources for their education when adults and students collaborate to build a conscious community that sustains the work of the school, although this means growing past the myth of the complete control of childhood. Students with significant disabilities and their parents can liberate and organize much creativity in the school community. To do this, all that is required is the courage to renegotiate familiar boundaries, relationships, and structures, the commitment to learn the way through the difficulties that arise, and the fidelity to renew the sense of community when it is threatened.

REFERENCES

Ackhoff, R. (1991). *Ackhoff's fables: Irreverent reflections on business and bureaucracy.* New York: John Wiley & Sons.

American Management Association. (1994). *The learning organization in action: A special report from Organization Dynamics.* Saranac Lake, NY: AMA Publication Services.

Cooper, P. (1993). *Safety net: The development of "at risk" services for all children and youth.* Saint Francisville, LA: West Feleciana Parish Schools.

Ferguson, D. (1994). Is communication really the point? Some thoughts on intervention and membership. *Mental Retardation, 32*(1), 7–18.

Fullen, M. (1993). *Change forces: Probing the depths of educational reform.* London: The Falmer Press.

Gharajedaghi, J. (1985). *Toward a systems theory of organization.* Seaside, CA: Intersystems Publications.

Giangreco, M., Cloninger, C., Dennis, R., & Edelman, S. (1994). Problem-solving methods to facilitate inclusive education. In J.S. Thousand, R.A. Villa, & A.I. Nevin (Eds.), *Creativity and collaborative learning: A practical guide to empowering students and teachers* (pp. 321–346). Baltimore: Paul H. Brookes Publishing Co.

Johnson, R., & Johnson, D. (1994). An overview of cooperative learning. In J.S. Thousand, R.A. Villa, & A.I. Nevin (Eds.), *Creativity and collaborative learning: A practical guide to empowering students and teachers* (pp. 31–45). Baltimore: Paul H. Brookes Publishing Co.

Logan, K., Fiaz, E., Piperno, M., Rankin, D., MacFarland, A., & Bargamin, K. (1994). How inclusion built a community of learners. *Educational Leadership, 52*(4), 42–44.

Martin, J. (1992). *The school home: Rethinking schools for changing families.* Cambridge, MA: Harvard University Press.

Martin, R. (1990). *The hungry tigress: Buddhist legends and jataka tales.* Berkeley, CA: Parallax Press.

Noddings, N. (1992). *The challenge to care in the schools: An alternative approach to education.* New York: Teachers College Press.

O'Brien, C. (1994). [Field notes on visits to inclusive school classrooms in Georgia]. Unpublished data.

O'Brien, J. (1992). [Field notes on visits to inclusive schools in the Kitchner-Waterloo, Ontario, Separate School Board]. Unpublished data.

O'Brien, J. (1993). [Field notes on visits and interviews with students, teachers, and parents involved in inclusive schools in Colorado, New Hampshire, and Oregon]. Unpublished data.

O'Brien, J., & Forest, M. (1989). *Action for inclusion.* Toronto: Inclusion Press.

O'Brien, J., & Lyle O'Brien, C. (1994). *Everybody's here, now we can begin....* Lithonia, GA: Responsive Systems Associates.

Pearpoint, J., & Forest, M. (1993). *The inclusion papers: Strategies to make inclusion happen.* Toronto: Inclusion Press.

Pearpoint, J., O'Brien, J., & Forest, M. (1993). *PATH.* Toronto: Inclusion Press.

Rankin, D. (1994). *Vignettes from inclusion classrooms in Gwinnett County, Georgia Public Schools.* Lawrenceville, GA: Gwinnett County Board of Education.

Rankin, D., Hallick, A., Ban, S., Hartley, P., Bost, C., & Uggla, N. (1994). Who's dreaming? A general education perspective on inclusion. *Journal of The Association for Persons with Severe Handicaps, 19*(3), 235–237.

Sapon-Shevin, M. (1994). *Playing favorites: Gifted education and the disruption of community.* Albany: State University of New York Press.

Sapon-Shevin, M., Ayres, B., & Duncan, J. (1994). Cooperative learning and inclusion. In J.S. Thousand, R.A. Villa, & A.I. Nevin (Eds.), *Creativity and collaborative learning: A practical guide to empowering students and teachers* (pp. 45–58). Baltimore: Paul H. Brookes Publishing Co.

Sarason, S. (1990). *The predictable failure of educational reform.* San Francisco: Jossey-Bass.

Schnorr, R. (1990). Peter? He comes and goes…First graders' perspectives on a part-time mainstream student. *Journal of The Association for Persons with Severe Handicaps, 15*(4), 231–240.

Senge, P. (1994). Thinking strategically about building learning organizations. In P. Senge, C. Roberts, R. Ross, B. Smith, & A. Kleiner (Eds.), *The fifth discipline fieldbook: Strategies and tools for building a learning organization* (pp. 15–47). New York: Doubleday.

Sergiovanni, T. (1994). *Building community in schools.* San Francisco: Jossey-Bass.

Shanker, A. (1994, January 6). Inclusion and ideology [advertisement]. *The New York Times,* p. E-7.

Tashie, C., Shapiro-Barnard, S., Dillon, A., Schuh, M., Jorgensen, C., & Nisbet, J. (1993). *Changes in latitudes, changes in attitudes. The role of the inclusion facilitator.* Durham: University of New Hampshire Institute on Disability.

Taylor, P. (1992). Community. In E. Keller & E. Lloyd (Eds.), *Keywords in evolutionary biology* (pp. 52–53). Cambridge, MA: Harvard University Press.

Thousand, J.S., Villa, R.A., & Nevin, A.I. (Eds.). (1994). *Creativity and collaborative learning: A practical guide to empowering students and teachers.* Baltimore: Paul H. Brookes Publishing Co.

U.S. Department of Education. (1994). *To assure the free appropriate public education of all children with disabilities: Sixteenth annual report to Congress on the implementation of the Individuals with Disabilities Education Act.* Washington, DC: Author.

Wang, M., Reynolds, M., & Walberg, H. (1994). Serving students at the margins. *Educational Leadership, 52*(4), 12–17.

York, J., Giangreco, M., Vandercook, T., & Macdonald, C. (1992). Integrating support personnel in the inclusive classroom. In S. Stainback & W. Stainback (Eds.), *Curriculum considerations in inclusive classrooms: Facilitating learning for all students* (pp. 101–116). Baltimore: Paul H. Brookes Publishing Co.

II

BASIC STRATEGIES

4

Ten Critical Elements for Creating Inclusive and Effective School Communities

C. Beth Schaffner and Barbara E. Buswell

THE PRINCIPLES OF inclusion apply not only to students with disabilities or at risk, but to *all* students. The challenging issues facing students and educators in today's schools allow no one the luxury of singling out and focusing on an isolated need or a target group of students. Furthermore, a piecemeal approach to school reform does not successfully meet the needs of any student:

> Comprehensive school reform entails two components. The first is a firm vision of the way schools could or should be. The ability to imagine schools otherwise—not stratified by ability, not beholden to a fixed curriculum, well staffed with innovative, engaging teachers who are themselves well supported —is the first requirement. But the second essential component of wide-ranging school reform, as opposed to program innovation or school tinkering, is a shared agenda: the understanding that fixing the school for some children must mean fixing the school for all children. (Sapon-Shevin, 1995, p. 70)

All advocates for improving schools to better meet diverse student needs must join together and recognize the principle that *good schools are good schools for all students*, and then act on that principle.

The elements that follow are those features that, when present in a school and a school system, contribute to the success of everyone. Furthermore, these elements are interdependent parts of creating a successful, dynamic, caring, learning community rather than discrete, unrelated components.

STEP 1: DEVELOP A COMMON
PHILOSOPHY AND STRATEGIC PLAN

The first and perhaps primary step for creating a quality inclusive school is to *establish a school philosophy* based on the democratic, egalitarian principles of inclusion, belonging, and provision of quality education to all students.

A quality inclusive system of education by its very nature focuses on the needs of the whole student, not merely on academic achievement. If schools are to achieve this emphasis on the *whole* student, their underlying philosophy needs to be that the education they provide will be

germane and relevant for each student, encompassing at the least three spheres of development: (1) the academic... (2) the social and emotional... and (3) personal and collective responsibility and citizenship.... (National Association of State Boards of Education, 1992, p. 12)

Schattman (1992) outlined the following key benefits of developing a school philosophy or mission statement:

1. Helps communities to define their purpose in terms that address the needs of all children
2. Provides educators and community members with the opportunity to communicate together about beliefs and possible goals
3. Establishes a standard with which discrete educational practices can be evaluated (p. 146)

The mission statement developed by a school or school system is the first step in a process of strategically planning how all students will be welcomed and supported as fully participating members of general classes in their neighborhood schools.

Communities that have embarked on the journey toward restructuring schools where everyone belongs and everyone is educated successfully have learned the critical importance of having *all* stakeholders participate in the process of developing the mission statement and the strategic plan. *Any discussions and planning for school reform must include the people who will be directly involved: students, parents, educators, administrators, support personnel, and community members.*

For far too long, those people most directly influenced by what happens in schools have been excluded from the planning and decision-making process. Students with diverse needs and their family members have rarely had an equal say in educational decisions. The "myth of clinical judgment" described by Biklen (1988) has kept educational programming decisions primarily in the hands of "experts," whose approach has been deficit focused and based on an outdated "fix-it" model by which the amount of a student's time in the mainstream of school and community life depends on the professional's judgment of whether the student has acquired the skills that prove his or her "readiness" for inclusion.

In schools surveyed that successfully include and support all students, teachers, parents, students, support staff, administrators, community members, and others are involved through decision-making teams or task forces that largely determine the school's procedures and practices (Stainback, Stainback, Moravec, & Jackson, 1992). These task forces are then responsible for the ongoing process of planning, monitoring, and fine-tuning school reform efforts in the school to ensure their continued success.

In addition to serving as general advocacy groups for the inclusion of students with diverse abilities, another role of these task forces is to help all individuals involved with the school gain a better understanding of the rationale for, and methods of, developing and maintaining a caring inclusive school community. This group must also ensure that all of the school's reform efforts be considered in terms of the benefits to all students. By establishing such task forces, community members, students, and a variety of personnel within the school can become involved and take pride in achieving an inclusive school.

The nine other elements listed in this chapter provide a guide that the task force and the entire school community can follow in developing and implementing a strategic plan for school inclusion.

The strategic plan needs to include specific objectives and, if the school is welcoming students who have been excluded in separate programs or placements, a timetable for achieving inclusion and quality supports for all students. The plan needs to outline how resources and personnel (especially those involved in special education, Chapter 1, and other programs that have been providing separate services to students) can be utilized to provide reduced teacher/pupil ratios, team teachers, consultants, teacher assistants, and support facilitators in the mainstream.

Once the mission statement is written and the strategic plan for inclusion is in place, steps toward implementation can begin.

STEP 2: PROVIDE STRONG LEADERSHIP

The school administrator must recognize his or her responsibility to set the tone of the school and to ensure that decisions are made, challenges are met, and interactions and processes are supported that are consistent with the school's philosophy. "To lead an inclusive school requires a personal belief that all children can learn and a commitment to providing all children equal access to a rich core curriculum and quality instruction" (Servatius, Fellows, & Kelly, 1992, p. 269).

The school administrator's role in ensuring that the school successfully educates all students is 1) providing support for teachers as they learn new educational practices, 2) finding meaningful ways to make personal connections with all students in the school, 3) developing with teachers a schoolwide approach to discipline that is consistent with the approach used in the classroom, and 4) helping the school as a whole to become and maintain a supportive, caring community (Solomon, Schaps, Watson, & Battistich, 1992, p. 50).

An administrator must be firm and unwavering when challenges arise supporting students with diverse needs. If a school administrator communicates ambivalence about school policies concerning including and supporting all students, then staff members will also waver and inclusive schooling efforts will be unsuccessful. (See Chapter 7 for more detail about the school administrator's role.)

STEP 3: PROMOTE SCHOOLWIDE AND CLASSROOM CULTURES THAT WELCOME, APPRECIATE, AND ACCOMMODATE DIVERSITY

Schools are mandated to meet students' ever-increasing needs in many areas of their development; schools must move beyond their traditional sole focus on basic academic learning. "While schools have responded, albeit sluggishly, to technological changes with various additions to the curriculum and narrowly prescribed methods of instruction, they have largely ignored massive social changes. When they have responded, they have done so in piecemeal fashion" (Noddings, 1995, p. 365).

Schools are microcosms of society; they mirror both positive and negative aspects, values, priorities, and practices of the culture that exists outside the school's walls. Schools also are training grounds where the youngest members of society develop attitudes, interests, and skills that they will use throughout their lives. Therefore, schools must assume responsibility for improving negative societal conditions. In other words, if we want society to be a place where an increasingly diverse group of people get along with each other, where all people are valued as contributors to the common good, where all people share basic rights as described in the U.S. Constitution, then schools must reflect those values by providing environments in which the values are modeled by adults and students and in which the very structures, teaching practices, and curricula reflect and model those same values.

> Our understanding of the mission of schooling must go beyond the merely measurable to a consideration of more profound purposes. (An) aim of fundamental importance in schools is helping children realize that they are part of a caring community. Such a realization will not occur unless the school itself becomes a community. (Eisner, 1991, p. 16)

For schools to become caring communities requires much more than implementing a social skills curriculum or having a school counselor available to help students cope when problems arise. Developing a caring learning community necessitates a pervasive school culture that communicates clearly, publicly, and intentionally that the school philosophy is based on principles of "equity, justice, and fairness for *everyone*" and for every one to "enjoy equal measures of respect and dignity..." (Flynn & Innes, 1992, p. 211).

Deliberate efforts are required to ensure that this message is communicated through the culture of the school. Sapon-Shevin wrote, "Creating an inclusive school where all students are acknowledged, valued, and respected involves attending to what is taught as well as to how it is delivered" (Sapon-Shevin, 1992, p. 19).

School personnel have not always recognized that, in order to educate the whole child, they must attend to students' needs for acceptance, belonging, and friends. In fact, some parents of students with disabilities relate that they have been told during school meetings that friendship facilitation and support are the parents' responsibilities, not the schools'.

However, school is where young people spend a substantial amount of time and the place where many of their social connections are made. Furthermore, friendships and relationships are actually preconditions to learning in schools (Forest, 1990). If a student feels unconnected and as if he or she does not belong, then the student is not able to learn to his or her fullest potential. Therefore, people working in schools must share with parents the responsibility for helping students make positive connections with each other in their schools and neighborhood communities. Educators and families have found that intentional, deliberate efforts often must be made in order to create and support opportunities for friendships to develop in school that carry over to after-school and weekend social opportunities for students.

Some strategies that can be used to develop friendships are

1. Promoting cooperative rather than competitive goal structures in the classroom and school (Johnson, Johnson, Holubec, & Roy, 1984)
2. Establishing classroom and school rituals or traditions in which everyone is provided the supports necessary in order to participate equally and fully (Pearson, 1988)
3. Finding opportunities throughout the school day to present students perceived as different in a positive way to their peers and to other adults in the school (Schaffner & Buswell, 1992)
4. Ensuring that in every classroom and school activity accommodations are made so that everyone, including students with challenging needs, can participate actively (Schaffner & Buswell, 1992)
5. Infusing positive values of respect, appreciation of people who are different, and cooperation into the curriculum itself (Noddings, 1995)
6. Involving students in decision making regarding classroom and school policies for supporting each other in school (Villa & Thousand, 1992)

Schools clearly must become caring communities where *all* students feel valued, safe, connected, and cared for in order for school reform efforts to succeed. If this critical element of community is overlooked or if its importance is underestimated, then students who present various kinds of diversity will continue to be disenfranchised and the schools' desired outcomes for all students will continue to miss the mark.

STEP 4: DEVELOP SUPPORT NETWORKS

Because of the range of student needs in general education classrooms and schools and the recent dramatic shift in the paradigm for the delivery of support services, it is important to develop school support networks for both teachers and students needing encouragement and assistance. Teachers who are new to including students with diverse needs in general education classrooms frequently need as much as or more support than the individual students.

A support team is a group of people who come together to brainstorm, problem-solve, and exchange ideas, methods, techniques, and activities in order to assist teachers and/or students requiring support to be successful in their roles. The team can include two or more people such as students, administrators, parents, classroom teachers, paraprofessionals, psychologists, therapists, and learning and behavior consultants. Support teams in schools can take on a variety of configurations. The special education referral and assessment team is one example of a working school support team. Many schools have grade-level interdisciplinary teams that include general education and special education staff who meet on a regular basis to plan curriculum and supports for all students in that grade. Sometimes, teams are developed to plan accommodations and support for a particular student or to problem-solve around a particular issue that requires attention.

Along with the student who needs assistance, it is helpful to include classmates of the student on the team. Classmates can provide practical suggestions regarding how the student can become integrally involved in school and feel welcome, secure, and successful in the classroom. With the assistance of school personnel, students often are able to mobilize a group of friends in the classroom around a particular student. Two major advantages of involving students on teams are that 1) they are available to provide friendly and accepting overtures as well as assistance and encouragement, and 2) they can offer culturally congruent support strategies because they have a better understanding than adults of the needs, desires, and interests of their peers. Also, unless they are involved in a team, students may not formulate clearly in their own minds what is needed or think about how they could specifically help another student. However, it is important that the student who is the recipient of help in one situation be involved in supporting other classmates in other situations. All students should be involved in helping each other rather than always focusing on nonlabeled students helping those who have special needs.

Many school teams designate a person to serve as an inclusion support facilitator for a particular student or for an entire school or school district (Ruttiman & Forest, 1986). An inclusion or support facilitator can assume a variety of responsibilities. He or she can encourage or formally organize support teams such as those described. The facilitator can help teams utilize strategies for promoting creative problem solving and ensuring accountability by team members for successfully implementing supports for a student.

A major role of the inclusion facilitator is to encourage natural networks of support for students. Particular emphasis is placed on facilitating friendships for students through identifying opportunities for students to make connections, interpreting individual students in a positive way to others in the school, and ensuring that accommodations are made so that students can actively participate in classroom and school activities (Schaffner & Buswell, 1992).

In addition, the inclusion facilitator functions as a resource locator, because a classroom teacher cannot be expected to have all the expertise necessary to meet the needs of all students in a heterogeneous classroom. This role may involve locating appropriate material, equipment, or specialists, consultants, teachers, and other school personnel who have expertise in a particular area. For example, the inclusion or support facilitator may assist in the recruitment and organization of classroom assistants or helpers such as teacher assistants and volunteers.

Inclusion facilitators can play a larger role by helping all students with or without disabilities who are having difficulty in educational tasks or in gaining peer acceptance. It is crucial that support facilitators provide support only when it is needed and that they not be overprotective. Finally, the inclusion facilitator is the teacher's resource and support and should not assume the role of a personal teacher for students needing support in the general education classroom.

Individuals who have served as support facilitators note that the most difficult part of the job is withdrawing from a situation once a student begins to experience success. This involves recognizing the point at which the facilitator's efforts begin to work and when the teachers and students no longer intensively need support and assistance. The facilitator literally intends to work him- or herself out of a job by encouraging natural networks of friendship and support in general education classes.

Some school districts have established individuals or teams to serve as district-wide support facilitators and consultants to building-level teams working to include and support students with diverse needs. Individuals in this role can provide much needed encouragement and support to people working to include students at the grass-roots level in schools, especially in situations in which there is building-level resistance to the process. The support network for a particular school may include various types of teams and other support systems that help ensure that the mission of the school to effectively meet the needs of all students is operationalized.

STEP 5: USE DELIBERATE
PROCESSES TO ENSURE ACCOUNTABILITY

Even support teams that are fully committed to including students can fail if they do not establish proactive processes to ensure efficient, effective, and ongoing planning and monitoring for the students. There often exists a tremendous discrepancy between a student's support plan as written in the individualized education program (IEP) and actual implementation of the student's day-to-day support. An additional problem is that traditional IEP meetings frequently become perfunctory sessions for filling out forms in order to comply with government regulations instead of dynamic problem-solving and strategy sessions. Many IEP documents are written and then filed away. This would not be such a problem if the IEP meeting were often not the only time a student's team came together to plan for the student. In this case, the IEP meeting becomes a deficit-focused session to certify the student's need for special education, and little or no time is devoted to strategizing what the student's support needs are. Even if the group designs sound strategies, there may be no system in place for implementing the strategies in the student's day-to-day support plan and monitoring their effectiveness.

The bottom line is that teams responsible for designing and implementing supports for diverse learners in general education classrooms often operate in a dysfunctional manner. The resulting inefficiency gravely affects the success of the student. In such cases, the student becomes a scapegoat when problems arise, and the student's lack of success is then used as justification for him or her to be excluded from the classroom. Such unhealthy practices demonstrate an inherent lack of understanding of the key elements that are needed in order to successfully deliver support for an individual student.

Key elements for success involve the recognition of

1. The importance of having a deliberate planning process that is ongoing rather than an isolated, annual or semiannual event. Teams need to meet on a regular basis so that a student's supports can be continually monitored in a proactive way to avert challenges. If challenging situations do arise, the team is then able to modify the support plan in a timely, efficient way, avoiding the necessity for a crisis to occur to precipitate a response.
2. The importance of focusing on strengths
3. The importance of including parents and students as equal, participating members
4. The importance of a proactive focus

Planning processes such as Making Action Plans (MAPs) (Falvey, Forest, Pearpoint, & Rosenberg, 1994) (formerly known as McGill Action Planning System [Lusthaus & Forest, 1987]), Planning Alternative Tomorrows with Hope (PATH) (Pearpoint, O'Brien, & Forest, 1993), Choosing Options and Accommodation for Children (COACH) (Giangreco, Cloninger, & Iverson, 1993), Personal Futures Planning (Mount, 1994), and Creative Problem Solving (CPS) (Giangreco, Cloninger, Dennis, & Edelman, 1994) can provide excellent ways for helping the team develop a clear focus on who the student is and what is important for the student and for establishing standards or norms for how team members will work together for the student in an ongoing and proactive manner that focuses on the student's strengths. Planning sessions must be treated as part of an ongoing process and not as ends in themselves. Regular and efficient team meetings are necessary in order to monitor progress.

A goal/activity matrix (for an example of one type, see Chapter 16, and COACH [Giangreco et al., 1993, p. 115]) is used by many teams to apply support strategies generated during team meetings to the general education classroom schedule. Without such a tool, this step is easily overlooked. The matrix serves other purposes as well:

1. Provides a structure for planning specific adaptations and accommodations to ensure active participation by the student in classroom and school activities
2. Helps the team to see where gaps exist in identified student needs that are not being adequately addressed and to make adjustments
3. Reassures general educators and others who may have doubts that the student's needs are being addressed through his or her participation in the general education classroom and about what goals should be targeted at a particular time of day

4. Clarifies the specific types and amounts of support a student needs at various times
5. Gives individual team members a clearer picture of their roles in supporting the student
6. Helps teams prioritize the activities or times of the day that present particular challenges that need to be addressed in a team meeting

The way in which the team meeting itself is structured can affect the efficiency and productivity of the team. Some key strategies that can help teams ensure efficient meetings are

- Designate roles (facilitator, recorder, timekeeper, transcriber).
- Stick to an arranged agenda with time limits for discussion items.
- Always begin with a celebration of successes.
- Always conclude with an action plan that specifically designates *who* will do *what* by *when.*
- Record the proceedings on charts on the wall using colors and graphics.
- Provide a transcription of the meeting's proceedings to all participants as soon as possible after the meeting.

Teams have found that, although utilizing the kinds of planning processes and strategies recommended here may at first be time consuming, they save time and frustration over the long term. As a result, the adults involved feel more effective and competent, and the outcome for the students is a richer and more successful school experience. Teachers have also expressed that learning to support a student with different needs in this way helps them improve their skills in teaching all students.

STEP 6: DEVELOP ORGANIZED AND ONGOING TECHNICAL ASSISTANCE

When educators are asked to implement educational practices that represent a significant departure from their traditional approaches and policies, they can feel inadequate and in need of training, information, and support. In addition, researchers following school reform efforts in the United States note that the reform movement is not achieving its aims: Substantive reform is not happening.

What's the problem? Our research suggests that (1) the "new kinds of teaching" required to implement the reforms are described in terms too general for teachers to use, and (2) even if these new kinds of teaching were clearly defined, current staff development practices are inadequate to effect meaningful changes. (Goldenberg & Gallimore, 1992, p. 69)

These issues point to a growing need for more comprehensive and innovative staff development opportunities in schools. A major role of the task force responsible for developing and implementing a school's or district's inclusive education policy is to establish a plan for providing technical assistance for all individuals involved. Participation on this task force by key school–district staff development personnel is advisable in order to ensure that the plan developed coordinates with and enhances existing staff development efforts. Regular needs assessments should be conducted to identify the types and content of the technical assistance activities that are most needed.

An effective technical assistance plan can include the following varied approaches:

1. Resource people from within and outside the district brought in to serve as consultants and facilitators
2. A readily accessible library of current print, video, and audio resource materials that can educate all members of the school community about school reform and recommended inclusive education practices. This resource library should also include a continually updated list of local, state, and national resource people and calendar of upcoming training events.
3. A comprehensive, responsive, and ongoing plan for inservice programming on relevant topics offered at districtwide and building levels
4. Opportunities for educators supporting diverse learners to come together to address common issues and help each other creatively develop new strategies
5. Opportunities for educators new to inclusive practices to visit other buildings and districts that have implemented inclusive education in conjunction with school reform efforts
6. Opportunities for educators to be mentors to increase their skills by observing, talking with, and modeling the practices of individuals experienced in supporting diverse learners in general education classrooms

In addition to involving all members of the school staff in these technical assistance activities (including custodians, secretaries, and other school support staff), participation by parents is essential. In order to promote a shared vision of the school's goals and how to achieve them, all constituents need to have the opportunity to hear and respond to the same information.

Restructuring staff development practices to achieve substantive change in schools is difficult. Nevertheless, "Staff development practices can change teaching practice, enhance student learning, and re-form school culture" (Hirsh & Ponder, 1991, p. 47). The outcome of creating schools that are responsive to diverse learners and embody a rich culture of acceptance and belonging for everyone is well worth the effort required.

STEP 7: MAINTAIN FLEXIBILITY

The element of flexibility has broad implications in the discussions of how to build quality schools that include students with disabilities.

> In some ways educators about to integrate students with disabilities are analogous to parents who have just given birth to a child with a severe disability. They are asked to make a leap of faith, to believe that what they are about to undertake will be good for them and the students. Like parents, they may envision a profoundly trying existence,

one clouded by anxiety. Yet, by working together, however difficult the experience, schools have the chance of discovering, as many parents have, that a commitment to working with and relating to youngsters with disabilities is good both for the person with a disability and for her allies and friends. (Biklen, 1989, p. 245)

From observing many families who have a child with disabilities, one can see clearly demonstrated the same qualities that enable a school to successfully welcome and educate all students. These families show flexibility and the ability to respond spontaneously with whatever strategy is required to "make the moment work" and include their child in the activities of their family. Parents become masters of persistence by asking challenging questions, trying new things, taking risks in order to discover what works, and by doing what works rather than the accepted way most others do it.

Similarly, educators must develop these same abilities to quickly respond to the challenges of supporting students with diverse abilities in participating in school activities. In addition to a strong belief in inclusive schooling and the commitment to making it work, spontaneity, flexibility, and the courage to take risks are key qualities.

In their book, *Enlightened Leadership*, Oakley and Krug (1991) discussed the critical role attitude plays in how individuals approach challenges and changes in their lives. The authors described two extremes of thinking style: reactive thinking and creative thinking. Among other things, reactive thinkers are resistant to change, blinded by problems, see reasons why they cannot do things, and are limited by what worked in the past. Conversely, creative thinkers are open to change, are "can-do" oriented, build on successes and strengths, and seek the opportunities in situations. The authors stressed that this is not an either/or situation. In a given situation, any individual falls somewhere on the continuum between these two extremes. School leaders need to cultivate environments in which individuals are encouraged to do creative, rather than reactive, thinking.

York and Vandercook (1989) also recommended that educators assume a problem-solving approach. When problems occur, the best strategy is to go back to the drawing board and determine a different way to proceed rather than retreat to placement in segregated special education classes. Although retreat may appear to be the easiest route, it is not in the long-term best interest of the students or the ultimate achievement of inclusive communities. The above point is especially critical in situations in which students exhibit challenging behavior in the classroom. Challenging behavior probably requires the most creativity and flexibility from individuals planning for a student, and yet it is the area in which individuals are often the least flexible and the least able to problem-solve.

Another dimension of developing flexibility relates to the abilities of educators to move beyond the traditional roles that their title or professional expertise has dictated that they play. When using a team approach to creatively design and implement supports for individual students, brainstorming and building on each other's ideas commonly become the typical operational patterns. Individuals then find themselves moving beyond traditionally defined roles and utilizing areas of interest and expertise unrelated to their professional titles. They also find that the assistance they provide is what is really needed at a particular time and not necessarily related to their traditional roles.

Teachers in successful schools do not view themselves as specialists, but more as generalists working across disciplines in a diagnostic fashion to solve student learning problems. Both general education and special education teachers describe this new role as rejuvenating. (National Association of State Boards of Education, 1992, p. 15)

Educators who are working on these kinds of dynamic teams report that they receive new energy, develop new skills, and become empowered to renew their commitment to providing a quality education to all students.

STEP 8: EXAMINE AND ADOPT
EFFECTIVE TEACHING APPROACHES

Effectively educating diverse learners requires that educators use a variety of teaching approaches to meet their students' needs. This frequently necessitates reevaluating the teaching practices with which they are most comfortable in order to assess if these are the best possible methods for facilitating the active learning of desired educational outcomes by all students in the class.

Many teachers become accustomed to using a "one-size-fits-all" approach to teaching. In a study of a number of schools throughout the nation, Goodlad (1984) found little variation in the narrow range of teaching practices used, although other characteristics of the schools varied significantly. The obvious problem with using only a few standard teaching methods is that students, even those who do not have identified special challenges, naturally have varying strengths, needs, and styles of learning.

The theory of multiple intelligences suggests using teaching approaches that tap each student's individual "gifts" as well as the modality through which he or she best learns (Gardner, 1993).

By chunking the broad range of human abilities into seven basic intelligences, we now have a map for making sense out of the many ways in which children learn and a blueprint for ensuring their success in school and in life. (Armstrong, 1994, p. 28)

Educational reform leaders assert that educating students to be productive citizens of the 21st century requires using teaching strategies that promote active rather than passive learning, cooperation instead of competition, and critical thinking skills in lieu of rote learning (Benjamin, 1989).

In addition to using a limited repertoire of teaching approaches, general education teachers have been led to believe that they do not have the skills or expertise to successfully educate students with disabilities. This is due to the fact that special education has evolved into a separate educational system focused on meeting the needs of students whose abilities fall outside traditional definitions. The existence of two parallel educational systems, one labeled "special education" and one labeled "regular education," reinforced the myth that students with disabilities learn so differently as to require teaching methods distinct from those used for typical students (Schaffner & Buswell, 1991).

> Fortunately, the long-standing assumption that there are two methodologies or psychologies of learning…is beginning to erode. It is being replaced with the view that the actual teaching strategies used with any child are but a part of the continually changing pattern of services provided in response to the individual and changing needs of the child. (Stainback, Stainback, & Bunch, 1989, p. 16)

A dynamic school environment in which adults support each other and work together to create strategies to ensure student success provides nonthreatening opportunities for teachers to learn about and try varied instructional approaches. Teachers can then incorporate those approaches that they find successful into their teaching repertoires.

STEP 9: CELEBRATE SUCCESSES
AND LEARN FROM CHALLENGES

As stated previously, it is important that school systems cultivate the ability of their staff members to think creatively rather than reactively. Creative thinkers demonstrate a positive focus and recognize the importance of acknowledging, celebrating, and building on successes. Creative thinkers also respond to challenges that inevitably arise as new opportunities to learn and grow present themselves.

The following "framework for continuous renewal" (Oakley & Krug, 1991) demonstrates how school teams can maintain a proactive, success-oriented focus:

1. Celebrate the small successes you are achieving.
2. Research extensively what you are doing to generate these successes.
3. Continually reclarify in great detail your specific objectives.
4. Help all parties understand the benefits of achieving the objectives.
5. Continually search for what you could be doing more of, better, or differently in order to move closer to the objectives. (p. 116)

Successful innovations implemented by individuals or groups in schools can have minimal effects on changing how teachers and schools better meet student needs unless deliberate efforts are made to incorporate them into school policy and day-to-day practice.

> It is not enough to achieve isolated pockets of success. Reform fails unless we can demonstrate that pockets of success add up to new structures, procedures, and school cultures that press for continuous improvement…. The failure to institutionalize an innovation and build it into the normal structures and practices of the organization underlies the disappearance of many reforms. (Fullan & Miles, 1992, p. 748)

It is common that a successful school reform model instituted by a particular person disappears when that key person is no longer involved and people drift back into old practices. Furthermore, schools that have included a student with significant needs because of the advocacy of an assertive parent or a visionary teacher but that do not incorporate what was learned with that student into standard practice diminish the potential benefits for present and future students and staff. To truly reform, successful innovations must become pervasive elements of the school's culture.

STEP 10: BE KNOWLEDGEABLE ABOUT THE CHANGE PROCESS, BUT DO NOT ALLOW IT TO PARALYZE YOU

Change–process theory is sometimes used by educators as a rationale for slowly phasing in new practices in schools. The belief is that change can occur only in small increments and that accelerating the process might cause individuals to reject the new practices and sabotage reform efforts.

Sensitivity to the reactions of individuals and organizations that are experiencing change is important. However, it is critical that this change–process theory not be used by individuals who are responsible for educating students as an excuse to keep them from making changes and taking actions in a morally and ethically coherent way on behalf of the students. Educators who have successfully changed educational practices to create quality inclusive schools report that an incremental view of change in which individuals move step by step through the process and in which new steps are not taken until everyone is "on the same page" is not necessarily an effective view. In fact, phase-in or other sequential processes for implementing this kind of educational change actually delay acceptance and allow the opposition to the change more time to organize (Noblit & Johnson, 1982).

Research has shown that attitude changes do not have to precede behavior changes. Therefore, it is not effective to wait for people's attitudes about a particular innovation to change before the change is implemented (Guskey, 1984). In fact, some studies have found that the only way attitudes *do* change is if individuals are guided in changing their behavior—then the attitude change follows (McDonnell & Hardman, 1987).

McDonnell and Hardman (1987) recommend that change be implemented simultaneously on a districtwide basis rather than by creating small-scale models. This strategy minimizes resistance and facilitates comprehensive planning. School boards and school administrators at all levels must play a significant role in promoting change. Organizational change theories indicate that "lack of top management support is one of the most frequent causes of implementation failure" (Daft, 1983, p. 285). As mentioned previously, administrators set the tone and communicate to staff the expectation that adopting practices that are consistent with the school's mission statement is not optional.

The most detrimental result of putting inclusive education on hold until all individuals involved are prepared or of phasing it in gradually is that these methods ignore the urgency of the need for inclusion for the students, *who have no time to lose*. Ultimately, including and ensuring a quality education for all students is an issue of social justice, which can either uphold or negate the values professed to be important by schools, school districts, and society as a whole.

CONCLUSION

Schools and communities must join together to ensure that principles of quality education for all students are established and followed. The critical steps outlined in this chapter can provide a guide for individuals committed to this goal of implementing substantive, lasting change that benefits all students.

The urgency with which this change must be implemented is evident. In spite of intense efforts to improve schools, too many reform plans are missing the mark.

Our society does not need to make its children first in the world of mathematics and science. It needs to care for its children—to reduce violence, to respect honest work of every kind, to reward excellence at every level, to ensure a place for every child and emerging adult in the economic and social world, to produce people who can care competently for their own families and contribute effectively to their communities. In direct opposition to the current emphasis on academic standards...I have argued that our main educational aim should be to encourage the growth of competent, caring, loving, and lovable people. (Noddings, 1995, p. 366)

Thoughtful dialogue and strategic planning involving all stakeholders are critical. Although students with disabilities may be the primary focus of the individuals reading this book, it is critical that these students and the reforms needed to successfully support them not be seen as a separate, "add-on" issue by advocates, policy makers, or those who implement policy in schools.

All advocates must join together in recognizing that schools that implement sound educational practices are good schools for *all* students. The presence of students with disabilities in general education classrooms and their successes or failures can serve as a barometer for how well all children are being educated in those classrooms. The most critical element of all is possessing the courage to do what is right in spite of the challenges and barriers that arise. The outcome is a stronger, more effective educational system for all students.

REFERENCES

Armstrong, T. (1994). Multiple intelligences: Seven ways to approach curriculum. *Educational Leadership, 52*(3), 26–28.

Benjamin, S. (1989). An ideascape for education: What futurists recommend. *Educational Leadership, 47*(1), 8.

Biklen, D. (1988). The myth of clinical judgment. *Journal of Social Issues, 44*(1), 127–140.

Biklen, D. (1989). Making difference ordinary. In S. Stainback, W. Stainback, & M. Forest (Eds.), *Educating all students in the mainstream of regular education* (pp. 235–248). Baltimore: Paul H. Brookes Publishing Co.

Daft, R.L. (1983). *Organization theory and design*. San Francisco: West Publishing Company.

Eisner, E.W. (1991). What really counts in schools. *Educational Leadership, 49*(5), 10–11, 14–17.

Falvey, M., Forest, M., Pearpoint, J., & Rosenberg, R. (1994). Building connections: All my life's a circle. In J.S. Thousand, R.A. Villa, & A.I. Nevin (Eds.), *Creativity and collaborative learning: A practical guide to empowering students and teachers* (pp. 347–368). Baltimore: Paul H. Brookes Publishing Co.

Flynn, G., & Innes, M. (1992). The Waterloo region Catholic school system. In R.A. Villa, J.S. Thousand, W. Stainback, & S. Stainback (Eds.), *Restructuring for caring and effective education: An administrative guide to creating heterogeneous schools* (pp. 201–217). Baltimore: Paul H. Brookes Publishing Co.

Forest, M. (1990, February). *MAPS and circles.* Presentation at PEAK Parent Center workshop, Colorado Springs.

Fullan, M.G., & Miles, M.B. (1992). Getting reform right: What works and what doesn't. *Phi Delta Kappan, 73,* 745–752.

Gardner, H. (1993). *Frames of mind* (2nd ed.). New York: Basic Books.

Giangreco, M.F., Cloninger, C.J., Dennis, R.E., & Edelman, S.W. (1994). Problem-solving methods to facilitate inclusive education. In J. Thousand, R. Villa, & A. Nevin (Eds.), *Creativity and collaborative learning: A practical guide to empowering students and teachers* (pp. 321–346). Baltimore: Paul H. Brookes Publishing Co.

Giangreco, M.F., Cloninger, C.J., & Iverson, V.S. (1993). *Choosing options and accommodations for children (COACH).* Baltimore: Paul H. Brookes Publishing Co.

Goldenberg, C., & Gallimore, R. (1991). Changing teaching takes more than a one-shot workshop. *Educational Leadership, 49*(3), 69–72.

Goodlad, J. (1984). *A place called school.* New York: McGraw-Hill.

Guskey, T.R. (1984). Staff development and teacher change. *Educational Leadership, 42*(7), 57–60.

Hirsh, S., & Ponder, G. (November, 1991). New plots, new heroes in staff development. *Educational Leadership, 49*(3), 43–48.

Johnson, D., Johnson, R., Holubec, E.J., & Roy, P. (1984). *Circles of learning.* Alexandria, VA: Association for Supervision and Curriculum Development.

Lusthaus, E., & Forest, M. (1987). The kaleidoscope: A challenge to the cascade. In M. Forest (Ed.), *More education integration* (pp. 1–17). Downsview, Ontario, Canada: G. Allan Roeher Institute.

McDonnell, A., & Hardman, M. (1987). *The desegregation of America's special schools— A blueprint for change.* Salt Lake City: The University of Utah.

Mount, B. (1994). Benefits and limitations of personal futures planning. In V. Bradley, J. Ashbaugh, & B. Blaney (Eds.), *Creating individual supports for people with developmental disabilities: A mandate for change at many levels* (pp. 97–108). Baltimore: Paul H. Brookes Publishing Co.

National Association of State Boards of Education. (1992). *Winners all: A call for inclusive schools.* Alexandria, VA: Author.

Noblit, G.W., & Johnston, B. (1982). Understanding school administration in the desegregation context: An introductory essay. In G.W. Noblit & B. Johnston (Eds.), *The school principal and school desegregation* (pp. 3–39). Springfield, IL: Charles C Thomas.

Noddings, N. (1995). A morally defensible mission for schools in the 21st century. *Phi Delta Kappan, 76*(5), 365–368.

Oakley, E., & Krug, D. (1994). *Enlightened leadership—Getting to the heart of change.* New York: Fireside.

O'Brien, J., & Forest, M. (1989). *Action for inclusion—How to improve schools by welcoming children with special needs into regular classrooms.* Toronto: Frontier College Press.

Pearpoint, J., O'Brien, J., & Forest, M. (1993). *PATH—A workbook for planning positive futures.* Toronto: Inclusion Press.

Pearson, V.L. (1988). Words and rituals establish group membership. *Teaching Exceptional Children, 21*(1), 52–53.

Ruttiman, A., & Forest, M. (1986). With a little help from my friends: The integration facilitator at work. *Entourage, 1,* 24–33.

Sapon-Shevin, M. (1992). Celebrating diversity, creating community: Curriculum that honors and builds on differences. In S. Stainback & W. Stainback (Eds.), *Curriculum considerations in inclusive classrooms: Facilitating learning for all students* (pp. 19–36). Baltimore: Paul H. Brookes Publishing Co.

Sapon-Shevin, M. (1995). Why gifted students belong in inclusive schools. *Educational Leadership, 52*(4), 64–70.

Schaffner, C.B., & Buswell, B.E. (1991). *Opening doors: Strategies for including all students in regular education.* Colorado Springs: PEAK Parent Center, Inc.

Schaffner, C.B., & Buswell, B.E. (1992). *Connecting students: A guide to thoughtful friendship facilitation for educators and families.* Colorado Springs: PEAK Parent Center, Inc.

Schattman, R. (1992). The Franklin Northwest Supervisory Union—A case study of an inclusive school system. In R. Villa, J. Thousand, W. Stainback, & S. Stainback (Eds.), *Restructuring for caring and effective education: An administrative guide to creating heterogeneous schools* (pp. 143–159). Baltimore: Paul H. Brookes Publishing Co.

Servatius, J.D., Fellows, M., & Kelly, D. (1992). Preparing leaders for inclusive schools. In R.A. Villa, J.S. Thousand, W. Stainback, & S. Stainback (Eds.), *Restructuring for caring and effective education: An administrative guide to creating heterogeneous schools* (pp. 267–283). Baltimore: Paul H. Brookes Publishing Co.

Solomon, D., Schaps, E., Watson, M., & Battistich, V. (1992). Creating caring school and classroom communities for all students. In R. Villa, J. Thousand, W. Stainback, & S. Stainback (Eds.), *Restructuring for caring and effective education: An administrative guide to creating heterogeneous schools* (pp. 41–60). Baltimore: Paul H. Brookes Publishing Co.

Stainback, W., Stainback, S., & Bunch, G. (1989). A rationale for the merger of regular and special education. In S. Stainback, W. Stainback, & M. Forest (Eds.), *Educating all students in the mainstream of regular education* (pp. 15–26). Baltimore: Paul H. Brookes Publishing Co.

Stainback, W., Stainback, S., Moravec, J., & Jackson, H.J. (1992). Concerns about full inclusion—An ethnographic investigation. In R.A. Villa, J.S. Thousand, W. Stainback, & S. Stainback (Eds.), *Restructuring for caring and effective education: An administrative guide to creating heterogeneous schools* (pp. 305–324). Baltimore: Paul H. Brookes Publishing Co.

Villa, R., & Thousand, J. (1992). Student collaboration: An essential for curriculum delivery in the 21st century. In S. Stainback & W. Stainback (Eds.), *Curriculum considerations in inclusive classrooms: Facilitating learning for all students* (pp. 117–142). Baltimore: Paul H. Brookes Publishing Co.

York, J., & Vandercook, T. (1989). *Strategies for achieving an integrated education for middle school aged learners with severe disabilities.* Minneapolis: Institute on Community Integration.

5

MAPs, Circles of Friends, and PATH

Powerful Tools to Help Build Caring Communities

Jack Pearpoint, Marsha Forest, and John O'Brien

ONE OF THE basic components for building connections and friendships is that people are in close proximity and have frequent opportunities to interact with each other. Research has demonstrated that, in order for children and adults to form the bonds necessary for friendships, they must have frequent access to one another. So it follows that students who attend the same schools and classes as their neighborhood peers are more likely to form bonds that are strong enough to result in friendship (Grenot-Scheyer, Coots, & Falvey, 1989; Stainback & Stainback, 1990).

Unfortunately, frequent opportunities and close proximity are not always sufficient for children and adolescents to feel connected to each other and to build a network of friends. Several tools have been used successfully to facilitate such connections and eventual friendships. These tools are designed to tap into the creative energy of students and educators. Circles of friends, Making Action Plans (MAPs) (formerly McGill Action Planning System), and Planning Alternative Tomorrows with Hope (PATH) are three person-centered tools that assume that everyone is valued. These tools are based on hope for the future and begin with the assumptions that all people belong, all people can learn, everyone benefits from being together, and diversity is one of our most critical strengths. These tools are described in detail in the remainder of this chapter.

MAKING ACTION PLANS (MAPs)

MAPs Beliefs

The following constitute the core beliefs upon which MAPs is based:

- All students belong in regular classrooms—no ifs, ands, or buts.
- General education teachers can teach all children.
- Necessary supports will be provided when necessary.
- Quality education is a right, not a privilege.
- Outcomes must be success, literacy, and graduation for all.
- Creative alternatives will be available for populations who do not succeed in typical ways.

What Is MAPs?

MAPs is a collaborative planning process for action that brings together the key actors in a child's life. The student, his or her family and teachers, and other significant persons in the student's life gather to discuss the student's and family's personal dreams and goals and to brainstorm ways of making them a reality. In the spirit of cooperation, this team creates a plan of action to be implemented in a general education classroom setting. It is a *not* a case conference or an individualized education program (IEP), but the results can certainly be used on any IEP form.

A MAP is facilitated by two people: One person is the MAPs recorder who makes a record (preferably using graphics) on a large piece of chart paper. This is an essential element of a MAP. The other person is the process facilitator, who welcomes the group, explains the process, and facilitates the MAP.

MAPs—Part I

Essential Elements of a MAP The following are essential elements of a MAP. Without these eight essential elements, the plan is not a MAP. It may be something similar, but a MAP must have the following eight elements or there must be a good reason to eliminate an element.

1. Cofacilitation (MAPs recorder and process facilitator) (can be interchanged)
2. Graphic recording with colored markers on chart paper
3. Hospitality—a personal and informal atmosphere (snacks, beverages, and tokens of thanks)
4. All key factors in the child's life present and participating
5. Focus person and their siblings and friends present and participating
6. Key issue addressed: *What does the child and family want?*
7. Decision to meet again (with a date)
8. Concrete plan of action with actual things to do right away—First Steps

A MAP is made up of questions, each of which can be conceptualized as a circle. The MAP questions are shown in Figure 1. Each question must be used, but there is no prescribed order to follow. The facilitators decide on the direction, depending on the needs of the group.

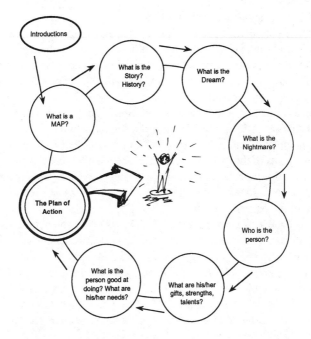

Figure 1.   The MAP questions—A mandela.

Setting the Tone and Introductions   Before the MAP begins, the facilitators set up the room with comfortable chairs in an informal semicircle. Chart paper and clean markers are ready for use. Snacks are available for people before the session begins. Colorful name tags have been prepared. The facilitators invite the group to be seated and introduce themselves, and then the facilitator asks everyone, "Please tell us who you are and explain your relationship to Mark [the focus person]."

Question 1: What Is a MAP?   The facilitator asks the participants to think of a map and asks, "What is a map?" Participants in one group provided these answers: "A map shows directions." "It tells you how to get from one place to another." "It shows you how to find stuff." "A map tells you where to go."

The facilitator answered: "That's exactly what we're here to do. To show direction for Mark's life, to help him and his family get from one place (the segregated class) to another place (the general education class). The MAP will also help us figure out how to find what Mark needs. If we all work together, we can decide where to go next. Together we can create a plan of action that we can put into practice for Mark starting right away."

Question 2: What Is the Story? (Can Also Merge with Question 3)   For example, the facilitator asked, "Please tell us your story. What are the most important things that have happened since Mark was born? I know you can go on and on with this, so I'll limit you to 5–7 minutes. Tell us what you feel is really important for all of us to hear and to know about Mark's story."

The MAPs facilitator must be careful not to let this be a case history. He or she must listen with his or her heart, soul, and body. The MAPs recorder writes the story in words, pictures, and images. The process facilitator asks the participants to also listen with their hearts: "Don't listen just with your ears. Listen with your whole body. Don't be judgmental. This is not a trial. Try to feel, hear what the person is telling you from inside—as if it were your own story."

We often ask this question before the question "What Is the Dream?" depending on the tone and mood of the group. The recorder summarizes the story after the family or person has completed stating their thoughts and ensures that all facts are correct and the essential elements of the story are recorded. The recorder requests the assistance of the MAPs team in this process. Making simple errors (especially with people's names) can be very upsetting, so it is important to make corrections and request assistance. This increases group participation and ownership.

Question 3: What Is the Dream?   This is really the heart and soul of the MAP. The MAPs facilitator must create an atmosphere in which the family feels comfortable to say what their dreams, hopes, and wants really are.

For example, the facilitator asked: "If you could dream the dream you really want, if you could have anything with no holds barred, what do you really truly want for yourselves and for Mark? Money is no object. Don't hold back. Let yourselves be free to really say what you want. Don't ask for what you think you can get. This is different. This is what you really want and dream about or pray for."

There is often a deathly silence at this moment—it is essential to the process. Do not interrupt; wait; allow the family time to build up their courage to express their real feelings and hopes. If this is rushed, the entire MAP may be a futile exercise.

When a facilitator asks this question about people's dreams with a full heart so that people gain the confidence to risk stating their buried dreams, profound things often happen. A pattern has emerged after years of asking this question. Parents all over North America have told us that the MAPs process enabled them to dream again. As one Colorado parent stated, "A MAP is a way of restoring the dream to a family." With older teenagers or adults, the focus person states his or her own dream. The MAP restores a dream to the individual.

"But what about the person who can't speak?" We have done many MAPs with children who are labeled nonverbal. Although these children do not speak with their voices, they certainly communicate. And if the group knows a child well, someone will be able to articulate his or her own dreams for the child and also the dreams he or she thinks the child might have. For example, the facilitator might ask, "If Mark could speak, what do you think his dream would be?"

Families often weep openly as a participant tells us, "My dream is that my child be happy, be included in school, walk or ride to school with his sister, be invited to birthday parties, have a hamburger with a friend, and have the phone ring just for him."

One 12-year-old girl told us, "I want a trip to Hawaii and a job with computers. Also a pet dog." She was clear as a bell!

One parent of a child with major medical issues told us, "I want my child to have one real friend before she dies. My nightmare is that my child will never know friendship." This little girl did die soon after the MAPs meeting, but, because she had moved into a school district that welcomed her, the mother did get her wish. The entire third-grade class attended her daughter's funeral. The family knew that their daughter had made real friends in her all-too-short life.

Question 4: What is the Nightmare? Many facilitators consider this question the hardest to ask. We believe it is important because the MAP must identify the nightmare in order to avoid it. Unless the MAP prevents the nightmare, it is a waste. Unless the *outcome* of the plan of action is to prevent the worst from happening, all we are doing is merely busywork.

In 10 years of doing MAPs, the following are examples of the most consistent responses to this question: "My nightmare is that my child will end up in an institution with no one to love him [or her]." "We will die and my child will be alone and put in a group home." "My child will never have a friend."

No one has ever said, "I'm afraid my child will not get an A in math or learn phonics."

No one has ever said, "I'm afraid there won't be a proper history curriculum."

This question often provides common ground between warring factions. When school staff see that these parents want what every other parent wants for his or her children, barriers break down. We have seen wars resolve into peace treaties. A Kentucky woman broke down when describing how her 18-year-old son was currently living out his nightmare, institutionalized after having blinded himself. "Our family is in the nightmare," she wept. "All we wanted, all we want now, is some shred of human kindness and friendship to our son." We had to stop for coffee because all participants, both factions, were in tears. For the first time, they were meeting as human beings rather than as combatants on opposing sides of a placement review table.

Facilitators do not have to be familiar with the person or the family, but they must know the MAPs process inside out. The facilitators must first and foremost believe 100% in the fact that inclusion is possible for all! The facilitators must be good listeners who are able to hear expressions of great pain without jumping to provide immediate advice and solutions.

The facilitators can be school personnel or an external team. The facilitator's role is to pull information from the group and shape it into an action plan. The recorder creates a picture of what the group says through color and graphics and also summarizes what has been said before the group goes to the next step. Questions 1–4 constitute Part I of a MAP. It is often necessary to take a break at this point. The second part is lighter in tone and faster paced and moves toward the action plan itself.

MAPs—Part II

We consciously try to change the mood and the motion of the MAPs process in Part II.

Question 5: Who Is Mark? To begin to think about this question, we draw an outline of a person on the chart paper and hand out self-stick notes. We need to brainstorm to come up with the answers to this question. Each participant writes a word or phrase (one per self-stick note) and posts it on the outline. These give us a snapshot of the person. For example, an outline of a 12-year-old boy had these words and phrases posted: curious, handsome, determined, likes good snacks, always hungry, potential, my son, dimples, pretty ordinary, my brother, very active, pest, a little brat, somebody's great friend someday, an interesting boy, lively, likes to play with drums, great family.

The MAPs recorder grouped the words in an attempt to get a picture of Mark. We sometimes ask, "What have other people said about Mark in the past? What words have been used before in other meetings?" For example, these words were previously used to describe Mark: retarded, developmentally delayed, autistic, severely autistic. These should be posted separately, but the recorder may want to highlight the dramatic differences between the two portraits of the same person. See Figure 2 for an illustration of this outline.

Question 6: What Are Mark's Strengths and Unique Gifts? To answer this question, another list of phrases and words was generated: happy, beautiful boy, loving, friendly, he can look you in the eye and smile, gives a lot, he has a "look," helps to put things in perspective, makes you feel good.

Question 7: What Does Mark Like to Do? What Is Mark Good at? What Are His Needs? Participants again brainstorm to generate this list, which is important because it gives the group many ideas for the curriculum and daily program. For example, these answers to Question 7 were provided for Mark: Mark likes to throw balls, play with ropes and strings, climb in parks, eat, relax, swim laps in the pool, play in water puddles, go skating, play in clothes closets, be with people.

By this point in the process, we have generated an enormous volume of information on Mark. The facilitator then asks, for example, "First and foremost, what do we all need to make this [the dream] happen? What does Mark need? What does Martha [his teacher] need? What does the family need?"

At this MAP, the participants were Mark's mother, father, teenage sister, and a dedicated teacher/friend. There was a real consensus that Mark needed to be involved and to meet people his own age. The family wanted him to meet other children and spend time with them so that his mother could begin to build a life of her own. The

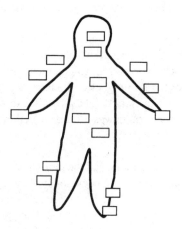

Figure 2.   The outline of the focus person with self-stick notes used to answer Question 5.

family agreed that a "worker" to help with community integration would be a godsend. The family wanted that person to take Mark to local places where he could get involved with other kids. The job description for that person was developed from what was said at the MAP: to find places where Mark can meet kids; to find kids to spend time with him; to go to the youth center with Mark; to get Mark involved in trips, swimming, and other activities; and to help Mark develop more communication skills.

Question 8: The Plan of Action   When the question "What does this person need?" is framed carefully, the answers flow directly into a plan of action. In some circumstances, such as planning a curriculum, we might draw the timetable and have the other students brainstorm about all the activities that Mark likes and can do. Then, we explore the logistics. If Mark is going to get from history to gym and be dressed in 10 minutes, he will need help—a guide. Who is willing to help? We link specific people to specific times, places, classes, and activities.

In this example, the family enthusiastically agreed to plan a pizza party at their home and invite some neighborhood kids that weekend. Together with Greg, Mark's teacher/friend, they started to look for a community integration facilitator. Greg agreed to facilitate another MAP with a wider group in 1 month, and a date was set.

Concluding a MAP

A MAP meeting must be concluded. The MAPs recorder guides the group through a summary of the charts and presents the charts to the family as a gift along with other gifts such as a plant and a cake—something that grows, something sweet. Before the MAP meeting ends, the facilitator asks each participant one more process question: "Will you give me one word or a phrase to sum up your experience of this MAP? Off the top of your head, the first word that springs to mind."

The participants in this group answered: "I'm relieved. Great session" [mother]. "Very positive. Thanks" [father]. "Awesome" [sister]. A very big smile [Mark]. "Fabulous and positive" [Greg].

A MAP IS NOT/A MAP IS...

It is important at the outset of the process to state clearly what a MAP is and what a MAP is not:

1.   A MAP is not a trick, gimmick, or quick solution to complex human problems. It is *not* a one-shot session that will provide the magic bullet that blasts a vulnerable person into the life of the community. MAPs is a problem-solving approach to complex human issues. It can and must be done as often as needed. At its core, it is *personal, common sense,* and *from the heart.* A MAP must ask over and over again, "Does what we are doing make sense for this person or organization?"

2.   A MAP is not a replacement for an IEP. A MAP session may help provide information for an IEP or some other needed documentation, but it is not a substitute for these and must not be treated as such. In a MAP, the people who give input are personally or professionally involved in the person's life. MAPs participants and

contributors must be people who know the person or organization intimately, not simply people who have tested or provided occasional intervention for a person.

3. A MAP is not controlled by experts in order to design a neat program package. The outcome of a MAP session is a *personalized plan of action* that has three criteria: 1) The plan is personalized and tailored to the person or organization. It is a one-of-a-kind MAP. 2) The person is at the heart of the MAP. 3) The plan assists in bringing the person or organization more and more into the daily life of the school or community.

4. A MAP is not a tool to make segregated settings better. MAPs was designed to liberate people from institutional care. It is for people and organizations trying to figure out together how to get a person included fully in the life of the community.

5. A MAP is not an academic exercise. A MAP is a genuine personal approach to problem solving. A MAP is for people who are vulnerable, and the outcome decisions of a MAP session have life and death implications for how the person will live his or her life. It is not a professionally controlled, expert-model, top-down management tool. A MAP is a group, problem-solving, cooperative, collaborative team approach to planning.

6. A MAP is not a neutral tool. The process facilitator must be skilled in group process, have leadership ability, have a problem-solving orientation, and, most of all, have values that clearly favor inclusive education and living. MAPs makes the value judgment that it is better for all of us to figure out how to live together than to put people in little (or big) segregated boxes. MAPs facilitators must have clear vision and share beliefs favoring the path of inclusion in all aspects of life.

7. MAPs is not talk—it is talk and action. A MAP gives clear direction and takes active steps that move in the direction of inclusion. Most of all, MAPs is ongoing. It is a life-long process of figuring out how to prevent the nightmare of segregation and how to enter into relationships that will lead to physical, mental, and spiritual well-being.

8. The metaphor for the MAP is a *kaleidoscope.* The kaleidoscope is a magical toy, a mysterious and beautiful tool that changes images constantly. Through the eyepiece we see little bits of color turning together into an ever-changing luminous melody of color and light. We see the kaleidoscope as a metaphor for the outcome of each MAP. A MAP is a medley of people working together to make something unique and better happen. A MAP is more than any one person can do alone.

CIRCLES OF FRIENDS

A circle of friends is something that we take for granted unless we do not have one. A circle of friends provides us with a support network of family and friends. In the absence of a natural circle of friends, educators can facilitate a circle process, which can be used to enlist the involvement and commitment of peers around an individual student. For a student who is not well connected or who does not have an extensive network of friends, a circle of friends process can be useful.

The circle of friends process starts with the exercise of a social scan. This gives a quick picture of who is in a person's life. This process is very useful to gain clarity about who might be involved in certain activities or circles that need to be filled. We recommend this exercise for everyone and consider it an essential preventive health check for students, teachers, and citizens. To begin this process, draw four concentric circles. Imagine yourself in the heart of the circles and then take a few minutes to fill in the people who are in each of your four circles. The inherent question that is the key to this process is, "Who loves this person?"

In the first circle, the circle of intimacy, list the people most intimately connected in your life—those people you cannot imagine living without.

In the second circle, the circle of friendship, list your good friends—those who almost made the first circle.

In the third circle, the circle of participation, list people, organizations, networks you are involved with (work colleagues, the choir, the square dance club, your softball team)—people and groups with whom you participate.

In the fourth circle, the circle of exchange, list people you pay to provide services to you (e.g., medical professionals, tax accountants, mechanics, hairdressers, barbers, teachers).

It is important to note that people can be in more than one circle. For example, your doctor or teacher could also be a very close friend. Figure 3 illustrates a circle of friends.

To illustrate a circle of friends process, a high school teacher's experience with a circle of friends process is described. This teacher decided to avoid burnout and wanted to inject life back into her students, herself, and the school where she taught. She knew she could not change everything, but she could at least make some changes for a few of her students who had been labeled as at risk or with significant disabilities and who were on the verge of dropping out of school. Her goal was to restore hope for them and herself and to help them build relationships with other students.

Circle 1: The Circle of Intimacy

The teacher gathered about 50 students together and told them she wanted to have a frank discussion about friends and how to build more solid relationships in the school. She did not single out any individual but talked in general for about a half hour about

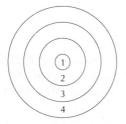

First Circle: **Circle of INTIMACY**
Second Circle: **Circle of FRIENDSHIP**
Third Circle: **Circle of PARTICIPATION**
Fourth Circle: **Circle of EXCHANGE**

Fill the circles from the outside in!

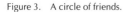

Figure 3.   A circle of friends.

her own visions and her beliefs in relationships and friendships as the core of a good school. She played music softly in the background and drew colorful images as she spoke. She then drew the four concentric circles on the chalk board. She gave each student a sheet of paper that also had these four concentric circles and requested that they each put their name in the center of the inner circle. She modeled this by putting her name in the center of her circle. Then she directed them to write, in the first and smallest circle, the names of all the people closest to their hearts and those whom they would be miserable without. She gave the example of her own life by putting her husband, her mother, her two children, and, for fun, her computer (she was an avid computer user) in the first circle. She also put in this first circle a friend who had died 2 years previously.

Circle 2: The Circle of Friendship

This teacher then explained that the second circle indicated people who were friends but who were not as close as those in the first circle. Again, she modeled this by using the example of her own life. She put in this circle six friends whom she called all the time and two others whom she saw once a year but who called her frequently. She also included some family members, a few teachers she worked with, and her cat. She then asked the students to fill in their second circle, and she found that the classroom grew very quiet and that the students were taking this activity very seriously.

Circle 3: The Circle of Participation

The teacher explained that the third circle was made up of individuals or groups of people whom they really liked but who were not very close to them. She modeled this circle by identifying teachers at the high school, members of the church choir in which she sang, her tennis partners, and members of her exercise class. She also listed individuals she saw occasionally, but who came and went, and three relatives she likes but seldom sees.

Circle 4: The Circle of Exchange

After the students had completed the third circle, she explained that the fourth circle was made up of people who were paid to be in their lives, such as teachers and doctors. She identified her doctor, chiropractor, and housekeeper as people who were paid to be in her life and who were in the fourth circle. The students followed by identifying those people in their lives who were paid to be there. The circles were now complete.

THE CIRCLE OF FRIENDS PROCESS

The teacher told the students that she could learn a lot about a person by looking at his or her completed circles. She asked for a student volunteer to share his or her completed circles. She held up the student's completed circles and read the names of the people in each circle. The circles were relatively full, representing a student who had a high quality of life experiences and opportunities. She stated that this student had a full life, but it was not perfect.

Then the teacher showed the students a completed set of circles for Jane, which reflected the relationships of a student who had a disability and was at risk and asked them to describe how they would feel if those were their circles. The circle of intimacy and the fourth circle, the circle of exchange, were relatively full, reflecting the pattern common among students with disabilities and at risk. The most frequent response of the students was that the only people who were involved in this student's life were her family and those people who were paid to be there.

The teacher then asked the students, "How would you feel if you had no friends?" The students responded with the following descriptors: lonely, confused, upset, rejected, isolated, depressed, unwanted, horrible, humorless, distraught, suicidal, and frustrated. Then she asked the students to identify what they would do if they had no friends, and their responses were the following: commit suicide, die, try to make friends, move to a deserted island, do something really drastic, stay in bed, kick, have a baby, take drugs, drink, kill someone, and get a tutor.

For Friends and Intimacy, Build from the Outside in

After answering these questions, a passionate discussion poured out of the students. They began talking about all the pressures they felt from their families, the school, their teachers, and society in general. They identified that they felt pressure, as they put it, "to look good, to do well, and to achieve a lot." They felt the general attitude of teachers was that if students could not make it to university, they were total failures. The teacher listened and contributed to the discussion. She explained that she had started the process to see how many students would be interested in helping her figure out how to fill in the circles of those students who were isolated and without friends.

She explained that her strategy was to fill in the circles from the outside circle inward. She continued, using the example of Jane. For example, if Jane felt lonely, we would start by getting Jane involved in groups and organizations in order to gradually find people who would be interested in personal relationships with her. She explained that she was not asking who wanted to be Jane's friend, which is a question searching for failure. Rather, she asked, "Who knows Jane and is willing to brainstorm ideas for getting Jane more involved?" For example, if Jane liked films, maybe we could identify someone who would invite her to join the film club.

The teacher asked the students if anyone wanted to continue this discussion and help figure out ways to build community and circles of friends in the school. To her surprise, all but three students signed up to continue and said they wanted to meet again and often.

A circle of friends is not a trick or a gimmick, it is a powerful tool. Like a chisel, it can pry open one's heart, soul, and thoughts or create a work of art. A work of art does not happen overnight; neither does building circles or communities. Circles and community building are commitments. Circles and community building are as important as math, physics, or history and are part of a curriculum of caring. A circle of friends is holistic, powerful, and not a process you do once and then walk away. It is an ongoing strategy for growth, change, and development.

PLANNING ALTERNATIVE TOMORROWS WITH HOPE (PATH)

PATH is a powerful strategy for solving complex individual, family, or systems issues. Developed by Pearpoint, O'Brien, and Forest (1993) PATH takes people through an eight-step process and provides them with a concrete PATH evolved from the MAPs process. It offers an opportunity to extend the MAPs process, delve into issues in more depth, and develop a more thorough plan of action. In the MAPs process, information is collected, and often the action plan is evident. When more complex issues arise, PATH is the tool to take out of your toolbox. It deepens the problem-solving process into one of creating a possible and positive future.

To Begin, Decide Whether You Want to Be a Pathfinder

A pathfinder is a person or a group of people who want to explore ways to realize a socially important vision in a complex and dynamic environment. In our experience, PATH usually generates a good understanding of the hard work a pathfinder must do to move forward. Because the process actively encourages sharing intuition, insight, and wisdom, the results are often surprising and exciting, but they invariably call for hard, although meaningful and potentially satisfying, work. Some of this work is in developing new skills and new relationships; some of it calls for the courage to face difficult personal and social barriers; some of it means letting go of familiar patterns of thinking and habits of action in order to make room for new development. Before embarking on PATH, answer these four questions:

1. Do we share a problem that we want to solve? (This may seem like an odd question, but we have noticed that many people and organizations act as if they enjoy their problems, or at least the chance to complain about them and lament their insolubility and complexity. There is no time in the PATH process for repeating familiar complaints.)
2. Do we share an important purpose, or do we want to find out whether we do?
3. Are we willing to face the possibility that, because important problems frequently call for shifting power arrangement and renegotiating roles and rules, we may have to confront significant conflicts, and we will certainly have to consider big changes in the way we do things?
4. Do we have the energy for the kind of action learning that PATH demands? People or organizations whose total focus is on day-to-day survival probably need to find other ways to grow stronger before attempting PATH.

People and organizations unready to consider reallocating some of their time and money to new pursuits may find PATH a waste of time. Remember, PATH is a process that unfolds over time. If it is hard to imagine getting a few hours away from daily demands for an initial PATH meeting, it may be very difficult indeed to make the time for the follow-up work and reflection required for action learning. Negative answers to these questions do not rule out PATH as a useful activity; many people and groups have found the process an energizing way to discover common purposes and shared action goals. But negative or equivocal answers to these questions point to possible limits on the effectiveness of PATH.

PATH is a facilitated process that uses a graphic record to focus energy and to support memory. It calls for two people as team guides: The first person is a process facilitator, who monitors the time and pace of the process while assisting the pathfinder through the steps and questions. The process facilitator attends to the process as revealed through words, voice, and expressions.

The second team guide is a graphic recorder, who captures the pathfinder's words and images on paper, offers the pathfinder occasional summaries of the work, and helps the pathfinder identify emergent themes that unify the ongoing process. The graphic recorder focuses on imagery, attending to ears and hands to highlight intuition.

In our experience, individuals who are not part of the focus group provide the most effective guidance for the PATH process. We have seen good, often surprising, results from people who are assuming the PATH guide roles for the first time. It would be extraordinary for someone who is part of the group to guide as well as an outsider and most uncommon for one person to be both process facilitator and graphic recorder.

It is absolutely necessary that the guides themselves have the experience of being a pathfinder. There is no substitute for the personal experience of discovering the texture of feelings and the pace of the questions in the process.

Because the situations pathfinders face generate intense emotion, pathfinders need to choose guides they can trust to deal constructively with the individual's and the group's feelings of pain, fear, and anger. Expression of such feelings is not the goal of PATH, as it is in some kinds of group work, but these feelings are real and part of the situation, and guides need skill and willingness to encourage pathfinders to face them and learn from them rather than flee them.

Invite People to Join in the Process

PATH is a social process. Even if focused on an individual's intensely personal issues, the process is immeasurably enriched by the active involvement of others who know and care about the person.

If the focus is on an organizational or a community issue, the more diverse the group with a common purpose, the better. For example, in working with a school we would much prefer to involve opinion leaders among the faculty, the student body, family members, and other concerned citizens than just involve representatives of one group. In situations that involve many people, we prefer many PATH sessions involving diverse groups. These many PATHs can be unified by ensuring that some members of each team take responsibility for linking up with other teams or by holding a PATH festival at which different teams share their findings.

The PATH process should not be thwarted if a particular person is reluctant to be involved. PATH joins people who share a common situation and the willingness to explore a common purpose. In our experience, all the people who should be there never attend a PATH meeting. That is why there is an explicit step in the process that focuses attention on the individuals who must be part of the team's vision and on how team members will go about involving them.

Participation in PATH must be voluntary. The idea of enrollment is central to the process. For us, enrollment suggests the image of people freely coming forward to sign up for hard work, perhaps even overcoming personal obstacles in order to enroll. This sometimes means that the pathfinder group is small, at least initially, because only a few people care enough about a problem to work on it. We have seen pathfinders work successfully to change organizations from the outside or from positions with little formal power, although more change will happen if people in authority genuinely enroll.

The PATH Process

The following are guidelines for the eight steps of the PATH process. Examples, approaches, and questions facilitate the appreciation that there is not one single correct question. With practice, the facilitator team will develop a style and a sense of when to push and when to ease off and move on. To begin the process, the process facilitator explains that there are eight steps in the PATH process. A chart, such as that in Figure 4, may be helpful in the initial explanation.

Step 1: Touching the Dream A situation becomes difficult when there is no reliable procedure that guarantees a desired outcome. The situation becomes more complex when people define what is going on in different ways and have different expectations. Being in a complex difficult situation is like being in an unmapped forest. To find a way through such an environment, pathfinders need the sort of direction that comes from being able to sight the North Star. There is often a physical image that cap-

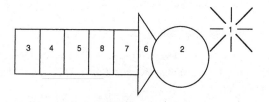

1 Touching the *Dream* - the "North Star"

2 Sensing the *Goal*

3 Grounding in the *Now*

4 Identifying People to *Enroll*

5 Recognizing Ways to Build *Strength*

6 Charting Action for the *Next Few Months*

7 Planning the *Next Month*'s Work

8 Committing to the *First Step*

Figure 4.   The eight steps of the PATH process.

tures the pathfinder's dream and direction and what matters most in the pathfinder's future. What dream for the future does the pathfinder want to work toward and enroll others to work toward? The dream is an expression of the pathfinder's identity and orientation.

The process facilitator invites the pathfinder to direct the search to his or her dream. Here are examples of the kinds of questions that may be helpful in nurturing a dream from a mere flicker to robust images with color, texture, tastes, and smells:

- What are some of the key words and images that express your dream?
- What are the words and images that capture your North Star direction finder?
- What ideals do you most want to realize along this PATH?
- What values do you want to use to evaluate your choices along this PATH?
- Do you have a physical image of his or her dream as a result of previous work, such as a MAPs session or a vision retreat, that you would like to use for this session. (Ask them to display their image and to briefly describe it.)
- How strongly do you feel committed to this dream?

The graphic recorder completes Step 1 by summarizing the pathfinder's dream and asking the pathfinder for confirmation that the summary is accurate.

Step 2: Sensing the Goal   The dream is an expression of identity and orientation. It gives direction. However, the dream is not the pathfinder's goal. The goal is for the pathfinder to realize and deepen the understanding of some of the values expressed in the dream. Identifying the goal for a PATH depends on having a vivid, colorful, multisensory image of what the results of effective work toward the dream would be. The more specific the images, the better. To describe the sense of success, the pathfinder uses the thinking tool of looking backward. The pathfinder vividly and concretely imagines that success has already been achieved and describes the changes that have resulted as if they were real. This process of "trying on" the future can seem awkward at first, but it can be enlightening.

Invite the pathfinder to travel forward in time in order to vividly imagine what he or she wants to create: Do you think that you could accomplish some important results in a year's time? In 1½ years? 2 years? When the pathfinder agrees on a time frame, ask the date by which there will be some important results. Write the date on the record. The ideal time frame is something that is "just beyond your grasp." If the pathfinder already has a 1-year plan, push it into uncertainty, but not too far—just enough to create some tension.

The process facilitator continues: "Imagine that today is [the future date specified]. You are taking time out to reflect on how far you have come since [today's date]. You have done an incredible amount of hard work over the last months. There were ups and downs and times when you felt lost, and there is still much to do. But when you look back and see how far you have come since [today's date], you feel a real sense of accomplishment and pride. Your dream is even more clear now because of what you have been able to do. Tell us what has happened. What, specifically, can you point to as the signs of what you have created? What you have done?" (For example, if a school team "remembered" that the Grade 10 class planned a trip together and everyone went, push them to remember the details. "Where did you go? Who was on the committee? What was the funniest incident? Who was involved?")

The process facilitator keeps asking for specific details: "Help us to see, hear, smell, taste, and touch (remember) what you have done." Let the pathfinder describe whatever accomplishments seem significant. There may be accomplishments in a number of different areas. The graphic recorder notes them all. If this step yields accomplishments in a variety of different areas, invite the pathfinder to focus on the area of accomplishment that seems most important to explore now. It usually works better to have more than one meeting than it does to explore several paths at the same time. Ask the pathfinder to quietly review the record of accomplishment, to add anything, and then to share key feeling words associated with the accomplishments. The graphic recorder adds the feeling words to the record. The process facilitator concludes this step by summarizing the pathfinder's sense of success and by getting confirmation that the summary is accurate.

Step 3: Grounding in the Now The energy to discover and follow a PATH is generated when the pathfinder accepts the tension between what he or she wants to create in the future and what he or she is now doing. The pathfinder can avoid this creative tension by diminishing what he or she wants to accomplish or by inflating or ignoring how things are now. Step 3 grounds the PATH process in a clear description of where the pathfinder is now.

Invite the pathfinder to ground the search in an honest description of the now: "Let's move back to the present. It's [today's date]. This [motioning to the area of accomplishment the pathfinder identified in Step 2] is what you want. As of today, looking around at the present situation, coolly and objectively, how would you describe where you are now? Give us a snapshot of the present." The facilitator keeps asking for facts or best guesses about facts: "Help us to see exactly where you are now in relation to where you want to be." He or she checks to make sure that the pathfinder feels a real stretch between the now and the image of success. Sometimes, pathfinders discover they have scaled down their images of accomplishment too much. If this happens, go back and add to the image recorded in Step 2.

The facilitator asks the pathfinder to quietly review the record of the now and to add anything and then to share key feeling words associated with now. The graphic recorder adds the feeling words to the record.

The process facilitator concludes this step by summarizing the pathfinder's sense of the now and getting confirmation that the summary is accurate.

Step 4: Identifying People to Enroll People other than the pathfinder control resources necessary to the pathfinder's success. The pathfinder must enroll some of these people in his or her vision of accomplishment in Step 2. Enrolling someone means more than just getting permission or trading favors; it means honoring a shared commitment. This step allows recognition of those people with whom the pathfinder wants to work to build a shared commitment. The process facilitator invites the pathfinder to identify the people they want to enroll: "You will meet many people along your PATH. Some will help you; some will try to block you. You will be able to ignore some people, get the minimum that you need from others, and negotiate truces and trades with others. But there are some people you have the opportunity to enroll in what you want to create. As you think about your situation, identify the people with whom you want to share and strengthen your commitment. Whom do you need to enroll to achieve your dream?"

The facilitator reminds the pathfinder that he or she should identify people whom the pathfinder assumes already share his or her commitment. The enrollment of no one should be assumed or go without affirmation. For each person identified, the facilitator asks, "What contribution can this person make to what you want to create?"

When the list seems complete, the facilitator asks the pathfinder to highlight the people he or she feels comfortable about approaching to help achieve goals. If there is no one the pathfinder feels uncomfortable approaching, ask the pathfinder to stretch a bit more. If there are a lot of people the pathfinder feels uncomfortable asking, the facilitator suggests that the pathfinder may want to schedule some planning time to develop a strategy for enrolling people. The facilitator reminds the pathfinder that it is usually possible to discover a way to negotiate an exchange with those who will not enroll, or failing that, a way around the person.

The process facilitator concludes this step by asking the pathfinder to quietly review the record and add any names and then to share key feeling words associated with the list of people the pathfinder wants to enroll. Add the feeling words to the record.

Step 5: Recognizing Ways to Build Strength   Sustaining the work that it takes to realize a dream demands that the pathfinder become stronger. As a pathfinder moves along the PATH, he or she must gain knowledge, learn skills, maintain mutually helpful relationships, and grow in healthy ways.

The facilitator invites the pathfinder to recognize the strengths needed: "Moving from what is now to what you want to create will take energy and skill. There will be challenges, there will be problems, there will be stresses, and there will be defeats. What do you need to do to become strong and stay strong as you move along your PATH? What knowledge do you need? What skills do you need to develop? What relationships do you need to maintain? How can you stay healthy and well as you work toward creating what you want?"

The graphic recorder briefly notes initial ideas that the pathfinder has about building strengths. (Pathfinders may need to schedule a separate time to work on ways to build strengths.)

The process facilitator concludes this step by summarizing the pathfinder's ideas about how to build strengths and by getting confirmation that the summary is accurate. It is important to note that building strengths includes, but is not limited to, personal growth. Building strengths is grounded in the commitment to build one's ability to be of service to people. The balance between personal strengths and social commitment is an important issue. The process facilitator should help the pathfinder attempt to achieve a healthy viable balance.

Step 6: Charting Action for the Next Few Months The pathfinder will not find a way through a complex situation without taking action (doing it) and learning from it (reflecting). The pathfinder needs to chart his or her main actions for the first few months of work.

The process facilitator invites the pathfinder to chart his or her actions for the next 3 months: "Go back and briefly review your image of what you want to create (Step 2). Think about the next 3 months. This should be time enough to take some important action toward what you want to create. What are the most important steps to take in the next 3 months?" The facilitator encourages the pathfinder to be concrete and specific in describing each step.

The facilitator ensures that the pathfinder has considered each aspect of what he or she wants to create. The pathfinder may decide not to take action yet on a particular aspect of what he or she wants to create, but this should be an explicit decision.

The facilitator asks the pathfinder to take a minute to check and confirm that the actions chosen are consistent with his or her dream (Step 1). If the pathfinder identifies actions that do not uphold the values expressed in the dream, the facilitator encourages the pathfinder to make revisions. The facilitator also asks the pathfinder to identify the actions that seem possible to undertake without additional resources. If the pathfinder has selected a long-term goal (i.e., 2 years), he or she may prefer to chart action for 6 months or 1 year.

The facilitator concludes this step by summarizing the pathfinder's action plans for building strengths and by confirming that the summary is accurate.

Step 7: Planning the Next Month's Work Specifying who will do what and by when in the upcoming month clearly focuses the process on action. The facilitator invites the pathfinder to plan the next month with the following questions: "If you are going to accomplish what you want in the next 6 months, you will have to take actions now. Exactly what will you have to do? By what day in the next month will this be done? Who will do what and by when will they do it?"

The facilitator ensures that the pathfinder plans, or schedules a time to plan, for each of the areas he or she charted for the next 3 months (Step 6).

The facilitator concludes this step by summarizing the pathfinder's plan for the next month and by confirming that the summary is accurate.

Step 8: Committing to the First Step Moving from thinking to action requires commitment to a clear first step. The nature of the step matters less than do specific pledges to take action soon by a definite time. Breaking the grasp of inertia is critical. The facilitator invites the pathfinder to commit to a specific first step by asking, "What is the first step? What are the biggest barriers to taking this step? Who, specifically, will support you in this step? How will you enlist their support?" The facilitator concludes this step by summarizing the pathfinder's first step and by getting confirmation that the summary is accurate.

In many situations, people can identify a first step with ease. However, because of lifelong habits, they might neglect to begin their journey with a new essential step—asking for support. Thus, the facilitator needs to ensure that no one takes the first step on the journey alone. The extent of support may be slight, but the new habit of asking for support is vital. It can be as simple as asking a colleague to phone at noon to ask if the pathfinder has made the "first step" call yet. In effect, the pathfinder is giving a supporter "permission" or an invitation to nag. Giving permission to someone to become involved is a very important ability to add to the pathfinder's repertoire. In other instances, a pathfinder may seem to be blocked about taking a first step. This is vital information and must be treated delicately. It is a good practice to talk about blocks with every group because we all encounter them from time to time. However, if a pathfinder is genuinely struggling with taking the "first step," there are probably deeper issues that need to be teased out. Good questions for the facilitator to ask in such a situation are the following: "Is there anything blocking? Is there anything that isn't on the PATH that needs to be there? Is there anything missing?"

One possibility for explaining a pathfinder's stalling is that the pathfinder began the process and suddenly realized that his or her dream is possible—achievable—if he or she is willing to make a commitment and work hard. This can be very unnerving because it means that the pathfinder actually must decide whether to make the appropriate commitment. Some people choose not to proceed, but it is a conscious choice and can be very difficult to face.

Alternatively, there may well be an underlying unresolved issue that has been ignored, avoided, or simply forgotten until now. In some instances, this can be sorted out on the spot. In other instances, it may well be that until that issue is resolved the entire PATH process must be put on hold. Some might think that this is a terrible waste, but if the process does nothing but strip away layers and reveal a central underlying issue, this can be enormously helpful—if the pathfinder chooses to work with it and through it.

CONCLUSION

MAPs is a process that can be used by the key people in a student's life (e.g., parents, friends, teachers) to carefully consider the life of a student—who he or she is and what the student, family, and friends dream for the future. It culminates in a concrete plan of action for helping the student reach a dream. However, sometimes this is not enough, and the student needs a circle of friends to help him or her toward realization of the dream. With the help of the team or other school personnel and friends, often a circle of friends can be formed around the student to facilitate realization of the dream and to help ensure that he or she is included in school and nonschool community activities and provided encouragement and support when needed. When issues become complex and difficult to address and solve, there may be a need to implement the PATH process. PATH is an in-depth eight-step process for helping a team of people assist a student by addressing complex individual, family, and systems issues.

We believe that communities of diversity are richer, better, and more productive places in which to live and learn. We believe that inclusive communities have the capacity to create the future. We want a better life for everyone. We want inclusion! We believe that the tools outlined in this chapter can help you in your efforts to foster inclusion of everyone.

REFERENCES

Grenot-Scheyer, M., Coots, J., & Falvey, M. (1989). Developing and fostering friendships. In M.A. Falvey (Ed.), *Community-based curriculum: Instructional strategies for students with severe handicaps* (2nd ed., pp. 345–358). Baltimore: Paul H. Brookes Publishing Co.

Pearpoint, J., O'Brien, J., & Forest, M. (1993). *PATH*. Toronto: Inclusion Press.

Stainback, W., & Stainback, S. (1990). Facilitating peer supports and friendships. In S. Stainback & W. Stainback (Eds.), *Support networks for inclusive schooling: Interdependent integrated education* (pp. 51–63). Baltimore: Paul H. Brookes Publishing Co.

6

Practical Strategies for Communicating with All Students

Maureen A. Smith and Diane Lea Ryndak

THE INDIVIDUALS WITH Disabilities Education Act of 1990 (IDEA) (PL 101-476) and the Individuals with Disabilities Education Act Amendments of 1991 (PL 102-119) ensured each student with a disability of the right to an education in the least restrictive environment. More and more, this mandate is serving as the premise for including students with disabilities in general education classes with appropriate support and aids. With the proper support, a student with a disability who is educated in general education settings with peers without disabilities has more opportunities for academic and social progress than are possible in self-contained settings. This progress, however, does not occur by chance. Proximity alone does not facilitate academic growth; systematic teaching is required. Similarly, mere proximity does not facilitate high-caliber social interactions; carefully planned social interactions are necessary. Central to development in both academic and social domains is the ability to communicate and interact with peers and adults. All students need to have some way to indicate to their teachers that curricular goals are being achieved. In addition, all students need to have some way to interact socially with both classmates and adults. Communication is the key to success in both areas.

Most of us typically use oral and written language to communicate with others. The presence of a disability, however, may limit the extent to which a student can communicate through these traditional avenues. Adaptations may be necessary if the student is to participate fully and reap the benefits of an inclusive placement. Some adaptations are managed fairly easily. For example, Bill has a learning disability that makes it difficult for him to process auditory information. His teacher provides him with an advanced organizer and makes use of visuals during her lessons. For another example, Mark's learning disability interferes with his ability to write coherently. His teacher targets the development of note-taking skills, and he uses a tape recorder to dictate, rather than write, his responses. Other students may have disabilities that interfere with communication in more fundamental ways. Ann, for example, has cerebral palsy that renders her speech unintelligible and makes it extremely difficult for her to write. Mary has autistic disorder and does not make or sustain eye contact, a very basic communication skill. In addition, she is nonverbal. It was not all that long ago that these students' disabilities made them candidates for placements in restrictive settings; however, this situation has changed drastically as more parents and professionals urge consideration of the general education class as an appropriate educational placement. What has not changed, however, is the complex nature of the communication difficulties experienced by these students. Adaptations are necessary for them to communicate effectively in the general education class. Fortunately, advances in assistive technology and augmentative communication have increased the quality and quantity of options available to maximize the communication among a student with disabilities, the teacher, and peers without disabilities.

There are two purposes of this chapter. First, we briefly review the ways in which various disabilities can affect communication abilities and how these can undermine success in inclusive settings. Second, we identify several options for enhancing communication abilities. There is a diverse range of options; some of them are rather complex. Not all options have a sufficient research base supporting their use. We want to caution the reader not to feel overwhelmed. Although a successful inclusive placement requires appropriate levels of support, a single teacher should not be solely responsible for assessing the student's needs and abilities, identifying an appropriate communication option, ensuring instruction of its application, or evaluating its use in the general education setting. All the educational team members, including parents, the student, and professionals, must work cooperatively toward these goals (Ryndak & Alper, 1996).

THE EFFECTS OF A DISABILITY ON COMMUNICATION SKILLS

A major factor in the development of communication skills is the acquisition of language. Although typical children vary in their acquisition of language, most American children speak and comprehend standard English by the time they enter the first grade. The presence of a disability, however, may place a child at risk for delayed or nontypical development of language skills. Students with disabilities may demonstrate difficulty in receptive (understanding) language, expressive (oral/written) language, or both. Obviously, a student who has a speech impairment (e.g., an articulation disorder, voice disorder, stuttering) has some difficulty communicating through speech. Communication problems, however, are not restricted to students identified as having a speech impairment; other disabilities also affect a student's communication. By definition, students with learning disabilities may experience difficulties with listening comprehension and/or oral and written expression. Typically, students with mental retardation have difficulty learning and using language. Physical disabilities such as cerebral palsy may affect the muscles needed in articulation, making it difficult for the student to use speech. Often, students with behavioral or emotional disorders have difficulties with language. In fact, difficulties with language and communication are key considerations in the diagnosis of these disorders. Some of the most extensive work in the area of pervasive developmental disorders has been conducted with students identified as having autistic disorder. Nearly half of these students are identified as being nonverbal, while some of those who demonstrate verbal ability use language in an unusual manner (Wicks-Nelson & Israel, 1984). For example, they may make inappropriate or seemingly random remarks or use words and phrases in idiosyncratic ways. Students with autistic disorder may be echolalic, repeating the last word of a phrase or an entire sentence spoken to them with no apparent comprehension of its meaning.

Receptive and expressive communication disabilities have a tremendous impact on a student's functioning. The results of formal and informal assessments can be compromised because a student may have limited ability or the inability to demonstrate the extent of his or her knowledge or skills. As educational team members, we must question the appropriateness of goals, objectives, materials, and instructional techniques selected on the basis of such assessment results. In addition, a student who lacks effective communication skills may be unable to express feelings and concerns and may resort to disruptive, even violent, behaviors. Ultimately, a student's academic and social progress is undermined if he or she has limited abilities to communicate effectively with peers and adults.

For some of the communication difficulties we have outlined, accommodations can be made relatively easily within general education settings. As suggested earlier, a student whose learning disability interferes with auditory perception may benefit from the teacher's use of advanced organizers and visuals in instruction. More intensive efforts are required, however, to address more severe communication difficulties. Given the communication problems associated with various disabilities and their effects on successful communication, it is essential that educational team members collaborate to identify alternatives to traditional methods of interacting with a student with a disability that affects communication. We now turn our attention to these options.

AUGMENTATIVE AND ALTERNATIVE COMMUNICATION SYSTEMS

Augmentative and alternative communication (AAC) systems can be used either as primary or supplemental communication aids for individuals for whom speech is difficult. AAC systems that use symbols may be categorized as aided or unaided. Each of these categories has several options.

Unaided AAC Symbol Systems

In an unaided AAC symbol system, the student uses only his or her body to communicate. Examples of unaided systems include gestures, manual signs, vocalizations, and facial expressions. People without disabilities use unaided symbols frequently to indicate preferences or express opinions. We wave good-bye; we shake our heads to indicate we do not want anything more to eat; we crook a finger or make eye contact to summon a waiter. Some students whose disabilities interfere with their use of traditional communication skills are able to use unaided symbols. In fact, students who have not been exposed to formal training may use unaided symbols as their only augmentative communication option.

Sign language is an example of an unaided symbolic communication system. There are several distinct sign languages, and they range in the extent to which they parallel spoken English. Manual sign languages offer several advantages. Sign language is always available for use because there is no equipment to carry around or turn on, because additional devices are not necessary. Also, some signs are very iconic, that is, very clear and easily understood even by those unfamiliar with them. Such signs include those for drink and eat. There are disadvantages as well. First, not all signs are iconic, clearly or easily understood. For example, a person unfamiliar with sign language is not likely to understand the sign for bathroom. Thus, it helps if all communication partners have a working knowledge of sign language, which is a difficult goal to accomplish. An alternative to everyone learning to understand and use sign language is to use an interpreter; however, the constant presence of an interpreter may in fact undermine the benefits of inclusion (Clark, 1984). Another disadvantage is that using manual signs does not produce a permanent product for easy reference. A student must be able to recall the signs he or she wants to use. Finally, the results of a substantial body of research indicate that students with mental retardation who require significant supports and students with autistic disorder can learn a core of basic signs; however, these students do not learn more than a few basic signs, and they do not use them spontaneously (Mirenda & Iacono, 1990).

Aided AAC Symbol Systems

Aided AAC symbol systems require tools or equipment in addition to the student's body to produce a message. Many of these symbol systems are very simple, or low tech; others are technologically complex, or high tech. Low-tech examples of aided symbol systems are tangible symbols, real objects or partial objects, or representational symbols. High-tech systems include symbol systems presented on personal communicators and personal computers. Some devices, such as communication boards, can be either low or high tech.

Communication Boards   A communication board may be either portable or attached to a student's desk or wheelchair. Figure 1 is an illustration of a communication board attached to a student's wheelchair. This example is nonelectronic, offering advantages such as being low-cost, easy to make and update, and portable. It can also serve as a backup for a more sophisticated electronic AAC system. There is one major

Figure 1. A communication board.

disadvantage, however, to a communication board such as this. Because there is no written or spoken output, the person with whom the student is interacting (the communication partner) must be able to see the board and immediately interpret the symbol system.

Using a nonelectronic communication board, the student selects items on the board directly by using touch or other type of physical pressure or by pointing without physical contact, such as with eye pointing. The student who is unable to use one of these methods may need to have someone point out options from those displayed. The student can then signal a selection by moving his or her eyes or other body part. An electronic communication board can be adapted to be operated by a finger, pointing stick, head pointer, beam of light, or switch that enables the student to select a desired picture, symbol, letter, word, phrase, or sentence.

Whether nonelectronic or electronic, the communication board should be easily adaptable as the student's needs change. The board should be individually designed for the student so that it matches his or her skills. A student who has a limited range of movement should have items on the communication board positioned so that he or she can have access to them easily. Similarly, the communication board must be dynamic; that is, it must keep pace with a student's changing needs. The communication board designed for a young student obviously cannot meet his or her needs over a lifetime. A student's first communication board may display only pictures. As the student's communication skills and needs increase, pictures can be added and combined with printed matter.

There are several varieties of communication boards. Mirenda and Iacono (1990) identified several very clever "homemade"communication devices, including communication books, wallets, eye-gaze aprons and vests, and easels.

Personal Communicators Technologically more sophisticated than the communication boards described, yet not as complex as personal computers, are personal digitized speech and nonspeech output devices such as the Canon Communicator, TouchTalker, Liberator, and IntroTalker. These devices are the size of calculators or cellular phones. As can be seen in Figure 2, these devices include keyboards and liquid crystal displays (LCDs). Some also include the option of a printout. They offer the advantages of being less noticeable than a communication board, easily transported, and, because the output is in standard written or spoken English, are easily used by communication partners. Obviously, they require the student to be able to understand and use the symbols and to be able to physically press the keys with their fingers or other body part or by using a pointer of some type.

Personal Computers The tremendous developments in computer technology have substantially improved the AAC systems available to students with special needs. Computers are becoming smaller, increasing the ease with which they can be transported across settings. They also are becoming more powerful, making them more flexible and more easily adapted for individual use. For example, expanded keyboards increase the ease of use for a student with a physical disability. Messages such as frequently

Figure 2.   A personal communicator. (Photograph courtesy of Canon U.S.A., Inc.)

used phrases and questions can be entered and retrieved from the computer's memory with a single keystroke. The incorporation of synthetic speech devices with PCs enables output to be easily understood by individuals with whom the student interacts. Personal computer systems include two categories. In the first category are dedicated systems, which are composed of both hardware and software (i.e., the computer itself and the programs). These systems have been developed specifically for individuals who have limited speech abilities. In the second category are integrated systems that feature commercially available hardware (e.g., the computer, a speech synthesizer, and communication software). Refer to Lewis (1993) and Lindsey (1993) for detailed information on available dedicated and integrated systems.

Combining AAC Components   More than one AAC component may be needed to maximize the quality and quantity of a student's interactions. We encourage those working with a student to identify both the settings in which he or she participates and the communication partners with whom he or she interacts. A variety of components may be combined in an AAC system so that the student can move freely across environments and communicate effectively with the people he or she meets. For example, a student could use a computer for lengthy conversations and schoolwork. A personal communicator or a communication wallet could be used in the community. Head nods, simple gestures, and vocalizations can be used for rapid informal communication.

Considerations in Choosing an Aided Symbol System

We have discussed only some of the low- and high-tech AAC devices appropriate for use in an inclusive setting by a student with a disability. However, the picture is not quite complete. We have mentioned that AAC components such as communication boards use symbol systems (e.g., objects, pictures, symbols, words). In addition, we have mentioned that students may need assistive devices (e.g., hand-held or head pointers) to select items. We now address these topics.

Symbol Systems   There are a variety of symbol systems that may be selected for use by a student in order to convey a message. These include tangible objects, pictures, drawings, rebus symbols, Blissymbolics, letters, and words. The choice of an appropriate symbol system should not be left to random chance but should reflect the same careful consideration and assessment that goes into selecting any other AAC options.

Tangible Objects   Attaching objects to a communication board can be cumbersome but may be appropriate for a student with limited cognitive ability and/or multiple disabilities, for whom something less concrete may be hard to understand. Complete objects can be used (e.g., coins). To save space, partial objects can be used (e.g., a piece of a drinking straw). In addition, miniature objects can be used, but must be selected with care as they may be difficult to recognize by students with intellectual disabilities (Beukelman & Mirenda, 1992).

Representational Symbols   An AAC system may incorporate pictures or drawings of people, places, things, and actions that are relevant to the student. Using pictures or photographs may be ideal for the student who does not require the concrete reference of objects. Fewer pictures that are large in size and highly relevant may be used at the beginning of a program that teaches a student to use the symbol system, with more but smaller pictures used as a student's and partner's communication skills improve. We recommend covering pictures with plastic or laminating them to guard against damage resulting from normal daily use.

Rebus Symbols A rebus is a picture that represents a word or a syllable. A rebus system that was developed in the United States, uses approximately 950 pictograph symbols (Clark, 1984; Clark, Davies, & Woodcock, 1974), each of which represents a single morpheme or basic unit of meaning. Rebus symbols have been found to be more iconic than some other signs, so students may find them easy to understand. Rebus symbols can be used in combination to construct sentences that vary in complexity. Sample rebus symbols are presented in Figure 3.

Blissymbols Blissymbolics (Bliss, 1965) was developed originally as a language for international written communication but began to be used in augmentative communication systems in the 1970s. It includes approximately 100 basic symbols that can be combined in a logical manner for communication. Each symbol is based on a geometric shape and can represent more than one concept. For example, the Blissymbol for house also means building (Clark, 1984).

The meaning of each Blissymbol is usually obvious after a brief explanation, which means that they are translucent in terms of iconicity. Blissymbols can be combined to create simple line drawings depicting actual objects or ideas. As illustrated in Figure 4, a symbol can be pictographic in that it actually resembles the concept it represents. An ideographic Blissymbol represents ideas or feelings about a concept, while an arbitrary symbol represents a grammatical marker. The Blissymbolics system can convey complex linguistic concepts such as plurality, action, number, and tense. Meanings of symbols change by altering the size, orientation, or position of the symbol. This system has been used with students with a variety of communication disorders who are unable to use writing but who can learn a large vocabulary. To facilitate use with communication partners, symbols are always accompanied by written captions.

Traditional Orthography: Letters and Words Letters, words, and sentences may be incorporated into AAC devices used by students who can read. There is a major advantage to using these traditional orthographic symbols; namely, they can be used to convey an unlimited number of messages, and they are understood by any communication partner who can read.

Letters on a communication board or displayed on a personal communicator or a PC can be arranged alphabetically or in typical keyboard format. Words on a commu-

Knife

Chair

Drink

Open

Figure 3.   Sample rebus symbols.

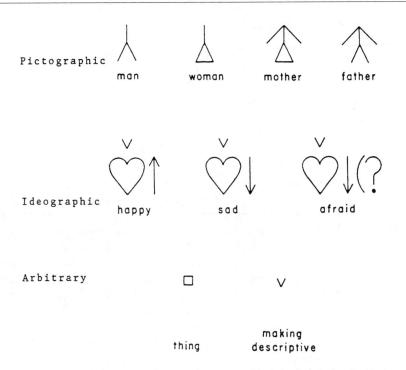

Figure 4.   Sample Blissymbols. (Blissymbolics used herein derived from the symbols described in the work, Semantography, original copyright © C.K. Bliss 1949. Blissymbolics Communication International, Toronto, Canada, Exclusive License, 1982; reprinted by permission.)

nication board can be grouped according to their parts of speech. For example, separate groupings of proper nouns (e.g., names of significant others), common nouns, verbs, adverbs, and adjectives can be displayed. Words can be combined in frequently used sentences to form another separate category (e.g., "I am hungry," "I don't understand"). In addition, a number could be assigned to each of several words. For example, *happy* and *sad* could be assigned the numbers 10 and 11, respectively. A student then would have an array of numbers attached to the communication board. He or she would point to 1 and 0 to indicate happiness, or point to the 1 twice to indicate sadness.

Assistive Devices   The exact nature of the student's abilities determines what assistive devices are appropriate for him or her. For example, a student with cerebral palsy may not be easily able to point to options on a nonelectronic communication board or physically depress computer keys. Various assistive devices have been developed to help individuals. For example, a student who is unable to use his or her fingers to select items or keys might be able to hold and use a pointing stick. The student might be able to use a head pointer to select from the items on a communication board. A switch, such as a joystick, can be adapted so that the student can activate automatic selectors and scanners without assistance.

SELECTING AND USING AAC SYSTEMS

At the beginning of this chapter, we made it clear that the responsibility for selection, implementation, and evaluation of an augmentative communication system should be shared among educational team members. Following the intentions of the legislation previously cited, the ideal people to assume this responsibility are those who develop and implement the student's education program. For a student with a serious disability, this typically includes the student, parents, the classroom teacher, and various professionals with expertise specific to the student's needs, such as a speech-language pathologist, physical therapist, occupational therapist, or audiologist.

The student's needs and abilities are the primary consideration in the selection and development of an AAC system. Therefore, the team first must conduct a thorough assessment of the student's strengths, abilities, and present and projected needs across a variety of areas. Some of this information should be available as a result of existing mandated assessments procedures. Of particular interest are the student's cognitive/linguistic abilities, motor abilities specifically related to accessing various AAC devices, sensory/perceptual abilities, and social functioning. Other assessment data are needed to describe the individual's needs and the environments in which the student functions, as well as verbal and nonverbal communication skills.

In deciding which augmentative communication option or options are appropriate for the student, it is essential that team members be fully informed about all available options and their appropriateness to the individual based on assessment data. The key concern is which option, or combination of options, will empower a student to communicate more effectively. Team members must consider the portability, durability, and naturalness of the options under consideration.

As part of the process of selecting an AAC system, the team should identify the alternative access methods most appropriate for the student. Some direct selection techniques have been discussed previously. In addition, a student may convey messages by scanning or encoding. A system that incorporates scanning may be appropriate for a student with motor control difficulties. In scanning, symbols are displayed and the student in some way stops the scan on the desired symbol. Encoding may enable a student to increase the rate of communication. Rather than construct a message item by item, a student can send a complete message by selecting a code. For example, a student may press a key to convey a greeting that has been stored in the device's memory or a prerecorded introduction. Message output options include visual output in the form of print and visual displays and auditory output in the form of digitized and synthesized speech. A speech synthesizer is an electronic device that can produce a variety of human voices. Correctly used, a speech synthesizer enables a student to speak.

The team must also select the symbol system or systems appropriate to the needs and abilities of the student. Chapman and Miller (1980) identified three factors to guide this selection. The first factor is the student's cognitive abilities. As mentioned previously, some students can use abstract symbols such as Blissymbols and written letters. Some students can use a system that involves tangible objects or visual representations. The second factor is visual acuity. Objects and pictures may be easier for a student to see than some rebus symbols or Blissymbols. These, in turn, may be easier to see than letters or words. The third factor is environmental receptivity. The system should be easily usable by the student and his or her communication partners, including educational team members and classmates.

The student and communication partners need to learn to use the AAC system. At first, the student may work exclusively with one person, such as a paraprofessional, to ensure that instruction is consistent and systematic. Instruction needs to address learning how to use all components of the AAC system. In order to engage in typical classroom activities, the student and communication partners need to learn how to initiate and respond to a variety of communication intents (e.g., expressing personal needs, asking and answering questions, making and responding to requests, and engaging in conversation). Communication partners should be added as they become adept at using the AAC system. The student needs to practice using the AAC system across a variety of environments. If future needs indicate that more than one system will be used eventually, the educational team may first choose an AAC system that has the greatest potential for immediately increasing communication accessibility and providing communication success. Incorporation of other AAC systems should proceed as student needs and abilities progress.

Ideally, all class members, family members, and school personnel should be able to use the AAC system to interact with the student. Because most AAC systems require more time to access and use than normal speech, communication partners need to develop patience and be advised against dominating a conversation. Increasing the number of communication partners who can communicate with the student through an AAC system will enhance the quality and success of an inclusive placement. As part of learning to use an AAC system, the student learns to be as responsible as possible for the transportation, care, and maintenance of the AAC system.

Finally, the appropriateness of the AAC system must be evaluated consistently. Several questions need to be answered during evaluation. Are the student and significant others at home and in school using the AAC system? Is the student initiating communication more frequently with a wider variety of communication partners? Are significant others initiating communication more frequently with the student? Is the student better able to meet curricular goals and objectives? Have previously identified behavior problems been reduced? Does any component of the AAC system need to be adjusted? Have there been improvements in AAC technology or methodology that would help the student?

FACILITATED COMMUNICATION

No matter how clever it is, no AAC device works unless the student and his or her communication partners use it. Unfortunately, the disability that makes traditional communication options unavailable may make it difficult for a student to use the AAC options that we have described. For example, a student with autistic disorder who does not speak may not focus on a communication board. This student may also display behaviors that are not conducive to using AAC devices. Other students with disabilities may not demonstrate capabilities to communicate in traditional ways. In the 1990s, a communication accommodation termed facilitated communication (FC) has emerged as a possible method for assisting these students by helping them overcome motor planning and initiation difficulties.

Facilitated Communication Defined

Through FC, a student has access to an AAC system and communication partner, known as a facilitator, who provides physical assistance to the student while he or she types out messages or selects letters, pictures, or symbols on the AAC device. Assistance begins as support (not actual guidance) to the student's hand or wrist and is faded over time by moving support from the hand or wrist to the arm, elbow, and shoulder, toward the ultimate goal of independent communication (Figure 5). This support is intended to reduce both demands on the student's fine motor skills and the need for motor planning and memory. The student develops functional movement patterns (e.g., pointing) so that he or she can make requests, insert comments, or express feelings with greater levels of independence.

Consider the following example. A student with autistic disorder may demonstrate perseveration; that is, he or she may demonstrate a tendency to repeat the same

Figure 5.   The backward support provided during facilitated communication. (Photograph courtesy of Steve Sartori.)

pattern of behavior. This student may correctly answer "yes" to a question but, because of perseveration, may continue to indicate "yes" in answer to subsequent questions that require a different response. The facilitator can withdraw the student's hand from the AAC device after each selection, thus ensuring there is a pause before the student makes the next selection. The facilitator's role is reduced as the student's skills and confidence increase (Crossley, 1990, 1993).

Facts and Fallacies Associated with Facilitated Communication

Supporters have claimed that FC has enabled individuals with serious disabilities, such as cognitive impairments or autistic disorders, to demonstrate unexpected levels of understanding and academic potential (Biklen, 1993; Crossley, 1993). There have been reports that some individuals whose disabilities have affected their communication have acquired some literacy skills from incidental exposure to written language. Family members or professionals may have been unaware of these skills because students had been unable to communicate through traditional avenues. FC, it is claimed, has enabled these students to provide some valuable clues about the true nature of their abilities. Other gains attributed to FC include a decrease in aggression and significant increases in on-task behavior, positive social interaction, improved eye contact, and meaningful speech.

The professional literature is replete with anecdotal evidence of the benefits of FC. In our own experience, we have encountered numerous professionals and parents who speak glowingly of FC. These anecdotal reports have contributed to the rapid growth of the use of FC across the country, along with other contributing factors. For example, the media's inexhaustible appetite for human interest stories, including unexpected achievements by people with disabilities, ensures that the existence of a new treatment such as FC is widely reported (Crossley, 1993).

Not everything written or reported about FC is true. For instance, Crossley (1993) has identified several myths associated with the use of FC. First is the belief that FC is the best or only communication strategy available for students without speech. A second myth is that FC is only useful to people who can spell. Crossley (1993) argued that it can be used when appropriate to assist nonspellers to make selections from their communication displays. Third is the notion that behaviors typically displayed by students with severe disabilities should not be challenged or changed. Crossley (1993) has argued strongly against this belief. Unwillingness to interfere with unnatural behaviors is demonstrated when facilitators allow students to point or type without looking. A student who glances occasionally at the AAC device, appears to use peripheral vision, or not to look at all is done no favor when a facilitator excuses such poor attention with comments like, "He's using peripheral vision" or "She has an image of the keyboard in her head" (Crossley, 1993, p. 5). The student who can't speak still has to learn appropriate interactive strategies. It would not be sensible to believe that a student with a serious communication disability would require less instruction than anyone else. A fourth myth is that all information obtained using FC is reliable. It is not; ensuring reliability is discussed later in this chapter.

Research Involving Facilitated Communication

More disturbing than myths, however, is the strong possibility that FC is not the effective, reliable method of assistance that its supporters proclaim it to be. A major factor contributing to this possibility is the lack of sound empirical evidence supporting its use. Biklen (1993), a major FC supporter, has been reluctant to evaluate FC through established methods of scientific rigor, believing efforts to validate FC with controlled scientific procedures will undermine the technique. Unfortunately, as Eberlin and McConnachie (1993) point out, there is a history in the special education field of unquestioned acceptance and implementation of treatments and programs that have not been tested for efficacy or negative side effects. Despite the lack of empirical support, procedures gain widespread acceptance and absorb valuable and ever-dwindling treatment resources. Furthermore, valuable student and practitioner time is wasted pursuing benefits that may not exist. This may be the case for facilitated communication.

Eberlin and McConnachie (1993) evaluated the anecdotal reports used to support FC. They noted the omission of reliable information on student communicators' diagnoses, their abilities prior to implementation of FC (including intellectual and adaptive functioning levels), and the amount and type of FC training the facilitators and students received. Wheeler, Jacobson, Paglieri, and Schwartz (1993) subjected FC to more rigorous testing. In their study, a facilitator and participant sat at one end of a long table that was divided lengthwise. The facilitator and participant then were shown pairs of photos. These pairs were not always identical, nor could facilitators and communicators see each other's pictures. The communicator was asked to use FC to identify the photo he or she saw. Results indicated that the communicators only correctly named items in pictures that had been seen by the facilitators.

In another study, Wheeler et al. (1993) pointed out that some programs have been implemented by caregivers or teachers who have heard about FC but have not had access to adequate training or instructional material to develop facilitation skills. Lack of information on what FC is, or how and why it is used, has led to misunderstandings and mistakes in implementation.

Issues and Cautions Concerning Facilitated Communication

FC's goal of increasing independence and choice among students with disabilities is an admirable one. However, we agree with Eberlin and McConnachie (1993) that "uncritical and unverified acceptance of FC output could lead to more oppressive practices and less control for the participant than if the facilitator produced output that is against the participant's wishes" (p. 11). The lack of empirical support to date does not mean that a successful case will never be confirmed (Eberlin & McConnachie, 1993). It does mean, however, that we should proceed with great care and be prepared to discontinue a program if the responses cannot be validated to be the communicator's. We cannot recommend adoption of FC without adherence to a set of very strict guidelines. Members of the student's educational team who are considering use of FC should plan carefully and adhere to the following cautions.

1. Students for whom training in FC is considered should be carefully assessed. Typically, these students have autistic disorder or a related developmental disability. They either do not speak or do not use speech in a functional manner and may be presumed to have serious intellectual abilities. They may also exhibit poor eye–hand coordination, low or high muscle tone, problems with finger isolation and extensions, and perseveration (Biklen, 1993; Crossley, 1990).

2. Informed consent from parents or legal guardians should be obtained before initiating FC. They should be aware of the problems associated with FC and the lack of empirical support.

3. Facilitators should be trained. Educational team members are advised to locate facilitator training programs that may be available in their area.

4. Biklen (1993) encourages paying close attention to issues surrounding physical support. Seating arrangements, positioning, backward resistance, and facilitator neutrality must be examined.

5. A student's introduction to FC should be carefully monitored. During the first session, the facilitator should explain to the student what will be done. The facilitator should speak in a normal supportive way and treat the student as competent, assuming the student understands. How much support a student needs can be partially determined by watching for muscle tone or tremors.

6. Emotional support for the student is important. At all times, the facilitator should treat the student with dignity and respect. The facilitator should not say "wrong," but encourage the student to try again. At the same time, the facilitator should be direct and firm about the need for practicing and staying on task.

7. Important interactive skills that are prerequisites to successful communication must be taught. Just as we look at each other when talking, so too should a student look at the AAC device. Developing improved eye–hand coordination helps the student using FC to gain independence and protects against leading a student to say something he or she doesn't intend (Crossley, 1993). The facilitator should monitor the student's eye contact and encourage him or her to look at the board. Pointing before the student is looking at the target area and extraneous actions (e.g., screeching, slapping of objects, and hand flapping) will impair communication.

8. If the student is using traditional orthography, conventional spellings, grammar, and word usage should be adhered to.

9. Students need sufficient time to respond. The time a student takes to respond should be factored in to any evaluation of the efficacy of FC.

10. Some of the criticism garnered by FC involves the failure to validate information. When in doubt, the facilitator should verify the student's communication. For instance, the facilitator should indicate that a request or piece of information was not understood and instruct the student to type or point again. The facilitator should note whether a student consistently uses the same unconventional spelling or grammar regardless of who the facilitator is. On occasion, the facilitator can use naturalistic message passing (Moore, Donovan, Hudson, Dystra, & Lawrence,

1993; Wheeler et al., 1993). The teacher can show a picture to the student when the facilitator is not present and then have the facilitator return to the room and ask the student to indicate what he or she has seen.

11. Promotion of maintenance and generalization of skills should be part of an FC program. Physical support should be faded over time. Other facilitators and functional situations are also important to generalization.

12. Procedures, progress, and assessment techniques should be documented. Videotaping FC sessions allows examination of techniques used by the facilitator. In addition, the effects of FC on a student's communication ability should be carefully evaluated. Of specific interest are items such as the level of communication without facilitation, alternatives prior to using facilitation, the quality and quantity of communication with facilitation, degree of support required, number of people with whom the student facilitates, and the settings in which facilitation is used.

SUMMARY

In this chapter, we briefly described the impact various disabilities can have on the development and use of communication skills. We identified aided and unaided AAC symbol systems that we believe are appropriate for use in the general education classroom. For each system, we provided a rationale for its selection and identified its advantages and disadvantages. We also recommended a set of procedures for selecting and using AAC devices and symbol systems. In addition, we discussed the use of facilitated communication under carefully controlled conditions.

This chapter has allowed us to only touch on the information most relevant to the needs of a student and an educational team working in an inclusive classroom. Teachers interested in learning more about AAC, symbol systems, and FC are encouraged to locate and review items listed in the reference section.

Running throughout this chapter is a message to educational team members to collaborate and document carefully every aspect of a student's communication skill development program. There must be a match between a student's skills and needs and the communication options selected. It is essential that the student, family members, general education and special education teachers, paraprofessionals, and peers receive adequate training in the correct use of these options. Most important, the effect of the program must be documented to ensure that it is maximizing a student's communication ability. This point cannot be minimized or overlooked, given limitations in the research conducted to support some of the options described in this chapter. We are aware that selecting, implementing, and assessing an augmentative or alternative communication system add to the responsibilities already shouldered by the educational team. However, given the importance of communication to academic and social success in school and adult life, we believe such efforts are critical. Finally, as a student's communication abilities develop and improve, we advise reassessment of academic performance and social skills. A student who is equipped with an appropriate method of communication may be able to demonstrate a level of knowledge and expertise previously untapped.

REFERENCES

Beukelman, D.R., & Mirenda, P. (1992). *Augmentative and alternative communication: Management of severe communication disorders in children and adults.* Baltimore: Paul H. Brookes Publishing Co.

Biklen, D. (1993). *Communication unbound: How facilitated communication is challenging traditional views of autism and ability/disability.* New York: Teachers College Press.

Bliss, C.K. (1965). *Semantography.* Sydney, Australia: Semantography Publications.

Chapman, R., & Miller, J. (1980). Analyzing language and communication in the child. In R.L. Schiefelbusch (Ed.), *Nonspeech language and communication: Analysis and intervention* (pp. 159–196). Baltimore: University Park Press.

Clark, C.R. (1984). A close look at the standard rebus system and Blissymbolics. *Journal of The Association for Persons with Severe Handicaps, 9,* 37–48.

Clark, C.R., Davies, C.O., & Woodcock, R.W. (1974). *Standard rebus glossary.* Circle Pines, MN: American Guidance Service.

Crossley, R. (1990). *Communication training involving facilitated communication.* Paper presented to the annual conference of the Australian Association of Special Education, Canberra.

Crossley, R. (1993). Facilitated communication: Training in North America: An Australian perspective. *IEEIR Interchange,* (April), 1–11.

Eberlin, M., & McConnachie, G. (1993). Facilitated communication: Employing research results to develop ethical practice guidelines. *The Forum, 19*(3), 9–12, 30.

Individuals with Disabilities Education Act of 1990 (IDEA), PL 101-476. (October 30, 1990). Title 20, U.S.C. 1400 et seq: *U.S. Statutes at Large, 104,* 1103–1151.

Individuals with Disabilities Education Amendments of 1991, PL 102-119. (October 7, 1991). Title 20, U.S.C. 1400 et seq: *U.S. Statutes at Large, 105,* 587–608.

Lewis, J.D. (1993). *Computers and exceptional individuals.* Austin, TX: PRO-ED.

Lindsey, R.B. (1993). *Special education technology: Classroom applications.* Pacific Grove, CA: Brooks/Cole.

Mirenda, P., & Iacono, T. (1990). Communication options for persons with severe and profound disabilities: State of the art and future directions. *Journal of The Association for Persons with Severe Handicaps, 15,* 3–21.

Moore, S., Donovan, B., Hudson, A., Dystra, J., & Lawrence, J. (1993). Brief report: Evaluation of eight case studies for the multihandicapped. *Journal of Autism and Developmental Disorders, 23,* 531–540.

Ryndak, D.L., & Alper, S. (1996). *Curriculum content for students with moderate or severe disabilities in inclusive settings,* Boston: Allyn & Bacon.

Wheeler, D., Jacobson, J.W., Paglieri, R., & Schwartz, A.A. (1993). An experimental assessment of facilitated communication. *Mental Retardation, 31,* 49–60.

Wicks-Nelson, R., & Israel, A.C. (1984). *Behavior disorders of childhood* (2nd ed). Englewood Cliffs, NJ: Prentice Hall.

7

Administrative Strategies for Achieving Inclusive Schooling

Daniel D. Sage

THE TITLE OF this chapter, in fact the title of this entire book, may be misleading in that it suggests the idea that there are simple actions (tricks, gimmicks, or interventions) that can be employed to bring about inclusive schooling. In the context of administrative behaviors, it is particularly unrealistic to imply that tinkering (even major tinkering) with what goes on in schools can bring about the necessary changes to accomplish this goal. Rather, we should recognize that inclusive schooling calls for major systems change. Furthermore, we should recognize that change is resisted because it is at best uncomfortable and often frankly feared. Finally, we should recognize that school administrators carry an ambiguous role expectation because, although they are expected to lead, they are also expected to maintain stability in the system. This makes the promotion of fearful or discomforting change a formidable administrative challenge.

THE NATURE OF NECESSARY SYSTEMS CHANGE

Inclusive schooling cannot spontaneously or readily occur, regardless of what any one individual does. However, it is a goal toward which systems can evolve. The changes that must take place for inclusive schooling to be realized should not be seen solely as *prerequisites,* but also as *co-requisites.* We cannot expect to have every component in place in advance. Some things will have to accrue over time. Changes involve multiple levels of the administrative system, including the central district structure, individual building organization, and classroom instruction. The administrator's role is vitally important at each level, and different levels of administrative staff are involved. Moreover, although much of what needs to be done by administrators is the facilitation of change for others (the people for whom they have supervisory responsibility), a significant arena of necessary change is the role and day-to-day practice of the administrators themselves.

One expression of the recognition of the need for change and the processes for accomplishing it can be seen in the work of the Council of Administrators of Special Education (CASE) in their document *CASE Future Agenda for Special Education: Creating a Unified Education System* (Council of Administrators of Special Education, 1993). The issues, recommended actions, and implications discussed in that document concern the following:

1. The responsibility of *all* stakeholders for *all* students
2. The development of a vision and mission for a *unified* system that includes *all* students
3. Accountability through a system of unified outcomes
4. Preparation of *all* educators to educate *all* students
5. A unified funding system emphasizing shared resources without labels
6. Site-based management as a means for building a community of learners
7. A unified curriculum framework as a means to conduct dialogue about outcomes for planning and organizing
8. Staff development fostering ad hoc problem solving, shared resources, and continuous improvement
9. Access to integrated community services at or near the school site
10. Access to and training in appropriate technology

The CASE agenda suggests that, to bring about the change toward more inclusive schooling, there should be a cycle of "centrally driven policy and locally driven actions within a community of stakeholders" (p. 5). The central policy component of the cycle involves the first five items listed above, while the local action component involves the latter five items. A graphic representation of the *total* cycle is shown in Figure 1. An elaboration of the steps within the *action* phase of the cycle follows:

> The first order of school governance is to build an inclusive school learning community based upon the school's defined purpose. The design and development of curricula leading to state and district valued outcomes should follow close behind. Preparing staff to work collaboratively and to share their expertise is the fundamental purpose of an on-going staff development program. A larger investment in technology to support individual and group decision-making is a key responsibility for sub-teams of staff. Technology serves as a major communication device to connect the school to the community and instruction to outcomes. Technology also serves to support staff reflection on practice. Time for reflection on practice needs to be built into the structure of the school and the school day to prepare and benefit from teams of teachers functioning as planners, instructors and evaluators of programs leading to valued outcomes. (Council of Administrators of Special Education, 1993, p. 5)

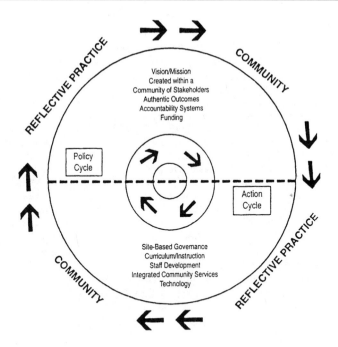

Figure 1. Policy and action cycles—centrally driven policy and locally driven actions within a community of stakeholders. (From Council of Administrators of Special Education. [1993]. *CASE future agenda for special education: Creating a unified system* [p. 5]. Albuquerque, NM: Author; reprinted by permission.)

THE CENTRAL DISTRICT STRUCTURE

The achievement of inclusive schooling calls for a perception of the school system as a *unified whole* rather than as two parallel, separate structures: one for typical students and another for students with disabilities or other special needs. This requires administrative personnel at the central level who not only believe that such unification is desirable and possible, but who also will communicate that vision in all their public behavior, in both words and actions. The inclusive behaviors of teachers and grassroots administrators are seriously diminished if policy-level administrators fail to be overtly supportive. Pronouncements of such support must be reinforced by organizational steps that demonstrate a truly unified system.

One concrete example of such a demonstration is the assignment of administrative and supervisory responsibilities within the central, districtwide staff. Rather than assigning some personnel solely to special education leadership tasks and other personnel to general curriculum and instruction roles, the responsibilities can be merged. Where specialization is deemed necessary, it should be based on functions of administration and supervision—not based on differences or classifications among students. A model of this type of organization, found in Johnson City, New York, is described by Sage and Burrello (1994) who noted that

In Johnson City, the role relationships between the central office staff and the building-level administrators are characterized by placing major responsibility for all programs and all children on the principals, with the central office administrators acting as enablers to help the building-level personnel exercise their role. The structure for these central office functions reflects considerable overlap among four persons carrying the title of Director or Deputy Superintendent, who each report to the general Superintendent of Schools. Three of these are involved rather directly with instructional programs (the other being the district's business official), but care is taken to address the concerns of students with disabilities, those with English as a second language, and all other programs associated with external grants, in the regular instructional program. In this way, specialization among the leadership personnel is avoided and the lines between domains of expertise and responsibility are intentionally blurred. While one of the three directors is primarily responsible for the merger of special and regular education, and is therefore concerned with curriculum and instruction at all levels, the other two directors are each responsible for activities and functions that also contribute in some measure to the successful inclusion of all students, regardless of individual differences, within one integrated school environment. (pp. 156–157)

The administrative strategy in this example is one employed by the chief school administrator and transmitted to the entire administrative staff. This strategy involves embracing an innovative organizational structure, discarding conventional roles and responsibilities, and "selling" one's belief that the change will lead to an improved system for everyone. Although administrative pronouncements and revised organizational charts can scarcely be expected by themselves to bring about systemic change, their contribution to the process is crucial.

At the Building Level

The emphasis on decentralization and the corresponding deemphasis on specialization have major implications for the administrator at the building level. The role of the principal is significantly affected by the changes in the role of the central director of special education, which are absolutely necessary for paving the way to more inclusive schools. Although it has long been recognized that the behavior and symbolic leadership of the principal establishes the cultural climate of the school, the extent to which his or her responsibilities include *all* students has remained unclear. It has been quite acceptable for the principal to defer to a central office specialist for many questions and decisions about students with disabilities. The shift of primary responsibility from the specialist to the generalist constitutes a major role change for both parties.

Burrello and Lashley (1992) have suggested that the leadership role of an inclusive school organization is to

build a joint model for the school, a way of believing and seeing the patterns, relationships, and linkages between one another and their shared values and purposes.... Leaders create a shared culture that challenges staff and students to take responsibility for their own learning and to assist in modeling education in a democracy.... Visions of inclusive schools emerge from tough debate and analysis of the beliefs that school stakeholders have about human potential and the role of education in reaching it. (p. 81)

Building on these visions, the task is to develop policy that supports the shared culture of inclusiveness. Beliefs that are necessary for such support are as follows:

1. everyone in the school is responsible for the education of each student from the school's attendance area regardless of learning needs;
2. everyone in the school is focused on meeting the needs of all students in a unified system of education. Labeling and separation of students are counterproductive to educational excellence;
3. all educators have skills and knowledge which should be used to support the efforts of all teachers to ensure the success of all students in typical classrooms;
4. all students benefit from participation in inclusive classrooms and schools;
5. prevention of learning problems is the proper province of special education;
6. assessment of students' needs is a regular part of curricular and instructional planning for all teachers and related service personnel;
7. special education and related service personnel serve as full members of teacher teams under the leadership of the school principal;
8. special education and related service personnel provide services to students in the context of the general school program;
9. funding and budgeting models support the provision of services for students with special needs in the home school and local community;
10. community human services for children are coordinated at the school;
11. evaluation of the effectiveness of a school's program includes consideration of the post-school adjustment of students with special needs. (pp. 82–83)

In the Classroom

The changes necessary at the classroom level, like those at the administrative level, involve sharing. A variety of terminology may be used to describe the processes, such as cooperation, collaboration, and teaming. The major constraint is that well-established norms of independence among classroom teachers are not easily overcome. In spite of considerable attention in the professional literature arguing for and giving testimony to collaborative efforts as well as to in-service staff development with this focus, a significant proportion of the teacher population still finds the practice "unnatural."

Collaborative teaming can be considered from at least two perspectives: concerning 1) the planning and decision-making activities that occur outside the classroom, and 2) the shared instructional activities that occur inside the classroom. Thousand and Villa (1992) have presented rationale for collaborative teaming within schools in terms of school restructuring, teacher empowerment, and basic need satisfaction. In reviewing the literature, they noted five elements that define the collaborative teaming process:

1. Face-to-face interaction among team members on a frequent basis
2. A mutual "we are all in this together" feeling of positive interdependence
3. A focus on the development of small group interpersonal skills in trust building, communication, leadership, creative problem solving, decision making, and conflict management
4. Regular assessment and discussion of the team's functioning and the setting of goals for improving relationships and more effectively accomplishing tasks
5. Methods for holding one another accountable for agreed-upon responsibilities and commitments (p. 76)

The elements listed above have primary relevance to the activities of team members engaging in meetings for instructional planning or other decision-making processes. These elements do not speak directly to *team-teaching* situations in which two teachers (usually one general educator and one special educator) share a classroom and responsibility for a group of students (usually a mix of typical students and students with special needs). However, such team meeting characteristics are important *precursors* to successful team-teaching arrangements in the classroom. Learning to work together in a shared space is the next step in successful team teaching. The development and routine practice of such skills are of vital importance because successful inclusion of students with disabilities depends largely on bringing support services (personnel) into the general education teacher's classroom.

The role of teams in enhancing the climate for collaboration and inclusion is discussed by Sage and Burrello (1994), who noted that school districts need support systems and problem-solving structures characterized by

- Teams focusing on outcomes for all students and the different environments where these outcomes should be demonstrated—classroom, hallway, cafeteria, home neighborhood, and job setting, and so forth
- Teams co-planning for instruction in multiple settings and measuring performance on the basis of agreed-upon criteria
- Teams planning and encouraging through natural peer supports in the classroom, school, and out-of-school settings
- Teams ultimately accepting responsibility for one another and all students they share
- Teams adopting a problem-solving approach and regularly reflecting on their practice
- Teams planning their own staff development as their need for information, reflection, and evaluation emerges (p. 265)

The administrator's role in bringing about the necessary system changes at each level—the central school district, the individual school building, and each classroom—is essentially one of facilitation. Change cannot be legislated or forced into existence. The fear of change cannot be ignored. The administrator can help others face the fear, encourage attempts at new behaviors, and reinforce honest efforts toward the goal of inclusion.

STRATEGIES FOR FACILITATING CHANGE

It has been noted that a foundation stone for the promotion of inclusive schools is the development of collaborative behaviors among all stakeholders in the school environment. The challenge of such an objective lies in the fact that schools, as most enterprises within our culture, are hierarchically organized. Schools operate with established expectations regarding authority and responsibility relationships. Skrtic (1991) makes the point that, although the process of education suggests that schools should be structured as *professional* bureaucracies, they are generally managed and governed as *machine* bureaucracies. This structure tends to reduce teacher discretion, leaving students with less personalized and therefore less effective services. Skrtic emphasizes that the existing structure of schools causes them to respond to public demands for change by building symbols and ceremonies (e.g., the individualized education program [IEP] and parent participation) that create the illusion of change while the fundamental functions of schools in fact remain largely the same. However, when we talk about collaboration, we must emphasize equality among peers. To get beyond accustomed views of school structures and personnel relationships, educators must experience a significant paradigm shift.

As long as special education is perceived as a separate subdivision of the total school enterprise—a parallel system—it must be considered a minority subsystem. Based purely on magnitude (numbers of students, personnel, and budget) and regardless of perceived values associated with its mission, the special education program is accorded a low rung on the school hierarchy. This aspect of the paradigm can be changed only by developing the concept of a single *unified* system of education that encompasses *all* students without discrimination.

Collaboration Among Peers

Among administrative personnel, collaboration (with equality among partners) entails negotiating and clarifying the roles of the principal and the special education director or supervisor in ways that emphasize the responsibility of the principal for *all* students and a *support* function for the specialist that carefully avoids a "takeover" of any student's educational program. That is, special educators should never accept *sole* responsibility for the education of a student with a disability independent of the general education staff. In systems in which separate structures for special education are strongly entrenched, this may be difficult regardless of the status hierarchy that may exist between central office specialists and building principals. Furthermore, the relative status of central office and building level personnel in a particular system may help or hinder the negotiation of desired role responsibilities.

At the teacher level, a similar concern for equality among partners must be recognized. It is important that any perception of hierarchy be clearly dismissed when collaborative participation in the instructional setting is desired. When two teachers collaborate in a classroom, it is critical that we avoid the perception of one as an "assistant." Most teachers, as a function of maintaining control in the classroom, are in the habit of being the sole authority in that setting. Visitors (including the principal) may come and go, but the classroom is the teacher's territory. It has been traditionally understood that the authority is not shared. For the teacher to become comfortable in a collaborative instructional setting requires a definite shift in attitudes and a letting go of customary individual control.

Symbolic Leadership

The administrators of a system that is moving toward a more inclusive environment play an important role in modeling collaborative behavior. Both the principal and the central office director or supervisor are able to influence the climate by the ways they exercise their functions. In discussing the role of the principal, Sage and Burrello (1994) cited the forces of leadership identified by Sergiovanni (1984), which provide a framework for examining principal behavior. These forces are described as

1. Technical—derived from recommended management practices
2. Human—derived from social and interpersonal resources
3. Educational—derived from expert knowledge in matters of education and schooling
4. Symbolic—derived from focusing attention on matters of importance to the school
5. Cultural—derived from developing a unique school culture

The manner in which administrators exercise symbolic and cultural forces through their attitudes and behavior is particularly significant when modeling the actions and attitudes necessary for an inclusive environment to prevail. First, the behavior of the principal establishes the climate that sees all children as belonging to the local school. Second, collaborative behavior among administrators provides a model for teachers who may need help to break away from the practice of "going it alone."

Sage and Burrello (1994), drawing conclusions from a series of case studies of principalship, note that "The beliefs and attitudes of the principals toward special education are the key factors influencing their behavior toward students with disabilities" (p. 238). Principals whose personal philosophies recognized the benefits of inclusion "communicated their attitude consistently in a variety of ways to students, staff, and parents and expected them to support this attitude through their own behaviors" (p. 238). Furthermore, "the most important role the principal plays" in the inclusion of students with disabilities in the school is that of symbolic leader" (p. 239). This is consistent with the idea expressed by Tyler (1983) that effective principals are very much aware of the symbolism of even the most mundane of their administrative actions and that they use even the most ordinary occasions to demonstrate their beliefs.

Given the importance of the beliefs and attitudes held by principals,

School officials responsible for the selection and professional development of principals should attempt to determine the beliefs and attitudes of candidates and search out those who are willing to assume responsibility for all students, regardless of individual differences. The need for principals who are willing to work with students with disabilities despite any fears or misconceptions must be met if special education programs are to be accepted in a school.

Beyond modeling and symbolic behaviors, the principal must also encourage staff development among both regular and special education personnel. This need for knowledge about students with disabilities is substantial, and staff members can be important sources of information to one another. Opportunities for collaborative staff development activities can result in an increase in professional knowledge, as well as the development of a positive relationship between regular and special education personnel. (Sage & Burrello, 1994, p. 242)

Staff Development

It should also be noted that the process of staff development at the school site provides an opportunity to identify leadership ability within the school. By encouraging teachers to help other teachers and by reinforcing such cooperative behaviors, the administrator can not only determine previously unrecognized skills, but also help establish the norm of collaboration throughout the school environment. A model for accomplishing the norm of collaboration has been described by Porter (1994) in a videotape and manual, *Teachers Helping Teachers*. Although the school administrator can facilitate this process, the major benefits come through peer interaction. The principal should be the chief reinforcer of teacher behavior that demonstrates collaborative thinking and action in the service of inclusion. It is not unusual for teachers who attempt innovation and take risks to be viewed negatively and with suspicion by peers who are clinging to the familiar models. The administrator is particularly crucial to overcoming such predictable barriers and can do so by well-placed words and actions that reinforce support.

We should recognize, however, that such "cheerleading" on the part of the principal requires some careful balancing. In promoting inclusion for students and collaboration among teachers, administrators must avoid the impression of devaluing teachers who are not yet comfortable with the application of these concepts. Even the strongest advocates of progressive inclusion acknowledge that teachers must be allowed to grow voluntarily into the practice and cannot successfully be forced to change. The principal, more than any other personnel in the school system, is in a position to understand and be sensitive to the status and needs of the teachers and other direct service personnel in order to develop the attitudes and skills necessary for inclusive practices to flourish. Whether by formal needs assessment or by just knowing the people with whom one works, the alert principal should be able to discern what the staff as a whole, as well as individual members, need in order to grow.

Time Management

Regardless of the strength of the commitment to collaboration, the realities of time schedules are inescapable. Existing organizational arrangements in a school can totally frustrate the good intentions of teachers who are willing and learning to work together. A most practical contribution of the school principal is to somehow create time for teacher-to-teacher contact and interaction to occur. One way to accomplish this is by attending to scheduling in the school. Scheduling is an area that the principal is typically expected to control. Priority must be given to reserving time within the day's schedule for face-to-face planning and conferencing among personnel who are sharing responsibility for an instructional group. It is quite typical to find that the commitment to providing time for planning and conferencing evaporates in the crunch of day-to-day pressures. The principal can be the guardian of such time commitments, protecting the schedule and opportunities for teachers to work together. Crawford and Porter (1992) discuss the provision of flexible planning time for teachers and describe a number of settings in Canada in which school system administrators arranged for such time through budget and policy mandates. Although individual principals, with their teaching staffs, are free to organize this time to suit their situations, it is compulsory that the time be provided and used. Crawford and Porter note that teachers need time to

(a) work with one another or work individually on planning lessons and class activities;
(b) modify materials and do needed curriculum revisions;
(c) participate in various other activities, including consultations with parents. (pp. 45–46)

In some of the settings described by Crawford and Porter (1992), budgetary arrangements for supply (substitute) teachers freed time for the general and special education teachers to plan activities. In other settings, special education teachers served as substitutes so that general education teachers could get away from the classroom to plan for the inclusion and learning of all students. It is clear that, by whatever mechanisms are used to guarantee time for planning and face-to-face collaboration, the support and management of such arrangements can occur only with the active involvement of the school principal.

CONCLUSION

Strategies for promoting inclusive practices in schools, regardless of which particular administrative role or position is the focus of concern, primarily involve the facilitation of change. Although the central office director must maintain a perspective that is system wide and the building principal must concentrate on site-specific issues, the actions of both administrators must be guided by identified needs in order to change existing attitudes and practices. The type of proactive leadership that is required has been described by Lipp (1992):

The administrator's role has been changed from one which could be managed with simple, mechanical processes to one demanding complex strategies that must be pursued on many fronts simultaneously. New leadership imperatives call for a fundamental shift in leadership style, from gatekeeper of tradition to catalyst for change. The new leader must be one capable of maintaining collaborative working relationships among the stakeholders in the pursuit of a common goal. To this end, administration must

- Make all leadership strategies pluralistic.
- Ensure that all perspectives have been solicited.
- Use a multicultural perspective to interpret the patterns of expressive nuance in communication.
- Ensure that all processes respect the autonomy of both the individual and the group.
- Develop strategies for collaboration among interest groups. (Lipp, 1992, p. 32)

Drawing on Lipp's analysis of the necessary shifts in perspective, Sage and Burrello (1994) compared the concerns of the generalist and specialist in terms of administrative orientation and practice. The culture of school systems as a whole is appropriately moving

from an emphasis on	to an emphasis on
• Centralization	• Decentralization
• Teachers' responsibilities	• Teachers' rights
• Identifying incompetence	• Developing competence
• Bureaucracy	• Child centeredness
• Applying pressure	• Applying resources
• Surrendering responsibility	• Participation

With these shifts in emphasis, program development and the design and implementation of inclusive school cultures become a site-specific function, carried out by the school-based stakeholders—students, teachers, and principals. "The special education leadership role should move from providing direct services to students to providing more technical assistance to principals and their staffs in the design and implementation of student programming" (Sage & Burrello, 1994, p. 22–23).

Skrtic (1994) notes a political-economic justification for inclusive practices in schools that goes beyond the familiar moral argument. Unlike the era when society's needs were served by schools structured as machine bureaucracies or even professional bureaucracies, our postindustrial society is beginning to recognize the need for democratic, interdependent, reflective, problem solvers. The thrust toward personalization of instruction, decategorization of students, and despecialization of professional personnel reflects a movement toward meeting this need. However, the type of collaboration necessary in order to make schools really different calls for abolishing the bureaucratic order and adopting an "adhocratic" structure that emphasizes innovation and problem solving (Skrtic, 1994).

Both generalist and specialist administrators must direct their efforts to encouraging the new and different (inclusive) culture to grow rather than attempting to force the strategies of inclusion into the traditional and largely inhospitable structure that characterizes most schools. The administrative strategies required for inclusion are those that promote opening oneself and others to the possibilities of change, that model the taking of risks, and that reinforce any and all attempts at creating an inclusive climate for learning by all students.

REFERENCES

Burrello, L., & Lashley, C. (1992). On organizing the future: The destiny of special education. In K. Waldron, A. Riester, & J. Moore (Eds.), *Special education: The challenge of the future* (pp. 64–95). San Francisco: Edwin Mellen Press.

Council of Administrators of Special Education. (1993). *CASE future agenda for special education: Creating a unified education system*. Albuquerque, NM: Author.

Crawford, C., & Porter, G. (1992). *How it happens: A look at inclusive educational practice in Canada for children and youth with disabilities*. Downsview, Ontario, Canada: G. Allan Roeher Institute.

Lipp, M. (1992). An emerging perspective on special education: A development agenda for the 1990s. *Special Education Leadership Review, 1*(1), 10–39.

Porter, G. (Director). (1994). *Teachers helping teachers.* [Video and manual]. Downsview, Ontario, Canada: G. Allan Roeher Institute.

Sage, D., & Burrello, L. (1994). *Leadership in educational reform: An administrator's guide to changes in special education.* Baltimore: Paul H. Brookes Publishing Co.

Sergiovanni, T. (1984). Leadership and excellence in schooling. *Educational Leadership, 41,* 4–20.

Skrtic, T. (1991). *Behind special education.* Denver: Love Publishing.

Skrtic, T. (1994, December). *A political and economic justification for inclusive education.* Paper presented at a meeting of The Association for Persons with Severe Handicaps, Atlanta.

Thousand, J., & Villa, R. (1992). Collaborative teams: A powerful tool in school restructuring. In R.A. Villa, J.S. Thousand, W. Stainback, & S. Stainback (Eds.), *Restructuring for caring and effective education: An administrator's guide to creating heterogeneous schools* (pp. 73–108). Baltimore: Paul H. Brookes Publishing Co.

Tyler, R. (1983). A place called school. *Phi Delta Kappan, 64,* 462–464.

8

What Do I Do Monday Morning?

Mary A. Falvey, Christine C. Givner, and Christina Kimm

IN INCLUSIVE EDUCATIONAL environments, learning is centered in the strengths, interests, and needs of the students who are the community of learners as well as focused on the explicit and implicit core curricula. The focus of this chapter is on the pragmatics of how to create and orchestrate the day-to-day practical context for learning and teaching that is deeply connected to the dynamics within classrooms. The skills and strategies discussed here are based in recent research and the common practices of "good teaching," which include both the science and the art of teaching. Although there is no magic formula for creating effective inclusive classrooms, there are several critical elements that can assist educators to facilitate effective learning in heterogeneous communities.

CREATING A COMMUNITY OF LEARNERS

Building a community of learners is critical to establishing inclusive schooling and is one of the first components that must be addressed. The community of learners is at the heart of inclusive schooling. Implicit in the meaning of inclusion is belonging (Kunc, 1992). Each student must acquire a sense of belonging to the group, a sense of connectedness, for authentic learning to take place. Each student must feel welcomed and valued. Teachers play a major role as mediators and facilitators in creating a community of learners. The process of building a community should begin at the beginning of the school year, when students come together for the first time. This is a time for establishing the rules and patterns of behavior that set the stage for how learning is conducted in the classroom and school.

117

The first set of activities in the process of building community must be centered around having students feel welcomed and getting to know one another. An extremely useful resource for teachers developing getting-acquainted activities is *Tribes* (Gibbs, 1987, 1994). The next important step in the process of building community is establishment of a social contract—an agreement about how to behave and what behaviors are acceptable, and unacceptable, in the classroom. Students need to be involved in developing this social contract for several reasons. Two of the most important are, first, that it is an opportunity for them to practice participating in the democratic process, a role they will be expected to assume as adults, and second, student involvement ensures that students will assume ownership of the social contract. There are three types of behaviors that must be addressed in the social contract: 1) rules about how to relate to one another in a humane, respectful, caring, and helpful manner; 2) rules about how to behave in a positive and productive manner during daily learning activities; and 3) guidelines about how daily learning is to be conducted. The teacher acts as a facilitator in finding ways to translate the social contract into routines that can be rehearsed and practiced with students until the rules are internalized.

Another important factor in creating a community of learners is establishment of a positive learning climate. As the instructional leaders, teachers need to consistently and explicitly communicate academic expectations. Examples of this type of communication are introductory discussion prior to a learning activity with specific expectations for students' performance and behavior; wall signs stating general academic expectations that generalize across all learning activities (e.g., Try your best!, When in doubt, ask for help), bulletin boards displaying student work and classroom newspapers in which the writings and drawings of students are published.

Teachers need to develop a safe, orderly, and academically focused environment for work. Teachers can facilitate the message that the classroom is a safe and orderly environment in many ways. Safety is important for learning because if a student does not trust that the environment is supportive and nurturing, he or she will not be comfortable and will not learn effectively.

The teacher can establish an orderly and academically focused environment for learning by using a number of instructional strategies. Teachers can structure the physical environment to communicate order and academic focus. Furniture should be flexibly arranged so that all students have access to different types of learning activities (e.g., small-group cooperative learning activities, individual work, whole classroom discussion, active construction projects, formal and informal learning activities). The learning environment should be arranged so that there are a variety of spaces for learning (e.g., a quiet, warm area with rugs for silent reading, listening to audio/video tapes, or class meetings; an area appropriate for "messy" productions such as building a diorama or miniature engine; an area for computers that minimizes distractions). Teachers must also consider such things as typical traffic patterns, extraneous stimuli, equipment needed by individual students such as wheelchairs or computers, and students who need additional individual support, when arranging the physical environment and organizing the daily routines to optimize learning and minimize distractions.

Another set of instructional factors controlled by teachers that have a tremendous impact on creating order and an academically focused learning environment involve decisions in time allocation and management, transition, pacing, and grouping decisions. In planning for instruction, teachers decide how much time will be devoted to each daily learning activity, how the activity should be structured (e.g., small-group work, individual work, or a combination), how students are to make the transition between activities, and what pace of instruction is to be used to maximize student enthusiasm and attention and to minimize disruptive off-task behavior. Another important consideration is how much time students need to satisfactorily understand and complete the task. When an instructional plan has been established, the teacher needs to monitor and adapt the plan as he or she finds that individual students need additional time to complete the task or need additional explanation, for example. In addition to these general components, the strategies that are presented in this chapter contribute to building a community of learners.

ASSESSMENT, CURRICULUM, AND INSTRUCTION

All students must have access to a core curriculum that is rich in content, although specific strategies for facilitating student learning of the core curriculum need to be based on individual learning styles. Sometimes the curriculum is precisely prescribed by the school, district, or state department of education; in other situations, it is broadly stated and used only as a guidepost for teachers. Regardless of how precisely the curriculum is followed, in order to ensure that students who learn differently acquire the knowledge and skills reflected in the curriculum, personalized or individualized approaches to learning must be developed for each student. The teaching process involves a highly complex and dynamic set of tasks that require an extraordinary level of competence in making decisions in complex and dynamic environments (Berliner, 1988). *Assessment* is a critical component of the teaching and learning processes. Educators must have a broad and deep understanding of their students if they are to construct a learning environment that is suited to each individual student. Assessment can be defined as the gathering of information from a variety of tasks and a variety of sources for the purpose of making educational decisions about a student (Salvia & Ysseldyke, 1991). Although there are several reasons for educational assessment, in the context of this chapter, assessment for instructional planning and student progress are discussed. In order to make thoughtful and meaningful instructional decisions that are sensitive to the individual needs of students, teachers must use data. That is, they must maintain a comprehensive and ongoing knowledge base of their students' changing strengths, interests, and needs. Assessment must be an interactive aspect of the instructional process in order to plan and implement learning activities that are student-centered, emerge from the core curriculum, and promote authentic learning.

Formal and Informal Assessment

There are various kinds of assessments used in education. One typology of categorizing assessments defines formal and informal assessment. *Formal assessments* or standardized tests are "developed with specific standard administration, scoring, and interpretation procedures, which must be followed precisely to obtain optimum results" (Overton, 1992, p. 19). Standardized tests have established technical adequacy, which means they have established validity, reliability, and have been normed on a defined representative sample. Although this definition sounds impressive, the reality is that formal assessments typically provide very little relevant information for instructional planning.

In comparison, *informal assessments* are "any class of assessment procedures used or constructed for use so as to allow for maximal adaptations of administration procedures, content, materials, and scoring criteria to the needs of the particular assessment situation" (Bennett, 1982, p. 337). Although informal assessments are not standardized, they are carefully planned, systematically administered, and precisely interpreted teacher-made tests designed to obtain specific information useful in educational decision making (Zigmond & Silverman, 1984). Examples of informal assessments include teacher-made curriculum-based tests, classroom observations, checklists, and interviews. Informal assessments, because of their maximum flexibility and connectedness to the curriculum taught in the classroom, provide teachers with a wealth of instructionally relevant information. Therefore, discussion in this chapter focuses on the use of informal assessments.

A specific subtype of informal assessment is the *authentic assessment.* In authentic assessment, students are required to generate, rather than choose, a response. Students are required to actively accomplish complex and meaningful tasks while bringing prior knowledge, recent learning, and relevant skills to solve realistic or "authentic' problems (Herman, Aschbacher, & Winters, 1992). Authentic assessment is often referred to as alternative or performance-based assessment. Examples of authentic assessment include exhibitions, investigations, demonstrations, written or oral responses, journals, and portfolios.

A wide variety of assessment instruments can be used to collect data to ascertain current student performance levels across appropriate academic and functional domains for instructional planning and evaluating student progress. A number of different student assessments should be conducted across a variety of tasks in order to increase the validity and credibility of data-based interpretations. Some of the most pertinent types of assessment follow: *Ecological inventories* (EI) are surveys or observations used to identify skills within current or projected settings in which the student functions (Brown et al., 1979). *Student repertoire inventories* (SRIs) are necessary assessments after ecological inventories have been completed. An SRI is a way of measuring a student's performance of a skill identified in the ecological inventory by comparing it with the performance of age peers without disabilities (Falvey, Brown, Lyon, Baumgart, & Schroeder, 1980). Measurement of behaviors (academic or behavioral) from direct observation, known as behavior counts, is another powerful informal assessment. Types of direct observation assessments include event, duration, latency, or time sampling recording, all of which allow teachers to precisely document student performance along one or more behavioral dimensions (Alberto & Troutman, 1990).

Curriculum-based assessment is yet another type of informal assessment that provides teachers with excellent data for decision making. Curriculum-based assessment involves measures developed from the school curriculum that are administered to all students in a target group (e.g., fourth graders in a classroom). The results provide data that are used to determine standards of performance (Mercer & Mercer, 1993). *Portfolio assessment,* another type of authentic assessment, is a process in which a collection of a student's work is evaluated using a predetermined set of rubrics. The portfolio might include work samples across a variety of subjects or a variety of work samples within a single subject area. Samples of students' work compiled in the portfolios, which involve the student in determining topics, include the time allocated to the task, the number of drafts or attempts, and the conditions under which performance was generated (Meyer, 1992).

Teachers need to develop an initial understanding of each learner as well as of the learners as a group. Some areas for initial assessment include student interests, motivation, academic strengths and needs, social skills, communication skills, fine and gross motor skills, level of self-management skills, and functional (i.e., daily living) skills. It is of critical importance to ensure that assessments are conducted across the various environments in which the student participates. Any student, not just a student with an identified disability, may be having difficulties in learning because of a mismatch between learner characteristics, characteristics of the learning environment, and the curricular content (Kameenui & Simmons, 1990). When teachers determine a mismatch, instructional methodology, curriculum, and/or materials that reflect this student's learning style need to be developed and made available to this student.

Another important consideration in determining individual student needs is to solicit information from various significant others in the student's life, as well as from that student. Parents, friends, siblings, and the other educators who work with students are a tremendous resource of relevant information for instructional planning. For students with identified disabilities, the team process is a mandated aspect of assessment. In spite of this mandate, parents are often relegated to a superficial role in planning the student's individualized education program (IEP). There are several strategies for soliciting meaningful input from significant others in the student's life. *Making Action Plans* (MAPS) (formerly McGill Action Planning System) (Forest & Lusthaus, 1990) is a process that allows educators to obtain information from several significant others (Falvey, Forest, Pearpoint, & Rosenberg, 1994) (see Chapter 5). The MAPs process is a gathering of people significant to the student who share information, dreams, and plans for that student at a meeting or series of meetings. The process involves a facilitator who asks the participants to respond to the following questions:

- What is this person's history? (Usually answered by family members and close friends)
- What dreams do you have for this person's future?
- What fears or nightmares do you have for this person's future?
- Who is this person?

- What are this person's strengths, gifts, and talents?
- What are this person's needs?
- What actions or action plans need to be developed in order for the dreams to be actualized and the nightmares to be avoided?

The answer to the final question, how to develop a plan of action, sets in motion the steps that need to be taken in order for this student to participate effectively in all environments, including the school and classroom.

After initial assessments, such as those discussed, are conducted to identify the student's most critical educational strengths and needs, current performance level, and level of participation in various activities and environments, it is important to conduct ongoing assessment concerning *what to teach, how to teach,* and *when to change instruction.* These are the three primary questions related to teaching and learning in the classroom.

What to Teach and How to Teach

The question of what to teach is answered by interfacing the student's individual strengths and needs (e.g., IEP instructional objectives) with the core curriculum identified by the teacher. Maximum flexibility should be used to ensure that topics are motivating to the student, that curriculum emerges from the student's interests as well as from the school district curriculum framework, and that the student is provided with as many opportunities as possible to choose options or to create his or her own options. These instructional strategies have many benefits, two of which are 1) the student becomes a more active, self-managed learner instead of a passive recipient of "wisdom," and 2) student ownership of the task increases the motivation to be a productive participant in learning (Bereiter & Scardamalia, 1989).

The question of how to teach is answered as the teacher initially interacts with each student in a "typical" instructional manner. The majority of classrooms in the world include a heterogeneous group of learners. The amount these learners differ from one another varies across geographic regions of the world. However, it is likely that in all classrooms, no matter how similar the students may appear, students who learn differently from one another are members of the same class. As a result, classroom teachers have become more creative and willing to try multiple teaching strategies in educating their students. Traditional classrooms that do not meet the needs of these diverse learners are those in which teachers stand in front of the class and lecture, with an occasional written explanation or direction on the chalkboard, or those in which students are expected to concentrate and complete large numbers of worksheets involving pencils and papers and in which the teachers do most of the talking and students listen, concentrate, and take notes. Instead, classrooms that are alive and that motivate a diverse population of learners are becoming more commonplace, even in secondary schools where these traditional classroom characteristics have been most frequently present (Goodlad, 1984; Sizer, 1992).

Multiple Intelligence Theory

Such classrooms are most likely to be successful in teaching all students, including those who have been classified and labeled as having differences and disabilities or being at risk or difficult to teach. The multiple intelligence theory of Gardner (1983) and refined by Armstrong (1987, 1994) provides a useful framework for identifying multiple teaching strategies. Classrooms that offer multiple teaching strategies are more likely to provide a heterogeneous population of students with access to meaningful learning experiences. In addition, repeated learning opportunities in areas in which students do not have strengths assist students in broadening their learning and strategies for learning. Students who have strengths in the area of linguistic intelligence are likely to benefit from the numerous traditional teaching strategies because this area of intelligence has been the focus of much of the instruction in the traditional school. Learning activities associated with the whole language approach involve strategies that assist linguistic learners as well as facilitate linguistic intelligence in every student. In addition, the following strategies can assist educators in broadening their students' learning in the area of linguistic intelligence: storytelling, brainstorming, the use of tape recorders, journal writing, and publishing in its many forms (Armstrong, 1994).

Students who have logical-mathematical intelligence have been able to succeed and excel in math and science classes in traditional schools. However, in schools and classes that honor logical-mathematical intelligence, numerous opportunities to learn other subjects through this form of thinking are provided. The following strategies can help to develop logical-mathematical intelligence across all school subjects: the use of calculations, quantifications, classifications, and categorizations; and critical thinking and problem-solving opportunities, including socratic questioning (instead of talking at students, talking with students) and heuristics (logical problem-solving strategies) (Armstrong, 1994).

Spatial intelligence involves strengths in responding to and learning information that is presented visually. In traditional schools, this area of intelligence has been relegated to art classes and often not incorporated into the rest of the curriculum. Schools that have effectively met the needs of heterogeneous students, including those who learn best through visual strategies, have incorporated a variety of such strategies. The following strategies can help to facilitate learning through spatial intelligence: giving students opportunities to create visualizations; using color cues on worksheets, chalkboards, textbooks, and other printed materials; having teachers or students develop pictorial metaphors of concepts they are learning or need to learn; and having students sketch or draw solutions or responses to questions across all areas of the curriculum (Armstrong, 1994).

Bodily-kinesthetic intelligence is reinforced and activated when educators teach students using a variety of gross motor activities. Often, students with bodily-kinesthetic intelligence are offered instruction in the format most accessible to them in physical education and, possibly, vocational education classes. However, traditional academics can be taught using activities involving a variety of movements. The following activities can be incorporated to reinforce this area of intelligence: using body movements to answer questions (going beyond students just raising their hands); using the classroom as a theater to act out or enact content in textbooks, problems, or other material; having students pantomime specific concepts; learning through hands-on materials (e.g., not just reading about soil erosion but constructing the land and water elements and relationships); and using specific body movements to create specific knowledge (e.g., using fingers for math) (Armstrong, 1994).

Students who have musical intelligence are not necessarily gifted singers or musicians, although this can be the case. The critical aspect for educators is that students with strength in musical intelligence learn rhythmically, and this strategy should not be relegated to music classes. Therefore, presenting information in rhythmical patterns can dramatically assist students in learning critical information for whom traditional memorizing or flash card formats have not been very successful. The following are ways to incorporate musical intelligence into the entire curriculum: using rhythms, sounds, raps, and chants to teach concepts; using musical selections that represent or reflect curricular content; playing music in the background while teaching; and using musical selections to depict the events and feelings in a story or book (Armstrong, 1994).

Students who demonstrate strong interpersonal intelligence are often described as gregarious, outgoing, and empathetic. These students are often referred to as the social learners of their environment and respond well to collaborative or cooperative activities. The following activities are suggested for teaching approaches that incorporate interactions among students: peer sharing of materials and responsibilities; having students construct "sculptures" of concepts using other students (e.g., each student is a weekly vocabulary or spelling word and the students together build a story); cooperative groupings; using games to teach and reinforce learned concepts; and using simulations to learn about events, people's feelings, and alternative strategies for behaving (Armstrong, 1994).

The final area of intelligence discussed in multiple intelligences theory (Gardner, 1983) is intrapersonal intelligence, which is manifested in students who are autonomous learners; that is, students who are more likely to learn when given opportunities to learn on their own. Although there has been a recent resurgence of cooperative groupings, teachers need to be cognizant of learners who struggle with cooperative activities and need to offer sufficient opportunities for intrapersonal learners to learn on their own. The following activities are suggested methods for incorporating intrapersonal intelligence into daily routines: using reflective activities in which students are asked to stop whatever they are doing and reflect on what they have learned (these reflections do not need to be shared); connecting the curriculum to students' personal lives and future expectations; giving students choices of what to do, when to do it, and how to do it, including establishing their own goals; and encouraging students to express their feelings (even if no one else feels that way) (Armstrong, 1994).

Figure 1 provides an example of an assessment tool that can be used by educators, related direct service personnel, parents, and administrators to assess a student's learning style.

Assessment of Multiple Intelligences

Name of Student: _____

Check items that apply:

Linguistic Intelligence

_____ Writes better than average for age

_____ Spins tall tales or tells jokes and stories

_____ Has a good memory for names, places, dates, or trivia

_____ Enjoys word games

_____ Enjoys reading books

_____ Spells words accurately (or, if preschool, does developmental spelling that is advanced for age)

_____ Appreciates nonsense rhymes, puns, tongue twisters, etc.

_____ Enjoys listening to the spoken word (stories, commentary on the radio, talking books, etc.)

_____ Has a good vocabulary for age

_____ Communicates to others in a highly verbal way

Other Linguistic Strengths:

Logical-Mathematical Intelligence

_____ Asks a lot of questions about how things work

_____ Computes arithmetic problems in his/her head quickly (or, if preschool, math concepts are advanced for age)

_____ Enjoys math class (or, if preschool, enjoys counting and doing other things with numbers)

_____ Finds math computer games interesting (or, if no exposure to computers, enjoys other math or counting games)

_____ Enjoys playing chess, checkers, or other strategy games (or, if preschool, board games requiring counting squares)

_____ Enjoys working on logic puzzles or brainteasers (or, if preschool, enjoys hearing logical nonsense such as in *Alice's Adventures in Wonderland*)

_____ Enjoys putting things in categories or hierarchies

_____ Likes to experiment in a way that shows higher-order cognitive thinking processes

_____ Thinks on a more abstract or conceptual level than peers

_____ Has a good sense of cause–effect for age

Other Logical-Mathematical Strengths:

(continued)

Figure 1. Assessment of multiple intelligences. (From Armstrong, T. [1994]. *Multiple intelligences in the classroom,* pp. 18–20. Alexandria, VA: Association for Supervision and Curriculum Development; reprinted by permission.)

Figure 1. *(continued)*

Spatial Intelligence

_____ Reports clear visual images

_____ Reads maps, charts, and diagrams more easily than text (or, if preschool, enjoys looking at more than text)

_____ Daydreams more than peers

_____ Enjoys art activities

_____ Draws figures that are advanced for age

_____ Likes to view movies, slides, or other visual presentations

_____ Enjoys doing puzzles, mazes, "Where's Waldo?" or similar visual activities

_____ Builds interesting three-dimensional constructions for age (e.g., LEGO buildings)

_____ Gets more out of pictures than words while reading

_____ Doodles on workbooks, worksheets, or other materials

Other Spatial Strengths:

Bodily-Kinesthetic Intelligence

_____ Excels in one or more sports (or, if preschool, shows physical prowess advanced for age)

_____ Moves, twitches, taps, or fidgets while seated for a long time in one spot

_____ Cleverly mimics other people's gestures or mannerisms

_____ Loves to take things apart and put them back together again

_____ Puts his/her hands all over something he/she has just seen

_____ Enjoys running, jumping, wrestling, or similar activities (or, if older, will show these interests in a more "restrained" way—e.g., running to class, jumping over a chair)

_____ Shows skill in a craft (e.g., woodworking, sewing, mechanics) or good fine-motor coordination in other ways

_____ Has a dramatic way of expressing herself/himself

_____ Reports different physical sensations while thinking or working

_____ Enjoys working with clay or other tactile experiences (e.g., fingerpainting)

Other Bodily-Kinesthetic Strengths:

Musical Intelligence

_____ Tells you when music sounds off-key or disturbing in some other way

_____ Remembers melodies of songs

_____ Has a good singing voice

_____ Plays a musical instrument or sings in a choir or other group (or, if preschool, enjoys playing percussion instruments and/or singing in a group)

_____ Has a rhythmic way of speaking and/or moving

(continued)

Figure 1. *(continued)*

_____ Unconsciously hums to himself/herself
_____ Taps rhythmically on the table or desk as he/she works
_____ Sensitive to environmental noises (e.g., rain on the roof)
_____ Responds favorably when a piece of music is put on
_____ Sings songs that he/she has learned outside of the classroom

Other Musical Strengths:

Interpersonal Intelligence

_____ Enjoys socializing with peers
_____ Seems to be a natural leader
_____ Gives advice to friends who have problems
_____ Seems to be street-smart
_____ Belongs to clubs, committees, or other organizations (or, if preschool, seems to be part of a regular social group)
_____ Enjoys informally teaching other kids
_____ Likes to play games with other kids
_____ Has two or more close friends
_____ Has a good sense of empathy or concern for others
_____ Others seek out his/her company

Other Interpersonal Strengths:

Intrapersonal Intelligence

_____ Displays a sense of independence or a strong will
_____ Has a realistic sense of his/her strengths and weaknesses
_____ Does well when left alone to play or study
_____ Marches to the beat of a different drummer in his/her style of living and learning
_____ Has an interest or hobby that he/she doesn't talk much about
_____ Has a good sense of self-direction
_____ Prefers working alone to working with others
_____ Accurately expresses how he/she is feeling
_____ Is able to learn from his/her failures and successes in life
_____ Has high self-esteem

Other Intrapersonal Strengths:

Accommodations for Students

Some students need more specific assistance in order to learn than that which multiple intelligence strategies provide. The Americans with Disabilities Act of 1990 (ADA) (PL 101-336) requires employers and community members to develop and offer reasonable accommodations so that persons with disabilities have access to their communities. Schools are also required to provide accommodations in order to facilitate students' access to learning. Accommodations in this context are individualized supports for a student that facilitates his or her access to learning in a situation in which academic expectations for the student have not been modified. For example, an accommodation might be extending the time for a student with a learning disability to take a test because he reads at a slower pace than his peers. Providing students with instruction in their first language, when the student is not proficient in English, can also be considered an accommodation. Technological and other adaptive devices can provide needed supports for students with physical and/or learning disabilities. Ensuring students physical access to schools, classrooms, and extracurricular activities is essential for students with physical disabilities.

The methods for assessing or evaluating the performance of students who have been provided with accommodations should in no way penalize their performance because of the accommodation. In other words, if a student is provided with a computer for answering questions on a final examination while other students write their responses by hand, no mention or consideration should be given to use of the computer when calculating that student's grade. It is, however, important to evaluate the effectiveness of an accommodation in order to determine future use. Individual support can range from periodic checks on a student, continuous support for a specific activity (e.g., supporting a student's personal care needs in the restroom), to continuous support across all activities. When students make transitions from year to year or from one service delivery system to another, move to a new town, or move from elementary to middle or high school, additional supports might be needed. Individual supports can be provided by same age or older peers, special or general education teachers, related service personnel, instructional or health care assistants, volunteers, or administrators (Udvari-Solner, 1994).

Accommodations should be provided to students only when they are necessary to facilitate access to the learning process. As a student's skills become more proficient and the need for the accommodation lessens, the accommodation should be faded and, if possible, eventually eliminated. There are, however, some students who will always require particular accommodations.

When a student is provided with an accommodation, care should be taken to assist the student's use of the accommodation in such a way that he or she is physically, socially, and emotionally included in all activities. This inclusion may require teaching students unfamiliar with a particular accommodation about its use and purpose. Giving all students the opportunity to use the accommodation can reduce any mystery about it and can facilitate the social and emotional inclusion of the student who uses an accommodation. For example, students who use communication books to interact should be encouraged to share them with their peers, which gives them an opportunity to become more familiar and comfortable with this assisted form of communication.

Multilevel Instruction

Occasionally, even with the use of multiple teaching strategies and accommodations, a student is still unable to understand the curriculum in a meaningful way, and so alternatives are necessary. Alternative instructional strategies are often referred to as *multilevel instruction*. Multilevel instruction provides a student with individualized supports in order to facilitate his or her access to learning in situation in which the academic expectations for the student have been modified. Multilevel instruction provides a student opportunities to participate in the classroom, even if only partially. The principle of partial participation encourages educators, parents, administrators, and others to create opportunities for all students to participate in all aspects of school and community life, even if their participation level is reduced because of disabilities (Baumgart et al., 1982). When a student is unresponsive to or less than successful on a typical task, multilevel instruction can be used and data collected (i.e., ongoing assessment of student performance) to determine its effectiveness. This process encourages teachers to be rational and data reliant in their decision making and exemplifies the idea of teaching as a scientific process. Multilevel instruction is designed individually for a student and can include 1) teaching the same curriculum but at a less complex level, 2) teaching the same curriculum but with functional or direct application to daily routines of life, 3) teaching the same curriculum but reducing the performance standards, 4) teaching the same curriculum but at a slower pace, and 5) teaching a different or substitute curriculum. One caution is in order: Teachers must remember that multilevel instruction should be as unobtrusive as possible. Stated differently, multilevel instruction should not be implemented unless it is necessary for success. Students may have such enduring learning needs that certain adaptations and modifications must be made in order to structure the learning task for student success. However, educators have no way of really knowing what kinds of adaptations or modifications, if any, need to be implemented to increase a student's opportunities for success until objective and comprehensive assessment information has been obtained. Such adaptations and modifications should not be used unless absolutely necessary, and they should be faded as soon as possible in order to liberate, not limit, a student's possibilities. Figure 2 provides a list of multiple teaching strategies, accommodations, and multilevel instructional options for teachers to consider when a student is experiencing difficulty in learning. It is important to note that some options, depending on how they are used, can serve as multiple teaching strategies, accommodations, or multilevel instructional opportunities. Teachers should keep in mind the specific definitions presented previously in this chapter when determining which option to use and how to use it.

The question of when to change is of critical importance in determining the effectiveness of instruction. Once goals and objectives have been established and interven-

Options for Facilitating Students' Access to Learning			
	Type of individualization		
Strategies for facilitating students' access to learning	Multi-strategy	Accom-modation	Multi-level
Change the physical environment			
Adjust pacing			
Extend time requirements			
Vary activity often			
Allow for breaks			
Send home texts for summer preview			
Give family a set of texts/materials for preview/review			
Make environmental accommodations			
Supportive seating arrangements (e.g., near front of classroom, next to peer support)			
Alter physical arrangement to reduce distractions (visual, spatial, auditory, movement) and ensure physical accessibility			
Teach students to effectively use the space			
Consider lighting for students (e.g., too much light to see the LCD display on a computer, not enough light for student with low vision)			
Change the organization of learning environment			
Vary group arrangements			
Use large-group instruction			
Use small-group instruction			
Use individual instruction			
Use peer/tutoring supports			
Use independent activities			
Use learning centers			
Vary methods of instruction			
Teacher directed instruction			
Student directed instruction			
Provide motivation and reinforcement			
Provide both verbal and nonverbal reinforcement			
Be positive			
Praise concrete/tangible accomplishments			
Plan motivating sequences of activities			
Reinforce initiation			
Offer choices			
Use strengths/interests often			
Send notes home			

(continued)

Figure 2.   Options for facilitating student access to learning.

Figure 2. *(continued)*

Strategies for facilitating students' access to learning	Type of individualization		
	Multi-strategy	Accom-modation	Multi-level
Use grades			
Motivate with free time			
Motivate with special activities			
Display progress charts			
Vary rules			
Differentiate rules for some students			
Use both explicit/implicit rules			
Teach self-management/follow-through opportunities			
Use visual/pictorial daily schedules/calendars			
Check often for understanding/review			
Request parent reinforcement			
Have student repeat directions			
Teach study skills			
Use study sheets to organize material			
Design/write long-term assignments/timelines			
Review and practice in real situations			
Plan for generalizations			
Teach in several settings/environments			
Change the methods of presentation			
Vary curricular strategies			
Teach to student's learning style (linguistic, spatial, logical-mathematical, bodily-kinesthetic, musical, interpersonal, intrapersonal)			
Utilize specialized curriculum			
Model experiential learning			
Tape lectures/discussions for replay			
Provide notes			
Provide NCR paper for peer to provide notes			
Demonstrate functional application of academic skills			
Present demonstrations (model)			
Utilize manipulatives			
Emphasize critical information			
Preteach vocabulary			
Make/use vocabulary files			
Reduce language level of reading assignment			
Use total communication			
Use facilitated communication			
Share activities			
Use visual sequences			

(continued)

Figure 2. *(continued)*

Strategies for facilitating students' access to learning	Type of individualization		
	Multi-strategy	Accom-modation	Multi-level
Vary amount to be learned			
Vary time to learn new information			
Vary conceptual level			
Establish relevancy and purpose of learning			
Modify materials			
Vary arrangement of material on page			
Provide taped tests and/or other class material			
Provide highlighted tests/study guides			
Use supplementary materials			
Provide note-taking assistance: NCR or copy notes of peers			
Type teacher material			
Use large print			
Use electronic equipment:			
Electronic typewriter			
Calculator			
Telephone adaptation			
Augmentative communication device			
Computer			
Video recorder			
Vary general structure			
Use advanced organizers			
Preview questions			
Use cues, mnemonic devices			
Provide immediate feedback			
Involve students throughout			
Vary amount to be practiced			
Time for practice			
Group/individual			
Teacher directed/independent			
Items ranging from easy to difficult			
Change the methods of assessment			
Use varying testing strategies			
Provide both oral/verbal and written testing			
Use demonstration			
Use taped tests			
Use pictures			
Read test to student			
Preview language of test questions			

(continued)

Figure 2. *(continued)*

Strategies for facilitating students' access to learning	Type of individualization		
	Multi-strategy	Accom-modation	Multi-level
Use applications in real setting			
Have test administered by resource person			
Use short answer			
Use multiple choice			
Modify format			
Shorten length			
Extend time frame			
Use varying assignments			
Give directions in small, distinct steps (written/pictorial/verbal)			
Use written back-up for oral directions			
Lower difficulty level			
Shorten assignment			
Reduce paper and pencil tasks			
Read or tape record directions to student			
Use pictorial directions			
Give extra cues or prompts			
Allow student to record or type assignment			
Adapt worksheets, packets			
Utilize compensatory procedures by providing alternate assignment/strategy when demands of class conflict			
Avoid penalizing for spelling errors			
Avoid penalizing for penmanship			
Offer social interaction support			
Encourage peer advocacy			
Encourage peer tutoring			
Structure activities to create opportunities for social interaction			
Focus on social process rather than activity/end product			
Structure shared experiences in school/extracurricular			
Use cooperative learning groups			
Use multiple/rotating peer supports			
Teach friendship skills/sharing/negotiation			
Teach social communication skills			
Greeting			
Sharing			
Conversation turn taking			
Negotiation			

tions have been initiated, the teacher must monitor individual student performance to determine if appropriate progress is being made and, if not, what needs to be revised to better ensure success. An error analysis of student performance on related instructional tasks should assist teachers in better understanding the dynamics of the student's understanding, or lack of it, related to specific instructional objectives as well as assist in deciding what accommodations or adaptations need to be implemented. In order to answer the question of when to change, teachers must reflect on the student's performance and the learning opportunities provided.

Scheduling and Planning Instruction

An organized plan must be created for each student in order to implement and individualize the teaching of meaningful explicit and implicit curriculum. Educators must implement the learning activities that they have planned for their students in daily instruction. In order to effectively and efficiently develop daily instructional plans, educators must work within the team of other educators, parents, and students who have information essential to the planning process and who will be affected by the plans. Creating communities of learners and individualizing instruction and curriculum are two of the three elements essential to creating inclusive classrooms. The third element in creating inclusive classrooms is systematic daily plans, which must be collaboratively developed in order to ensure orchestrated teaching. Teacher orchestration concerns the actions and decision making "associated with carrying out classroom activities in space and time" (Doyle, 1986, p. 414). Teacher orchestration involves the delicate and complex processes of sustaining order in the classroom while at the same time implementing planned daily individualized instructional activities. Ongoing monitoring of students' performances and of the effectiveness of teachers' instruction is a key process in the orchestration of classroom activities.

When students with disabilities were mainstreamed into general education classes in the traditional model (which required that they have certain prerequisite skills to qualify for mainstreaming), necessary supports rarely followed them (Falvey, 1995). As a result, educators were not successful in meeting all students' needs, and many students with disability labels were unable to participate in the learning process. To provide inclusive education, the supports necessary for students to be successful must be provided within the general education classroom and school environment. To integrate individual student supports (i.e., multiple strategies, accommodations, multilevel instruction), goals and objectives, and other student needs, Giangreco, Cloninger, and Iverson (1993) developed a *scheduling matrix*. A scheduling matrix is a format for aligning an individual student's needs, as identified by IEP goals and objectives, with the general education schedule and routine. Figure 3 provides an example of a matrix for an individual student. (See Chapter 16 for additional information about this process.)

Responding to individual student needs in lesson planning is facilitated by completing an IEP scheduling matrix. Lesson planning is essential for several reasons: It helps the educator to meet responsibilities, ensures that instruction is related to specific

Sample IEP Scheduling Matrix

Student's Name: Emily Yamashita   Age: 9   Grade: Third

IEP Goals	Opening	Lang. arts	Recess	Math	Social stud./ science	Lunch	Art/music	P.E.
1. Interacts with peers	5,A,B	3,5,A,H,a	A	3,A,d	3,5,A,C	A,C	3,5,B	3,5
2. Points to pictures in story	3,A,B	3,5,A,H,a		3,A,b	3,5,A,C		3,5,B	
3. Classifies objects	3,5,A,B	3,5,A,H,a		3,A,a	3,5,A,C		3,5,A,B	3,5,A,B
4. Greets adults	5,A,B	3,5,A,H,a	A	3,A,d	3,5,A,C	A,C	3,5,B	3,5
5. Delivers messages	3,A,B				3,A,B,c			
6. Shares materials	3,5,A,B	3,5,A,B		3,5,A,B	3,5,A,B	A,C	3,5,A,B	3,5,A,B

Code:

Multiple strategies
Linguistic = 1
Log/math = 2
Spatial = 3
Bod/kinesth = 4
Musical = 5
Interpers = 6
Intrapers = 7

Accommodations

Personal assistance
Peers = A
Gen ed teach = B
Spec ed teach = C
Related ser = D

Modifications
Physical space = E

Equipment/Materials
Wheelchairs = F
Other chair = G
Computers = H
Talk books = I
Video story = J

Assessment
More time = K
Alt. methods = L

Multilevel instruction
Less complex = a
Functional application = b
Reduce performance stand. = c
Slower = d
Subcurriculum = e

Figure 3.   Example of a student's completed scheduling matrix.

Table 1. Daily lesson plan format

Class/group objectives
Additional objectives for individual students (multilevel instruction)
Substitute objectives for individual students (multilevel instruction)
Procedures (including multiple strategies, accommodations, and multilevel instructional procedures)
    For class/group objective(s)
    For alternative/additional objectives
Materials needed
Evaluation procedures for all group and individual objectives identified

student objectives, gives information necessary for preparing the lesson, and assists educators in creating a learning process that builds upon previously learned information. In addition, and specific to the topic of this chapter, lesson plans can assist educators in providing the necessary supports that facilitate all students' learning in a heterogeneous setting. For individualizing lessons to accommodate the learning styles of all students, Table 1 provides an example of a daily lesson plan format. In addition, Figure 4 is a thematic unit plan format that can be used to design thematic instruction over a period of time.

This chapter provides educators with a conceptual framework as well as pragmatic tools and strategies to use in facilitating the learning of diverse students in heterogeneous classrooms and schools. Still, there are no easy recipes or formulas. Each educator must develop his or her own style of teaching as scientist, artist, and decision-maker and broaden his or her repertoire of instructional tactics in order to build the community of learners.

REFERENCES

Alberto, P.A., & Troutman, A.C. (1990). *Applied behavior analysis for teachers* (3rd ed.). Columbus, OH: Charles E. Merrill.

Americans with Disabilities Act of 1990 (ADA), PL 101-336. (July 26, 1990). Title 42, U.S.C. 12101 et seq: *U.S. Statutes at Large, 104,* 327–378.

Armstrong, T. (1987). *In their own way.* Los Angeles: Jeremy P. Tarcher.

Armstrong, T. (1994). *Multiple intelligences in the classroom.* Alexandria, VA: Association for Supervision and Curriculum Development.

Baumgart, D., Brown, L., Pumpian, I., Nesbit, J., Ford, A., Sweet, M., Messina, R., & Schroeder, J. (1982). Principles of partial participation and individualized adaptations in educational programs for severely handicapped students. *Journal of The Association for the Severely Handicapped, 7*(2), 17–27.

Bennett, R. (1982). Cautions for use of informal measures in the educational assessment of exceptional children. *Journal of Learning Disabilities, 15,* 337–339.

Bereiter, C., & Scardamalia, M. (1989). Intentional learning as a goal of instruction. In L.B. Resnick (Ed.), *Knowing, learning, and instruction: Essays in honor of Robert Glaser* (pp. 361–392). Hillsdale, NJ: Lawrence Erlbaum Associates.

Berliner, D. (1988). The half-full glass: A review of research on teaching. In E.L. Meyen, G.A. Vergason, & R.J. Whelan (Eds.), *Effective instructional strategies for exceptional children* (pp. 7–31). Denver: Love Publishing Co.

Thematic Unit Plan

Class/Group objective(s):

_____

Additional or substitute objective(s) for individual students:

_____
_____

Procedures (including multiple strategies)

Strategies for using spoken or written words:

Strategies for using numbers, cal- culations, classifications, logic, or problem-solving activities:

Strategies for using visual aids, visualizations, color, art, or symbols:

Strategies for using sounds, music, or rhythm:

Strategies for using hands-on manipulatives or activities that involve gross motor activities

Strategies for peer support and sharing, cooperative grouping, group simulations

Strategies for giving students choices and opportunities to work alone or providing students with opportunities to describe their feelings or memories

Accommodations needed:

_____
_____

Multilevel instructional opportunities needed:

_____
_____

Materials needed:

_____
_____

Evaluation procedures for all multiple teaching strategies, accommodations, and multilevel instruction planned and/or used:

_____
_____
_____

Figure 4. Thematic unit plan format.

137

Brown, L., Branston, M.B., Hamre-Nietupski, S., Pumpian, I., Certo, N., & Gruenewald, L. (1979). A strategy for developing chronological age appropriate and functional curricular content for severely handicapped adolescents and young adults. *Journal of Special Education, 13*(1), 81–90.

Doyle, W. (1986). Classroom organization and management. In M.C. Wittrock (Ed.), *Handbook of research on teaching* (3rd ed., pp. 392–431). New York: Macmillan.

Falvey, M. (1995). *Inclusive and heterogeneous education: Assessment, curriculum, and instruction.* Baltimore: Paul H. Brookes Publishing Co.

Falvey, M., Brown, L., Lyon, S., Baumgart, D., & Schroeder, J. (1980). Strategies for using cues and correction procedures. In W. Sailor, B. Wilcox, & L. Brown (Eds.), *Methods of instruction for severely handicapped students* (pp. 109–133). Baltimore: Paul H. Brookes Publishing Co.

Falvey, M., Forest, M., Pearpoint, J., & Rosenberg, R. (1994). Building connections: All my life's a circle. In J. Thousand, R. Villa, & A. Nevin (Eds.), *Creativity and collaborative learning: A practical guide for empowering students and teachers* (pp. 347–368). Baltimore: Paul H. Brookes Publishing Co.

Forest, M., & Lusthaus, E. (1990). Everyone belongs with the MAPs action planning system. *Teaching Exceptional Children, 22*(2), 32–35.

Gardner, H. (1983). *Frames of mind.* New York: Basic Books.

Giangreco, M.F., Cloninger, C.J., & Iverson, V.S. (1993). *Choosing options and accommodations for children: A guide to planning inclusive education.* Baltimore: Paul H. Brookes Publishing Co.

Gibbs, J. (1987). *Tribes: A process for social development and cooperative learning.* Santa Rosa, CA: Center Source Publications.

Gibbs, J. (1994). *Tribes: A new way of learning together.* Santa Rosa, CA: Center Source Publications.

Goodlad, J. (1984). *A place called school: Prospects for the future.* New York: McGraw-Hill.

Herman, J.L., Aschbacher, P., & Winters, L. (1992). *A practical guide to alternative assessment.* Alexandria, VA: Association for Supervision and Curriculum Development.

Kameenui, E.J., & Simmons, D.C. (1990). *Designing instructional strategies: The prevention of academic learning problems.* Columbus, OH: Charles E. Merrill.

Kunc, N. (1992). The need to belong: Rediscovering Maslow's hierarchy of learning. In R.A. Villa, J.S. Thousand, W. Stainback, & S. Stainback (Eds.), *Restructuring for caring and effective education: An administrative guide to creating heterogeneous schools* (pp. 25–39). Baltimore: Paul H. Brookes Publishing Co.

Mercer, C.D., & Mercer, A.R. (1993). *Teaching students with learning problems* (4th ed.). New York: Merrill/Macmillan.

Meyer, C. (1992). What's the difference between authentic and performance assessment? *Educational Leadership, 49*(8), 39–40.

Overton, T. (1992). *Assessment in special education: An applied approach.* New York: Merrill/Macmillan.

Salvia, J., & Ysseldyke, J.E. (1991). *Assessment in special and remedial education* (5th ed.). Boston: Houghton Mifflin.

Sizer, T.R. (1992). *Horace's school: Redesigning the American high school.* Boston: Houghton Mifflin.

Udvari-Solner, A. (1994). A decision-making model for curricular adaptations in cooperative groups. In J.S. Thousand, R.A. Villa, & A. Nevin (Eds.), *Creativity and collaborative learning: A practical guide for empowering students and teachers* (pp. 59–78). Baltimore: Paul H. Brookes Publishing Co.

Zigmond, N., & Silverman, R. (1984). Informal assessment for program planning and evaluation in special education. *Educational Psychologist, 19*(3), 163–171.

III

COLLABORATION

9

Friendships as an Educational Goal

What We Have Learned and Where We Are Headed

Jeffrey L. Strully and Cindy Strully

IN 1989 WE wrote a chapter entitled "Friendships as an Educational Goal" (Strully & Strully, 1989); some years later we are still involved, with a renewed sense of urgency, in helping to facilitate friendship in our daughter's life. What we have learned during this journey and what we are still learning about friendship is the focus of this chapter. We also discuss where we see our daughter headed in her journey in life as together we work to build an inclusive community that includes friendship.

The question was never whether friendship is a good idea or whether it is important to work on. The only questions that need be answered are: How do you facilitate, support, and maintain friendships within people's lives? How do people come to know one another and develop relationships and ultimately friendships that will last over time? How do we ensure that people's lives are not empty and lonely? How do we work together to support friendships between and among people?

Friendship is mostly magic, mystery, and wonder. There are some concrete strategies that people can use to help build and facilitate friendships in people's lives, but these are only strategies. There are no simple solutions that will work all of the time to build friendships between and among people. It takes hard work and energy to maintain friendships, especially if the people we care about have long histories of segregation, isolation, profound loneliness, and few, if any, opportunities.

The strategies that we have used are outlined in this chapter. It is important to remember that a friendship is still an issue of chemistry and wonder rather than of science. There really are no "how-to" books available to develop friendships. Even if there were books to tell you what to do, they would not help you with the day-to-day struggles associated with building and supporting friendships. However, it is critical to recognize that, without friendships, it is almost impossible for children and adults to spend their time learning or working. If our schools and communities cannot welcome and embrace diversity and support friendships among its members, then belonging will not take place. Without a sense of belonging, it is not possible to consider lower-level issues such as learning or working. Ultimately, facilitating friendships is about living and learning together. It is about intentionality, membership in the community, and inclusion. It is about confronting difficult, frustrating, and heart-wrenching issues, and it is about disappointment. But most of all, facilitating friendships is and always will be one of the most important things we continue to work on not only for our children, but for ourselves.

WHAT FRIENDS SAY

Our daughter Shawntell's best friend, Cyndi Peters, recently wrote the following letter presented by Strully, Strully, Strully, and Peters (1994) at the 1994 Shape Conference in Edmonton, Alberta:

> I'm very sorry I was unable to do the presentation, but I thought I would leave a few thoughts behind. Looking back I know that initially I was just as nervous as anyone when I first met Shawntell. Shawntell seemed so different and I (unfortunately) had never had the chance to learn in a fully integrated classroom before. I wasn't sure I was "good" enough for Shawntell. This may sound strange and perhaps I'm not wording it correctly, I just thought it would take more than I had to be friends with Shawntell. Now nearly six years later, Shawntell is most assuredly one of my best friends. I love her deeply. It didn't take anything unusual to be friends with Shawntell, just being human was enough and I trust that we're all human, right? Shawntell's life has gone separate ways than my own in the past. In high school I was grounded quite a bit, so our time together was sometimes limited. She went away to college, I moved to New Hampshire. But today our friendship continues because luckily it has been strong enough to last. Of course it's not all roses. We have our moments as all friends do, but we also see each other very frequently. I help her through bad times and she helps me. We've been through a lot; more than many. I believe, and I hope Shawntell does as well, that our friendship will outlast time. We are just friends like everyone else in the world. I love you Shawn. I apologize if this is sketchy, but it is 2:00 A.M. I just wanted to make the point that there is no limit to friendship. Love knows no "disability," if it did, I wonder if we could love anyone.

Shawntell's other friends, Natalie, Joyce, and Cheryl, have written similar letters since Shawntell moved from Colorado to California. Relocating is difficult for any of us. Leaving your friends and familiar surroundings behind to start a new life with new experiences and meeting new people is not an easy chore for many of us. We know that it will take time for Shawntell to develop the sort of friendships she had in Colorado, and at the same time it will take effort on everyone's part to continue to support her long-distance friendships.

Shawntell's new support people are getting to know her, and Shawntell is getting to know them. They are just beginning to learn who Shawntell is and what she wants, needs, and desires. Finding support people who take the time to listen and learn is not easy. Everyone just wants to "run programs" or "teach Shawntell" rather than help introduce her to other people; help her join organizations, clubs, and associations; assist her in being known in her new community; and facilitate the development of relationships and friendships in her life.

Shawntell has not made any real friends since her move. She has met some people and maybe they will develop a relationship with her, but only time will tell. However, we are not discouraged because we know there are people out there who are just waiting to get to know Shawntell and waiting for Shawntell to get to know them. This will take time and energy as we move forward with a new stage in Shawntell's journey.

REMEMBERING AND LOOKING BACK

In February 1994, Shawntell almost died, and the medical professionals, with all their degrees, skills, and competencies, as well as their licenses and accreditation, were ready to blame Shawntell's friends for this situation.

Shawntell had gone out on a Monday evening with Joyce, a longtime friend from high school, who was supporting Shawntell in Shawntell's own home. Joyce and Shawn came home late, and Joyce forgot to give Shawntell her evening medication. The next morning Shawntell woke up and had a seizure. Her friend Cyndi called us. We told her to let Shawntell rest and we would see what developed. Later on in the morning, Shawntell was feeling better. Shawn and Cyndi decided to go out. Just before their departure, Shawntell had a second grand mal seizure; she cut her chin, and the paramedics were called. Shawntell was going to need stitches to repair the gash. Cyndi and Joyce were going to accompany Shawntell to the hospital in the ambulance and Cindy S. (Shawntell's mother and co-author of this chapter) would meet them there. At the hospital, Shawntell had her chin stitched.

Cindy S. decided to take Shawntell to her home for the evening. By the time they got home, Shawntell had another seizure. Her neurologist suggested additional medication. By the time a family friend came with the medication, Shawntell had several more seizures without regaining consciousness. At that time, it was felt she needed to go to the hospital. That evening Shawntell had approximately 13 more seizures. Her blood pressure dropped dangerously low. After administering medication, the hospital staff finally stabilized her condition sometime in the early hours of the next morning.

The following morning, Jeff arrived (Shawntell's father and co-author of this chapter). The physician informed us that Shawntell had cocaine in her body and that she (the doctor) was going to inform the police as well as Adult Protective Services. We informed the doctor that Shawntell's friends could never have done anything like that directly or indirectly. However, the physician was very sure that her friends had allowed Shawntell to have or be exposed to cocaine. We asked for another test to confirm the results. It would take 48 hours to get these results.

Over the next 2 days, we discussed what the doctor had said with Shawntell's friends and roommates. They could not believe what had happened or that we would even believe for one moment that they would allow something like this to happen to their friend. The tests came back—*positive results*. There was indeed cocaine in Shawntell's body. The doctor renewed her intention to call the police and Adult Protective Services to report this situation. At that time, Cindy S. was able to figure out, with help from the poison control center, that the medication given to Shawntell when she first arrived to have her chin stitched had a cocaine base. It was the hospital and the emergency room physicians who almost killed our daughter. (Cocaine is known to cause seizures in a person without a seizure disorder; in a person with a seizure disorder it can lower the seizure threshold causing numerous breakthrough seizures.) However, upon hearing this result, the doctor immediately changed her story, saying that it was the missed medication, not the cocaine, that caused Shawntell's seizures.

The lesson from this story is that people with credentials, certification, and white lab coats almost killed our daughter, and her friends, young 20-year-olds, were going to be blamed. This does not make all 20-year-olds perfect or all professionals bad; it is just that we put so much stock and credibility into professionalism and professionals and very little energy into relationships and friendships. We could not believe that Shawn's friends, who had known her for years, could have been involved in allowing something like cocaine near our daughter.

This story tests your faith and confidence in the people who are nearest to your son or daughter. Whom do you trust? Where do you put your faith and confidence? For us, putting our faith and confidence in Shawntell's friends was the right thing to do.

The lives of most people with developmental disabilities have been associated with programs with highly trained, licensed professionals caring for and doing something to make them better. There has been a predisposition to "fix" people with disabilities rather than accept people for what they bring to a situation. If we had to wait for Shawntell to learn prerequisite skills before developing friendships, she would never have had any friends. We decided to take another path than the traditional one in order to ensure that our daughter's life would be filled with people who love her and care about her as a friend. How did we come to this conclusion? In part, the answer lies in who Shawntell is and where her journey has taken us.

DESCRIBING OUR DAUGHTER

Depending upon who is providing the description, we would seem to have two adult daughters. We could describe our daughter in the following ways:

We Describe Shawntell

- Is 22 years old
- Lives in her own home with friends and roommates
- Attends classes at Colorado State University and changes her major constantly
- Volunteers on campus and in the community

- Works in the university recreational center
- Travels to Mexico, California, and Florida on winter and spring breaks
- Enjoys the freedom to get around in her own car
- Is becoming her own person with her own interests, likes, and desires
- Has a boyfriend
- Speaks out on issues of concern to her
- Is becoming a real adult who is no longer her parents' little girl

Hardly a day goes by without our thinking about the kind of future we would like for our daughter. Our dreams for her are close to what she is doing: having friends, living in her own place, working, volunteering, having someone to care about, learning, figuring out who she is, and what she wants to do with her life. It is exciting to be a 22-year-old. Hers is a rich journey with many different possibilities for a desirable future.

Others Describe Shawntell

Some other people have described Shawntell in the following ways:

- Is 22 years old
- Is severely/profoundly mentally retarded
- Is hearing impaired
- Is visually impaired
- Has cerebral palsy
- Has a severe seizure disorder
- Does not chew her food and sometimes chokes
- Is not toilet trained
- Has no verbal communication
- Has no reliable communication system
- Self-stimulates (hand in eye, hand in mouth)
- Has a developmental age of 17–24 months
- Loves Fisher-Price toys
- Loves music: "Row, Row, Row Your Boat"; "Three Blind Mice"; "London Bridge"

Most people have a difficult time thinking about a desirable future for Shawntell. They might imagine her in the future living in a group home with six or eight other people like her and spending her days in a sheltered workshop or day activity center. For recreation she would be involved in Special Olympics, and for social activities she would go on group field trips with friends who are "just like" her. She would need continual programming and might have volunteers to "work" with her on these programs.

How is it possible that one person could be described in such different ways? How do we determine what an individual's future should include?

What Is Most Important in Life?

When thinking about desirable futures for the people we care about, we need to think about issues such as what we generally think is important for our own lives, how we describe people, and what we dream about for our sons and daughters or the people we support. We hope that Shawntell's life journey will be filled with excitement and rich experiences and that she will enjoy life to the fullest. This includes, as noted earlier, our hope that she will continue to live in her own home with people she wants to live with, to work or have a career that she likes and that pays well, to be an active community member, to play and socialize in her community, and, most of all, to be surrounded by a group of friends who want to be with her because they enjoy her and she enjoys them.

Shawntell needs to be around people to socialize with, people to help her when she needs support, people whom she can help—in short, people who care about her and whom she cares about. We define friendship exactly the way you would determine friendship for yourself. The key ingredients are reciprocity, mutuality, common ground, and, of course, chemistry.

There remain many skills Shawntell has yet to master, such as independent toileting and eating, verbal communication, and walking with stability. However, despite our active efforts to help her in these areas, whether Shawntell achieves such skills in her lifetime is not what concerns us most as parents. Our biggest concerns are that there will be no one in our daughter's life who wants to be with her, that she will be at risk of being victimized, that she will be lonely, and that she will be without friends. Our biggest fear as parents is for Shawntell's safety and social security. How do we help ensure that neglect, victimization, abuse, and profound loneliness are not experiences that she has during her life? How do we ensure that after our death people will know what her favorite food is? It is these issues that concern us the most.

We do not want only paid human services workers who come and go in Shawntell's life. We do not want professionals who do not know our daughter making decisions about her future. How do we ensure that people will spend time getting to know Shawntell before deciding something for her? How do we deal with the possibility that her future could be isolated, lonely, and without friends?

Given these realistic concerns, what can parents, educators, and others do to help individuals develop friendships? How can we help ensure that our daughter and many other individuals with a label of disability will have a circle of friends over the long haul? How can we work toward Shawntell's having a best friend?

Developing friendships is not something that comes easily or naturally to most of us, children or adults. Most people simply have trouble connecting with other people. The schools, for their part, pay little attention to the social and educational values of friendships. Yet it is our friendships and relationships that are our only real way of being true members of our communities. Friendships protect us from being alone and vulnerable and ensure that our lives are rich and full. However, the lives of people who are labeled as having mental retardation or developmental disabilities seem to be filled with profound loneliness and isolation—that is, with few, if any, friends. This is something that all of us must work to change. It is becoming increasingly clear that, without friends, real school and community inclusion cannot take place.

We must start building and supporting friendships in schools. As noted by the New Mexico Board of Education in its inclusion policy, friendship is an educational goal for *all* children. Schools need to know that if you do not have friends, you cannot learn effectively. Why would anyone spend time learning if there was no one around to play with and hang out with?

FRIENDSHIPS: ISSUES TO CONSIDER

As we have struggled over the years with these concerns for our daughter, as well as for many other people, the following issues continually arose:

1. People need to be in many and varied ordinary places with ordinary people for relationships to develop. Where is the individual each hour of the day? What is he or she doing and with whom? For example, if you are by yourself or in a segregated school environment, how do you expect people to get to know you? If you are not in after-school clubs, groups, or organizations, how do you meet people? Why would anyone call you to see what you are doing on the weekends if the people you share your space with during the week are also sitting around waiting for someone to call?

2. People need to work on developing relationships. This includes parents, educators, human services workers, citizens, and students. We all need to work on supporting these relationships. It is our job to work on building friendships or at least to work on providing opportunities for friendships to blossom. What have you done today to help facilitate opportunities for friendships between students?

3. People need to see the gifts, talents, and contributions that each person has and can make and use these to help develop relationships. People like to share common experiences or likes and preferences. Where do people who like to listen to music go after school? Where do people play baseball or basketball? If an individual is interested in stamps, where do like-minded people get together? You first need to know the gifts and talents of your son or daughter or the people you support in order to help them become connected with others.

4. Friendships come and go, they change, are unpredictable, are "loose," and are hard to grasp. Do not make them into something they are not. Friendships are not simple solutions to life's problems. They are important, even critical, but they are not a panacea for all the woes facing people with disabilities. As a point of information, not all friendships are healthy and good. There are bad friendships and unhealthy friendships. These are issues that also need to be addressed.

5. Friendships are two-way: Both parties must give and take in the relationship. There is a difference between friendship and other types of relationships. Do not confuse these differences. People who are nice, helpful, and protective are not friends. They may be helpers, mentors, and advocates, but they are not friends. Everyone who says "hi" to you or helps you in class is not necessarily your friend.

6. Friendship is freely given. Friends are not paid to be with you; they are not getting extra credit for a project; they are not getting a Girl Scout badge or the Mother Theresa humanitarian of the year award. Friends are not the same as peer tutors, special buddies, or helpers. This is not to say that such forms of assistance are not helpful in certain conditions, but they are not friendships.

7. Friends come in a variety of different packages. Although this discussion primarily concerns people with labels coming together with people without labels, this does not preclude friendship between people with labels.
8. Most people are interested in having many different friends from many different walks of life.
9. Finally, friendships are at the heart of any community, including the school community. Friendships are the most important aspect of life that we can spend our time working on.

Developing friendships in school for all children is one of the most important accomplishments that we as parents and educators can undertake. Whether getting together means, for example, going out after school for a hamburger, just being in the schoolyard and talking, visiting a friend in his or her home, or having someone over to your house, schools need to help facilitate opportunities for friendships between and among people with varying abilities and characteristics.

WHAT NEEDS TO BE IN PLACE FOR FRIENDSHIPS TO DEVELOP

The following is a list of specific and general suggestions for nurturing friendships among all students:

- All children must attend their neighborhood school.
- All children must learn together in our general education program.
- All children must ride the school bus, walk, carpool, or ride their bikes to school. Getting there is half the fun.
- All children must be included in the associational life of school (this includes the Friday night dance or pep rally, the Saturday morning baseball game, clubs, and organizations).
- The concept of special education must be eliminated in favor of education for all children with the support each student needs.
- Schools must be inclusive, not exclusive, communities. They must invite people in and welcome them—all people!
- Parents must encourage and demand, if necessary, that schools facilitate children in learning to play and work together in inclusive classrooms.
- Educators must learn to embrace and support the efforts needed in order for friendships to blossom. We all need to help relationships develop. This is as important as reading, writing, and arithmetic.
- All children, whether labeled as disabled or nondisabled, must be involved in helping friendships develop.
- Children need to be introduced to one another by other friends and interested others such as support facilitators. Some children need support from a facilitator for friendships to develop. Without these supports, these children will not develop friendships. Without intentionality, many friendships would not develop.

- Facilitation of relationships may need to take place at first or even over time for them to develop. There is a belief that friendships just happen. Although this may be true sometimes, many of us know that getting and keeping a friend is hard work. It is like a marriage: You need to work on the marriage to keep it going. The same is true for friendships.

It is important to clarify what we mean here by inclusion and community. Inclusion does not mean a self-contained special education classroom with opportunities to be with nonlabeled children for recess, art, music, and lunch. Inclusion does not mean bringing nonlabeled children into a special education class and working on a project. Inclusion means the process of making whole, of bringing together all children, and having all children learn together. Inclusion means helping all people (children and adults) recognize and appreciate the unique gifts that each individual brings to a situation or the community.

Community is a reality that, for the most part, has not been experienced by people with labels. There is a great difference between being in a community of service professionals and being in a community of citizens. We need to work toward the day when churches, neighborhoods, and schools become places that are inclusive and respectful of everyone's individual differences rather than fearful and ignorant of differences. Embracing differences rather than avoiding differences is what community is all about. A community is not perfect, nor is it without pain. However, it is where we all belong.

All of this is easier said than done. How do we create communities that include our children or the individuals we support? The following story illustrates some of the measures that parents and educators can undertake in order to facilitate friendships for their children.

SHAWNTELL'S STORY

When we originally wrote "Friendships as an Educational Goal," Shawntell was finishing her first year at Arapahoe High School. That was almost 6 years ago—a long time ago in Shawntell's journey. Since that time, Shawntell finished high school, went off to Colorado State University for several years, and lived in her own home. She enjoyed life away from her family, working, learning, volunteering, partying, and getting connected with people in Fort Collins. She started a new part of her journey, which was becoming an adult with new interests and feelings that were part of her adult self. Shawntell enjoyed the chance to become a young woman, having a life away from her family.

However, this part of her journey was also filled with difficulties, problems, and frustrations. Shawntell's medical needs, especially surrounding her seizure activity, surfaced once again after many years. The medication that had controlled her seizures for years was no longer working. She started to have many more seizures each day. In addition to her medical needs, there were other difficulties. Her support people started arguing with each other; there were roommate problems. Some of her problems were the same as those of other students at the university (who took what food from whose shelf, boyfriends, responsibility for the phone bill, money, and cleaning chores). Other issues were specific to Shawntell (expectations from the family and conflicting messages from Shawntell). These issues caused problems and tensions.

Now, Shawntell has moved to California. She is currently trying to get to know people, learn about the California lifestyle, and get her medical needs under control. Her journey is on a changing course.

Good Old School Days

When we look back to Shawntell's time at Arapahoe High School, we are filled with many mixed emotions. The most important memory we have is of all the good friends Shawntell made over the years: Denise, Joyce, Brandi, Melissa, Ruth, and Cyndi. These young women were the reason that Shawntell's high school experience was an overall positive experience. They got to know Shawntell by being in class with her, through clubs and organizations, and through working together in and out of school and just being together. Over time, they became involved in Shawntell's life outside of school. Finally, they became friends, culminating in a strong circle of friends by Shawntell's senior year.

Looking back, friendships were the highlight of Shawntell's educational experience. This is very interesting because we hear the same thing so often from others that we know that this is also true for them. Without her friends, Shawntell's high school experience would have been a major disappointment no matter what skills or competencies she learned. However, Shawntell did meet people, and friendships did form.

This process was directly attributable to Leslie, Shawntell's integration facilitator at Arapahoe High School. Without the intentional efforts by Leslie, these friendships would never have formed. The high school students who came to know Shawntell and her family stayed involved in Shawntell's life not only during high school, but also as she moved on toward the university. For some of her fellow students, Shawntell would have remained a stranger without Leslie's involvement. Physically being in a general education class is only the beginning. There is so much more work and effort to be done in order to build friendships. One factor that would have helped in building friendships would have been a school that was inclusive.

However, Shawntell's high school was never really an inclusive community. The school district never really adopted the concept or believed it was important. The school district saw no benefit of inclusion to all students. While they "allowed" inclusion on a student-by-student basis, they never embraced it. Hence, Shawntell's high school experience, while personally very good, did not have the long-term benefit of changing the way her school viewed the needs of all of its students. This was, in our opinion, a tragedy not just for our daughter but for all young people who have not yet experienced learning in an inclusive school. The school district has not yet realized the importance and power of inclusion. The district just saw inclusion as one thing it had to do for one family who would make trouble if the school did not include Shawntell.

They also never imagined the possibilities that could be realized if they embraced this concept for all students. This has been their loss.

There were, however, several teachers who supported what we were trying to accomplish and embraced our daughter in their classrooms. There were some administrators who were supportive and flexible in accommodating Shawntell. We appreciate the commitment and dedication of the teachers, administrators, and others who supported Shawntell in attending her neighborhood high school, attending general education classes all day, working, volunteering, and participating in all school and after-school activities. So the message is that, even if your school is not perfect, something can happen.

In Shawntell's senior year, things were as good as they could be from our point of view. Shawntell was taking some wonderful classes with excellent teachers. She was involved with several clubs and organizations both during and after school. Most important, she had developed a strong and committed circle of friends. Shawntell's facilitator was spending less and less time with her as her friends replaced the paid support. In addition, Shawntell's friends were meeting regularly to discuss how Shawntell could become more and more involved in the school community. They were also involved in helping Shawntell think about the next step on the journey, going to Colorado State University.

Off to College

When Shawntell finished high school in the summer of 1991, her circle of friends and family met to discuss what would be the next step on Shawntell's journey. It was decided that Shawntell should attend college or a university. The reason was simple: that is where 18- to 21-year-olds are. Also, the other options were not appealing—work or the military.

Leslie was no longer able to be Shawntell's facilitator, and we had to find a new facilitator. The first person recruited did not work out, but the second individual, Cheryl, not only became Shawntell's facilitator for the next 2 years, but also has become a long-term friend of Shawntell's

Cheryl did essentially the same things that Leslie had done. She helped Shawntell take classes at the university (classes such as The Age of Reformation, movement and dance, human sexuality, writing your life, women's studies, psychology, and swimming). She also assisted in finding Shawntell a job at the recreation center, which was right in the middle of activity and where people got to know Shawntell. Shawntell started going to the student center and getting to know people. She volunteered for other activities on campus. Finally, it was felt Shawntell should move to the university. The reason lies in the difference between being *in* the community and being *part of* the community.

By moving to the university and living away from home, Shawntell became more involved in student life, just like other students. She was able to hang out at her favorite pub, attend sporting events and plays, and join the clubs and organizations on campus. She became a regular!

Shawntell attended the university for the next 2 years until she moved to California. We do not want to minimize the problems and issues surrounding these experiences, but Shawntell met many new people and several have become friends. Shawntell had many wonderful experiences and took a new journey in her life. As recounted earlier, there were also lessons to learn when things went wrong. There were problems surrounding support. There were questions about who did what and whose role was what. There were problems around communication between Shawntell's support staff and friends and her parents. There were fights and missing money. However, there were lessons to be learned from these experiences.

There is a difference between living in a dream and living a dream. The former has to do with pretending that things are better than they are or that the life experiences are just wonderful and going well. Although we would all love this to happen, it is not reality. Living a dream has to do with having a strong vision for a possible future and working to achieve it even when things go wrong or are far from perfect. Live a dream, just do not live *in* a dream.

IMPORTANT THEMES IN MAKING FRIENDSHIPS

Our experiences in helping promote meaningful relationships for Shawntell lead us to make the following suggestions for parents and educators:

- Believe that friendships are possible and are critical for your child's future as well as for those of other children and believe that people do want to get to know and spend time with your child or the people you support.
- Effort and intentionality are necessary in order to facilitate friendships. There are mistakes and ups and downs when working with human beings. Planning is sometimes difficult.
- For friendships to occur, opportunities for people to be together must be identified, such as in classes, at home, after school, or in the community. The more chances that a person has to be with other people, the greater the likelihood that relationships and friendships will form.
- Get adults out of the way and let children get to know one another.
- Utilize adults as facilitators of friendships only when needed and only for the amount of time required.
- *Ask, ask, ask.* Sometimes simply asking people to get to know another person is a real start; sometimes asking for advice from others is helpful.
- Understand the power of letting people solve problems and think about creative solutions. Let them come up with ideas; intervene only when needed or to provide initial direction or focus.
- Help people understand their similarities. People need to have a common bond, whether it is music, shopping for clothes, eating pizza, being in the mall, or riding horses. The issue is to find what people like to do and to use that to link them with one another.

- Do not place demands on people, especially young people, that they cannot live with. Take people as they are, and help them move forward.
- The ultimate spokesperson is the person him- or herself. Most young people are good at selling themselves to other people. Let them do it!
- Appreciate that creating friendships for the person has at least equal benefits for the nonlabeled individual.

CONCLUSION

Developing friendships is something that all of us, at any age, need to work on. There is no one way to go about facilitating and developing friendships; there are no books (including this one) with quick and easy answers.

Of course, there are paths that one can take to make the task easier. Family life is one path. Children need to grow up in a family—not in a group home, residential child-care facility, or institution—to learn the give and take in relationships. Of course, like friends, families have strengths and weaknesses. Children also need to go to school in their own neighborhood, to attend classes with typical children their own age, and to be involved with kids in activities outside of school. Adults should not interfere but at the same time should understand that some children may need help in being introduced to others, in sharing their gifts with them, and in making personal connections. This is a major role of the integration facilitator, who needs to know when to support, when to get out of the way, and when to offer a friendly suggestion. This is a difficult task and one that is not generally taught, but should be, in university programs.

For parents, the issue of friendships can be problematic, even frightening. Parents need to recognize that working on friendships takes time. They need to express that friendships with other students and adults are critical in their children's lives. Many parents think that if their child receives another hour of speech therapy or of individualized instruction, he or she will get what they need. Sometimes parents even feel guilty if their children are not receiving instruction that one professional or another has told them should be provided in a self-contained special education class. However, the issues of friendship and quality education are not mutually exclusive. In fact, it is our opinion that one cannot take place without the other.

Many parents have been placed in an either/or situation and forced to choose between quality education in a special education class and friendships in a general education class. In fact, it is impossible to have a quality education without having friendships, and friendships go a long way toward ensuring quality education. It should be remembered that it is possible to offer both within the framework of a general education classroom. However, it is impossible for friendships with typical peers to take place when children are locked away in self-contained special education classes or schools.

For some children and parents, the promise of a future is a new idea. For the formerly special student, being part of a general education class, being just another student, entails some limitations and difficulties. For example, it may mean standing outside in the rain waiting for the school bus instead of staying inside the house until the special van beeps its horn. For parents, it means picking up and taking kids all over to meet friends, attend parties, go swimming, or go to the gym. It means sending your children out with their friends to concerts, parties, and malls. It means making sure that your child dresses in style, that he or she has the "right" possessions, that his or her room looks the way other children's rooms look. Other likely components include soft drinks, loud music, and lots of talking in the bedroom with the door closed, telephone calls, and strange hairdos. *It means struggling with issues of life, not issues of disability!*

Friendships are indeed at the heart of what we all need for one another. It is our friendships that enable us to be active and protected members of the community. Friendships help ensure that being a part of the community, rather than just being in the community, is a reality for everyone!

REFERENCES

Strully, J., & Strully, C. (1989). Friendships as an educational goal. In S. Stainback, W. Stainback, & M. Forest (Eds.), *Educating all students in the mainstream of regular education* (pp. 59–68). Baltimore: Paul H. Brookes Publishing Co.
Strully, J., Strully, C., Strully, S., & Peters, C. (1994, May). Paper presented at the 1994 SHAPE (Severe Handicaps Alliance for Public Education) Conference, Edmonton, Alberta.

10

Facilitating Friendships

Kathryn D. Bishop, Kimberlee A. Jubala,
William Stainback, and Susan Stainback

THE IMPORTANCE OF children's friendships has long been acknowledged by families and educators and has been a frequent topic of research. In reviewing the literature discussing the value of friendships for children, Grenot-Scheyer (1994) stated that friendships serve to enhance a variety of communicative, cognitive, and social skills as well as provide children with nurturance, support, and a sense of well-being. The friendships established in childhood are the basis for the formal, informal, and intimate relationships in adulthood.

The development of friendships by students with significant disabilities was often neglected because educators and support personnel focused their efforts on functional and academic skill development (Strully & Strully, 1989). In addition, it has been determined that the opportunity for close, mutual, and ongoing relationships has been lacking in the lives of most people with significant disabilities (Taylor, Biklen, & Knoll, 1987). Increasingly, parents and individuals with disabilities have stressed the value of friendship and meaningful relationships between both children and adults with significant disabilities and their peers without disabilities (Barber & Hupp, 1993; Strully & Strully, 1989; Van der Klift & Kunc, 1994). Strain (1984) argued that friendships for children with disabilities may be even more important than for more typical children because of their increased needs for language, cognitive, social, sexual, and academic development.

This chapter presents strategies that have been helpful to parents and educators in facilitating friendships specifically between students with significant disabilities and their peers without disabilities. It is important to note that there are no proven skill requisites (e.g., IQ scores, verbal communication abilities, motor responses) for developing friendships. In a study completed by Grenot-Scheyer (1994), none of the factors of developmental age, language age, functional movement, social competence, or communicative competence of students with significant disabilities were determined to be related to the development of friendships with peers without disabilities. Given that a student need not spend valuable time on "friendship readiness" skills, this chapter outlines some of the strategies that can be used to support the development of friendships regardless of a student's particular strengths or needs.

STRATEGIES FOR FACILITATING FRIENDSHIPS

Friendships have been considered "highly individualistic, fluid and dynamic, varying according to the chronological age of the participants, and largely based on free choice and personal preference" (Stainback & Stainback, 1990, p. 52). Although friendships cannot be forced, their development can be encouraged, nurtured, and facilitated in educational and community environments. The strategies suggested in this chapter have been used by parents, educators, and advocates to facilitate friendships and informal relationships between students of all ages, backgrounds, and abilities.

Proximity as a Prerequisite

Although there are no skill requisites for developing friendships, a critical variable in the establishment of friendships is physical proximity (Asher & Gottman, 1981; Grenot-Scheyer, Coots, & Falvey, 1989). If a student is to have the opportunity to develop friendships with typical peers, he or she must be in the presence of these peers. Educational services for students with disabilities have evolved from no services, to segregated services, to integrated services, to inclusive services and supports. It has been logically argued that relationships between students with disabilities and their peers without disabilities are more likely to develop when all students receive their education in shared environments (Hamre-Nietupski, Shokoohi-Yekta, Hendrickson, & Nietupski, 1994).

Physical proximity occurs when students with and without disabilities ride the same school buses; attend the same classes on integrated campuses; and participate in school clubs, church groups, recreational sports programs, Boy and Girl Scouts, community theaters, and informal "hangout" spots like shopping malls or fast-food restaurants. The opportunities for physical proximity within the classroom have increased significantly with the inclusion model of service delivery. However, if students are not attending their neighborhood schools or are not supported in after-school activities, the friendships initiated in the classroom will not extend beyond the school day.

Jaime Jaime, a 10-year-old boy who is hard of hearing and legally blind, has a great sense of humor, and has significant cognitive delays, had his first opportunity for inclusive education in the fifth grade. Although he attended a general education fifth-grade class with special education supports, he rode a bus 25 miles from his home each day because his neighborhood school was not "ready" to provide him with an appropriate education. Jaime was able to develop friendships with a number of the boys who were in the fifth-grade class with him and became well known across the campus. Jaime was elected by the students to the student council office of commissioner of the environment.

Jaime's social opportunities were extensive during the school day. However, after school and on weekends he continued to be isolated because of the geographic distance from his school friends and the lack of regular contact with the children in his neighborhood who attended the local elementary school. When it came time for Jaime to make the transition to junior high school at age 13, his opportunities for social interactions and friendship development were considered carefully. The individualized education program (IEP) team decided that Jaime would attend the local junior high school with his neighborhood peers. The proximity to those peers both during the school day and after school hours allowed Jaime's relationships to grow, and his afternoons, evenings, and weekends were shared with new friends. Because he no longer had to leave school immediately to begin the long journey home, Jaime was able to participate in after-school activities and eventually earned a varsity letter in wrestling alongside his many proud teammates.

Eric In another example, this student's involvement and participation in his neighborhood led eventually to inclusion in the local school. Eric came from a family of two sisters and three brothers and parents who made their house the neighborhood hangout. Eric, who had cerebral palsy and used a wheelchair, was always an integral part of family and neighborhood activities. He could be frequently seen in the street, helmeted and covered with pads, his chair buttressed with reinforced cardboard. As the goalie for the neighborhood street hockey games, he was simultaneously cheered and cursed by any number of children.

Eric's natural involvement in family and neighborhood activities begged the question of why he spent 30 minutes each weekday on a special bus riding to a special school while everyone else he knew well was walking to the school a few blocks away. When the school district began to offer inclusion as a service option, Eric "walked" the few blocks to receive his education with his siblings and neighborhood friends.

Opportunities for Interaction

Although physical proximity is a necessity for the development of friendships, by itself it is not enough. There are many examples of poorly executed attempts at mainstreaming or inclusion in which students with disabilities were placed in a general education classroom, perhaps given adapted assignments, and then left to fend for themselves or otherwise placed with an aide in a corner of the classroom. The development of friendships requires ongoing opportunities for social interaction between students with and without disabilities.

Educational practices have shifted from didactic exercises that discourage student–student interaction to practices that require student–student interaction for optimal learning. Classroom strategies such as cooperative learning, community circles, job pairs, lunch/recess organized activities, partner work, and group homework assignments support student–student interactions as well as seating arrangements that include shared tables, round tables, and group study areas as opposed to individual desks (Gibbs, 1987; Johnson & Johnson, 1989; Jubala, Bishop, & Falvey, 1995; Putnam, 1993; Thousand, Villa, & Nevin, 1994).

Students with disabilities must be provided with a contributing role to social interactions in the context of academic, physical, or social activities. For example, in a science unit on botany, a student with a cognitive disability can be in charge of physically organizing the plant structures as dissected and directed by group members. In physical education class, a student with a physical disability can be involved as a team captain, coach, statistician, equipment manager, or free-throw shooter in a basketball game or designated runner in a baseball game. Cooperative games can be structured around the specific abilities of a student. Parachute games, for example, would allow full participation of a student who uses a wheelchair. In social activities, it is important that the student with a disability pay his or her share of dues, wear the appropriate uniform, and assume as many of the same responsibilities as their peers as possible. For example, students who are not able to drive might provide snacks for others on the ski club trips or pay for the gasoline.

Opportunities to contribute in meaningful ways are important not only for the self-esteem of the student with a disability but also to earn the respect of his or her peers. The role of parents and educators is to create ways for a student with a significant disability to provide valuable contributions in ways that are not readily apparent. As relationships grow and friendships develop, the need for extrinsic contributions diminishes as the student is acknowledged for his or her intrinsic worth and as peers gain an understanding of each other's strengths and inherent abilities.

Michael   Michael's friendships were nonexistent when he entered the second grade at his local elementary school. Michael was a child with autistic disorder and along with this label came an inability to verbally communicate, a tendency to bite adults, and a propensity for engaging in self-stimulatory behaviors not typical of his classmates. Although there was an attempt to introduce Michael to his classmates through a modified circle of friends strategy (Forest & Lusthaus, 1989), there was little meaningful interaction between him and his peers. As the class routine became established, Michael's parents worked hard to collaborate with his teachers to create areas of expertise for Michael. For social studies, he brought in pictures and artifacts of the countries being studied; he often housed many of the supplies for art projects or math manipulatives in his desk; and he led students through the obstacle courses set up on the playground. The school personnel helped his peers develop a "Michael dictionary," which provided interpretations of Michael's behaviors: "When Michael flaps his hands he might be bored; you can ask him to play a game or read a book with you." "When Michael makes a loud shriek, he is happy and wants you to come and look at what he is doing." As the students began to understand Michael and realize his interests, they spent more time interacting with him. Eventually, more meaningful relationships developed with two of his peers, who spent time at his house as he did at theirs.

Marci   Marci's friendships were initially limited to the friends of her younger sister and to her cousins. Marci had significant multiple disabilities and spent most of her life in a segregated school. Her opportunity for inclusion came when she entered high school and attended her neighborhood campus where there were no special education supports. Because the school was less than pleased to undertake inclusion, much of Marci's support came from her parents and high school counselor. The school district hired an aide for Marci who was trained to attend to all of Marci's physical and medical needs during the school day. The primary support for Marci's participation in classes came from her high school peers, who were supported by the general education teachers. The teachers provided many opportunities for group projects and activities while her peers brainstormed other ways for Marci to participate. Because Marci had very little muscle control, which limited her voluntary movement, had no systematic means of effective communication, and had mental retardation with extensive support needs, her active participation was a challenge to all. Even with such challenges, Marci was more alert and involved in her inclusive high school classes than she was in her special day class for students with significant disabilities.

One positive aspect of Marci's inclusion was the relationship she developed with her best friend. Heather shared several classes with Marci and immediately took an interest in her well-being. After several weeks of school had passed, Heather began walking home from school with Marci and Marci's mother and learned more about Marci's physical and medical needs. Soon Heather began calling and asking to come over and take Marci with her on long walks through the park and the neighborhood. When Heather and her family went on a ski trip during winter break, Heather sent Marci a postcard nearly every day. When Heather was asked why she considered Marci her friend she said, "At first I liked to be around Marci because it made me feel important and helpful, and I thought she had a beautiful smile. Then I just started talking to her and sort of never stopped. I tell her all of my secrets and my fears and my dreams. She never judges me or tells my secrets…she can't tell my secrets! I really need her right now, she balances me and makes me feel peaceful."

In order to support the development of friendships, it is helpful for families to get involved and include classmates and potential friends in the home life of their children. One parent recalled the first time they had a birthday party at their home with their child's typical peers: "The kids were so surprised that Jose had a bedroom with Power Ranger posters and a swingset in the backyard!" It is helpful for peers to see that, although a child has disabilities, he or she is part of a family and lives a life not all that different from their own. In addition, some families have found that inviting one or both of a classmate's parents over for coffee or lunch while the children play together or socialize increased the likelihood that their child will, in turn, be invited over to the friend's house. Once a typical peer's parents learn about the child's interests, interaction style, and physical or behavioral needs, they become more comfortable in supporting the children's relationship too and include the child with disabilities in their family activities.

Creating an Awareness of Friendship and Respect for Diversity

When physical proximity has been achieved and social interactions facilitated, it may be helpful to promote an awareness of the importance of friendships for all students.

Often, friendship seems such a natural thing that people do not step outside of their daily interactions and consider the value of friendship from a broader perspective. To encourage an awareness and appreciation of friendship, one sixth-grade class (including a student with significant disabilities) developed a unit on friendship. One of their exercises was to determine the meaning of friendship. Bishop and Jubala (1994) reported the following student statements:

I think friendship is having fun together and talking about our problems together. I also think friendship is sharing our special possessions and fun places we've been. Friendship is going places together.

Friendship means people who are there for you whenever you need them. There to cheer you up when you're down and to help you out when needed.

Friendship to me means having a person who's considerate and caring. Someone who has both the same and different interests as you.

Friendship means to be loyal and to feel sympathetic toward your friend. In order to be a true friend you have to build up a lasting relationship and don't rush it.

It is hanging out with each other at school or at home and just plain being nice to each other and once in awhile arguing but mostly being friends and helping each other when it's needed.

In my opinion, in this world most people all need at least one friend to survive today.

A friendship is the best thing out of all others that you could ever achieve in your whole entire lifetime. (p. 38)

The classroom teacher noticed that, by talking about friendships and belonging, the students in her class began to look out for each other and to be more supportive of peers who had previously been left alone during lunch and recess.

Several high schools have encouraged the establishment of friendship clubs, which allow students the opportunity to meet different people and to acknowledge in a safe atmosphere that they are interested in having someone to eat with, go to games and movies with, and call on the telephone. Students who are new to a school, who are shy and uncomfortable initiating interactions, who were teased at an earlier age, or who just want more support than they are getting are able to take advantage of relationship possibilities in a nonthreatening environment.

Other strategies described in detail in Chapter 5, such as the Making Action Plans (MAPs) (Falvey, Forest, Pearpoint, & Rosenberg, 1994) (formerly McGill Action Planning System [Lusthaus & Forest, 1987]), and circles of friends (Forest & Lusthaus, 1989), can be used not only to enhance the awareness of an individual's need for friends and support, but also to create specific plans for developing new friendships. As noted in Chapter 5, in a circle of friends, students represent the relationships in their lives by placing people in a series of concentric circles. By reviewing these circles and discussing the results, students analyze the pattern of their friendships and those of others (Sherwood, 1990).

In the MAPs process, a group of peers and people significant in a student's life are brought together to discuss who the student is as a person, his or her hopes, dreams, fears, immediate needs, and future goals. The participants develop suggestions for solving a current problem or for progressing toward a goal and then take responsibility for specific actions that will make a difference in the life of that individual. Two case examples follow that illustrate the application of these strategies.

Lauren Lauren, a high school student, was devastated because her parents would not allow her to attend after-school functions with her boyfriend because they considered her too young to date. As a solution, her support circle decided that none of them would have dates for school functions. The girls would travel together, arriving and departing in one car, and the boys would travel in another car. This solution was helpful not only in this situation, but throughout the year because when someone in the group did not have an official date for an event, he or she was always included as part of the group.

Kristen and Garret In another situation, Kristen and Garret, two students with disabilities, got into trouble with teachers at their middle school for their public displays of affection with each other. The peers at their support meeting decided that what they were doing was not any different from what other students were doing on the campus; the problem was when and where they were doing it. These supportive peers took it upon themselves to provide helpful hints to the young couple and to keep an eye out for them at school. The relationships established during the problem-solving sessions eventually led to invitations to attend parties, to watch TV at each other's homes, and to hang out during schoolday breaks.

Care must be taken so that friendship building and awareness activities do not inadvertently make the student with a disability stand out or be treated in any way that diminishes his or her dignity. It is possible that these strategies can mistakenly be used to highlight a person's disabilities and promote an artificial "be nice to the handicapped" mentality (Van der Klift & Kunc, 1994). Emphasis should be placed on the premise that all students benefit from a circle of support and the knowledge that there are caring people surrounding them in their lives who are willing to be involved and who can make a difference.

In order to develop an awareness of friendship needs and possibilities, it is necessary to create a caring classroom community and an appreciation of diversity. Gibbs (1987) outlined a "Tribes" process for providing students with a lasting sense of classroom membership and respect for peers. The Tribes process is a synthesis of theories and methods that

1. Places students in long-term support groups;
2. Builds inclusion and trust within the groups prior to working on tasks;
3. Sets aside time to reflect upon individual and group learning experiences;
4. Has a set of protective "norms" (groundrules) that assure a safe positive climate;
5. Transfers responsibility from the teacher to students to help maintain the learning environment, solve problems, and be accountable for completion of tasks; emphasizes teacher and peer role modeling to teach interpersonal skills and caring behaviors;
6. Focuses on children's social development to enhance academic achievement; and
7. Promotes a respect for and acceptance of individual differences.... (Gibbs, 1987, p. 22)

Tribes and other strategies for implementing supportive classroom environments (Jubala et al., 1995) are essential for ensuring a sense of value and belonging in each student. Without a sense of belonging, it is difficult to have the self-esteem necessary to establish a genuine friendship (Kunc, 1992).

Give it Time; Friendships Cannot Be Forced

Mai   Mai's fifth-grade teacher was concerned about her success in school. Mai was making progress on her IEP objectives and was an active participant in class activities. However, Mai was not developing friendships with her peers as successfully as her mother and teacher had hoped. Other students with disabilities whom the teacher had taught in the past had developed friendships easily with little adult intervention. In an effort to encourage friendships for Mai, the teacher asked a few of the students to consider starting a friendship play group at recess that included Mai. One student wrote the teacher a response that politely declined; she had enough friends and was happy with the things she did at recess, but maybe at another time she might be interested.

Although the teacher's efforts to directly facilitate friendships were thwarted for the most part, Mai, in time, established an important relationship on her own. Her friendship with Holly didn't develop until the spring of that year, but the two have already been best friends for 1½ years at this writing, which is close to a record for 11-year-old girls! When Holly was asked about her friendship with Mai, she said, "We're just friends, she comes to my house, I go to her house, we're friends. We talk about school and boys and stuff and she makes me laugh. Usually we do what I want to do. It's no big deal, we're just friends." The friendship between Holly and Mai developed not by any special activity or directed process—it evolved over time. By sharing experiences, by having opportunities to interact day after day, week after week in a natural fashion, this relationship grew—it could not be forced, it could not be rushed.

Sarah   Relationships may grow from acquaintances to friendships with proximity and opportunity, but they also need a certain amount of chemistry to develop fully. Joachim was given plenty of opportunities to develop a friendship with Sarah, a girl with disabilities, who sat by him in his fourth-grade class. When asked if Sarah was his friend, Joachim thought carefully and responded, "She spits on my desk, she steals my pencils and eats the erasers, she makes funny noises...no, I would say Sarah is not my friend." However, Therese became friends with Sarah almost immediately. When asked about their friendship, Therese responded, "She makes funny noises that make me laugh, she's really good at jump rope, and she's nice to me. She's my friend, but sometimes people think I'm her babysitter because she is so short and I'm pretty tall—but I'm not. We're really friends. I don't think of her as someone with a disability, she's just Sarah."

Van der Klift and Kunc (1994) proposed that friendship is "one third proximity and two thirds alchemy" (p. 393). Indeed friendships, like marriages, cannot be forced, dictated by others, or randomly assigned. In some situations, friendships develop because two individuals have a great deal in common—for example, they are both sports fanatics or love the same mystery novelist. In other situations, friendships develop based on opposites—a person who is shy becomes friends with the class clown, a child who feels lost in the middle of a large family befriends an only child and spends most of her time in the calm atmosphere of that home. Although parents and educators cannot choose a child's friends, they can observe interactions and nurture the possibilities they present.

Helper–Helpee versus Reciprocal Friendships

Definitions of friendship vary nearly as much as the relationships that characterize them. Stainback and Stainback (1990) stated that friendships

> may range from simple, short-term events, such as saying hello in the hallway or one student helping another find his or her way to the cafeteria, or with a homework assignment during study hall, to more complex, long-term relationships where two or more students "hang out" together, socially interact, and freely help and assist each other inside and outside of school. (p. 52)

Grenot-Scheyer et al. (1989) defined friendship as "a bond between two individuals that is characterized by mutual preference for one another, a positive affective style, an ability to engage in social interactions, and to have interactions that last over a period of time" (p. 348). Clearly, there are a range of interactions that make up the continuum of friendship.

Concerns have been raised (Van der Klift & Kunc, 1994; Strully & Strully, 1989) that, although the opportunities for children with disabilities to have relationships with their typical peers have increased through inclusion, the relationships have often not become friendships. Van der Klift and Kunc (1994) expressed the concern that overuse of buddy systems, friendship circles, and peer pals can exacerbate the stereotyping of a student with a disability as needing help and the peers without disabilities relegated to the role of helpers. Van der Klift and Kunc stated:

> An overemphasis on the "helper-helpee" relationship can easily skew the delicate balance of giving and receiving that is the precursor of true friendship. It is critical, therefore, to examine regularly and carefully the nature of the interaction we facilitate and the attitudes that inform it. (p. 392)

Opportunities for a range of friendships and social interactions are a valued part of all of our lives. When a new student enters a school or classroom, teachers can be supportive by assigning a welcoming committee to show the student around and help him or her become familiar with the campus and connected with others in the environment. Tutoring groups can help any student who is struggling with academics, and peer counseling teams allow students to support each other in ways in which adult support would be less effective. However, students whose primary social interactions are restricted to such generic assistance programs may lack opportunities to experience the depth of a reciprocal relationship that is the basis for a genuine friendship.

In contemporary society, a healthy, well-rounded individual may be considered to be someone who is able to both give and receive help as necessary for continued growth and self-esteem. The ability to perceive oneself as both the helper and helpee in any friendship is valuable to the maintenance and growth of that relationship. Too often, people with disabilities are presumed to be able to participate in relationships only as the helpee, which is detrimental to the depth and longevity of the relationship. It is important to realize that "helping" comes in many forms and does not require specific skills or abilities. Students with disabilities have much to share and to benefit from in the role of helper.

Rashaan   Paul was initially introduced to Rashaan when he was hired as Rashaan's personal assistant and job coach. Over time, a genuine friendship grew between the two young men and continued after Paul moved on to begin a new career. When talking about Rashaan, Paul reflected:

> Our friendship doesn't seem extraordinary to me. Rashaan is a great listener and even though he is not verbal he is very sympathetic and empathetic. I can just tell by watching his body and facial expressions that he understands me. I could always tell what he was feeling too, it's hard to explain if you don't know Rashaan, but he has a tremendous capacity for emotion. It's neat because he gives me the opportunity to be a really good friend to him and some of my other friends don't let me be there for them in that way.

Jaime   Jaime's three best friends in fifth grade were asked to comment on what they learned from being his friend. The following responses reflect the reciprocity of their relationships:

> He makes me feel good when I am sad, and when I get mad he slows me down. I helped Jaime run a 7:15 in the mile run, and I won't forget that ever.
> I learned that he could fit in with everyone in the school and he wanted to be friends and he is my friend. Being friends with Jaime has its advantages. He is very nice, considerate, kind, polite, and my favorite, a cool kid.
> I learned what a real friend would be like. He is truly a good friend. I learned that a friend has to be kind and I learned that from Jaime.
> When Jaime was asked to talk about his friends, he replied, "I have three friends, Zach, Jose, and Mark, one, two, three. I like my friends. I like to tease and run and play." (Bishop & Jubala, 1994, p. 39)

Parents and educators who attempt to facilitate and support potential friendships and meaningful relationships between students must consider and nurture opportunities for reciprocity. It may not be readily apparent in any given relationship what form that reciprocity should take, but, over time, the participants will be able to articulate the factors that create the bonds in a genuine friendship.

Teach the Skills that Support Interactions

Students with and without disabilities may benefit from specific skill instruction in behaviors that can enhance the development of friendships and social interactions. As mentioned previously, it is not a prerequisite that students have any or all of such skills in order to be involved in a friendship, but awareness of, exposure to, and mastery of these skills may encourage a greater number of friendships or enhance the quality of existing friendships. Stainback and Stainback (1990) identified and described the following categories of behaviors and skills that may be of value in building and maintaining friendships.

Positive Interaction Style   An interaction style that promotes a positive attitude and an appreciation of others is an asset to any relationship. Teaching students to be active listeners, to give positive feedback, to ask questions, and to respond to the needs of others can be a step toward greater peer acceptance.

Establishing Areas of Compatibility   Introducing students to peers who have interests or experiences in common is a way to foster a potential friendship. In addition, teaching a student how to ask questions of peers about hobbies, interests, talents, experiences, and beliefs as well as how to acknowledge and share their own enables students to initiate relationships on their own. Asking specific questions of others and being able to respond to questions with more than yes or no help enhance the likelihood of establishing areas of compatibility. Students who use augmentative communication systems need individual accommodations to indicate the range of interests they wish to ask about or share with others.

Taking the Perspective of Others   Considering the needs, feelings, and interests of a variety of people helps students to be appreciated as friends. Learning to compromise on activity choices, listening to the ideas and needs of others, and putting themselves in the position of another can enhance relationships. Learning to interact with tact and sensitivity as well as the ability to "read" a social situation are skills helpful in establishing positive friendships.

Sharing and Providing Support   Learning to share belongings, ideas, and feelings and providing comfort, help, and support to others are also components of friendships. Again, students of all abilities and backgrounds benefit from the role of helper and supporter and can be shortchanged if always relegated to the role of needing help.

Trustworthiness and Loyalty   An individual's ethical and moral character often determines the depth of his or her relationships. A student can prove worthy of a peer's trust as they learn to keep a friend's secrets and not break promises. Standing up for a friend in a difficult situation and supporting his or her rights upholds the integrity of the individual. In young students, trustworthiness and loyalty are frequently tested, and loyalties shift often. Teaching students to value themselves and to appreciate their own character can help in times of shifting allegiances.

Conflict Resolution   The ability of students to resolve their own conflicts and support their peers in doing so has gained wide attention in the literature (Drew, 1987; Kreidler, 1984; Prutzman, Stern, Burger, & Bodenhammer, 1988). Interactions that occur during appropriate student–student conflict resolution provide a safe way to air grievances, feelings, and differences of opinion (Jubala et al., 1995). Skills learned through these practices can generalize to situations encountered throughout life.

Teaching Friendship Skills   Friendship skills can be taught in the classroom and reinforced at home in the same ways that other areas of the curriculum are addressed. Providing students with specific examples to analyze and discuss is one way of introducing some of the concepts related to social interactions and relationships. Role playing, coaching, and small-group discussions also aid social skill development and awareness. Community circles provide a format for whole-class discussions of particular incidents and help students learn the perspectives of their peers and gain strategies for solving problems in the future (Gibbs, 1987; Jubala et al., 1995). Perhaps the most effective strategy for teaching specific skills is to provide the student with support and feedback during actual situations. Giving students information and suggestions in a specific situation allows them to practice their skills. For example, the fifth-grade class has an important test scheduled first thing in the morning. It is helpful to tell Angel (a student with significant disabilities) before she walks into the classroom that the students are all very anxious about a big test and to help her to enter the room quietly. Angel can offer to sharpen pencils, which may prevent her from upsetting her classmates by running in and showing everyone her new toy. Encouraging students to think first and to consult their peers when they are struggling supports the students in becoming better decision makers. Also, teaching students to provide honest, helpful feedback to each other (e.g., "It hurt my feelings when you teased me about my shoes at lunch") encourages open communication and provides concrete feedback that is necessary for behavior change and growth in the area of social competence.

Get Out of the Way

The well-intended efforts of adults to facilitate friendships for their children and students can backfire if not carefully chosen and executed. How many young people have been forced on blind dates with Aunt Sally's best friend's son or daughter or as a child endured miserable playtime or lunch get-togethers with a parent's boss's obnoxious child? Such efforts can be interpreted as intrusive and unwanted even if arranged with the best intentions. As mentioned earlier, relationships cannot be forced, and the more artificially arranged the opportunities for interactions are, the less likely they will be met with an open mind and positive attitude. Subtlety paired with natural opportunities provides an atmosphere that is more likely to facilitate genuine friendships and positive interactions.

A challenge specific to facilitating friendships for students with disabilities is the entourage of adults who are often involved in the student's support system in the general education classroom. General education teachers often report difficulty in assuming responsibility for a student in their classroom when special education classroom aides or support personnel are constantly hovering over the student. Similarly, peers are hampered in their efforts to initiate interactions when it appears as if these "professional adults" are the only ones allowed to interact with the student. Children can be easily intimidated by adults with whom they are not familiar, and they may not make the effort to initiate interactions with a child surrounded by so many different adults. Even one-to-one aides can significantly interfere with a student's opportunities to develop relationships.

One suggestion to counter this is that the adults in a student's life support relationship development by modeling interactions, by helping to establish common interests and similarities, and by creating opportunities for student–student interactions without interference. Students who need full-time support can be helped when their aides position them for an activity and then move to a respectful distance and read or write (and not listen to the student's conversations) while still monitoring the students' needs. Classroom aides can also create situations that allow a greater amount of active participation by a student with a disability. After setting up the activity and teaching all of the students how to participate and allow each other to participate, the aide can move to another area of the room, gym, playground, or field and let the activity be enjoyed with all of the jokes, banter, and silliness that accompanies play that is not directed and supervised by an adult.

Students benefit from being trusted by adults and from assuming responsibility in many areas. Although a peer may not be skilled in helping a student with physical disabilities eat his or her lunch, the peer may well be able to hold an ice cream cone for the student to lick. Providing peers with skills that enable them to be comfortable and competent with a student's physical and communication devices can enhance the depth of the relationship. This is not to say that peers should be placed in caregiver roles but that they should be encouraged to interact in a variety of settings with as little adult assistance as is reasonable considering the age, needs, and skills of the students. For example, elementary school students may learn to safely manipulate a peer's wheelchair around the campus and neighborhood or to program a communication device so that they can discuss the baseball game on the weekend. High school students may learn to empty a peer's catheter bag so that they can go to the mall together or to help a peer calm down if the environment is too stimulating.

Essentially, adults' responsibilities in facilitating friendships are necessary but tenuous. Adults are required to interpret situations and intuit possibilities for friendships between students. Adult facilitators serve as models through friendships in their own lives and promote the values of all individuals. It is necessary for parents and educators to teach, facilitate, support, and nurture friendships and to get out of the way as friendships both stumble and flourish. Attempts at facilitating friendships can at times be frustrating or discouraging, but, when successful, the results provide incomparable rewards for both students and adults.

CONCLUSION

Friendships are treasured by children and adults throughout the world. Most people cannot imagine a life without the support, nurturance, and good times experienced with their closest friends. Although easily taken for granted, the importance of friendship is clearest to those who lack such relationships in their lives. The education of students with and without disabilities in shared environments has brought the need for meaningful relationships to the forefront. When strategies such as those discussed throughout this chapter are implemented, the benefits for all students are increased. Parents, educators, community members, and students themselves share the responsibility for reaching out to others, valuing and appreciating diversity in our peers, and supporting the rights of our neighbors. Friendship encompasses the casual greetings exchanged while passing on street corners and school hallways as well as the intimate sharing of hopes and fears. The experience of friendship can be extended to everyone in a school, neighborhood, and community as people work together to create opportunities for understanding, supporting, and enjoying others for who they are and what they are willing to give and receive.

REFERENCES

Asher, S., & Gottman, J. (Eds.). (1981). *The development of children's friendships.* Cambridge, MA: Harvard University Press.

Barber, D., & Hupp, S.C. (1993). A comparison of friendship patterns of individuals with developmental disabilities. *Education and Training in Mental Retardation, 28*(1), 13–21.

Bishop, K.D., & Jubala, K.A. (1994). By June, given shared experiences, integrated classes, and equal opportunities, Jaime will have a friend. *Teaching Exceptional Children, 27*(1), 36–47.

Drew, N. (1987). *Learning the skills of peacemaking.* Rolling Hills Estates, CA: Jalmar Press.

Falvey, M.A., Forest, M., Pearpoint, J., & Rosenberg, R.L. (1994). Building connections. In J.S. Thousand, R.A. Villa, & A.I. Nevin (Eds.), *Creativity and collaborative learning: A practical guide to empowering students and teachers* (pp. 347–368). Baltimore: Paul H. Brookes Publishing Co.

Forest, M., & Lusthaus, E. (1989). Promoting educational equality for all students: Circles and maps. In S. Stainback, W. Stainback, & M. Forest (Eds.), *Educating all students in the mainstream of regular education* (pp. 43–57). Baltimore: Paul H. Brookes Publishing Co.

Gibbs, J. (1987). *Tribes: A process for social development and cooperative learning.* Santa Rosa, CA: Center Source Publications.

Grenot-Scheyer, M. (1994). The nature of interactions between students with severe disabilities and nondisabled friends and acquaintances. *Journal of The Association for Persons with Severe Handicaps, 19,* 253–262.

Grenot-Scheyer, M., Coots, J., & Falvey, M. (1989). Developing and fostering friendships. In M. Falvey, *Community-based curriculum: Instructional strategies for students with severe handicaps* (pp. 345–358). Baltimore: Paul H. Brookes Publishing Co.

Hamre-Nietupski, S., Shokoohi-Yekta, M., Hendrickson, J., & Nietupski, J. (1994). Regular educators' perceptions of facilitating friendships of students with moderate, severe, or profound disabilities with nondisabled peers. *Education and Training in Mental Retardation and Developmental Disabilities, 29*(2), 102–117.

Johnson, D.W., & Johnson, R.T. (1989). *Cooperation and competition: Theory and research.* Edina, MN: Interaction Books.

Jubala, K.A., Bishop, K.D., & Falvey, M.A. (1995). Creating a supportive classroom environment. In M. Falvey (Ed.), *Inclusive and heterogeneous schooling: Assessment, curriculum, and instruction* (pp. 111–129). Baltimore: Paul H. Brookes Publishing Co.

Kreidler, W.J. (1984). *Creative conflict resolution.* Springfield, IL: Scott, Foresman and Co.

Kunc, N. (1992). The need to belong: Rediscovering Maslow's hierarchy of needs. In R.A. Villa, J.S. Thousand, W. Stainback, & S. Stainback (Eds.), *Restructuring for caring and effective education: An administrative guide to creating heterogeneous schools* (pp. 25–40). Baltimore: Paul H. Brookes Publishing Co.

Lusthaus, E., & Forest, M. (1987). The kaleidoscope: A challenge to the cascade. In M. Forest (Ed.), *More education integration* (pp. 1–17). Downsview, Ontario: G. Allan Roeher Institute.

Prutzman, P., Stern, L., Burger, M., & Bodenhammer, G. (1988). *The friendly classroom for a small planet.* Philadelphia: New Society Publishers.

Putnam, J.W. (Ed.). (1993). *Cooperative learning and strategies for inclusion: Celebrating diversity in the classroom.* Baltimore: Paul H. Brookes Publishing Co.

Sherwood, S.K. (1990). A circle of friends in a first grade classroom. *Educational Leadership, 48*(3), 41.

Stainback, W., & Stainback, S. (1990). Facilitating peer support and friendships. In W. Stainback & S. Stainback (Eds.), *Support networks for inclusive schooling: Interdependent integrated education* (pp. 51–63). Baltimore: Paul H. Brookes Publishing Co.

Strain, P.S. (1984). Social interactions of handicapped preschoolers. In T. Field, J. Roopnarine, & M. Segal (Eds.), *Friendships in normal and handicapped children* (pp. 187–207). Norwood, NJ: Ablex.

Strully, J.L., & Strully, C.F. (1989). Friendship as an educational goal. In S. Stainback, W. Stainback, & M. Forest (Eds.), *Educating all students in the mainstream of regular education* (pp. 59–70). Baltimore: Paul H. Brookes Publishing Co.

Taylor, S.J., Biklen, D., & Knoll, J. (Eds.). (1987). *Community integration for people with severe disabilities.* New York: Teachers College Press.

Thousand, J.S., Villa, R.A., & Nevin, A.I. (Eds.). (1994). *Creativity and collaborative learning: A practical guide to empowering students and teachers.* Baltimore: Paul H. Brookes Publishing Co.

Van der Klift, E., & Kunc, N. (1994). Beyond benevolence: Friendship and the politics of help. In J.S. Thousand, R.A. Villa, & A.I. Nevin (Eds.), *Creativity and collaborative learning: A practical guide to empowering students and teachers* (pp. 391–401). Baltimore: Paul H. Brookes Publishing Co.

11

Student Collaboration

An Essential for Curriculum Delivery in the 21st Century

Richard A. Villa and Jacqueline S. Thousand

Many of our most critical problems are not in the world of things, but in the world of people. Our greatest failure as human beings has been the inability to secure cooperation and understanding with others. (Hersey & Blanchard, 1977, p. 1)

THE HISTORY OF collaboration among educators in North American schools in the development, delivery, and modification of the curriculum and instruction has been relatively short. Emerging in the 1960s in the form of team-teaching arrangements (Bair & Woodward, 1964; Beggs, 1964) and evolving and expanding in the 1970s and 1980s to consultation and special education prereferral approaches, such as child study teams (Graden, Casey, & Christenson, 1985), teacher assistant teams (Chalfant, Psych, & Moultrie, 1979), consulting teacher systems (Knight, Meyers, Paolucci-Whitcomb, Hasazi, & Nevin, 1981), and collaborative consultation approaches (Idol, Nevin, & Paolucci-Whitcomb, 1992; Nevin, Thousand, Paolucci-Whitcomb, & Villa, 1990; Tharp, 1975), collaboration has become a buzzword in futurist conceptualizations of the effective 21st century school (Benjamin, 1989).

Although collaboration is not yet the norm in North American schools, it is generally thought of as adults (professional educators) sharing the planning, teaching, and/or

Portions of what is presented in this chapter are based on material previously published in Villa, R., & Thousand, J. (1992). Student collaboration: An essential for curriculum delivery in the 21st century. In S. Stainback & W. Stainback (Eds.), *Curriculum considerations in inclusive classrooms: Facilitating learning for all students* (pp. 117–142). Baltimore: Paul H. Brookes Publishing Co.

171

evaluation responsibilities for students. The purpose of this chapter is to examine forms of school collaboration that use the resources of students in determining and delivering the school community's curriculum. For example, there have been calls for the inclusion and empowerment of students in decision-making processes regarding discipline (Curwin & Mendler, 1988) and the delivery of instruction and social support to peers (Glasser, 1990; Johnson, Johnson, & Holubec, 1994; Thousand, Villa, & Nevin, 1994). The recognized benefits of and rationale for greater involvement of students in the determination of the form and content of their own education include enhanced motivation (Glasser, 1990; Johnson & Johnson, 1987b) and achievement (Johnson & Johnson, 1989).

The most powerful arguments for enhanced student collaboration, however, are concerned less with traditional notions of (tested) performance and motivation than with the development of information-seeking and problem-solving citizens who will be able to thrive in the complex, diverse, information-rich, and technologically driven 21st century. Education futurists observe interdependent, international societal trends that make it increasingly difficult for school curricula to keep pace with the exponential growth of information and technological and scientific discoveries. "There is simply too much for any one of us to know, never mind teach to dozens of students in a crowded day. Such a tragic fact leads to a liberating realization: wisdom matters more than knowledge" (Wiggins, 1989, p. 58).

Wisdom, in the futurist's eye, includes "habits of mind" (Wiggins, 1989, p. 48), such as the ability to suspend disbelief, to listen to someone who knows something "new," and to question in order to clarify an idea's meaning or value; openness to new and strange ideas; and the inclination to question confusing or "pat" statements. Wisdom involves having strategies for coping with diversity and for being a lifelong learner; it means having the social competence to communicate and interact with others, including people in international democratic workplaces.

How, then, do futurists see schools operating in the 21st century so that graduates have acquired wisdom? In the educational futurist literature, the most frequently occurring recommendation for 21st-century schools is to increase active learning on the part of the student. Active learning involves students participating in all aspects of the learning process. Active learning also means empowering students to determine what and how they will learn. Given the projected information explosion of the next century, futurists also recommend that schools concentrate on teaching students how to be lifelong learners rather than only learners of facts. Additionally, futurists consider the school responsible for helping students to extend their concerns beyond themselves and to gain a community service ethic through real-life service experiences and in-school analyses of the experiences.

The future world suggests "a new collaborative role for teachers and students in which students accept an active senior partnership role in the learning enterprise" (Benjamin, 1989, p. 9). Therefore, teachers in 21st-century schools must become familiar with existing methods and be encouraged to experiment with strategies for actively engaging students in their own and others' acquisition of humanistic public service ethics; communication, information-seeking, and problem-solving skills; and the core curriculum deemed essential by the school and greater community.

This chapter describes a number of collaborative arrangements and strategies that engage students in instructional and advocacy roles for and with their peers with and without disabilities and in decision-making roles that determine the school's curriculum, organization, and governance. However, before examining these strategies, the reader should reflect on his or her personal experiences as a student and assess the extent to which those experiences exemplified or incorporated a collaborative spirit by responding to the questions in the Student Collaboration Quiz, presented in Figure 1.

After reading the remainder of this chapter, the reader should envision him- or herself as a student enrolled in a school that uses the recommended peer empowerment strategies and then, retaking the quiz, find dramatic positive shifts in collaboration scores. In addition, this chapter should enable readers to further explore and implement some of the discussed student collaboration strategies in community schools so that future high school graduates who take this same quiz not only give themselves and their schools high scores but also are able to articulate what life is like in the 21st century and how their schooling has prepared them for this life.

The authors have grouped the *peer power* (student collaboration) strategies discussed in this chapter into three categories. These are strategies that involve students as 1) members of the instructional team, 2) advocates for themselves and their peers, and 3) decision makers.

STUDENTS AS MEMBERS OF THE INSTRUCTIONAL TEAM

Teaching Teams

Teaching teams are a promising instructional arrangement for providing intensive services to students; they are based on the assumption that all students can be educated effectively in the same school and classroom structures.

> A teaching team is an organizational and instructional arrangement of two or more members of the school and greater community who distribute among themselves planning, instructional, and evaluation responsibilities for the same students on a regular basis for an extended period of time. Teams can vary in size from two to six or seven people. They can vary in composition as well, involving any possible combination of classroom teachers, specialized personnel (e.g., special educators, speech and language pathologists, guidance counselors, health professionals, employment specialists), instructional assistants, student teachers, community volunteers (e.g., parents, members of the local "foster grandparent" program), *and students themselves* [emphasis added]. (Thousand & Villa, 1990, pp. 152–153)

Teaching teams enable any student to receive intensive instructional support within the classroom, thereby eliminating the need for a separate special education system and a referral process for gaining access to that system. Teaching teams take advantage of the diverse knowledge and instructional approaches of the team members as well as of a higher instructor/learner ratio, which allows for more immediate and accurate diagnosis of student needs and for more active student learning.

1. Did you as a student observe or experience your teachers modeling collaboration in instruction (e.g., team teaching), planning, or evaluation?

   Never   Rarely   Sometimes   Often   Very often

2. Were you as a student given the opportunity and training to serve as an instructor for a peer?

   Never   Rarely   Sometimes   Often   Very often

3. Were you as a student given the opportunity to receive instruction from a trained peer?

   Never   Rarely   Sometimes   Often   Very often

4. How often was the instruction you received structured in such a way as to encourage the use of higher-level reasoning skills (e.g., analysis, synthesis, evaluation, creative problem solving, meta-cognition)?

   Never   Rarely   Sometimes   Often   Very often

5. How often were you expected to support the academic and social learning of other students as well as be accountable for your own learning?

   Never   Rarely   Sometimes   Often   Very often

6. Were you as a student given the opportunity and training to serve as a mediator of conflict between peers?

   Never   Rarely   Sometimes   Often   Very often

7. How often were you asked to evaluate your own learning?

   Never   Rarely   Sometimes   Often   Very often

8. How often were you given the opportunity to assist in determining the educational outcomes for you and your classmates?

   Never   Rarely   Sometimes   Often   Very often

9. How often were you given the opportunity to advocate for the educational interests of a classmate or asked to assist in determining modifications and accommodations to the curriculum?

   Never   Rarely   Sometimes   Often   Very often

10. How often were you as a student encouraged to bring a support person to a difficult meeting to provide you with moral support?

    Never   Rarely   Sometimes   Often   Very often

11. How often were you involved in a discussion of the teaching act with an instructor?

    Never   Rarely   Sometimes   Often   Very often

12. How often were you asked to provide your teachers with feedback as to the effectiveness and appropriateness of their instruction and classroom management?

    Never   Rarely   Sometimes   Often   Very often

13. How often did you participate as an equal with teachers, administrators, and community members on school committees (e.g., curriculum committee, discipline committee, hiring committee, school board)?

    Never   Rarely   Sometimes   Often   Very often

14. How often did you as a student feel that the school "belonged" to you, that school experiences were structured primarily with student interests in mind?

    Never   Rarely   Sometimes   Often   Very often

Figure 1.   Student Collaboration Quiz.

Partner Learning or Peer Tutor Systems

Same-age and cross-age partner learning systems can be established within a single classroom, across classrooms, or across an entire school. The benefits of students receiving instruction from peers are well documented (Harper, Maheady, & Mallette, 1994; Topping, 1988) and include significant academic gains, the development of positive social interaction skills with other students, and heightened self-esteem. Tutors also benefit from this instructional relationship; they receive training and coaching in the effective communication skills they are to use in tutorial sessions (e.g., giving praise and corrective feedback). By assuming the status of teacher, the tutor's own self-esteem may be enhanced (Gartner, Kohler, & Riessman, 1971). Also, the preparation for effective teaching requires the use of higher-level thinking skills (e.g., synthesis, task or concept analysis) and promotes a deeper understanding of the curricular content being taught (Johnson, Johnson, & Holubec, 1994).

Teachers who are most effective in collaborating with students in peer tutoring arrangements have well-organized strategies for recruiting, training, supervising, and evaluating the effectiveness of the peer tutors. Readers may refer to Harper et al. (1994), LaPlant and Zane (1994), McNeill (1994), and Topping (1988) for models and suggestions for organizing same-age and cross-age tutor systems that add instructional resources to the classroom without additional adult personnel.

Formalized schoolwide peer tutoring systems cannot be organized overnight. Teachers unaccustomed to or skeptical of tutoring arrangements need to become familiar with the research and the strategies for establishing such systems, directly observe successful partner learning relationships, and have access to technical assistance in initiating and supervising peer tutor programs.

Example: Evolution of a Peer Tutoring System in an Elementary School Over a 3-year period in the late 1980s and early 1990s in the Winooski, Vermont, elementary school, the informal use of several peer tutors in three classes evolved into a formalized training and supervision program involving more than 80% of the student body as tutors and tutees in 18 of 21 classrooms. This occurred as a result of the faculty setting as a priority the establishment of peer power strategies such as peer tutor systems and cooperative learning groups in order to strengthen the in-class model of delivering special services as well as collaboration among general and special education personnel.

In the first year, three teachers took the first step by using cross-age peer tutors who were recruited from the junior high school and trained and supervised by the classroom teachers. In the following year, this cross-age peer tutoring arrangement continued. In addition, a fourth-grade teacher and one of her collaborating support staff established a peer tutoring system in the class that involved all of the students as tutors and tutees. Within a few months, a first-grade teacher requested that the fourth-grade tutors become cross-age tutors in her classroom. Aware of the potential benefits to her students (e.g., enhanced self-esteem, practice with higher level thinking skills, content mastery), the fourth-grade teacher arranged for seven tutors to provide math review to ·

the first graders for 30 minutes every other Friday. Each tutor worked with three or four first graders, allowing all students in the class to receive tutorial instruction. The specialized support person, who worked in both classes, trained and monitored the tutors in the procedures of instruction and correction. This support was phased out over a 2-month period, and supervisory responsibilities were shifted to the first-grade teacher, although the support person continued to conduct brief pre- and postinstructional conferences with tutors, tutees, and the teacher. Tutors eventually became responsible for creating their own instructional materials.

At the end of the school year, a number of the fourth-grade tutors approached their assigned fifth-grade teachers, requesting reassurance that they would be able to continue their tutoring roles. Furthermore, one tutor presented the benefits of the tutoring experiences at a summer leadership course that focused on integration strategies and included 10 of the elementary school staff. Finally, job descriptions for all teachers were changed to include shared responsibility for training, supervising, and evaluating peer tutors.

In the third year, the established same-age and cross-age tutoring programs continued. In addition, a system was put in place for negotiating a contract with each tutor and for gaining permission from parents and sharing information about tutoring with them. By the third year, as mentioned, over 80% of the elementary school students were involved in this tutoring program, with four dozen fourth- and fifth-grade tutors teaching in first-, second-, and third-grade classrooms every other week. On the alternate weeks, tutors engaged in an intensive training session, during which specific instructional procedures and behavior management and communication skills were modeled and coached.

An important feature of this program was that many of the students who served as tutors had special needs of their own that teachers believe were helped through the tutoring experience (e.g., high-achieving students in need of experiences that require creative problem solving; students eligible for special education; students identified as withdrawn, shy, or having low self-esteem; students needing incentives and contingencies, such as the opportunity to teach, to motivate work completion). Tutors with their own areas of academic challenges may tutor younger students in those same academic areas, thus enabling them to experience success in the esteemed teacher role while simultaneously addressing individualized education program (IEP) objectives and practicing basic skills in nonstrength areas.

A second important feature was that classroom teachers could be periodically relieved by tutors so that they could observe their students performing in other contexts. It is considered particularly important for teachers to see students who pose academic or behavioral challenges in their own classrooms performing successfully and exhibiting responsible and appropriate social behavior elsewhere.

Example: Peer Tutoring Roles for Learners Experiencing Behavioral Challenges Serving as tutors has had a powerful positive impact on learners identified as having emotional and behavior difficulties. For example, a sixth grader in one

Vermont middle school served as a cross-age tutor the last 45 minutes of the school day. His tutoring is contingent upon appropriate behavior as outlined in his behavior contract. Although this young man still presented intensely challenging behavior to his own teachers and peers, he was described as a model of appropriate behavior and a valuable instructional asset by the second-grade teacher who was responsible for his training and supervision as a tutor in her classroom (M. Steady, personal communication, January 2, 1990). A Christmas story illuminates the importance of this collaborative relationship to this student. The week before the Christmas break, the sixth-grader chose to forego his own class party to attend the second-grade class celebration; he presented individual presents to each student in the class and a large stuffed teddy bear to the teacher.

In the same school district, a fourth-grade student described as hyperactive was placed in a tutoring role to help her identify and moderate her own inattentive and rule-violating behaviors. Following each of her tutoring sessions with second-grade students, she was "debriefed" and asked to analyze the effectiveness of the instructional and behavior management strategies she used. Emphasis was placed upon the discussion of behaviors exhibited by her tutees that interfered with their learning and management. Analogies were drawn with regard to the tutor's own behaviors, their effects upon her learning, and strategies for effectively moderating the behaviors.

Cooperative Group Learning Systems

Cooperative group learning systems are the most researched of instructional strategies that allow for and promote heterogeneous student grouping (Davidson, 1994; Johnson & Johnson, 1987b; Johnson & Johnson, 1994; Slavin, 1984, 1989). In this learning structure, students are responsible not only for their own learning, but also for the learning of the other members of their group. They are also responsible for exhibiting certain prosocial behaviors with their peers. The role of the teacher who structures cooperative groups shifts from that of a presenter of information to a facilitator of learning. The five major jobs of the teacher in this student–teacher collaborative arrangement are to 1) clearly specify the objectives of the lesson, 2) make decisions about placing students in learning groups to ensure heterogeneity, 3) clearly explain what learning activities are expected of the students and how positive interdependence is to be demonstrated, 4) monitor the effectiveness of collaborative interactions and intervene to provide task assistance (e.g., answer questions or teach task-related skills) or to increase students' interpersonal and group skills, and 5) evaluate student achievement and group effectiveness (Johnson & Johnson, 1987a).

A major responsibility of the teacher in structuring cooperative groups is to adapt lesson requirements for individual students. This can be accomplished in numerous ways. Each group member may have different success criteria; the amount of material each group member is to learn may be adjusted; or group members may rehearse different math problems, spelling or vocabulary lists, or reading materials. If a test is given, all group members may receive a common grade based upon the extent to which members exceed their individual success criteria. (See Thousand, Villa, & Nevin, 1994, for sample cooperative group lesson plans, which contain adaptations that include and enhance the learning of students with disabilities.)

Example: A Cooperative Group Lesson Adapted for a Young Learner with Multiple Disabilities A group lesson that included Sarah, an 8-year-old girl with multiple disabilities, illustrates effective adaptation strategies. When this lesson took place, Sarah had been in her local school for 1 month and was integrated into the combined first- and second-grade classroom. Although Sarah occasionally vocalized loudly, she did not use vocal behavior to communicate. A major educational goal in developing an augmentative communication system was to assess and develop Sarah's use of various switches on communication devices such as tape recorders. Behavior goals were for Sarah to remain with a group throughout an activity, refrain from grabbing others' materials, and refrain from making loud vocalizations when in a group.

In this particular lesson, students were assigned to groups of five. All group members, including Sarah, were expected to sit in a circle, remain with the group throughout the activity, and keep their voices at a conversational level. Groups were first assigned the task of listening to an audiotape while following the illustrations and text in the original storybook. Members of each group were assigned specific jobs or roles to perform during the lesson. One job was to turn the pages of the storybook in coordination with the tape; another was to turn the tape recorder on and off. Sarah was assigned the latter role for her group. The role was adapted so that Sarah operated the tape recorder by pushing a switch that needed to be depressed continuously in order for the tape to play. Sarah received hand-on-hand assistance from one of the two teachers, as needed, to activate the switch.

This assignment not only gave Sarah a valuable and needed role in her group, but also addressed two of her IEP goals. First, it introduced her to a new switching mechanism and created an opportunity to assess the potential for using the switch in a meaningful real-life situation. Second, the incompatible response of pushing a switch to activate the tape recorder inhibited Sarah from reaching for others' possessions (at least with her engaged hand). A tape recorder is a popular educational and leisure device among children and adults and was appropriate for Sarah to learn to use independently.

When each group finished listening to the story, members generated and agreed on answers to a set of related questions. Each group joined to form a large group and to share their responses. Sarah's objectives for this portion of the lesson continued to focus on behavior—to stay with the group and to refrain from making loud noises or touching others' materials.

Example: A Cooperative Group Lesson Adapted for an Adolescent with Multiple Disabilities Bob, a young man with multiple disabilities, illustrates how a cooperative group lesson can be adapted to involve an adolescent with multiple disabilities. At the time of this lesson, Bob was 13 and in the seventh grade in the local junior high school. The cooperative group lesson described took place in Bob's biology class, and this teacher regularly used cooperative group learning structures in her lessons.

Students were clustered in groups of threes and engaged in dissecting a frog and identifying body parts. While the other groups used lab tables to do their dissection work, Bob's group used the lap tray attached to his wheelchair as their work space. Bob's objectives for this lesson were different from those of the other class members and focused on communication. For example, he was engaged in indicating choice and discrimination among objects that were familiar to him. In addition to the dissecting equipment and the frog, there were several of Bob's objects on the lap tray. Occasionally, during the course of the activity, Bob's teammates would ask him to look at one or another of his items. Bob's responses to the questions were recorded by an instructional assistant who collected data on the programs and assisted the groups as needed. The students easily incorporated Bob's objectives into the dissection activity.

Another communication objective was to increase Bob's vocalizations. A powerful motivator for vocalizing was the conversation and verbal reinforcement of his peers, which occurred naturally during this and other group activities. Bob laughed and squealed as readily as any other student when a teammate invariably held up a part of the frog and wiggled it in front of his face. Although no adult was directly involved in guiding peer interactions with Bob, before the lesson the classroom teacher and her special education teammate briefed Bob's group members on his discrimination and vocalization programs. Knowing Bob's objectives, the students easily included him within planned activities, enabling him to address his objectives while simultaneously working on their own.

A Teacher–Student Team Teaching Arrangement

"It is pretty neat when you can help out students who are having trouble learning, challenge someone like me at the same time, and it doesn't cost the school district a dime." This statement was made by Bill, a high school student who exhausted his school's mathematics curriculum offerings in his sophomore year and attended university mathematics courses in his junior and senior years. In his senior year, he arranged an independent study course in mathematics that included team teaching in the high school's most advanced math class. Bill wanted to initiate this arrangement in order to refine his instructional skills. He also tutored students in mathematics after school.

In the first week of this team-teaching arrangement, Bill observed the classroom teacher. At the end of the second week, he began teaching the last 10 minutes of the class, and his responsibility was to introduce the math concept or operation that would be addressed in the next day's lesson. The classroom teacher and Bill met daily so that the teacher could review and approve his instructional plan for these mini-lessons. After a month in the classroom, Bill taught his first full-length class. He continued to teach one full-length lesson approximately once a week for the remainder of the semester.

When Bill was not instructing the group as a whole, he worked individually with students who had missed work because of absences or who had difficulty with a concept. He continued to observe the teacher's instructional methods and conferred with the teacher on a daily basis to receive feedback on his instruction. He also solicited regular feedback from the class members. Bill was available to any class member for help after school. Several students even called him at home for assistance.

Good and Brophy (1987) have suggested that peer instructors may be more effective than adults in teaching certain concepts, such as mathematics (Cohen & Stover, 1981). They speculate that their superior effectiveness may be attributed to their tendency to be more directive than adults, their use of age-appropriate language and examples, and their recent familiarity with and awareness of their peers' potential frustrations with the content. These speculations are validated by the comments made by one of the students in the advanced class who said, "Bill is easier to understand and uses better examples."

Bill's membership on this mathematics team had additional positive effects. Bill reported that he was furthering his math education and learning about people at the same time. He noted that his self-confidence grew as a result of this experience. Also, having been a student in the class just 2 years before, he empathized with the students' struggles with the material and believed the students recognized and appreciated this empathy. The classroom teacher was impressed with the professional and serious manner with which he conducted himself, the positive response of students to his presence, and his growth in the use of effective instructional strategies.

Students Determine Accommodations for Classmates with Intensive Educational Needs

One of the challenges that teachers face in a heterogeneous classroom is determining meaningful curricular adaptations and instructional modifications that enable students with intensive educational needs to be active members of the daily classroom routine. One effective and simple strategy for meeting this challenge is employed by a number of Vermont teachers who have students with significant disabilities as regular members of their general education classrooms (Giangreco, Cloninger, Dennis, & Edelman, 1994). These teachers ask as a part of the routine introduction of lessons, "In what ways might we make [student's name] a meaningful part of this activity?" Teachers report that their students are creative problem solvers who easily brainstorm numerous realistic and practical modification strategies.

Student Involvement to Improve Instructional Effectiveness

Schools throughout North America are actively engaged in a school improvement movement and are dedicating much in-service training to establishing "a common conceptual framework, language and set of technical skills in order to communicate about and implement practices which research and theory suggest will enable them to better respond to a diverse student body" (Villa, 1989, p. 173). Although school districts choose different instructional and discipline models, all have a common need for comprehensive in-service training agenda that moves teachers from acquisition to mastery of the selected model. One Vermont school community collaborated in generating a school restructuring proposal for creating a "community of high performers" for the 1990s (Villa, Peters, Zane, Ellenboden, & Soutiere, 1989). A writing committee with community, student, teacher, and administrative representation identified desired outcomes and strategies for achieving them. One of the more unconventional recommendations of the committee was to initiate a student training program that would complement the strategies (e.g., cooperative group learning, discipline strategies that teach responsibility) of the district's teaching staff. An expected benefit of the student training was empowerment, so that students experiencing difficulty in a lesson would be comfortable asking the teacher to review or represent a concept in another way. Additionally, students could better provide teachers with immediate feedback regarding their instructional effectiveness and engage with the teacher in active problem solving to identify ways to change the task, change the standard, or provide supports to enhance the likelihood of success. Finally, teachers could use student feedback as diagnostic information for setting professional growth goals.

STUDENTS AS PEER ADVOCATES

Students can act as advocates for their peers by participating in transition teams, planning teams, and peer support networks.

Peers on Transition Planning Teams

Peers have proven to be valuable in assisting in the transition of students with intensive needs from one educational setting to another. Bob's transition in and out of the Winooski School District illustrates this point. Bob, the student with multiple disabilities mentioned earlier, was 13 years old when he moved to Winooski from a segregated residential facility. The student body of the small junior high school met with school staff in small groups to plan Bob's transition. The students' participation in the planning helped develop a genuine sense of ownership and responsibility for Bob's success among his future classmates. The advice they gave faculty members greatly facilitated his immediate acceptance, and suggestions ranged from providing an augmentative communication device they thought would help Bob communicate to what kind of notebook, backpack, and musical tapes he should have to fit in (Scagliotti, 1987).

After 2 years at Winooski, Bob's family moved to a neighboring community. His classmates offered to talk with teachers and students in the new community to ease his adjustment and acceptance. Three students were invited to speak to Bob's new peers. A letter of thanks from the teacher responsible for Bob's program in the new community clearly summarized the importance and impact of peers in successful transitions:

> Moriah and Jason spoke to Bob's afternoon classes. They spoke articulately and with humor and covered many important aspects of Bob's integration at your school. Most important was the regard and fondness for Bob evident in their presentations. They were excellent. Chardra Duba, who came to school at 7 A.M. to speak with Bob's morning classes, discussed not only Winooski's experiences with Bob but also her own experiences with handicapped siblings.
>
> Although Bob was the focus of their work, the impact of these young people went far beyond Bob. The attitudes and behaviors they modeled were lessons for us all about friendship and mutual respect. What they taught made the way easier for many handicapped students here. (K. Lewis, personal communication, November 20, 1989)

Many high schools now have effective formalized transition planning processes for linking high school students with postsecondary work, living, and social support services. A core team that includes community agency personnel, a parent, a school counselor, a collaborating teacher, an administrator, and a student oversees the planning and implementation of transition plans for individual students. Student representation and input is important to bring a youth perspective to the group as well as to provide a peer advocate for any student who needs or requests personal support to make the transition from school to postsecondary options.

Peer Advocacy on Planning Teams

Schools across North America include students on their own IEP planning teams and invite them to bring in peers as their educational advocates. Peers serve a number of functions on the team—they can provide a voice for a student who is not able to speak for him- or herself (e.g., a nonverbal student), or they can provide moral support and assistance in self-advocacy, particularly when students differ with parents or professional educators concerning the focus of their education or the goals and objectives of their IEPs.

Making Action Plans (MAPs) is a structured process "to help individuals, organizations, and families determine how to move into the future effectively and creatively" (Falvey, Forest, Pearpoint, & Rosenberg, 1994, p. 353). Formerly known as the McGill Action Planning System (Lusthaus & Forest, 1987), this strategy is increasingly used in schools to determine the educational program of students with disabilities in integrated general education environments. In combination with an extension process, Planning Alternative Tomorrows with Hope (PATH), teams of people who are concerned about a student develop detailed plans of action to avoid the nightmares and facilitate the short- and long-term educational and social outcomes desired for a student (Falvey et al., 1994). Critical to both the MAPs and PATH processes is the inclusion of peers in all stages. Peer involvement is beneficial not only to the focus of students, but also to the peers who through this intensive experience have the opportunity to learn and practice valuing diversity. In both the MAPs and PATH processes, participants collaborate by responding to a series of questions that help them creatively dream, plan, and produce results. (See Falvey et al. [1994] and Chapter 5 of this book for specific examples of the effective use of MAPs and PATH.)

Peer Support

Historically, students with intensive needs were excluded not only from academic but also from cocurricular and nonacademic aspects of school life (e.g., school clubs, school dances, athletic events). Peer support networks have been established in some schools to rectify these situations. The purpose of peer support was clearly articulated by a student who helped organize a network for herself.

Peer support is a bunch of kids working together to break down the barriers that society has built into the public's idea of what the norm is. Teachers and peers need to be trained; they need to understand that the goal of peer support is not competitive academics. The goal is to belong, to meet new people, to learn to break down the barriers. (Budelmann, Farrel, Kovack, & Paige, 1987, n.p.)

Peer Buddy Network A peer buddy network is a type of peer support in which classmates voluntarily help a classmate negotiate the school day and be involved in before- and after-school activities throughout the year. Students themselves stress the importance of recruiting a diverse group of peers active in a wide variety of cocurricular, social, and community activities to be peer buddies. This networking strategy is effective because peer buddies are active and motivated and have a rich social network into which another student can be introduced.

The range of social supports that buddies can provide to other students is unlimited. For example, a buddy might assist a student with physical limitations to use school lockers, get on and off the school bus, hang out in the halls before and after classes, or attend school sporting events or dances. Peer buddies can assist a student's transition by talking with other students, teachers, and community members about the unique characteristics and daily challenges of their friend.

In some schools, peer buddies meet periodically with a faculty facilitator or a veteran peer buddy to receive important information about individual students (e.g., how to respond to a student's hyperactive choke reflex) or to discuss how they could better support their friend.

Circle of Friends In Snow and Forest (1987), Falvey et al. (1994), and Chapter 5 of this book, a process for building a circle of friends around a new student with intensive needs is described. In the process, an adult facilitator gathers a group of potential peer buddies and has them construct four concentric circles that become progressively larger around a central stick figure (themselves). Each participant includes his or her closest relationships in the first circle (e.g., family members, best friends). Other people are placed in the second and third circles based upon closeness to the student. In the fourth circle are the people who are paid to be in the students' lives (e.g., doctors, teachers). The task is repeated for the new student. The objective of this circle of friends activity is to sensitize peers to a new student's friendship needs through a visual representation of the imbalance between the number of people in their own friendship circles and the number in the new student's circles. Forest and Lusthaus (1989) emphasized that the outcome of the process is not to engage peers in a special, short-term helping relationship but to create "a network that allows for the genuine involvement of children in a friendship, caring, and support role with their peers" (p. 47).

Collaborative Enterprises Among Peers Peer support, in its various forms, can quickly become the norm within a school. In a school in which peer support networks had developed over several years, over 25% of the seventh grade volunteered to be buddies for a new student whose only previous school experiences had been in segregated special classes. In this same school, social support for one person expanded to mutually beneficial collaborative enterprises among students with and without disabilities. Cota's Cool Cookies, a student business partnership, illustrates this evolution. The company derived its name from the name of a student with severe disabilities who was the company's founder (i.e., Cota) and the cool mint chocolates used in the product. Four students and their families formed the business, with each student having a specific role. The student with disabilities was the chief executive officer (CEO), responsible for mixing the cookie batter through the use of a panel switch and the assistance of a student business partner. Other student partners were responsible for the jobs of baking, packaging, and delivering the product to several school and community sites. The broader school community also became involved in the business—art students competed to produce the best label for the product, and one of the business classes developed the company's contract. Within the first few months, the company turned a profit and was featured in a newspaper article (Hemingway, 1989).

Assumptions and Cautions Regarding Peer Support Networks Stainback and Stainback (1990) suggested that within each classroom there should be a peer support committee with a rotating membership and the goal of determining ways that class members could be more supportive of one another and be a more caring community. This recommendation, as well as the other peer support approaches presented, are based on the proposition that school is a place where children practice being caring members of a community. Whatever approach a school employs to empower students to support one another, "the assumption underlying the students' involvement is that it is a valid and vital educational experience for students to participate in planning their own lives and also in helping others" (Forest & Lusthaus, 1989, p. 46).

Van der Klift and Kunc (1994) issued a serious caution about using any process intended to bring children together for social support and relationship building. Simply put, it is to be sure not to confuse friendship with help. Both are valuable, but they are not the same.

> Clearly, there is nothing wrong with help; friends often help each other. However, it is essential to acknowledge that help is not and can never be the basis of friendship. We must be careful not to overemphasize the helper–helpee aspect of a relationship... Unless help is reciprocal, the inherent inequity between helper and helpee will contaminate the authenticity of a relationship... Friendship is about choice and chemistry... Realizing this, we can acknowledge... that we are not, nor need to be, friendship sorcerers.
> However, teachers and others do have some influence over the nature of proximity. Thus, to create and foster an environment in which it is possible for friendship to emerge might be a more reasonable goal. (p. 393)

STUDENTS AS DECISION MAKERS

Equity and parity among students and adults in educational decision making are more likely to promote active student participation and problem solving, community spirit, and a climate of mutual respect than situations in which most or all decisions are made by adults. Students may join in decision making in areas that are generally controlled by the adults in the school community. The following discussion offers ideas for student–teacher decision-making partnerships in the management of student behavior; the improvement of teacher and administrator job performance; and the determination of the curriculum, in-service training, and overall school governance.

Student Accountability and Responsibility

Student accountability and responsibility involve, at minimum, behaving within limits of agreed-upon social norms established for and by a school community. Beyond this, they involve students learning to resolve their own conflicts and the conflicts of their classmates (Schrumpf, 1994). Curwin and Mendler (1988, p. iii) began their book, *Discipline with Dignity,* with a poem that asks, "Whose school is this, anyway?" They concluded that schools are for children, that children learn about adulthood through their interactions with the adults who teach and discipline them, and that discipline methods and the values underlying them greatly influence the students' "development of self-concept; the ability to take responsibility for one's actions, the way children learn to communicate with others, and how they learn to work cooperatively with others" (p. 241).

Curwin and Mendler (1988), Glasser (1990), and others concerned with student discipline and empowerment (e.g., Villa, Udis, & Thousand, 1994) recommended procedures for determining classroom rules, schoolwide norms, and consequences for rule violation that are jointly determined by students and teachers. Discipline strategies suggested by these authors are more concerned with students acquiring responsible behaviors than they are with obedience. Developing responsible behavior involves students learning to determine and negotiate "natural" and logical consequences for their rule-violating actions and being willing and able to formulate a plan of action or a social contract for rule-following behavior in the future.

Among the many ideas advanced by Curwin and Mendler for student involvement is engaging students in determining, with the teacher, the rules and consequences of the classroom. Curwin and Mendler (1988) recommended that students develop rules for their teachers (e.g., homework is handed back to students within 3 days, the teacher cannot drink coffee in class if students cannot chew gum) as well as negotiate rules for themselves. They also presented the following recommendations for student empowerment formulated by a suburban middle school:

1. A student council of "poor achievers" and "in-trouble students" (different labels were used) [was established] to help set school policy and to help modify rules and consequences.
2. Students who served detention were given the job of commenting on how school climate could be improved.
3. Students took the job of running the school for one day once a year with the teachers and administrators taking student roles.
4. Each class was required to have at least two student rules for the teacher. (Curwin & Mendler, 1988, pp. 17–18)

Schrumpf (1994) described North American schools that tackled the issue of student accountability and responsibility by turning to conflict resolution programs that place students in the role of *peer mediators* or *peacemakers* (e.g., Schrumpf, Crawford, & Usadel, 1991). A peer mediation approach may be initiated within a single classroom or schoolwide, it can be adapted for elementary through high school students, and it can start on a small scale, with a few students selected and trained in the conflict mediation process. These student peacemakers then are available to conduct mediations between peers throughout the range of activities in a school day. Students, teachers, and administrators can request mediation. In some elementary schools, mediators are assigned to playground areas to settle disputes on the spot without adult intervention. The authors are particularly attracted to the idea of training all students in negotiation and mediation skills and processes through the elementary curriculum and secondary level subjects such as social studies, language arts, and health and wellness classes. When a conflict arises, students then can be asked to negotiate their own differences. If they cannot reach an agreement, a peer can be asked to assist. Adults intervene only if the peer mediator is unable to help resolve the dispute. In an elementary school in Minnesota that used this approach, principal referrals dropped to zero and student conflicts that teachers were required to manage decreased 80% (Johnson, Johnson, Dudley, & Burnett, 1992).

Graduates of schools that have empowered students to actively problem solve regarding their own behavior will be better prepared for the complexities of life forecasted in the 21st century. Specifically, they will have had opportunities to use creative problem-solving skills to address the behaviors of others—skills needed in their future work environments. They will have had opportunities to recognize that some solutions are more successful than others and that it is acceptable to have a second approach if the first fails. They will have observed teachers and peers modeling appropriate ways for coping with stress and adversity and for responding when caught breaking a rule. In short, they will have had multiple opportunities to develop a healthy appreciation for the complexity and diversity of human behavior.

Teacher and Administrator Accountability

Clearly, students are not the only performers in a school. Teachers and administrators have designated roles as managers and facilitators of the learning environment and as the instructional leaders. Students can play a very positive and active role in improving instruction in a number of ways. For example, students trained in the elements of effective instruction can use this knowledge to provide teachers with prompts and constructive feedback that promote more effective teaching and learning. Students can also provide teachers with feedback about their consistency in enforcing classroom rules, delivering consequences, and modeling an educational rather than emotional response to challenging behavior and stress.

Students are well qualified to notice and report to administrators information regarding 1) the school climate, 2) the visibility of school leadership personnel and their availability to listen actively to student concerns, and 3) the extent to which they (the students) are involved in learning and in determining schoolwide policies and procedures.

Student Representation on School Committees and the School Board

In order for student–adult collaboration to extend beyond the classroom, students need to be welcomed in the forums where global decisions are made regarding the school's mission, curriculum, in-service training, hiring policies, procedures for evaluating instruction, incentives and rewards for teachers, and restructuring of the school organization. One school redesign committee of which the first author was a member called for student representation on the school board on the curriculum, discipline, and in-service training committees and on a proposed creativity committee that would have the ongoing responsibility of determining future organizational, curricular, and instructional change needs (Villa et al., 1989). To welcome students as decision makers in this way is a radical step in school organizational restructuring. Yet it is exactly what is needed to actualize the sage advice to create "a new collaborative role for teachers and students in which students accept an active senior partnership role in the learning enterprise" (Benjamin, 1989, p. 9).

CONCLUSION

The role of the public school in North America has always been to prepare children for their roles in society. This role has seen dramatic change during the 20th century. In the early 1900s, a major function of the public schools was to induct the waves of immigrants into the culture, language, and democratic processes (Stainback, Stainback, & Bunch, 1989) and to prepare the masses for work in the factories of the industrial age. The public school was hallowed as the "great equalizer" because of the common knowledge and skills it imparted to children.

As an organizational structure, however, the school came to mirror the standardized and bureaucratic model of the factories (Skrtic, 1987). Like the factory, the school was structured to create a standard product; all students experienced and were expected to master the same curriculum, at the same rate, through the same instructional methodologies (e.g., large group). There was little tolerance of or appreciation for the natural differences among children in culture, learning style, interests, and values. This was a time when left-handed children were routinely forced to learn to write with their right hand, which was the standard. Students who did not do well in the standardized, lock-step curriculum were allowed or encouraged to drop out. Segregation of segments of the school population were entrenched. Native Americans and African Americans were educated separately; students identified as disabled were largely excluded from the public school; and tracking became popular, with poor and disadvantaged youth assigned to the lowest tracks.

Society at the end of the 20th century is much more complex, global, interdependent, rich in information, technological, and inclusionary in its values. There has been a shift in values and a steady trend to include all students in the mainstream of general education (Reynolds & Birch, 1982), making the schools more diverse and more reflective of the society that its graduates will enter. Wisdom at the end of the 20th century involves knowing strategies for embracing diversity. The future "world of work will require the abilities to manage information and to work with people. Workers will need high-level thinking skills as well as the ability to adapt" (Benjamin, 1989, p. 8). "The world's store of knowledge has doubled and doubled again during the 20th century" (Cornish, 1986, p. 14) and will continue to increase geometrically so that no one will be able to keep pace with this information explosion. As we enter the next century, we and our students know only half of what we need to learn and know in order to perform our jobs 5 years from now. As a result of the short life of useful knowledge, our children will need to learn to be inquiring lifelong learners.

Given these changes in society, what changes are needed in public education? Organizationally, there is a need for schools to model collaboration among school personnel, community members, and students (Idol et al., 1992; Thousand & Villa, 1992; Thousand et al., 1994) and for educators to share their power and decision-making responsibilities with their students in a climate of mutual respect. The curriculum must expand to include the development of students' values, attitudes, and character. Instructionally, there is a need for "responsive and fluid instructional options rather than pigeonholing of students into one of several standing, standard programs" (Thousand & Villa, 1989, p. 89). Finally, educational assumptions and practices must be examined regularly in order to eliminate those that impede student opportunities to actively determine and be involved in their education, to be contributing members of society through real-life experiences (e.g., peer tutoring, peer advocacy, community service), and to experience and value diversity. Teacher-dominated instruction, the emphasis on student competition over collaboration, the focus on academic performance over the development of social competence, segregated schooling, and tracking are all examples of educational practices that will come to be viewed as archaic in the 21st century as has the 20th-century practice of tying down a student's left hand to ensure a society of right-handed writers.

Benjamin (1989) forecasted that "the future will arrive ahead of schedule" (p. 12). Therefore, it is imperative for us to demonstrate wisdom and courage by acting to change schools now so that students may be more actively engaged in their own and others' acquisition of humanistic ethics, communication, information-seeking, and problem-solving skills, and the core curriculum deemed essential by their community. Starting points for change include the implementation of student collaboration strategies presented in this chapter.

We hope that by the 21st century, students taking the Student Collaboration Quiz (Figure 1) will be able to give themselves and their schools higher ratings than those given by graduates of 20th-century schools. These higher ratings will be the result of the multiple opportunities they had to participate in collaborative arrangements in learning, advocacy, and leadership.

School belongs to the children (Curwin & Mendler, 1988), and so does the future. "Your children are not your children. They are the sons and daughters of Life's longing for itself... Their souls dwell in the house of tomorrow, which you cannot visit, even in your fondest dreams" (Gibran, 1923, p. 18).

REFERENCES

Bair, M., & Woodward, R.G. (1964). *Team teaching in action.* Boston: Houghton Mifflin.

Beggs, D.W., III. (1964). *Team teaching: Bold new venture.* Indianapolis: Unified College Press.

Benjamin, S. (1989). An ideascape for education: What futurists recommend. *Educational Leadership, 47*(1), 8–14.

Budelmann, L., Farrell, S., Kovack, C., & Paige, K. (1987, October). *Student perspective: Planning and achieving social integration.* Paper presented at the Least Restrictive Environment Conference, Burlington, VT.

Chalfant, J., Psych, M., & Moultrie, R. (1979). Teaching assistance teams: A model for within building problem solving. *Learning Disabilities Quarterly, 2,* 85–96.

Cohen, S.A., & Stover, G. (1981). Effects of teaching sixth-grade students to modify format variable of math work problems. *Reading Research Quarterly, 16,* 175–200.

Cornish, E. (1986). Educating children for the 21st century. *Curriculum Review, 25*(4), 12–17.

Curwin, R., & Mendler, A. (1988). *Discipline with dignity.* Alexandria, VA: Association for Supervision and Curriculum Development.

Davidson, N. (1994). Cooperative and collaborative learning: An integrative perspective. In J.S. Thousand, R.A. Villa, & A.I. Nevin (Eds.), *Creativity and collaborative learning: A practical guide to empowering students and teachers* (pp. 13–30). Baltimore: Paul H. Brookes Publishing Co.

Falvey, M.A., Forest, M., Pearpoint, J., & Rosenberg, R.L. (1994). Building connections. In J.S. Thousand, R.A. Villa, & A.I. Nevin (Eds.), *Creativity and collaborative learning: A practical guide to empowering students and teachers* (pp. 347–368). Baltimore: Paul H. Brookes Publishing Co.

Forest, M., & Lusthaus, E. (1989). Promoting educational equality for all students: Circles and maps. In S. Stainback, W. Stainback, & M. Forest (Eds.), *Educating all students in the mainstream of regular education* (pp. 43–57). Baltimore: Paul H. Brookes Publishing Co.

Gartner, A., Kohler, M., & Riessman, F. (1971). *Children teach children: Learning by teaching.* New York: Harper & Row.

Giangreco, M.F., Cloninger, C.J., Dennis, R.E., & Edelman, S.W. (1994). Problem-solving methods to facilitate inclusive education. In J.S. Thousand, R.A. Villa, & A.I. Nevin (Eds.), *Creativity and collaborative learning: A practical guide to empowering students and teachers* (pp. 261–274). Baltimore: Paul H. Brookes Publishing Co.

Gibran, K. (1923). *The prophet.* New York: Alfred A. Knopf.

Glasser, W. (1990). *The quality school: Managing students without coercion.* New York: Harper & Row.

Good, T.L., & Brophy, J.E. (1987). *Looking into classrooms* (4th ed.). New York: Harper & Row.

Graden, J., Casey, A., & Christenson, S. (1985). Implementing a prereferral intervention system. *Exceptional Children, 57,* 377–384.

Harper, G.F., Maheady, L., & Mallette, B. (1994). The power of peer-mediated instruction: How and why it promotes academic success for all students. In J.S. Thousand, R.A. Villa, & A.I. Nevin (Eds.), *Creativity and collaborative learning: A practical guide to empowering students and teachers* (pp. 229–242). Baltimore: Paul H. Brookes Publishing Co.

Hemingway, S. (1989, November 10). High school feels loss of Bob Cota. *Burlington Free Press,* B1.

Hersey, P., & Blanchard, K.H. (1977). *Management of organizational behavior: Utilizing human resources.* Englewood Cliffs, NJ: Prentice Hall.

Idol, L., Nevin, A., & Paolucci-Whitcomb, P. (1992). *Collaborative consultation* (2nd ed.). Austin, TX: PRO-ED.

Johnson, D.W., & Johnson, R. (1987a). *Learning together and alone: Cooperation competition, and individualization* (2nd ed.). Englewood Cliffs, NJ: Prentice Hall.

Johnson, D.W., & Johnson, R. (1987b). *A meta-analysis of cooperative, competitive and individualistic goal structures.* Hillsdale, NJ: Lawrence Erlbaum Associates.

Johnson, D.W., & Johnson, R. (1989). *Cooperation and competition: Theory and research.* Edina, MN: Interaction Book Co.

Johnson, D.W., Johnson, R., Dudley, B., & Burnett, R. (1992). Teaching students to be peer mediators. *Educational Leadership, 50*(1), 10–13.

Johnson, D.W., Johnson, R., & Holubec, E. (1994). *The new circles of learning: Cooperation in the classroom and school.* Alexandria, VA: Association for Supervision and Curriculum Development.

Johnson, R., & Johnson, D.W. (1994). An overview of cooperative learning. In J.S. Thousand, R.A. Villa, & A.I. Nevin (Eds.), *Creativity and collaborative learning: A practical guide to empowering students and teachers* (pp. 31–44). Baltimore: Paul H. Brookes Publishing Co.

Knight, M.F., Meyers, H.W., Paolucci-Whitcomb, P., Hasazi, S.E., & Nevin, A. (1981). A four year evaluation of consulting teacher services. *Behavior Disorders, 6*(2), 92–100.

LaPlant, L., & Zane, N. (1994). Partner learning systems. In J.S. Thousand, R.A. Villa, & A.I. Nevin (Eds.), *Creativity and collaborative learning: A practical guide to empowering students and teachers* (pp. 261–274). Baltimore: Paul H. Brookes Publishing Co.

Lusthaus, E., & Forest, M. (1987). The kaleidoscope: A challenge to the cascade. In M. Forest (Ed.), *More education integration* (pp. 1–17). Downsview, Ontario: G. Allan Roeher Institute.

McNeil, M. (1994). Creating powerful partnerships through partner learning. In J.S. Thousand, R.A. Villa, & A.I. Nevin (Eds.), *Creativity and collaborative learning: A practical guide to empowering students and teachers* (pp. 243–260). Baltimore: Paul H. Brookes Publishing Co.

Nevin, A., Thousand, J., Paolucci-Whitcomb, P., & Villa, R. (1990). Collaborative consultation: Empowering public school personnel to provide heterogeneous schooling for all. *Journal of Educational and Psychological Consultation, 11,* 41–67.

Reynolds, M., & Birch, J. (1982). *Teaching exceptional children in all America's schools* (2nd ed.). Reston, VA: Council for Exceptional Children.

Scagliotti, L. (1987). Helping hands: School works to overcome student's handicap. *Burlington Free Press,* B1, 10.

Schrumpf, F. (1994). The role of students in resolving conflicts in schools. In J.S. Thousand, R.A. Villa, & A.I. Nevin (Eds.), *Creativity and collaborative learning: A practical guide to empowering students and teachers* (pp. 275–291). Baltimore: Paul H. Brookes Publishing Co.

Schrumpf, F., Crawford, D., & Usadel, C. (1991). *Peer mediation: Conflict resolution in schools.* Champaign, IL: Research Press.

Skrtic, T. (1987). An organizational analysis of special education reform. *Counterpoint, 8*(12), 15–19.

Slavin, R.E. (1984). Review of cooperative learning research. *Review of Educational Research, 50,* 315–342.

Slavin, R.E. (1989). Research on cooperative learning: Consensus and controversy. *Educational Leadership, 47*(4), 52–54.

Snow, J., & Forest, M. (1987). Circles. In M. Forest (Ed.), *More education integration* (pp. 169–176). Downsview, Ontario: G. Allan Roeher Institute.

Stainback, W., & Stainback, S. (1990). Facilitating peer supports and friendships. In W. Stainback & S. Stainback (Eds.), *Support networks for inclusive schooling: Interdependent integrated education* (pp. 51–63). Baltimore: Paul H. Brookes Publishing Co.

Stainback, W., Stainback, S., & Bunch, G. (1989). Introduction and historical background. In S. Stainback, W. Stainback, & M. Forest (Eds.), *Educating all students in the mainstream of regular education* (pp. 3–14). Baltimore: Paul H. Brookes Publishing Co.

Tharp, R.G. (1975). The triadic model of consultation: Current considerations. In C.A. Parker (Ed.), *Psychological consultation: Helping teachers meet special needs* (pp. 133–151). Reston, VA: Council for Exceptional Children.

Thousand, J., & Villa, R. (1989). Enhancing success in heterogeneous schools. In S. Stainback, W. Stainback, & M. Forest (Eds.), *Educating all students in the mainstream of regular education* (pp. 89–103). Baltimore: Paul H. Brookes Publishing Co.

Thousand, J., & Villa, R. (1990). Sharing expertise and responsibilities through teaching teams. In W. Stainback & S. Stainback (Eds.), *Support networks for inclusive schooling: Interdependent integrated education* (pp. 151–166). Baltimore: Paul H. Brookes Publishing Co.

Thousand, J., & Villa, R. (1992). Collaborative teams: A powerful tool in school restructuring. In R.A. Villa, J.S. Thousand, W. Stainback, & S. Stainback (Eds.), *Restructuring for caring and effective education: An administrative guide to creating heterogeneous schools* (pp. 73–108). Baltimore: Paul H. Brookes Publishing Co.

Thousand, J.S., Villa, R.A., & Nevin, A.I. (Eds.). (1994). *Creativity and collaborative learning: A practical guide to empowering students and teachers.* Baltimore: Paul H. Brookes Publishing Co.

Topping, K. (1988). *The peer tutoring handbook: Promoting co-operative learning.* Cambridge, MA: Brookline Books.

Van der Klift, E., & Kunc, N. (1994). Beyond benevolence: Friendship and the politics of help. In J.S. Thousand, R.A. Villa, & A.I. Nevin (Eds.), *Creativity and collaborative learning: A practical guide to empowering students and teachers* (pp. 391–401). Baltimore: Paul H. Brookes Publishing Co.

Villa, R. (1989). Model public school inservice programs: Do they exist? *Teacher Education and Special Education, 12,* 173–176.

Villa, R., Peters, M.J., Zane, N., Ellenboden, G., & Soutiere, L. (1989). *Reinventing Vermont schools for very high performance: Winooski challenge grant proposal.* (Available from Richard Villa, 6 Bayridge Estates, Colchester, VT 05446.)

Villa, R., Udis, J., & Thousand, J. (1994). Responses for children experiencing behavioral and emotional challenges. In J.S. Thousand, R.A. Villa, & A.I. Nevin (Eds.), *Creativity and collaborative learning: A practical guide to empowering students and teachers* (pp. 369–390). Baltimore: Paul H. Brookes Publishing Co.

Wiggins, G. (1989). The futility of trying to teach everything of importance. *Educational Leadership, 11*(3), 44–59.

12

Collaboration, Support Networking, and Community Building

William Stainback and Susan Stainback

HELEN HANSEN ELEMENTARY in Cedar Falls, Iowa; Winnsboro High School in Winnsboro, Texas; Elkins High School in Sugarland, Texas; Winooski High in Winooski, Vermont; Brook Forest School in Oak Brook, Illinois; St. Francis School in Kitchener, Ontario; Chapparal Elementary School in Albuquerque, New Mexico; and Ed Smith Elementary School in Syracuse, New York, are just a few of the schools that have recently had the attention of parents, educators, and concerned community members. These are examples of a new breed of schools developing across North America. What these and a growing number of other schools have in common is their attempt to develop educational settings into inclusive supportive communities. The goal in these schools is to ensure that all students, regardless of any individual differences they might have (be they classified at risk, homeless, gifted, or with disabilities), are fully included in the mainstream of school life. This goal also incorporates the idea that all students deserve to be safe, happy, secure, and successful learners within the mainstream of education.

Educators, parents, and students in schools oriented toward inclusion and community building have consistently stated in interviews, in conference presentations, and in various publications that a major key to their success is the involvement of students, teachers, specialists, and parents working in collaboration. Students have been involved in circles of friends, as advocates for fellow students, in cooperative learning situations, as peer tutors and partners, and on educational planning teams as equal members with teachers, administrators, and parents. Although there are a small but growing number of schools throughout the nation similar to those cited above, they are still the exceptions rather than the rule. There remains an enormous amount of work to be done in order to achieve effective, inclusive, and caring schools on a widespread basis.

In the early 1990s, a Massachusetts scholar clearly summarized a major obstacle to inclusion:

> Our society's current infatuation with the word "competitiveness" which has leached into discussions about education encourages a confusion between two very different ideas; excellence and the desperate quest to triumph over other people...
>
> At a tender age, children learn not to be tender. A dozen years of schooling often do nothing to promote generosity or a commitment to the welfare of others. To the contrary, students are graduated who think that being smart means looking out for number one. (Kohn, 1991, p. 498)

Growing numbers of practitioners, researchers, and scholars (e.g., Coleman & Hoffer, 1987; Flynn, 1989; Kohn, 1991; Sapon-Shevin, 1992; Solomon, Schaps, Watson, & Battistich, 1992; Stainback & Stainback, 1992; Thousand & Villa, 1992) have argued that far too many of today's schools have lost or are losing a sense of the community in which students and teachers care about, work cooperatively with, and support each other. There is growing empirical evidence that in schools in which students and teachers do *not* establish friendships, commitments, and bonds with each other (where there is an absence of community) there are increased problems with underachievement, student dropouts, drug abuse, gang activity, and exclusion of students with disabilities from the mainstream (Coleman & Hoffer, 1987; Maeroff, 1990). As a result, Coleman and Hoffer (1987) hypothesized that some of the problems in education, including the exclusion of some students from the mainstream, are due, at least in part, to a lack of community in many schools in an increasingly urban, complex, and depersonalized society.

WHAT IS COMMUNITY?

The need for community as part of school renewal has been discussed in detail in Chapter 3. In inclusive schools and classrooms, there is much emphasis on building community. Flynn (1989) provided the following background information about community:

> True community is rare in today's society even though there is a natural longing in each of us to be a part of something. Scott Peck, in his book "The Different Drum," says that we humans often have a sense that in the good old days we knew more of community than we do today. For example, John Winthrop, the first Governor of the Massachusetts Bay Colony, in 1630, speaking to his fellow colonists just before they stepped on land, said: "We must delight in each other, make others' conditions our own, rejoice together, mourn together, labour and suffer together, always having before our eyes our community as members of the same body."
>
> Two hundred years later the Frenchman Alexis de Tocqueville published a book in 1835 entitled "Democracy in America." In the book he marvelled at a characteristic

that he found in people throughout the United States that he described as individualism. He went on to caution however that unless this individualism was continually and strongly balanced by "other habits," it would inevitably lead to fragmentation of American society and social isolation of its citizens.

In 1985, Robert Bellah published a book entitled ironically enough "Habits of the Heart." In the book Bellah argues compellingly that our individualism has not remained balanced and that de Tocqueville's predictions have come true and that *isolation* and *fragmentation* have become the order of the day. (p.1)

Flynn (1989) went on to define community:

To respond to the call "to community" we must have some understanding of what community is—what it looks like when it happens.... I think that a...true community is a group of individuals who have learned to communicate honestly with one another, whose relationships go deeper than their composures and who have developed some significant commitment to "rejoice together, mourn together, to delight in each other, and make others' conditions their own." (p. 4)

As can be gleaned from these statements, community is hard to define, but if it is to be promoted in schools it is essential to develop a sense of what is meant by community. Many successful inclusive schools and classrooms that emphasize community focus on how to operate classrooms and schools where everyone belongs, is accepted, supports, and is supported by his or her peers and other members of the school community in the course of having educational needs met.

It should be stressed that in inclusive communities everyone's gifts and talents, including those of students traditionally defined as having significant disabilities or disruptive behaviors, are recognized, encouraged, and utilized to the fullest extent possible. In supportive communities, everyone has responsibilities and plays a role in supporting others. Each individual is an important and worthwhile member of the community and contributes to the group. This involvement helps foster positive self-esteem, pride in accomplishments, mutual respect, and a sense of belonging among community members. Such a community cannot occur if certain students are always the receivers of, and never the givers of, support. As noted by Wilkinson (1980), "People are interdependent; everyone has a function and everyone has a role to play, and that keeps people together and forms a community" (p. 452).

To reestablish a sense of community, educators and community leaders in some large impersonal schools in the United States and other countries have started dividing their schools into smaller units, each with its own principal, teachers, students, and self-identity. In these smaller schools, teachers and students stay together for most, if not all, of the school day. These schools also become a center of community activities that involve parents and community members. To form bonds and friendships and to create more personalized and sensitive institutions, people need opportunities to communicate with each other on a personal level.

In schools such as Saint Francis School in Kitchener, Ontario, and Helen Hansen Elementary in Cedar Falls, Iowa, students traditionally classified as having significant disabilities are included in the mainstream through the use of circles of friends (Snow & Forest, 1987) and other approaches that focus on connecting students and teachers in friendships and caring relationships. These efforts can lead to a better sense of community in the entire school (Flynn, 1989; Jackson, 1990).

Many chapters in this book provide numerous practical suggestions regarding how students can mature together by working cooperatively and caring about and supporting each other and why this is so critical to enhancing their social, educational, and life achievements. Circles of friends (Snow & Forest, 1987), Making Action Plans (MAPs) (Falvey, Forest, Pearpoint, & Rosenberg, 1994), Planning Alternative Tomorrows with Hope (PATH) (Pearpoint, O'Brien, & Forest, 1993), and adult collaborations are all examples of practical ways to build community in classrooms and schools. The authors of this chapter do not repeat these strategies but instead refer the reader to other chapters in the book, particularly Chapters 4, 5, 7, 9, 10, 11, 12, and 16.

PRINCIPLES OF SUPPORT NETWORKING

As you read the chapters of this book, it becomes evident that there is much emphasis on students and teachers helping and supporting each other in efforts to build inclusive, supportive communities. There are a number of basic principles of support networking that have emerged that may be helpful to keep in mind when working toward inclusive communities.

1. Support networking is based on the premise that everyone has capabilities, strengths, gifts, and talents, including students classified as having disabilities, which they can use to provide support and assistance to their fellow community members.
2. In support networking, all people are involved in helping and supporting one another in both formal and informal arrangements. Relationships are reciprocal rather than some people always being helpers and other people always being helped.
3. Naturally supportive relationships in which individuals support one another as peers, friends, or colleagues are as important as professional support. A focus on natural supports helps connect people in classrooms and schools and thus fosters supportive communities.
4. Individuals are unique and differ in what they require, and their needs usually change over time. Thus, components of a support network should not be based on a predefined, ironclad list of support options that cannot be modified to meet individual needs.
5. Support networking works best in integrated, heterogeneous classrooms and schools. The diversity of the members increases the likelihood that all class and school members, including students, teachers, parents, specialists, administrators, and other school personnel, have the assets and resources necessary to support the needs of, and become interdependent with, each other.
6. Supports should be consumer driven. The focus should be on what the consumer (the person receiving support) wants and needs as stated by the consumer. If the

person is very young or unable to communicate effectively to the provider, his or her advocate should present what the consumer wants and needs.

7. Any provided support should focus on empowering a person to assist him- or herself and others. This type of support includes empowering a person to seek assistance when required and provide assistance to others.

8. School personnel in administrative or decision-making situations not only need to provide opportunities for informal support development among all members of the school community but also, when possible, to empower and encourage people to provide support to each other.

9. Support networking should be a natural and ongoing part of the school and classroom. It should not be episodic or reserved for use only in t' nes of difficulty or crisis.

10. Support networking should be conducted by insiders (i.e., individuals directly involved in the school and classroom communities). Such individuals include students, teachers, secretaries, administrators, parents, specialists, community volunteers, and other school personnel.

11. Support networking is for everybody. Plans that focus on and operate for a single student or teacher generally are inefficient in promoting and maintaining an inclusive supportive community.

12. Support networking begins with an examination of the social interactions and supportive characteristics that are naturally operating in classrooms and other school settings and builds on these natural supports.

13. A danger inherent in providing some types of support is that, if a support is incorrectly provided, it can make an individual unnecessarily dependent on the support. For example, if someone helps a particular student find his or her way to the school cafeteria, without at the same time helping the student learn the route and the skills necessary to find it independently, then that student may never learn how to get to the cafeteria independently. Thus, it is critical in supportive classroom communities that, although everyone understands that the goal is to provide support to others whenever it is needed, they always work to empower people to assist and support themselves.

HOW CAN SUPPORT NETWORKING BE FACILITATED?

The informal and formal supports essential to inclusive communities, which are responsive to the needs of all students, can be facilitated by phasing out special schools and classrooms. Special educators can become general educators, team teachers, resource and collaborating specialists, and facilitators of support networks within general education. In addition, the wealth of materials, procedures, supports, equipment, and resources in special education can be integrated into general education.

There are literally billions of dollars being spent and hundreds of thousands of personnel working in segregated special education programs. All of these dollars and personnel can and should be integrated into the educational mainstream in order to facilitate support networking and whatever else is needed to achieve inclusive school and classroom communities. Schenkat (1988) estimated that $30–$35 billion was being spent annually in special education. This money could provide considerable support and assistance in establishing inclusive schools and support networking to enable teachers and students build community in the classroom. Furthermore, Reynolds (1989) estimated that

> One teacher out of eight in the United States is employed in Special Education. If we add the school psychologists, school social workers, occupational therapists, and other professional personnel who work mainly…[in special education]…we come to a total of about 400,000 professional employees in U.S. schools—about one-sixth of the total number of professional school employees. (p. x)

Another important element in facilitating support networking and community is that all of us appreciate the value of diversity. Diversity is valued in inclusive schools. Diversity strengthens the school and classroom and offers all members greater opportunities for learning. The quote from Barth (1990), included in the preface of this book, needs to be reiterated here:

> I would prefer my children to be in a school in which differences are looked for, attended to, and celebrated as good news, as opportunities for learning. The question with which so many school people are preoccupied is, "What are the limits of diversity beyond which behavior is unacceptable?" … But the question I would like to see asked more often is, "How can we make conscious, deliberate use of differences in social class, gender, age, ability, race, and interest as resources for learning?" … Differences hold great opportunities for learning. Differences offer a free, abundant, and renewable resource. I would like to see óur compulsion for eliminating differences replaced by an equally compelling focus on making use of these differences to improve schools. What is important about people—and about schools—is what is different, not what is the same. (pp. 514–515)

CONCLUSION

Inclusive schools and classrooms do *not* focus on how to assist any particular category of students, such as those classified as having disabilities, to fit into the mainstream. Instead, inclusive schools and classrooms focus on how to operate classrooms and schools as supportive communities that include and meet the needs of all students. Personnel in inclusive schools and classrooms intentionally foster a sense of community— a sense that everyone belongs, is accepted, supports, and is supported by his or her peers and all members of the school community in the course of having his or her educational needs met. Much emphasis is placed on students, as well as all school staff, caring about and accepting responsibility for each other.

Although this is still a relatively new approach used by a growing number of schools, the need for greater development of inclusive school and classroom communities is widely recognized. Although inclusive schooling was initially an effort to welcome and support students with disabilities in their neighborhood schools and general education classrooms, the need for this approach to the education of all children is important. There is a growing need for support among all students as evidenced by the rising incidence of suicides, gang violence, and school dropouts and failures. A high school student, speaking at a local school board meeting concerning the gangs in her midwest community, voiced the importance of involving students in school decision making as well as of students not only needing, but also seeking supports.

> You guys should deal with us... not with the public, not with the TV. Talk to us. Because if there's a problem, it's us and it's us that should be dealt with.... Ask us why we join gangs. It's simple. People want to belong...they want to have someone they can lean on. In gangs, that's what happens. ("Gangs Hearing," 1990)

REFERENCES

Barth, R. (1990). A personal vision of a good school. *Phi Delta Kappan, 71,* 512–571.

Coleman, J., & Hoffer, T. (1987). *Public and private high schools: The impact of communities.* New York: Basic Books.

Falvey, M.A., Forest, M., Pearpoint, J., & Rosenberg, R.L. (1994). Building connections. In J.S. Thousand, R.A. Villa, & A.I. Nevin (Eds.), *Creativity and collaborative learning: A practical guide to empowering students and teachers* (pp. 347–368). Baltimore: Paul H. Brookes Publishing Co.

Flynn, G. (1989, November). *Toward community.* Paper presented at the annual conference of The Association for Persons with Severe Handicaps, San Francisco.

Gangs hearing: School board's policy review draws wide range of opinions. (1990, April 17). *Waterloo [IA] Courier.*

Jackson, J. (1990, October 12). *Full inclusion at Hansen.* Paper presented at the University of Northern Iowa, Cedar Falls.

Kohn, A. (1991). Caring kids: The role of the schools. *Phi Delta Kappan, 72*(7), 496–506.

Maeroff, G. (1990). Getting to know a good middle school. *Phi Delta Kappan, 71,* 505–511.

Pearpoint, J., O'Brien, J., & Forest, M. (1993). *PATH.* Toronto: Inclusion Press.

Reynolds, M. (1989). Foreword. In R. Gaylord-Ross (Ed.), *Integration strategies for students with handicaps* (pp. ix–x). Baltimore: Paul H. Brookes Publishing Co.

Sapon-Shevin, M. (1992). Celebrating diversity, creating community: Curriculum that honors and builds on differences. In S. Stainback & W. Stainback (Eds.), *Curriculum considerations in inclusive classrooms: Facilitating learning for all students* (pp. 19–36). Baltimore: Paul H. Brookes Publishing Co.

Schenkat, R. (1988, November). The promise of restructuring for special education. *Education Week, 8,* 36.

Snow, J., & Forest, M. (1987). Circles. In M. Forest (Ed.), *More education integration* (pp. 36–47). Downsview, Ontario: G. Allan Roeher Institute.

Solomon, D., Schaps, E., Watson, M., & Battistich, V. (1992). Creating caring school and classroom communities for all students. In R.A. Villa, J.S. Thousand, W. Stainback, & S. Stainback (Eds.), *Restructuring for caring and effective education: An administrative guide to creating heterogeneous schools* (pp. 41–60). Baltimore: Paul H. Brookes Publishing Co.

Stainback, S., & Stainback, W. (Eds.). (1992). *Curriculum considerations in inclusive classrooms: Facilitating learning for all students.* Baltimore: Paul H. Brookes Publishing Co.

Thousand, J.S., & Villa, R.A. (1992). Collaborative teams: A powerful tool in school restructuring. In R.A. Villa, J.S. Thousand, W. Stainback, & S. Stainback (Eds.), *Restructuring for caring and effective education: An administrative guide to creating heterogeneous schools* (pp. 73–108). Baltimore: Paul H. Brookes Publishing Co.

Wilkinson, J. (1980). On assistance to Indian people. *Social Casework: Journal of Contemporary Social Work, 61,* 451–454.

IV

CURRICULUM CONSIDERATIONS

13

Curriculum in Inclusive Classrooms

The Background

Susan Stainback and William Stainback

THIS CHAPTER ATTEMPTS to put the issue of curriculum into perspective by briefly reviewing some of the basic goals of inclusion as they relate to curriculum. The basic assumptions and premises underlying the development and design of curriculum in inclusive general education classrooms are briefly outlined and discussed. Finally, the chapter addresses how to design or adapt curricula so they are appropriate for inclusive classrooms.

CURRICULUM IN PERSPECTIVE

When discussing what students should learn, care must be exercised not to overemphasize predefined curriculum concerns. While learning math, history, geography, daily living skills (e.g., driving, cooking), and vocational skills is important, this is not the only or the primary goal for students with significant disabilities. Strully and Strully (1985) made this point clearly:

> Our daughter, Shawntell, is not going to one day wake up with all the competencies and skills that she needs in order to live independently. The reality is that we have been working on teaching Shawntell to use the bathroom for the last nine years. At this point in time, Shawntell is approximately 58% toilet trained. This is a significant increase in her accuracy, but Shawntell may never achieve complete success. The same is true for lots of other areas such as eating independently, walking, and commu-

nicating. Though Shawntell has learned important things and will continue to do so, the issue that we face is, will the skills our daughter has learned keep her in the community? The answer, we are afraid, is no!

Yet imagine if you will, that she did achieve all these competencies, would that make everything perfect? Again, the answer is no! One's ability to know things or master skills is not a litmus test of the person's capability to be an active member of the community and to have friends. What matters, we believe, is trying to be the best person you can and having people accept you for who you are, with all of your strengths and weaknesses. If we can accept people for who they are and not for who we want them to be, our communities will have moved a considerable distance. In the final analysis, whether or not Shawntell obtains all the competencies and skills in the world, it really isn't significant. What is important is being cared about by another human being. If Shawntell is really going to be an integral member of her community, she will need to rely on her friends who want to be involved with her because they are her friends. (pp. 7–8)

As is evident in this statement, among the major educational goals that enable students to be active members of their communities are socialization and friendships. When adults focus on and foster buddy systems and implement other friendship facilitation activities, children can gain what will be most important to them in their lives— relationships with a wide range of people who genuinely care about them as individuals. Thus, if a child never learns any math or history, it is still critical that he or she be included in the educational mainstream so that all students have opportunities to learn mutual respect and to care about and support each other in an integrated society.

A focus on friendships does not mean, however, that teachers and others should not be concerned about fostering curricular goals for all students in reading, math, history, daily living skills, or vocational skills. It is important that all students learn as much as they possible can in these areas, but specific curricular goal achievement is not always the major factor in later success and happiness in life.

The authors have observed classrooms and schools that have been both successful and unsuccessful in implementing inclusion. The successful classrooms and schools tended to focus on making students feel welcome, secure, and accepted and on ensuring that they have friends among teachers and students while developing feelings of belonging, positive self-worth, and success. In some cases, the primary goal was that the student be accepted by his or her peers and teachers while developing friendships and supportive relationships. For these students, the focus on predefined curricular goals was put on hold until acceptance and friendships were developed, although major efforts were made to keep them actively involved with their peers through related classroom activities. These students were generally included or involved in what their peers were doing during class even if the long-term benefits were not always immediately clear. Being accepted, welcomed, and feeling secure in a learning setting with their peers were considered prerequisite to the later success of students on focused learning tasks. Gradually, as students became accepted, they became involved in classroom activities in ways that addressed daily living, academic, and vocational objectives.

In contrast, classrooms and schools that were typically unsuccessful with inclusion tended to focus almost exclusively on assessing the previously excluded students' competencies in daily living, academic, and vocational skills and on designing specific curricular objectives and activities for them (regardless of what a particular student found to be of interest or felt secure in doing) and put far too little emphasis on relationships, acceptance, and friendships. This is not to imply that previously excluded students should initially focus only on socialization in an inclusive classroom. From the first day, all students should be involved in interesting, worthwhile learning activities that include them as much as possible with their classmates. Doing nothing or isolated, boring, or frustrating activities can lead to any student's dislike of the setting, to disruption, and to initial rejection by peers and educators.

With a focus on friendships, numerous opportunities for meaningful learning begin to emerge as friendships develop. It is through socialization with a diversity of peers in mainstream settings that children learn, find meaning and purpose to, and gain a greater understanding of the many subject areas covered in school. Perhaps even more important, if properly organized, the socialization process can provide opportunities for students to get to know, respect, care about, and support each other as well as learn academic, daily living, social, vocational, and other skills (e.g., sharing, communicating, initiating, responding, making choices, dressing and acting appropriately) critical to living and working in integrated and inclusive communities. We all learn many of the necessary and practical communication and social skills we need to live happy productive lives through socialization with peers (Johnson & Johnson, 1987). Students do not learn only from teacher–student interactions; much of what is learned in school is learned through student–student interactions. Thus, although curricula for inclusive classrooms is the topic of this chapter, it is important to keep the curriculum in perspective in the overall educational experience offered to students.

BASIC PREMISES OF CLASSROOM CURRICULUM

Curriculum has long been perceived and implemented from the perspective that general education classrooms have a standardized set of curriculum requirements or pieces of knowledge and skills that every student must achieve to successfully complete the grade. This view is based on the assumption that there are predefined bodies of knowledge or information that when learned in sequence result in success in postschool life (Poplin & Stone, 1992). It is such a set of sequenced information that has been used in many classrooms as "the curriculum." This standardized sequenced curriculum is often delivered through such means as lectures by the teacher and by students reading textbooks and completing worksheets to learn and practice the terms, concepts, and skills essential to the subject. For the most part, when a child cannot learn the curriculum through this type of approach, he or she is failed and in some cases is excluded from general education classrooms.

Fortunately for the inclusive school movement, this view of curriculum is increasingly in disfavor among progressive general educators (Smith, 1986). Some of the reasons are

- The growing recognition that in a rapidly changing, complex, and dynamic society there is no longer (if there ever was) a single, discrete, and static body of information that will result in students' success in adult life. Instead, a more productive approach has emerged, which is to teach students the learning process—a process that involves learning how to learn or becoming adept at discerning what is needed to adapt to and become proficient at in a new situation, and how and where to go about locating needed information.
- The lack of accommodation for the inherent diversity of the background experiences and learning speeds, styles, and interests of all students. This diversity exists not only among students who have been labeled at risk, gifted/talented, or with mental retardation, but also among typical students.
- The predefined curriculum's emphasis on the curriculum itself rather than the child. There is now an emphasis on starting with the child and building the curriculum around his or her experiences, perceptions, and current knowledge, keeping firmly in mind what people generally need to know in order to live happy and productive lives.
- Many students' perception of the traditional curriculum as boring, uninteresting, and purposeless (Smith, 1986). Standardized curricula often do not evolve from or relate to students' lives and the world around them.
- The disempowerment of the individuals directly involved in the learning process. A standardized curriculum is generally predefined by individuals such as consultants in state departments of education and curriculum specialists who compile, for example, basal readers and math and history textbooks. The knowledge and experience of the teachers and students involved in the actual learning situation regarding the meaningfulness of the materials to them and the best ways to learn the material often go unrecognized.

As a result of these shortcomings of a standardized lock-step curriculum, greater attention and acceptance is being given to a more holistic, constructivistic perspective on learning. There are a number of common elements in the holistic perspective:

- The recognition of the student as the center of learning (Lipsky & Gartner, 1992). A holistic perspective starts with the student and builds on student strengths (what the student already knows) in order to facilitate learning and success.
- The reduced emphasis on remediating deficits and weaknesses. These are addressed as students become excited about learning and engage in purposeful projects and activities.
- The recognition that 1) curriculum content must take into account the dynamic nature of what students need in order to successfully live and work in a community (thus the focus on learning how to learn); and 2) in order for information to be learned, used, and remembered, it must be meaningful and make sense to the learn-

er (thus the focus on considering the student's experiences, interest, and understanding).

- The teacher as facilitator of students who are actively involved in the process of learning information, rather than as dispenser of a standardized curriculum (Smith, 1986). The teacher may teach or share his or her knowledge with students through mini-lessons or other means but primarily focuses on helping students to be actively engaged in their own learning.
- The emphasis on real-life purposeful projects and activities. For example, students read and discuss interesting books and stories rather than learn fragmented isolated reading skills (e.g., diphthongs) by completing worksheets. Keeping a diary or journal and writing letters, memos, stories, books, and editorials for the newspaper constitute other typical activities. There is little focus on practicing skills such as punctuation, capitalization, or noun–verb identification in isolation; such skills are learned in the context of actual writing activities.
- The encouragement of all children to read (or listen or discuss) stories or information of interest to them at their individual ability level and to write (or to communicate in some other way) information that is meaningful to them. This perspective does not advocate an ironclad, preset, lock-step, standardized curriculum that all children of the same age must master at the same time regardless of their individual backgrounds, learning characteristics, interest, and experiences.
- The movement away from teaching students isolated skills in isolated settings and toward students learning through engagement in purposeful, real-life projects and activities as they interact and cooperate with each other (e.g., see Smith, 1986, about the concept of learning clubs).

An example of this shift in perspective is illustrated in an exchange that took place between a junior high school music teacher and an inclusion facilitator as they collaborated to determine what a new seventh-grade student who had been labeled as being nonverbal and with an autistic disorder and mental retardation might enjoy learning in the music class. In this particular classroom, the teacher engaged the children in listening to music, reading about the basic principles of music, learning to play various musical instruments, and composing their own musical pieces. That is, she facilitated them in becoming involved in actual music projects and activities as much as possible. Although there were some traditional lectures and textbook readings, the focus was on the children actively enjoying and engaging in actual music activities while learning about music and how it is created. The initial exchange between the teacher and the inclusion facilitator occurred as a result of the teacher's question, "What am I supposed to teach this student?" When asked what she wanted the other children to learn, she said that it was the enjoyment of music and its vocabulary such as scales and notes. When asked if everyone was required to master all the content in order to pass, the teacher initially said yes but then reconsidered her answer and replied that individual students were expected to learn varying amounts. Some students entered the class with considerable knowledge and appreciation of music through their experiences with piano and other music lessons, while other students were totally unfamiliar with the material. After further discussion, the two educators agreed that all students, including the new student, could be expected to achieve varying degrees of appreciation of and involvement with music and mastery of terms and concepts. However, it was agreed that mastery of the curriculum or content taught in class was not the ultimate objective of attending the class. Rather, the music curriculum (as other curriculum areas such as history or science) simply provided a vehicle for students to better understand, appreciate, adapt to, and use to the best of their ability whatever is available in the world around them (in this case, music) to live a satisfying and productive life as members of their community. In such a class, the teacher uses the curriculum to challenge every class member to achieve as much as possible. From a holistic, constructivistic perspective, all children are engaged in the process of learning as much as they can in a particular subject area; how much and exactly what they learn depends on their backgrounds, interests, and abilities. From this perspective, all students are able to gain from the learning opportunities offered in classrooms, and the purpose of the curriculum is not to define some students as successes and others as failures.

CONCLUSION

The following chapters in this section include strategies that help to use curriculum to foster the diverse abilities of class members in inclusive classrooms. Some strategies described are holistic, and others are more traditional in an attempt to cover the broad range of teaching styles in classrooms and schools. Nevertheless, more classrooms are moving toward a holistic, constructivistic perspective concerning curriculum.

REFERENCES

Johnson, D., & Johnson, R.T. (1987). *Joining together: Group therapy and group skills* (3rd ed.). Englewood Cliffs, NJ: Prentice Hall.

Lipsky, D., & Gartner, A. (1992). Achieving full inclusion: Placing the student at the center of educational reform. In W. Stainback & S. Stainback (Eds.), *Critical issues confronting special education* (pp. 5–20). Boston: Allyn & Bacon.

Poplin, M., & Stone, S. (1992). A holistic, constructivistic perspective. In W. Stainback & S. Stainback (Eds.), *Critical issues confronting special education* (pp. 175–197). Boston: Allyn & Bacon.

Smith, F. (1986). *Insult to intelligence.* New York: Arbor House.

Strully, J., & Strully, C. (1985). Friendship and our children. *Journal of The Association for Persons with Severe Handicaps, 10,* 224–227.

14

Learning in Inclusive Classrooms

What About the Curriculum?

*William Stainback, Susan Stainback,
Greg Stefanich, and Sandra Alper*

> *We do not have to choose between socialization and friendships in general education classes and a quality education in special classes. We can provide a quality education in general education classes. (Strully & Strully, 1989, p. 77)*

GROWING NUMBERS OF previously excluded students are being integrated into the mainstream of general education (Alper & Ryndak, 1992; Falvey, 1995; Stainback & Stainback, 1992; Villa, Thousand, & Nevin, 1994). However, these students need more than mere placement in the mainstream. They also need to be *included* as equal and valued members of the classroom. There has been considerable emphasis on how to include all students in the social life of the classroom (see Stainback & Stainback, 1990), but considerably less attention has been given to how all students can be involved in actively learning in inclusive classrooms.

This chapter suggests some strategies that general educators, in collaboration with inclusion facilitators and other specialists, can use to make classroom curriculum adaptive, flexible, and challenging to *all* students. The strategies presented are based on a

Portions of what is presented in this chapter are based on material previously published in Stainback, W., & Stainback, S. (1992). Using curriculum to build inclusive classrooms. In S. Stainback & W. Stainback (Eds.), *Curriculum considerations in inclusive classrooms: Facilitating learning for all students* (pp. 65–84). Baltimore: Paul H. Brookes Publishing Co.

review of the professional literature and research regarding curriculum in education (e.g., Falvey, 1995; Giangreco, Cloninger, & Iverson, 1993; Sommerstein, Schooley, & Ryndak, 1992; Stainback & Stainback, 1992) and on the authors' own experiences in working in general education classes.

STRATEGIES FOR ADAPTING CLASSROOM CURRICULUM

Use Flexible Learning Objectives

With such a diversity of students included in the mainstream, we as educators must take a critical look at what is being required of each student. Although basic educational goals for all students may remain the same, specific curricular learning objectives may need to be individualized to fit the unique needs, skills, interests, and abilities of students. For example, a basic goal in a language arts class, such as effective communication, may be appropriate for all students, but the specific learning objectives that meet the goal may not be the same for all students. For many students, an objective may be to learn to write letters to friends. But for other students, a more appropriate objective might include dictating a letter into a tape recorder or expanding communication board vocabulary options in order to communicate with friends.

When what is required of students is *not* considered on an individual basis, apathy toward schoolwork can result. Persistence is a byproduct of success, and if success is repeatedly out of the reach of the student he or she learns not to try (Seligman, 1975). This "learned helplessness" is exhibited by students when there is not a good match between learning objectives and student attributes; therefore, one single set of standardized objectives cannot be expected to meet the unique learning abilities of individual students in inclusive classrooms. Individual abilities can and should be considered in light of curricular activities of the classroom peer group. Developing separate or different objectives for one or several students can lead to their isolation and segregation within the classroom. Building on activities that address the diverse abilities of students while maintaining a group context and having class members at various times address different objectives can help offset this potential problem.

An illustration of individualizing learning objectives occurred in a third-grade science class. The need to choose learning objectives appropriate to individual students resulted in the classroom teacher and the inclusion facilitator working together to develop the following plan of action. Although the basic curricular goal of the science unit, "Understanding the Physical World Around Us—What Is Temperature," was considered to be appropriate for all students, individual students had different skills and knowledge so that each needed to focus his or her energies toward different specific learning objectives in working toward the goal. Most of the students were learning to use Fahrenheit and Celsius temperature scales, while others were working with molecular movement at different temperatures. One student was learning to recognize the terms *hot* and *cold* and to create an operational definition by describing the term from experiences with different objects. In this general education science unit, each student was called on to contribute to real-life science projects involving temperature and to engage in activities appropriate to the objectives he or she was responsible for learning. That is, while all students were pursuing the same basic educational goal (what is heat and how is it measured) and learning together in class activities, it was necessary for students to focus on and be evaluated by different curricular objectives.

Everyone benefited from the diversity in this class. The activities of the student learning to differentiate and to use hot and cold items, for example, gave the other students who were learning temperature scales many opportunities to construct practical, real-life hot and cold situations and to practice measuring various temperatures. In addition, the student who needed experience in differentiating and using hot and cold items received many opportunities and ample assistance in learning to do so.

Another example occurred in a fourth-grade classroom math period. This example is based on a classroom situation cited by Ford and Davern (1989) but has been modified to illustrate several points about curriculum adaptations. This fourth-grade class was learning to multiply and divide three- and four-digit numbers. The teacher used the traditional approach of lecturing and asking the students questions about how to multiply and divide these numbers, worked several problems at the chalkboard to illustrate the concepts and procedures, assigned worksheets for student practice, and, toward the end of the class, discussed and asked the students questions about real-life math problems involving multiplying and dividing three- and four-digit numbers.

Because there were students with diverse abilities and achievement levels in the class, not all of them were ready to learn to multiply and divide three- and four-digit numbers. One student, Shawn, was reviewing number recognition, learning how to count from 1 to 100, and matching coins to money cards (graphic representations of coins).

The inclusion facilitator assisted by analyzing the math lesson to see how students who were at different levels in math could be included in the general unit. For example, for Shawn, questions such as the following were explored: Could the teacher ask Shawn to identify some of the numbers (e.g., 6) in the examples on the chalkboard in the same way that other students are asked if they could calculate 8 times 9 or regroup numbers? When worksheets were handed out, could Shawn receive one that required number recognition and coins to be matched with money cards rather than the worksheet with multiplication and division problems? When discussing real-life math problems involving three- and four-digit multiplication and division problems, could the teacher ask Shawn which number is larger, 3 or 5, in the problem written on the chalkboard in the same way another student is asked how to solve the problem? The danger this example presents is that the student might be perceived as separate or different because he was engaged in different math activities. However, in this particular class, a variety of students often engaged in different activities so it did not seem strange to the other students that Shawn worked on number recognition.

Furthermore, the classroom teacher, with assistance from the inclusion facilitator, organized a class activity in which *all* the students participated in a practical real-life experience that applied what they had been learning in the math class, and a hot chocolate business was set up (Ford & Davern, 1989). For 6 weeks, the class operated the business each day during math. Groups of five or six students were assigned on a rotating basis to a schedule drawn up by the classroom teacher and inclusion facilitator.

On Mondays, Tuesdays, and Thursdays the business operated in the classroom, and on Fridays the class operated the hot chocolate business during school recess. On Wednesdays, the students walked two blocks to a grocery store where they purchased supplies.

Planning the business, keeping records, and figuring expenses, prices, and profits provided many opportunities to practice a range of math skills and to learn community-based skills (e.g., traveling to the grocery store, locating and purchasing goods). A typical classroom lesson was planned to accomplish a variety of objectives. These included learning to apply the multiplication and division procedures that many students were working on. Objectives also included learning skills that Shawn and other students needed such as how to count money, how to match real coins to representations of coins on money cards, and community-based skills. In addition to the math skills all the students learned, it is important to acknowledge that this activity also presented opportunities for the students to develop social and communication skills, daily living skills (e.g., shopping, going to the store, cooking), and for some students, such as Shawn, motor skills.

Activity Adaptation

Teachers also may need to modify activities in which a particular student participates or the way he or she achieves objectives. The following example illustrates how modifications can be accomplished.

In a high school American history unit, students had a general curricular goal, "Understanding the Civil War." One primary objective for the students was to learn about the key figures in the war through readings, library research, and class discussion. One student had strong artistic talent but could not read or write and had considerable difficulty expressing himself verbally. While most students were given reading assignments for homework, this student had homework assignments to draw poster-size portraits of these key figures from their pictures in the textbook. Subsequently, his drawings were used as the stimulus for discussion about the people being studied. Students were requested to share with this student and others what they learned from readings and outside research concerning a particular person (e.g., personality, consequences of key decisions made during the war).

For evaluation, while most of the students wrote an essay about one of the Civil War figures to share with their classmates, this student, along with some of his classmates, conceptualized and constructed a Civil War mural to be displayed in the classroom that included the figures in some activity appropriate to them. The mural formed a basis for sharing the essays and for discussing these historic individuals among class members. In this way, this student, who did not have the skills necessary to learn and share information about historic figures of the Civil War in the same ways as the majority of the students, was nevertheless involved with his peers in classroom curriculum activities.

In the above example, the student contributed to the class by producing poster-size pictures and by developing a mural, all of which were used to stimulate class discussions. At the same time, he had opportunities to improve his skills in drawing, group participation, volunteering information (e.g., pointing to his pictures), and listening to and responding to classmates (e.g., show the picture of Robert E. Lee). In addition, he had an opportunity to share and learn with his classmates information about key figures in the Civil War.

Multiple Adaptations

In addition to curricular variations of single elements to accommodate diverse student abilities (e.g., adapting objectives, pursuing different objectives, adapting activities), several such modifications can be implemented simultaneously. Illustrations of multiple adaptations are given in the following examples.

In an integrated English literature class at a junior high school level, students were studying the concept of courage. Activities of the unit included becoming familiar with the story *My Friend Flicka* (O'Hara, 1988) and demonstrating or explaining how courage was an important element in the story and how such courage might relate to the students' own lives. A broad range of student abilities, interests, and knowledge in the class influenced the selection of diverse learning objectives, from simply recognizing characters and what was meant by courage to analyzing, synthesizing, and forecasting events in the story.

In order for students to pursue the individual learning objectives, the classroom teacher and inclusion facilitator working together organized a series of activities that presented and explored the elements of the story in a variety of ways. Various ways of learning and reporting on the story were provided to students, including reading the story silently, listening to tape recordings of the story, arranging picture sequences of the story, and writing summary reports. In this way, students with diverse abilities could participate in the unit. One student who could not read listened to a tape recording explaining the basic ideas of the story in simplified language and shared these elements and ideas in discussions with peers. Some students made a picture book and taped an explanation of the pictures to summarize what was learned, and other students wrote traditional book reports.

After initial exposure to the story, the teachers divided the class into small groups of students of differing abilities with the assigned task of reviewing the story and sharing and explaining facts, concepts, and insights about the characters and plot with each other. With prompting and support from classmates, each student shared his or her knowledge of the main character and what courage meant to him or her. Some students helped members of their group analyze and synthesize events in the story.

Another example of multiple adaptations took place in a high school biology class that was studying plants. The curricular goal was for class members to learn and understand various aspects of plant characteristics and growth. To ensure that students had experiences in observing plants, all class members visited a plant nursery and were involved in growing a variety of plants in the classroom. In addition to the traditional class textbook, the teacher and inclusion facilitator arranged to have a variety of books on plants, such as books with pictures of plants in various stages of development, simple pamphlets on plant care, books with stories about plants, videotapes of plant growth using time-lapse photography, and elementary- to college-level textbooks and plants. Many students were responsible for learning and understanding plant types (e.g., vascular, nonvascular), technical terminology for plant parts (e.g., herbaceous stems), and technical processes of plant life (e.g., photosynthesis).

However, during the unit students did have different specific objectives in the group activities. For example, one student was unable to read the technical words or comprehend the growth processes of plants. Nevertheless, she still could participate with her classmates in the study of plants by concentrating on learning objectives that included labeling parts of plants in everyday language, such as root, stem, and leaf. She also learned along with her peers how to plant seeds, cuttings, roots, and young plants into soil and was responsible for their care (water, fertilizing, placing in light). During class discussions, the teacher asked her questions in everyday language about plants and about practical procedures for growing plants in the same way he asked other students questions about technical terminology and growth processes.

All the students not only learned about plants but also worked cooperatively and contributed to the class by growing and nurturing a number of different plants in the classroom for everyone to observe and study. Everyone in the class benefited—the student who could not read learned practical, everyday terms for plants, how to grow plants, and a few technical words. Other class members related the technical terminology, concepts, and ideas they were learning in the biology class to actual live plants.

IMPLEMENTATION CONSIDERATIONS

A Team Approach

Some educators have had little or no experience in providing or adapting a general education curriculum to meet all students' needs. Thus, for some people, it may be seen as an overwhelming and intimidating task. This problem generally can be overcome by a team of people (i.e., teachers, parents, classmates, administrators, occupational and physical therapists, communications experts, school psychologists) meeting together when needed to brainstorm and provide suggestions about curricular objectives for a particular child or children and how these objectives can be achieved in general education classrooms. When educators have had some experience and practice in curricular design and adaptations that include and challenge all students, it becomes fairly easy and natural for the teacher, collaborating with colleagues, specialists, students, and parents, to develop ongoing curricular procedures or accommodations. However, at first, teachers are likely to need assistance from a team of people to learn how to provide appropriate learning experiences for the diverse students in their classrooms.

Peer Involvement

Students can help teachers implement the type of curriculum flexibility that has been discussed in this chapter. In fact, the involvement of students in their own learning experiences and in the planning and implementation of purposeful and meaningful learning experiences for their classmates is seen as critical to inclusive classrooms. Students can propose activities, gather materials, and organize and implement whatever help any one of them needs. The authors have observed a circle of friends volunteering their free time on weekends to gather materials and organize a classroom curriculum activity for a classmate as well as help the classroom teacher to implement the activity while achieving their own educational objectives. These students felt that becoming involved in helping someone else was a valuable learning experience and did not see this as a distraction from their studies or a drain on their time. In fact, many students reported that, for the first time, they had a real reason to thoroughly learn the material they were studying in the classroom and, as a result, got better grades. One student said, "I found out that when you help someone else, you often end up helping yourself."

Functional Skills

Curricular concerns, such as daily living and vocational skills, that were traditionally addressed because of their practical utility for students in segregated learning settings need not be eliminated when students are included in general education classrooms. Students who require opportunities to learn practical living, vocational, and social skills can be provided guidance and opportunities at natural times throughout the day. Lunch and snack time and home economics classes can provide opportunities for class members to learn food preparation, eating, and dining skills. Dressing and grooming skills can be fostered naturally before and after school or gym class, and bus riding skills can be taught when students travel back and forth to school and in the community. With guidance from and interactions with peers and adults, many daily living skills are learned naturally by students as they observe and share with their peers recreational and work activities in mainstream settings. The authors have observed students in a junior high school teaching a classmate, without prompting from adults, how to comb her hair, wear makeup, and dress in style. Within several weeks, the student dressed and looked like any other junior high school student, despite years of failure in teaching, collecting "hard data," and programming "generalization" of such skills "systematically" in isolated settings. Similarly, skills such as ordering and eating in fast food restaurants, going to the movies, hanging out, and shopping at the mall have been learned naturally while spending time with parents and peers.

In addition, community-referenced and vocational skills can be taught in general education work–study programs and in cooperative education programs. One parent described how her daughter (a student with Down syndrome) gained her most valuable vocational skills in a supervised after-school and summer-jobs program for teens in her community (Sylvester, 1987). Summer, weekend, and after-school jobs are natural, normal ways for all students to develop vocational skills as long as needed supports are provided.

It should be stressed that it is a mistake to place elementary or high school students classified as having disabilities in the community during school hours to learn "functional, community-referenced, or vocational skills" unless other students in general education classes are also doing this. This segregating practice decreases the opportunities for students classified as having disabilities to become integrally involved in and make friends in general education classes. As noted above, functional, community-referenced, and vocational skills can be learned in natural environments.

It is important *not* to assume that the general class curriculum is nonfunctional for some students. The following example illustrates this point. Each morning during the first 15 minutes of a sixth-grade class, the classroom teacher asked the students to report on a news story they had seen on television or read in the newspaper. The inclusion facilitator and classroom teacher had doubts about whether this was a functional activity for a 12-year-old student classified as having mental retardation and autistic disorder because, in their best judgment, he would never fully understand or become fluent in discussions of current affairs. However, because they were committed to inclusion, they arranged ways for him to participate. They recommended to his mother that he watch a television news story each night and look at pictures in the newspaper while she explained them to him. She also was asked to coach him on one story each night that he could share with the class. (He was particularly fond of sports so the stories often related to sporting events.) By learning a news story each night, the student had something to say when the teacher asked for volunteers to report on a news story. Prompting from the teacher and his classmates was often necessary, but the student gradually became an active participant in class.

After careful consideration, both the classroom teacher and inclusion facilitator concluded that this was functional for the student. He learned something that allowed him to participate with other students his age, which opened up opportunities for socialization and potential friendships. He also became more aware of his environment through news stories, increased his vocabulary, learned to take turns and interact with his peers, and practiced remembering, listening to, and sharing ideas. These were all considered functional and useful skills.

The definition of what is meant by functional needs to be broadened to include science, art, music, history, English literature, and other subjects. All students need to master whatever they can in these academic areas and use their knowledge to improve their quality of life with their peers in the community. Contrary to the arguments of some (e.g., Brown et al., 1990), learning history, geography, science, and math with classmates is functional and in the long-term best interests of all students, including those classified as having significant intellectual disabilities. Although not everyone can learn the same amount or the same knowledge in these academic areas, whatever is gained is of value and is worthwhile. There is more to anyone's life than learning to make a sandwich or sweep a floor. It also is worthwhile for any of us, regardless of individual characteristics, to have a sense of who we are, know who our ancestors were, and appreciate the environment and world around us. It is a serious mistake to underestimate or place limitations on some students by assuming that the only things they can learn that are useful to them are how to tie their shoes or ride a bus. In addition, it is critical to guard against educating a subgroup of students in such a way that they share few common experiences and understandings with the people they are expected to live, socialize, and work with in the community.

The arguments about learning practical living and vocational skills versus academic instruction are waning. Many people are beginning to see the need to integrate all these skills into the educational experiences of all students. It has been found that, although academic learning can lead to better community-referenced vocational competence, vocational community-referenced learning can provide more context and motivation for learning academic subjects and higher-order thinking skills (Rosenstock, 1991; Wirt, 1991).

Ryndak (in press) described a curriculum-blending process for developing individualized curriculum content for students in inclusive classrooms. This process draws on functional and age-appropriate skills typically included in special education and general education curricula. An overview of the curriculum-blending process described in detail by Ryndak is represented in Figure 1. First, information from a variety of sources is gathered in order to identify the functional curriculum needs of an individual student. Second, information is gathered to identify relevant curriculum objectives from an inventory of general education settings and curriculum content. Third, the educational team uses this information to negotiate annual goals for the student and make a decision regarding which settings would be most appropriate for pursuing the goals.

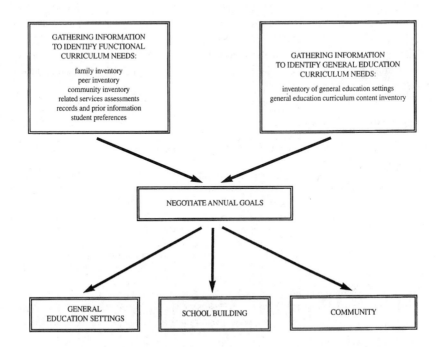

Figure 1. Blended curriculum content flowchart.

Educationally Challenge All Students

If the curricular objectives or activities are made too easy through curriculum adaptations when the student could, with persistence or different learning methods, master more challenging learning opportunities, the student is done a disservice. Research has shown that students are more successful educationally and socially when school personnel maintain high expectations for them (Jones & Jones, 1986). Thus, the curriculum provided to *all* students should challenge them to stretch their abilities as much as possible and to surpass previous achievements, with *the necessary adaptations and supports*. Although the goals and methods of teaching educational programs should be adapted to meet the individual needs of each student, high expectations and challenges for each student, based on his or her unique capabilities and needs, are essential in providing each student a quality education.

CONCLUSION

The major reason for inclusion is *not* that previously excluded students are necessarily going to become proficient in socialization, history, or math, although it is obvious that there are more opportunities for everyone to grow and learn in inclusive classrooms. Rather, inclusion of all students teaches the student with disabilities and his or her peers that all persons are equally valued members of society and that it is worthwhile to do whatever is necessary in order to include everyone in our society. The previously accepted mode of dealing with differences in people was segregation, which communicates the message that we do not want to accept everyone and that some people are not worth the efforts to include them. As stated by Forest (1988), "If we really want someone to be part of our lives, we will do what it takes to welcome that person and accommodate his or her needs" (p. 3).

REFERENCES

Alper, S., & Ryndak, D. (1992). Educating students with severe handicaps in regular classes. *Elementary Schools, 92,* 373–388.

Brown, L., Schwartz, P., Udvari-Solner, A., Kampschroer, E., Johnson, F., Jorgensen, J., & Gruenewald, L. (1990). *How much time should students with severe intellectual disabilities spend in regular education classrooms and elsewhere?* Madison: University of Wisconsin, Department of Behavioral Studies.

Falvey, M. (Ed.). (1995). *Inclusive and heterogeneous schooling: Assessment, curriculum, and instruction.* Baltimore: Paul H. Brookes Publishing Co.

Ford, A., & Davern, L. (1989). Moving forward with school integration. In R. Gaylord-Ross (Ed.), *Integration strategies for students with handicaps* (pp. 11–31). Baltimore: Paul H. Brookes Publishing Co.

Forest, M. (1988). Full inclusion is possible. *Impact, 1,* 3–4.

Giangreco, M., Cloninger, C., & Iverson, V.S. (1993). *Choosing options and accommodations for children: A guide to planning inclusive education.* Baltimore: Paul H. Brookes Publishing Co.

Jones, V., & Jones, L. (1986). *Comprehensive classroom management.* Boston: Allyn & Bacon.

O'Hara, M. (1988). *My friend Flicka.* New York: HarperCollins.

Rosenstock, L. (1991). The walls come down: The overdue reunification of vocational and academic education. *Phi Delta Kappan, 72,* 434–436.

Ryndak, D. (in press). The curriculum content identification process. In D. Ryndak & S. Alper (Eds.), *Curriculum content for students with moderate to severe disabilities in inclusive settings.* Boston: Allyn & Bacon.

Seligman, M. (1975). *Helplessness: On depression, development and death.* San Francisco: W.H. Freeman.

Sommerstein, L., Schooley, R., & Ryndak, D. (1992, November 19). *Including students with moderate or severe disabilities in general education settings.* Paper presented at the annual regional conference of the Genessee County Special Education Training and Resource Center, Genessee, NY.

Stainback, W., & Stainback, S. (Eds.). (1990). *Support networks for inclusive schooling: Interdependent integrated education.* Baltimore: Paul H. Brookes Publishing Co.

Stainback, S., & Stainback, W. (Eds.). (1992). *Curriculum considerations in inclusive schools: Facilitating learning for all students.* Baltimore: Paul H. Brookes Publishing Co.

Strully, S., & Strully, C., (1989). Friendships as an educational goal. In S. Stainback, W. Stainback, & M. Forest (Eds.), *Educating all students in the mainstream of regular education* (pp. 59–68). Baltimore: Paul H. Brookes Publishing Co.

Sylvester, D. (1987, October). *A parent's perspective on transition: From high school to what?* Paper presented at the Least Restrictive Environment Conference, Burlington, VT.

Thousand, J.S., Villa, R.A., & Nevin, A.I. (Eds.). (1994). *Creativity and collaborative learning: A practical guide to empowering students and teachers.* Baltimore: Paul H. Brookes Publishing Co.

Wirt, J. (1991). A new federal law on vocational education: Will reform follow? *Phi Delta Kappan, 72,* 425–433.

15

Designing Inclusive Curricula Right from the Start

Practical Strategies and Examples for the High School Classroom

Cheryl M. Jorgensen

IN THE PREVIOUS chapter, designing and adapting the classroom curriculum at both the elementary and secondary levels to meet the needs of all students was discussed. In this chapter, the focus is on designing inclusive curricula specifically for high school students, a topic about which little has been published to date. The chapter is divided into four parts. In Part 1, song lyrics by Billy Joel are used to begin the discussion about developing an inclusive high school curriculum. In Part 2, the foundations of curriculum design are outlined, and many everyday, practical examples of high school curriculum are discussed. Part 3 focuses on professional development strategies for supporting teachers who want to adopt this innovation. Part 4 discusses the still-puzzling difficulties in developing inclusive curricula.

Preparation of this chapter was supported by Grant no. H023R20018 from the U.S. Department of Education, Office of Special Education and Rehabilitative Services, Office of Special Education Programs, Division of Innovation and Development. The opinions expressed in this chapter are not necessarily those of the U.S. Department of Education or the University of New Hampshire.

PART 1: WHAT DOES A BILLY JOEL SONG HAVE TO DO WITH DEVELOPING INCLUSIVE HIGH SCHOOL CURRICULA?

At Souhegan High School in Amherst, New Hampshire, and at other schools in the Coalition of Essential Schools (Sizer, 1992), provocative learning materials and the use of a systematic curriculum design process can accommodate student diversity right from the start, instead of through later "modification," "remediation," or "enrichment." (Table 1 displays the principles of Coalition schools and Souhegan's unique mission statement.)

The song "We Didn't Start the Fire" by Billy Joel (1989) was used by a team of teachers from Souhegan to teach students about U.S. culture and history during the second half of the 20th century. "Essential Questions" that guided the 89 ninth-grade Souhegan students through the unit were: What is the fire? Who started the fire? Have any fires been put out? Are any fires still burning?

On a cold Monday morning in January, all 89 students gathered on Team 9A to listen to the song. Each student was given a copy of the written lyrics, several copies of the taped song were made available, and teachers explained the unit. The teachers wanted students to learn much of the cultural history of America since the 1940s through a cooperative interdisciplinary unit. For a final exhibition (a culminating demonstration that showed what students had learned), students were told to "wow" their classmates and teachers with a 15-minute presentation that would address at least two of the essential questions, explain a portion of the lyrics, and educate their peers. Student work was assessed in 11 categories ranging from "demonstration of prepara-

Table 1. Principles of the Coalition of Essential Schools and mission statement of Souhegan High School

Principles of the Coalition of Essential Schools

1. Focusing on helping students to use their minds well
2. A few simple but clear goals
3. Interdisciplinary learning
4. Personalization and interdependence
5. Student as worker
6. Teacher as coach
7. Diploma reflects achievement of performance-based skills and knowledge
8. An ethic of growth, development, and inquiry
9. A just community that reflects democratic principles

Mission statement

Souhegan High School aspires to be a community of learners born of respect, trust, and courage. We consciously commit ourselves:

To support and engage an individual's unique gifts, passions, and intentions.

To develop and empower the mind, body, and heart.

To challenge and expand the comfortable limits of thought, tolerance, and performance.

To inspire and honor the active stewardship of family, nation, and globe.

From Souhegan High School Program of Studies, 1994–1995.

tion time" to "effective use of selected medium." The grading scale included "distinctive," "effective," "acceptable," and "ineffective." Teachers applied discretionary grading points, referred to as the "wow" factor.

Students learned laser disc technology in order to view newsreel footage of historical events; they explored CD ROM media; and they mastered video technology, taping from discs, and dubbing soundtracks and voiceovers. They laughed when they discovered that, although they were surrounded by sophisticated audiovisual equipment, they could not find a record player in the building!

Final exhibitions ranged from a "Saturday Night Live" skit, in which Davy Crockett and Albert Einstein visited "Wayne's World," to a demonstration of a cycle theory model, in which every person or event is identified as either a problem, an inspiration, or a solution. One group staged a re-creation of the explosion of the bridge over the River Kwai, and another combined television footage of Nasser's funeral with music by Prokofiev. The variety of exhibitions—tapping talents in writing, speaking, acting, musical performance, and building—made this unit particularly inclusive of all students on the team.

The team's English teacher recorded her teammates' comments about what they as teachers had learned:

- We need to develop a new language to describe students—not LD, coded SPED, high level, or most challenged. These terms do not fit our experience when we design curriculum based on real world solutions to real world situations. (social studies teacher)
- Although 20 percent of our team population is labeled as educationally handicapped, visitors to our classroom have difficulty identifying those students "most labeled." We certainly acknowledge the need for "special services"; each of our 89 students requires special services at some point. (mathematics teacher)
- Some of our students need to learn to work with others, others need to learn to demonstrate learning without a pen or a multiple choice chapter test. Some of our students need help to write with clarity, to comprehend reading, to concentrate and complete a task, to become better organized, or to present work creatively. (science teacher)
- Our students represent great diversity of skill, ability, and interest, but the balance shifts according to the nature of the tasks. Every time we grapple with essential questions that require active student participation, we hear students testify that they have learned more in 1 week than they could have learned in a month in a lecture-oriented classroom. With such powerful testimony, how can we ever return to our old methods? (special education teacher)

PART 2: FOUNDATIONS OF INCLUSIVE CURRICULUM DESIGN

When students with widely varied talents, interests, learning styles, and support needs are fully included in content-driven high school classes, developing the curriculum and delivering instructions can be challenging. Although the formation of essential questions (Table 2) is a springboard from which inclusive curriculum can be developed, there are other components of curriculum design that are also necessary to ensure that

Table 2. Characteristics and examples of essential questions

Characteristics
1. They help students become investigators.
2. They involve thinking, not just answering.
3. They offer a sense of adventure and are fun to explore and to answer.
4. All students can answer them.
5. They require students to connect different disciplines and areas of knowledge.

Examples
1. How will the face of America change in the next century?
2. What is your sense of place?
3. What does having money do to people?
4. If we can, should we?
5. Is the world orderly or random?
6. Is it true that the more things change, the more they stay the same?
7. Can you be free if you're not treated equally?
8. How can you tell if something is living?

all students are challenged and included. These components comprise a planning/ teaching/evaluation model that can be used by individual teachers or teaching teams (Figure 1). Each step in the planning/teaching/evaluation process is briefly explained, and examples are given from a variety of subject areas for a variety of students. (Some examples are drawn from the author's experience at Souhegan High School; others are stories of students from other schools in New Hampshire.)

Meet Four Members of the Class of 1996

Colleen appears to sail through her academic work without lifting a finger. It is clear, however, that she is bored in some of her classes because she twirls her long blond hair around her pencil and appears frustrated with the time that it is taking her social studies group to decide on a topic for their project.

Amro spent the first 13 years of his life in segregated classes for students with disabilities. He communicates with lightening-quick speed by pointing to letters on an alphabet board—the same board that accompanied him out on the field in the fall when he kicked off in his first football game. Amro has great difficulty remembering facts and details about the subject areas he studies, but he has no difficulty making connections between some general topics (e.g., slavery) and his own life.

Brandon takes a long time to get to know, but he has a biting sense of humor and a playful personality. Last year his 10th-grade science class hiked to the Souhegan River to do water sampling, and his math teacher gave Brandon a piggy-back ride through the muddy fields. The teacher had to laugh because Brandon had his hands so tight around her neck, and she said, "Brandon, hold on tight, but just don't cover up my eyes or we're in trouble." Brandon's hands instantly went up to her eyes. This incident shows Brandon at his best, but many days at school are not happy ones for him. Some-

Planning Inclusive Performance-Based Curriculum

A. Unit topic/title: _____ Time needed: _____ weeks

B. Other subject areas this unit may connect with: _____

C. Outcomes/proficiencies/skills: What do you expect students to remember about this unit and to be able to do a year from now when they have forgotten all the details? Can all students achieve some of these outcomes? Do these outcomes take into consideration student diversity?

1. _____
2. _____
3. _____
4. _____
5. _____
6. _____
7. _____
8. _____

D. Essential questions—they "hook" students into wanting to learn. Can all students answer some of these questions? Are they provocative? Do they involve thinking, not just answering? Do they provide opportunities for students to begin the unit from their own past experience or understanding?

1. _____
2. _____
3. _____
4. _____

E. Performance-based exhibitions—ways students can show that they understand the material and perform the skills of the unit. What might students produce that will be interesting and useful for others? Who are some of the natural audiences for student work? Are there options for students who have different learning styles and talents?

1. _____
2. _____
3. _____
4. _____

F. Activities, materials, and resources: Do these activities include opportunities for students to utilize different "intelligences" or talents? Are the activities student-centered, requiring them to do the "work" of learning? Are the materials and learning resources representative of different reading levels and learning styles?

Activity   *Material resources needed*
1.
2.
3.

_____

(continued)

Figure 1.   Form for planning inclusive performance-based curriculum.

Figure 1. *(continued)*

G. Planning for students with extraordinary learning challenges

Student: _____

Priority learning goals:

1. _____
2. _____
3. _____
4. _____

Technology and materials needed:

1. _____
2. _____
3. _____
4. _____

H. Lesson plans—the schedule of lessons or activities that will be offered to help students learn about this topic. Are there opportunities for students to collaborate? Is the primary work of the curriculum accomplished by students actively thinking through, experimenting with, speculating about, researching, debating, discussing, and responding rather than by teachers lecturing? Are a variety of media available through which students can discover new information and ideas? Is enough support available to students in and outside the classroom?

Day	Monday	Tuesday	Wednesday	Thursday	Friday
Week 1					
Week 2					
Week 3					

I. How will student work be evaluated? Have standards and examples of quality work been shared with students? Do students have the opportunity to reflect on and judge their own learning? Is a larger audience involved in evaluating student work? Does feedback reflect constructive suggestions that will lead students to further their interest in learning? Are grades assigned based on individualized expectations rather than by comparing one student's work with that of another?

Portfolio for this unit consists of the following items (homework, tests, exhibitions)

1. _____
2. _____
3. _____
4. _____
5. _____
6. _____

Homework assignments

1. _____
2. _____
3. _____
4. _____

Tests

1. _____
2. _____
3. _____
4. _____

(continued)

Figure 1. *(continued)*

Exhibition #1

Description: _____

Outcome/proficiency/skill	Rubric
	1. 2. 3. 4.
	1. 2. 3. 4.
	1. 2. 3. 4.
	1. 2. 3. 4.

times he is able to articulate through facilitated communication, but other days his silence is very frustrating for him and for others around him.

Andrew gave his first presentation in class last year in 10th grade. He wrote a four-stanza poem about cars, entered it on a computer, and illustrated it with intricate drawings of a formula one race car. Andrew can add and subtract up to 20, use a calculator for multiplication and division, and read at a second-grade level. He is at constant risk for dropping out and needs to develop a work ethic as well as additional literacy and vocational skills before he graduates.

Planning Backward for Inclusive Curriculum

The process by which a teacher or team of teachers develops a curriculum unit that accommodates student diversity generally follows the steps outlined in Figure 1 (Fried & Jorgensen, 1994). Planning backward simply means that curriculum planning begins with the identification of the outcomes that teachers want students to demonstrate and that the nuts and bolts of the curriculum—the design of individual lessons and the selection of learning materials—follows from these outcomes and from the essential questions that guide the unit.

A. Unit Topic/Title When Souhegan High School Team 9B decided to teach an interdisciplinary unit one winter, each teacher on the team gave a brief overview of the curriculum content that he or she would typically introduce to students over the course of the next month or so. The teachers did not know where this sharing of information would lead, but they were open to ideas:

"I don't mean to be selfish," began the social studies teacher, "but the state of New Hampshire requires all ninth graders to have a unit in economics and I just don't know when I'm going to get that unit in. I need to deal with money, distribution of wealth, and the micro and macro forces of economic theory."

"I was planning to do something on ecosystems," offered the science teacher. "Probably using the rain forest as an example, since I have some ideas I've gathered from various Earth Day celebrations and from my trip to Costa Rica. Maybe some kind of unit having to do with the negative impact of overharvesting the Brazilian rain forest could help us tie together some of our disciplines?"

The team English teacher felt that, regardless of what unit they picked, she could identify literature that would support the theme. Piggybacking on the economic unit idea, she said, "You know, I've used *Raisin in the Sun* [Hansberg] and Studs Terkel's *Working* real effectively with ninth graders to give them an appreciation for some of the economic issues associated with poverty and social class.

The math teacher said, "I am so frustrated with my integrated math curriculum handbook. I would love to just ignore it for a month and do some real practical stuff on graphing, computer modeling, tax rates, and proportion that would fit into ideas about the economics and ecosystems units. Why don't you guys just count on me to blend what we do in math to the demands of their final exhibition."

The special education support teacher on the team said, "You know, one of the most effective techniques I have used to get kids to gain a personal understanding of some of the issues surrounding the distribution of wealth and natural resources was to have them experience a "hunger banquet." Oxfam even has some materials that we could use to help us plan it. It might be a great kick off for a unit focusing on the economic and environmental impact of overharvesting the Brazilian rain forest. I can think of all kinds of neat activities we could have the kids do that would really be hands on, that would tap into the talents of every kid on our team and really get them working together. What do you think?"

The seeds of an interdisciplinary curriculum unit were planted!

B. Connecting the Unit with Other Subject Areas   This team had experience working together and managed to arrive at a match between their subjects just through conversation. Another technique for discovering the overlap between disciplines is to draw a matrix of outcomes or proficiencies from each discipline participating in the unit and then to select provocative current issues or problems that would require students to apply skills from those disciplines in order to solve the problem or address the issue in a comprehensive way.

C. Outcomes/Proficiencies/Skills   Many constituencies are addressing the issue of what students need to know and be able to do when they graduate from high school. At Souhegan High School, for example, outcomes across subject areas have been adopted by both the local school board and the New Hampshire State Board of Education. Within each unit, teachers identify the priority outcomes on which they will focus. In the interdisciplinary "Lives of a Cell" unit, outcome goals included 1) acquire and integrate critical information (specified science and English content), 2) interpret and synthesize information, 3) express ideas clearly, 4) effectively communicate through a variety of mediums, 5) work toward the achievement of group goals, and 6) self-monitor individual behavior in the group.

Clearly, the teachers had different expectations for the students introduced at the beginning of this section, Colleen, Amro, Brandon, and Andrew. Andrew was expected to have an understanding of the functions of different cell structures, and Colleen was expected to describe how function was uniquely related to structure and form. If Brandon worked through an entire class period without attempting to scratch another student or his facilitator, he rated an A for goal 6 (above). Amro easily scored well on goal 5 because of his ability to inspire order and organization in his group. Achieving this goal was very difficult for Colleen, and at the beginning of the group project teachers did not expect her to be able to cooperate well.

D. Essential Questions As described earlier, essential questions are overarching questions, statements, or problems that require students to apply knowledge from several different domains. For example, two teachers worked together on a Civil War unit that focused around the question, "What Does It Mean to Be Free?" One teacher recounted:

> Some students in my class could answer that question using information from their Civil War reading and by thinking about the process of civil rights in the United States. One or two students in my class had to approach this question first from their own personal perspective. Amro knows that he is treated differently from his brothers and has a strong opinion about that. If we start with his personal experience, it's a little bit easier for him to make a connection with the Civil War. (Fried & Jorgensen, 1994, p. 22)

We imagine that any student can find a way to answer this particular essential question. Some students might have demonstrated that they understood the complex interrelationships between states' rights and the economics of slavery by writing opposing editorials for newspapers in Boston and in Atlanta in 1860. Another student might have shown her understanding of freedom on the first day that she used a voice output communication device to communicate.

E. Performance-Based Exhibitions The conclusion of the first section of the curriculum design process is the description of the exhibitions that students produce to demonstrate what they have learned. The word to describe this—exhibition—intentionally denotes action. Some examples of exhibitions at Souhegan High School were 1) participating in an all-day environmental summit in which students developed and presented position statements on whether the Brazilian rain forest should be harvested, 2) writing a letter to a student 30 years in the future describing the progress in civil rights for African Americans, 3) performing a play and producing a video depicting one of the major life processes occurring in a cell, and 4) completing the family's federal income tax forms.

In the unit "What Does It Mean to Be Free?" Amro learned that some people have skin that is a different color from others (he had never noticed before) and that a long time ago those people were slaves. He gained an understanding of what their lives were like by comparing their lack of freedom to some of this own experiences as a student with disabilities who was segregated in a special education class and who still did not have some of the freedoms of typical students. For his performance-based exhibition,

Amro made a collage depicting people of different ethnic backgrounds peacefully together, captioned with a computer-printed banner, "People Are Free."

F. Activities, Materials, and Resources   The questions in Section F in Figure 1 provide clear direction for teachers about the design of learning activities and materials appropriate for diverse groups of learners. The following example illustrates how the choice of teaching methodology affects the adaptability of lessons for all students.

The biology teacher used a hands-on activity to help the students learn the rules that govern the phenomenon of evolution known as natural selection. She knew that students would benefit more from discovering the principles involved in natural selection than from just reading about experiments and memorizing formulas. In this lesson, students worked with a hypothetical species (small squares of scrap paper) in a hypothetical environment (a newspaper spread out on a lab table). To begin the activity, species members with different characteristics—red squares of paper, white squares of paper, and squares of newspaper—were scattered all over the environment (the sheet of newspaper). In an apparently random way, one member of a four-student team "preyed on" (removed) members of the population. Another member of the group kept a tally of the number and type of members remaining after each "hunt." After a prescribed number of hunts, the students studied their data, and the two other members of the group recorded answers to the following questions: Do any of the three species have more survivors than the other two? Can you propose a hypothesis that might explain this phenomenon? Were the red individuals suited or unsuited to their environment? Can you write a formula that represents what happened in this experiment? Is appearance the only characteristic that determines whether an individual plan or animal is suited to its environment? In this activity, students who are skilled in mathematics can work on developing the formula. Students who have difficulty understanding abstract formula may find it easier to understand the laws of natural selection by seeing and experiencing the process in the classroom. If another student's learning goals included communication, sequencing, following instructions, and using fine motor skills, she would also be able to participate in this activity. Because the structure of the activity itself requires the application of many kinds of skills to successfully solve the problem, it is inherently "inclusive."

G. Planning for Students with Extraordinary Learning Challenges   A school is not truly inclusive unless every student, including those with significant disabilities, can participate in learning and work toward challenging outcomes. For students with significant disabilities, the framework of curriculum design must consider their individual learning needs by focusing teachers' attention on the support and adaptations that are necessary for each student to fully participate in the unit and to achieve his or her learning goals (Tashie et al., 1993). Some examples of individualized supports and accommodations are presented in Table 3.

To design inclusive curriculum, teachers must ask themselves a series of questions. First, *can the student participate in this lesson in the same way as other students?* Students with even the most significant disabilities can often participate in

Table 3.   Examples of individualized supports and accommodations

Examples of student participation without extra support:

Amro was able to participate in his chef's class with very few modifications, and he earned an A in the class.

Brandon was able to participate in cooperative activities on the ropes course (an activity in which people try challenging physical tasks, many of which require cooperation, to execute successfully) because support and choice for all students is inherent in the activity.

Examples of "people" supports that facilitate full participation:

Brandon has a visual impairment and needed to have written materials read to him or greatly enlarged.

In a social studies class, students worked in small groups to perform a short skit depicting homelessness, which they had been studying for several weeks. When it was Amro's turn to say his lines, a group-mate whispered them to him one-by-one, and he repeated them to the class.

Shawna needed someone to support her hand while she entered data on the computer in a keyboarding class.

Examples of modifying materials in order to facilitate full participation:

Jessica's lines in theater class were recorded by a classmate. During the class performance, she leaned her head against a pressure switch connected to a tape player, which played her lines at the appropriate time.

Amro used a variety of communication strategies and technology (low and high) depending on the situation. He did his seatwork or homework on a laptop computer. Sometimes the teacher gave him a choice of two responses by holding up her hands and asking him to touch "this hand for bituminous or this hand for igneous." In the hallway Amro greeted friends with a wave, high-five, or flip of his hat brim. During small-group discussions, he spelled on a laminated plastic letter board, which was then read by a peer or classroom assistant.

Brandon completed multiple choice tests by pointing to the letters *a, b, c,* or *d* written in the four quadrants of a portable board. A teaching assistant read the question and the answer choices, but the answer sheet needed to be adapted so that he could participate.

Brandon's 10th-grade biology class learned to be astute observers of natural phenomena. They walked through the woods to the banks of a nearby river and made micro, mid-macro, and macro drawings of what they saw on the river's edge. Brandon was unable to use his hands to draw so he used a copy of another student's drawings for follow-up classroom activities.

Examples of modifying expectations to facilitate full participation:

Matt was in a 10th-grade biology class and was unable to compose sentences. During lab experiments he was responsible for organizing his group's dissection tray and bringing it to the lab station. He took instant pictures of the various steps of the experiments and, with the assistance of another group member, pasted them into the group's lab notebook alongside the corresponding written report.

Amro's teacher was conducting a unit on geometry. She frequently drew geometric figures on the board, and while she explained the theorems associated with the figure, Amro was asked to spell the name of the figure on his letter board and indicate the sides that were shorter or longer. His goals in math were unique to his learning needs.

Although Taryn participated as fully as every other student in the 10th-grade classes, her priority learning goals did not include the content of science, social studies, English, and math classes. In science class, students categorized plants by species, kingdom, phylum, and order. The names of plants in the same species were mounted on red posterboard, those of the same kingdom on green posterboard, those of the same phylum on blue posterboard, and those of the same order on yellow posterboard. Taryn's goals were to sort the plants by color. She had numerous opportunities to use her fine motor skills in this activity and sometimes glanced expectantly at a tablemate for assistance if she could not reach a card. She worked on this at the same time that her group studied for a test on the plant classification system.

many lessons and activities without extra support or accommodation. Second, if the student is unable to participate fully without accommodation, *what supports and/or modifications are necessary for the student's full participation in this lesson?* Some students may not be able to participate independently, but can participate with support from classmates or an adult. For many students, modifying the materials used in the classroom is necessary for full participation. Such modifications may include adaptations of the learning environment or the learning materials or the provision of assistive technology.

Third, *what expectations must be modified to ensure the student's full participation in this lesson?* Modifying expectations means changing 1) how students demonstrate what they know, 2) the generally expected quantity or standard of work, or 3) the priority learning objectives of a particular lesson. For instance, instead of using the traditional written report, students may demonstrate what they know through the following products or projects: videotapes or slides, bulletin boards, cookbooks or recipes, displays or showcases, banners, photo albums, diaries or journals, songs or other musical productions, poems, game boards, mobiles, dioramas, speeches, inventions, commercials, comic strips, or models. The quantity or quality of output required may be modified, for example, by requiring that the student complete fewer problems to demonstrate mastery, setting a different standard of quality (must get 50% correct instead of 100% to move on to the next set of problems), or giving a student longer to complete an assignment. The priority learning objectives may be modified by adapting content or focusing more intensively on the communication, movement, organizational, and/or social skills embedded in the unit.

H. Lesson Plans   By this point in the planning process, teachers are ready to sit down with their lesson books and plan exactly what they will do on a day-to-day basis over the course of the unit. The scheduling of lessons and activities begins with identifying a target date for the students' exhibitions and then by planning lessons that lead to these exhibitions.

For example, the 10C team at Souhegan High School planned an "Evolution/Civil Rights" unit based on the essential question: Is change necessary for survival? A 1-week, three-subject lesson plan outline for this unit is presented in Table 4.

I. Evaluation   Every school has a unique set of constraints under which evaluation of student work must be developed that include teachers' professional judgments, local school board policies, state curriculum and/or testing requirements, pressure from national examinations (e.g., SATs), and requirements for acceptance into postsecondary training and education programs. The most difficult challenge of evaluation in an inclusive school, however, is merging the philosophy and the practicalities of valuing the learning needs of all students with the equally valuable expectation of excellence. A two-pronged approach to evaluation forms the framework of this successful merger.

The first component of the evaluation process is based on multiple sources of evidence, selected by both the students and their teachers, that provide an assessment of the proficiency with which a student demonstrates his or her mastery of the unit outcomes. For example, can Steve, given the option of demonstrating knowledge in indi-

Table 4. One-week three-subject lesson plan for the "Evolution/Civil Rights" unit

Day	Subject		
	Science	Social sciences	English
Monday	Conduct community meeting to explain unit	Respond to essential questions in journal	Read and discuss *Inherit the Wind*
Tuesday	Read article and frame question	Read original sources from 1860s	Read and discuss in small theme groups; each day small groups get to watch movie
Wednesday	Watch Mendel and Darwin movie	Do team semantic maps of viewpoints	Read and discuss characters in small groups
Thursday	Discuss natural selection theory and activity	Experience slave ship conditions	Assign roles for trial
Friday	Meet in exhibition teams	Lecture on states' rights issue	Practice trial segments in small groups

vidualized ways and with support from teachers, describe the relative importance of the four major factors contributing to the Civil War? Can Taryn, using assistive technology, press a switch, under the direction of her lab partners, that operates the centrifuge? Can all students, if provided with instruction and feedback from teachers, work cooperatively to produce their final exhibition?

For each major skill or outcome, teachers and students together must also develop a rubric for judging the students' demonstrations of that outcome. To use a very simple example, a four-level rubric for student mastery of writing mechanics could be the following: 1 = written work contains many mechanical errors—it is evident that this is a first draft; 2 = mechanics are weak and inconsistently used—another draft or two is clearly needed; 3 = between three and five mechanical errors per page, but student can correct them when they are pointed out; and 4 = written work needs little or no correction of writing mechanics.

An unresolved issue in evaluation (and, ultimately, in the debate concerning what a high school diploma indicates) is if there is a minimum standard (perhaps Point 2 or 3 in a 4-point rubric) of each skill that a student must attain in order to pass and graduate. Resolution of this debate in a way that considers all students will occur only when the differences of each and every student are celebrated, and when teachers use an equally diverse repertoire of curricula, teaching strategies, and materials to respond to those differences.

As students move from course to course and from year to year, a proficiency checklist should accompany them so that when they graduate their future employers or college admissions officers are able to assess what each of these high school graduates knows and can do.

The second component of the evaluation process—at least in most schools in the United States—is to label the students' work with a grade. That grade usually represents the ranking of students from the most proficient to the least proficient. Many teachers also try to use grades to evaluate students' efforts. It is easy to spot the schools that are earnestly trying to figure out how to authentically evaluate student performance without relegating students with learning difficulties to the "land of the C." Their report cards use a traditional letter grading system, and students whose learning objectives in a particular subject have been modified are given an asterisk next to their grade and effort marks of 1 through 4.

As long as schools support (or are resigned to accepting) the need to rank students, the following system might meet the need to communicate what students know and can do along with an assessment of effort. Proficiency- or outcome-based checklists can be completed by teachers at the conclusion of each major exhibition. A letter grade would indicate the student's actual performance relative to expected performance (e.g., assuming that no grade lower than C is acceptable, with C indicating expected performance; B, higher than expected; and A, outstanding performance). This system of grading might be a way to acknowledge the inevitable differences in achievement among a diverse student body, yet hold each student to very high expectations. The key, of course, is to ensure that what is expected of a student is neither too high—so that some students never have the satisfaction of receiving an A or being on the honor roll—nor too low—so that some students never have the satisfaction of learning important and challenging material.

Thus, when students have finished 4 years of high school, their diplomas would signify that they had achieved at least a grade of C in every class, and their portfolios and proficiency checklists would document exactly what they had learned and could do.

PART 3: PROFESSIONAL DEVELOPMENT STRATEGIES FOR SUPPORTING TEACHERS WHO WANT TO ADOPT THIS INNOVATION

The following strategies are devised to help administrators or community members avoid some common pitfalls while implementing these curricular designs and to introduce some supports that teachers have found to be helpful.

1. Begin a conversation at your school about what you think is important that all students know and be able to do when they graduate. Be sure that the needs and talents of students with disabilities are represented in your discussion.

2. Assess what your colleagues are ready for and what their greatest concern is. Make no assumptions, but ask, observe, and identify teachers who are willing to take risks and work with you to try new approaches.

3. Somehow, some way, find time away from school to work with a small number of teachers (no more than six) on developing inclusive, performance-based units. The opportunity to get away from the distractions in the school building, enjoy a relaxed lunch, and have the luxury of actually thinking about teaching is cited by teachers as the single most important support that they need in order to develop inclusive, performance-based units.

4. Establish a mechanism for getting feedback on the unit that you teach from another teacher, an administrator (not during your yearly evaluation!), your students, and/or a faculty member at a local university.
5. Use student work to evaluate your experimental unit. If more students than usual "got it," you did something right! If a student who had been silent all year read two lines of a presentation, cheer! If the tough kid rigged up a switch for a student who cannot easily use his hands, a small miracle has occurred. Try the same process with another unit, and see if the results are similar.

If something (or many things) bombed—getting students to work in cooperative groups was a disaster, exhibitions looked like bad middle school science fair projects, you finished the unit and had no idea how to tell if students had learned without having given a multiple choice test—analyze what happened and try something different the next time. Tell your students what you wanted to accomplish and have them work on developing options for the next round of exhibitions.

PART 4: WHAT IS STILL PUZZLING—CONCLUSION

The difficulties in developing inclusive, performance-based curriculum seem to be clustered in four general areas.

First, we must live with the unresolved question of whether there should be different outcomes for different students and whether all students should receive a high school diploma.

Second, implementing a curriculum design and teaching process such as this requires a radical change in the roles of special education staff, who must now assume the responsibilities of curriculum developers and subject area teachers and provide resources and supportive instruction for all students.

Third, few teachers—general or special education—have experience in working collaboratively with colleagues in different disciplines. Everyone can benefit from staff development focused on group processes and collaborative problem-solving skills.

Finally, the experience of many school districts has shown that high-achieving students and their parents express the most dissatisfaction with curriculum defined by the words *inclusive, nontracked,* and *performance based.* Just as teams may need to intentionally focus on students with extraordinary learning challenges, they may also need to ask whether they have provided a challenge for each and every student.

REFERENCES

Fried, R., & Jorgensen, C. (1994). Creating questions that all students can answer. *Equity and Excellence, 2*(Spring), 22.

Joel, B. (1989). We didn't start the fire. On *Storm Front* [CD]. New York: CBS Records.

Silva, P. (1993). Starting the fire in the heterogeneous classroom. *Equity and Excellence, 1*(Spring), 4–5.

Sizer, T. (1989). Diverse practice, shared ideas: The essential school. In H.J. Walberg & J.J. Lane (Eds.), *Organizing for learning: Toward the 21st century.* Reston, VA: National Association of Secondary School Principals.

Sizer, T. (1992). *Horace's school: Redesigning the American high school.* Boston: Houghton Mifflin.

Tashie, C., Shapiro-Barnard, S., Schuh, M., Jorgensen, C., Dillon, A., Dixon, B., & Nisbet, J. (1993). *From special to regular: From ordinary to extraordinary.* Durham: Institute on Disability/University Affiliated Program, University of New Hampshire.

Terkel, S. (1985). *Working.* New York: Ballantine.

16

Choosing Options and Accommodations for Children (COACH)

Curriculum Planning for Students with Disabilities in General Education Classrooms

Michael F. Giangreco

WHEN A STUDENT with disabilities is placed in a general education class, one of the most universal concerns expressed by families and school personnel is the need to develop a relevant educational plan that meets the student's individual needs and makes sense in the context of general education. This chapter presents information about Choosing Options and Accommodations for Children (COACH) (Giangreco, Cloninger, & Iverson, 1993), a planning tool designed to assist teams with their individual student planning efforts. The chapter is divided into three major sections. First, COACH is described. Second, the results of recent research pertaining to COACH are discussed. This section includes 1) national expert and social validation of COACH, 2) cross-cultural feedback on COACH, and 3) what has been learned about the use of COACH and its impact on students, families, and professionals. Third, implications for the future use of COACH are discussed.

Portions of this text are based on Giangreco, M., Edelman, S., Dennis, R., & Cloninger, C. (1995). Use and impact of COACH with students who are deaf-blind. *Journal of The Association for Persons with Severe Handicaps, 20*(2), 121–135. Used by permission. Unless otherwise noted, all quotes are from this source.

WHAT IS COACH?

COACH, Choosing Options and Accommodations for Children (Giangreco, Cloninger, & Iverson, 1993), is a planning process designed to assist individual student planning teams in identifying the content of individualized education programs for students with significant disabilities in general education settings and activities. Although COACH has been used primarily with this low-incidence population, its concepts and procedures are generally applicable for use with students who have a much wider range of characteristics, with minor adaptations to its content. COACH is based on a series of six underlying principles as well as on a set of five valued life outcomes (see Table 1). The valued life outcomes included in COACH originally were generated through interviews with 28 families with children with significant and multiple disabilities (Giangreco, Cloninger, Mueller, Yuan, & Ashworth, 1991) and were further validated as important indicators of a quality life by 44 additional families (Giangreco, Cloninger, Dennis, & Edelman, 1993).

COACH is organized into three major parts. Part 1 (Family Prioritization Interview) is used to identify a small set of priority learning outcomes for the student. These priority learning outcomes are individualized and selected by the family based on their proposed impact on valued life outcomes. Part 2 (Defining the Educational Program Components) is used to 1) translate the family-selected priority learning outcomes into individualized education program (IEP) goals and objectives, 2) assist the full team (which includes the family) in identifying other important learning outcomes in addition to those selected by the family, and 3) determine general supports and accommodations to be provided to or for the student to allow access and participations in the education program. This part of COACH ensures that the selection of a small set of priorities will not unnecessarily limit the breadth of the student's learning opportunities and explicitly documents the contents of the education program in a succinct format (i.e., Program-at-a-Glance) for practical use by classroom staff. Part 2 further assists team members by distinguishing between student learning out-

Table 1.   The basis of COACH

Underlying principles

1. Pursuing valued life outcomes is an important aspect of education.
2. The family is the cornerstone of relevant and longitudinal educational planning.
3. Collaborative teamwork is essential to quality education.
4. Coordinated planning is dependent on shared, discipline-free goals.
5. Using problem-solving methods improves the effectiveness of educational planning.
6. Special education is a service not a place.

Valued life outcomes

1. Having a safe, stable home in which to live now and/or in the future.
2. Having access to a variety of places and engaging in meaningful activities.
3. Having a social network of personally meaningful relationships.
4. Having a level of personal choice and control that matches one's age.
5. Being safe and healthy.

comes and supports or accommodations. Particularly with students who have significant disabilities, confusion regarding this distinction has led to conflicts among team members and to IEPs that are unnecessarily passive (Downing, 1988; Giangreco, Dennis, Edelman, & Cloninger, 1994). Part 3 (Addressing the Education Program Components in Inclusive Settings) is used to determine options for addressing students' education program components in general education class settings and in other settings (e.g., community, vocational) with people without disabilities through the use of a scheduling matrix and a set of lesson adaptation guidelines. Table 2 provides an overview of the various parts of COACH.

RESEARCH ON COACH

Although COACH has been publicly available since 1985, it has only been in the early 1990s that any systematic evaluation has been undertaken regarding its validity, use, and impact. The seven updated versions of COACH, which were available between 1985 and 1993, were influenced by anecdotal, although extremely valuable, feedback primarily from special education teachers, related service providers, and parents who used COACH.

National Expert Validation

Initial data exist establishing COACH as a tool that is congruent with a variety of exemplary educational and family-centered practices (Giangreco, Cloninger, Dennis, & Edelman, 1993). Seventy-eight experts in the area of multiple disabilities, all of whom met specified criteria, reviewed and rated COACH. Forty-eight percent ($n = 37$) of these experts had used or observed previous versions of COACH. Thirty-seven of the respondents were national or state experts, such as university faculty, state coordinators for deaf-blind services, and regional consultants for national technical assistance networks. Forty-one respondents were people who have expertise by virtue of their field-based involvement with students who have disabilities, such as parents, special educators, general educators, and related service providers. Respondents indicated that COACH was highly congruent with characteristics of family-centered practitioners (Capone, Ross-Allen, DiVernere, & Abernathy, 1991) and several exemplary practices in the categories of 1) family–school collaboration, 2) collaborative planning, 3) curriculum planning, 4) social responsibility, and 5) individualized instruction (Fox & Williams, 1991). Respondents supplemented their high ratings of COACH with positive written comments regarding its purpose, philosophical basis, content, process, and presentation (see Table 3). Respondents offered comments such as the following:

> I think the most valuable aspect of this tool is that it moves from assessment to program implementation without stopping. Too many assessments don't consider that their final purpose should be to develop a program that assists the child to learn meaningful skills. This one does!
>
> COACH is a comprehensive and sensitive approach to providing quality education for all students with disabilities. The utilization of the family-centered approach is key in the development and implementation of programming which effectively meets the

Table 2. Overview of COACH

Part of COACH	Divergent aspect	Convergent aspect
Part 1.1 Valued Life Outcomes	Gather information about the current status and desired future status of valued life outcomes to set a context for the rest of COACH.	Select one to three valued life outcomes that the family feels should be emphasized during the year as part of the school experience.
Part 1.2 Selecting Curricular Areas to Be Assessed	Consider all the curriculum areas in COACH to determine which areas need to be assessed in Part 1.	Select a subset of the curriculum areas in COACH to assess in Part 1, those that include potential priorities for this year.
Part 1.3 Activity Lists	Gather information on the student's level of functioning regarding activities listed in the curriculum areas being assessed.	Select activities needing work this year.
Part 1.4 Prioritization	Within each assessed curriculum area, reconsider all the activities identified needing work this year.	Select which activities needing work are potential priorities and rank the top five.
Part 1.5 Cross-Prioritization	Consider a maximum of the top five priorities from each of the assessed curriculum areas.	Rank the top eight overall priorities and determine which priorities to include in the IEP.
Part 2.1 Restating Selected Priorities as Annual Goals	Consider the contexts where the priorities to be included in the IEP might be used.	Determine the contexts within which the student will use the priorities and combine to write annual IEP goals.
Part 2.2 Breadth of Curriculum	Consider a variety of general education and other curricular areas for potential inclusion in the educational program.	Select curriculum areas and learning outcomes to be targeted for instruction this year in addition to the IEP goals.
Part 2.3 General Supports	Consider the variety of general supports/accommodations that may be needed for the student.	Select which general supports are needed for the student to have an appropriate education.
Part 2.4 Program-at-a-Glance	None	Summarize educational program components (Parts 2.1, 2.2, 2.3).
Part 2.5 Short-Term Objectives	Consider various conditions, behaviors, and criteria.	Write objectives based on selected conditions, behaviors, and criteria.
Part 3.1 Organizing the Instructional Planning Team	Identify the individuals who will be affected by team decisions, and consider possible tasks.	Determine which team members will make up the core and extended team and who will be responsible for identified tasks.
Part 3.2 Becoming Familiar with the Student	Consider a broad range of facts and needs about the student.	Summarize and document the facts and needs that pertain to the educational experience.

(continued)

Table 2. *(continued)*

Part of COACH	Divergent aspect	Convergent aspect
Part 3.3 Becoming Familiar with the General Education Program and Setting	Consider a broad range of facts about the general education curriculum, instructions, routines, and settings.	Summarize and document the information relevant for the student, and clarify what each team member needs to know.
Part 3.4 Scheduling for Inclusion	Consider possibilities for addressing the student's educational program in inclusive settings.	Develop a schedule addressing the student's educational program components in inclusive settings.
Part 3.5 Considerations for Planning and Adapting Learning	Consider specific lesson adaptations to meet student needs.	Select specific lesson adaptations to meet student needs.

From Giangreco, M.F., Cloninger, C.J., & Iverson, V. (1993). *Choosing options and accommodations for children: A guide to planning inclusive education.* Baltimore: Paul H. Brookes Publishing Co.; reprinted by permission.

needs of the student and the family. So often, professional disciplines fail to recognize the family as not only a viable, but necessary, member of the collaborative planning team. COACH certainly balances the professional and consumer input.... (Giangreco, Cloninger, Dennis, & Edelman, 1993, p. 112)

Feedback About Cultural Sensitivity in Family Interviewing

The perspectives of individuals from cultural minority groups were substantially underrepresented in the national expert validation of COACH (Giangreco, Cloninger, Dennis, & Edelman, 1993). The education community increasingly has placed importance on providing services for families and individual students in ways that respect, acknowledge, and promote their cultural diversity and strengths (Harry, 1992). Attention to cultural sensitivity is particularly important for special educators because 1) the number of non-Caucasian children in the United States is increasing, so that, by the year 2000, 38% of children under 18 will be of non-Caucasian heritage (Hansen, 1992); 2) the numbers of children who are from minority ethnic and racial groups who receive special education services are disproportionately high (Harry, 1992); and 3) the majority of educators in this country (over 80%) are white, and most are women (Banks, 1994). Because of minority underrepresentation in the validation studies, a group of 14 people were asked to review COACH from a cross-cultural perspective and provide their feedback (Dennis & Giangreco, 1994). Respondents were 1) members of a cultural minority group within the United States (i.e., African American, Hispanic/Latino, Chinese American, Japanese American, Native American/American Indian, Asian American, Native Hawaiian, and Native Alaskan); 2) knowledgeable about cultural issues related to their own heritage; and 3) knowledgeable about recommended practices in the education of students with significant disabilities in the United States. Each person read COACH, submitted a written report of his or her findings, and was subsequently interviewed by telephone.

Although there may be a number of approaches to culturally sensitive family interviewing, it is ultimately the quality of interaction and conversation between fami-

Table 3. Positive features of COACH identified by expert respondents

Purpose

Assists in developing individualized education programs and in setting priorities

Moves from assessment to program planning without stopping

Facilitates access to general education settings and activities

May assist with transition of students into integrated settings

Limits IEP goals to a reasonable number

Philosophical basis

Emphasizes inclusion

Is family centered

Is based on actual use in general education settings

Emphasizes valued life outcomes

Content

Is up-to-date, representative of current exemplary practices

Is thorough, complete, comprehensive

Includes curriculum areas and activity lists that are succinct yet complete

Includes activity lists that are functional and age-appropriate

Builds on existing general education curriculum rather than replaces it

Process

Provides ample opportunity for family input

Facilitates collaborative teamwork; balances professional and consumer input

Has practical, common sense approach

Is systematic, linear, yet flexible

Has sensitive, informal participatory tone

Stresses involvement with the general education program and staff

Moves quickly

Includes use of problem-solving strategies embedded in COACH

Includes guidelines for developing goals, objectives, breadth of curriculum, and general supports

Includes self-monitoring and peer coaching, which enhance proficiency

Uses staff time efficiently; streamlines assessment and planning

Presentation

In-depth description and explanation

Clear, easy to understand, readable

Well-organized, logically ordered

Program-at-a-Glance effective for keeping the team focused

Scheduling provides concrete way to show what is being worked on in integrated settings

ly members and professionals as individuals that yields the important information needed to design and implement meaningful educational programs for students with disabilities. Although Table 4 lists some of the respondents' major points regarding cultural sensitivity in family interviewing that were prompted by their review of COACH, these points are applicable to family interviewing in general.

Table 4.   Respondents' perspectives on cultural sensitivity in parent interviewing

1. Each family should be approached individually. The family is a cultural group, each unique and distinct from other families (including those from the same ethnic or racial group) by virtue of the values, beliefs, and experiences shared by its members. Therefore, we need to guard against stereotyping based on cultural affiliation.

2. Individual families may view their own roles (within the family), the role of children, and particularly children with disabilities, differently than do the professionals who serve them in school.

3. Professionals should develop an appreciation of the environments in which families live. Literally "knowing where families are coming from" can help professionals understand family priorities concerning community activities and social, recreational, and vocational goals they consider important for their children.

4. Professionals need to be aware that they introduce their own culture into their relationships with families. Their position, as a representative of public agency, can be perceived differently by the families with whom they work. The policies, forms, and other written materials that professionals commonly use may be based on concepts not necessarily valued by the families, which may cause them to seem illogical, overwhelming, or intimidating to families unfamiliar with special education rules, regulations, language, and procedures.

5. Personal interactions can bridge cultural differences experienced by both professionals and families if professionals are sensitive and respectful of cultural interaction styles. It is incumbent upon the professional to be open to different cultural norms and customs with which they may be unfamiliar.

6. The family's understanding of the purpose of the interview, use of family members' preferred language, issues of time, and preferred style for sharing information are important aspects of cultural sensitivity when interviewing families.

7. Professionals who acknowledge the importance of culturally sensitive practices must purposely seek ways to enhance their understanding and knowledge about "other ways of thinking and being." These ways may include study and reading on the topics of families and ethnicity in interdisciplinary professional and nonprofessional literature, coursework, or more experiential learning with the help of people and families from cultural groups other than their own.

8. The extent to which professionals need to learn specific details about a particular cultural group varies and must be balanced with an understanding of cultural processes and an appreciation for the individual family's experience, for family members' levels of acculturation, and for the changing nature of culture itself.

Use and Impact of COACH

Between 1991 and 1993, a multisite evaluation of COACH was conducted across eight states with 30 teams who served students with significant and/or multiple disabilities. This evaluation consisted of interviews, observations, and document analysis (e.g., completed COACH forms) (Giangreco, Edelman, Dennis, & Cloninger, 1995). This study yielded some valuable, if not surprising, data.

When Used in Ways Incongruent with Its Underlying Assumptions, COACH Was Less Effective   Professionals found it more difficult and less valuable to use COACH when they attempted to use COACH without 1) a thorough understanding of its underlying principles, 2) a working knowledge of the instructions for its use, and/or 3) the adequate involvement of other team members in deciding whether to use the tool.

As an adjunct to this study, a conceptual analysis of the COACH forms collected from the teams being studied was conducted in an attempt to identify adaptations to the

COACH process made by team members. Adaptations were defined as any documentation on the COACH forms that did not follow the instructions outlined in the manual. Because COACH is not designed to be a standardized process, adaptations to the process are not inherently positive or negative. As adaptations were identified, a judgment was made by this author (as the originator of COACH) whether each adaptation was congruent or incongruent with the underlying principles of COACH as listed in Table 1, and, if congruent, which underlying principles have been compromised. Table 5 lists examples of how individuals have adapted COACH in ways that were incongruent with its underlying assumptions; these examples are offered to assist future consumers of COACH in avoiding these same pitfalls.

When Used in Ways Congruent with Its Underlying Principles, COACH Was Considered Effective Professionals' attempts to interact more collaboratively with families were either facilitated or hampered by how they chose to familiarize themselves with the principles and instructions for using COACH (Giangreco et al., 1995). As with anything new, proficient use of COACH requires an investment of time and energy (e.g., reading the manual, viewing a competent model on videotape or in person, having discussions with team members to facilitate understanding, role playing prior to actual use, providing feedback after use). Results of the study suggested that relying on team members to learn together through practice and peer coaching could mitigate some of the problems inherent in solitary learning and application (e.g., difficulty explaining COACH to families, misunderstanding written instructions, individual errors in judgment, lack of motivation to complete various parts, lack of ownership by team members in using the results of COACH) (Giangreco et al., 1995).

In situations in which people used COACH as described in the manual or with minor adaptations congruent with its underlying principles (e.g., scoring variations, individualization of question-asking language), reaction to its use was positive. As two special educators said, respectively, "I very much like it because it's a very directed and organized way to be able to discuss things that are sometimes difficult to discuss." "It's a combination of structure, but flexibility...so we can tailor it to everyone's individual needs" (Giangreco et al., 1995).

Professionals and parents reported that the use of COACH caused them to think differently. A parent commented, "I like the structure because it enabled you to maybe think about things that you would not have considered before." The use of COACH "spurred on some conversations I don't think would have come up if we had not been doing COACH" (special educator). This thought-provoking aspect of COACH may be attributed primarily to the multiple and alternating use of divergent and convergent questions. This strategy is an adaptation of the Osborn-Parnes Creative Problem Solving Process (CPS) (Parnes, 1985, 1992). CPS methods for eliciting new ideas are facilitated by creating opportunities to actively defer judgment (divergence) as well as opportunities to actively engage judgment (convergence). The multiple fact-generating and decision points in COACH distinguish it from other planning tools, such as checklists, which may provide for reporting a student's level of functioning but offer no

Table 5. Adaptations incongruent with the underlying principles of COACH[a]

Section of COACH	Adaptations to written instructions	Principles with which the practice is incongruent	Why the practice is incongruent
General	Documentation of team involvement was incomplete (e.g., did not list all team members; did not document dates reviewed with other team members)	Collaborative teamwork is essential to quality education	Not sharing information or developing a shared framework and goals interferes with teamwork
	Completed Part 1 of COACH (Family Prioritization Interview) but did not complete Part 2	Pursuing valued life outcomes is an important aspect of education	Family Prioritization Interview provides an incomplete and unnecessarily narrow view of the student's educational program
	Family filled out the COACH forms at home by themselves	Using problem-solving methods improves the effectiveness of educational planning	Both the divergent/convergent problem-solving and interactive aspects embedded in COACH are lost
Part 1.2: Selecting Curricular Areas to Be Assessed	Did not complete this section	Using problem-solving methods…	The field of possibilities was not narrowed
Part 1.3: Activity Lists	Added the score NA (not applicable) to the existing range of scoring options	Pursuing valued life outcomes…	Addition of NA interferes with providing the greatest opportunity for, and least restriction on, student potential
Part 1.4: Prioritization	Skipped "Potential Priorities" column and went directly from Scoring to Ranking	Using problem-solving methods…	If more than 5 items were circled "y" under the heading "Needs Work", nonuse of the Potential Priorities column fails to take advantage of the divergent/convergent problem-solving approach

(continued)

245

Table 5. (continued)

Section of COACH	Adaptations to written instructions	Principles with which the practice is incongruent	Why the practice is incongruent
	Checked all items that "Need Work" as "Potential Priorities"	Using problem-solving methods...	Marking all items as potential priorities does not assist in narrowing the selection of priorities
	Ranked Activity Listing (e.g., Personal Management) items 1–9. (These were all marked "Yes" for "Needs Work" in Part 1.3.)	Using problem-solving methods...	Uses time inefficiently because only a maximum of the top five ranked items go on to be considered at the next level (1.5)
	Checked items as "Potential Priorities" and ranked them as priorities although they were marked as N in Part 1.3, indicating that they do not "Need Work" this year	Using problem-solving methods...	Only those items that "Need Work" are considered as "Potential Priorities"
Part 1.5: Cross-Prioritization	In "Other" category, added the item "Maintain range of motion by positioning/stretching"	Coordinated planning is dependent upon shared, discipline-free goals	Part 1.5 addresses learning outcomes only in an attempt to distinguish them from general supports
	Added "increase kicking" to "Other" category	Coordinated planning...	This item is not an "activity" but rather a "subskill"; it would need to be put into a functional context to be considered an activity
	Listed Overall Priorities as "Communication," "Academics"	Using problem-solving methods...	Such descriptors are merely curricular categories, not learning outcomes
	Did not list the Valued Life Outcomes that correspond with the family's "Overall Priorities"	The family is the cornerstone of relevant and longitudinal educational planning	May interfere with professionals adequately understanding the underlying meaning of the family's selected priorities
	Did not indicate whether the Overall Priorities should be "Included in the IEP," "Breadth of Curriculum," or "Home"	The family is the cornerstone...and collaborative teamwork...	Fails to clarify expectations among team members

Part 2.1: Annual Goals Worksheet	Did not set context for annual goals	Pursuing valued life outcomes...	Interferes with the pursuit of Valued Life Outcomes because it does not place learning outcomes in contexts that are individually meaningful for the student
Part 2.2: Breadth of Curriculum Worksheet and Listing	Listed only general education classes in which the student is currently placed rather than those available to all other students in that particular grade	Using problem-solving methods..., pursuing valued life outcomes... and special education is a service not a place	Listing does not account for the divergent consideration of all possibilities available to the student
Part 2.3: General Supports	Did not indicate the Valued Life Outcomes sought by providing the General Supports	Pursuing valued life outcomes...	May interfere with team members adequately understanding the underlying meaning of the selected General Supports

*See Table 1 for underlying assumptions of COACH.

process for decision making about the information that is gathered. Although some families are articulate and anxious to give their input when asked open-ended questions, the discrete, short-answer format of COACH provides a vehicle for many families to organize and communicate their ideas.

One of the most common comments about COACH was that it assisted people in focusing on priorities for a student. As one general education classroom teacher said, "I think COACH helps focus the families' priorities for the students and really makes them look at what's important to them and what's not important to them." Parents echoed this sentiment, and one mother said, "Of everything we've tried, and we've tried lots of different approaches over the years with Sandra of coming up with IEP goals, this just gave us so much assistance in really getting what we wanted for her and helping us crystallize what we really did want."

This focusing reportedly added clarity and relevance to the IEPs that were developed based on the family-selected priorities from COACH. Families reported that the priority learning outcomes they selected using COACH accurately reflected the needs of their child.

Breadth of Curriculum (Part 2.2) was found to be an effective mechanism for making decisions about a broader set of learning outcomes to complement the priorities selected by the family. Included in this broader view were learning outcomes from the general education curriculum, a source for outcomes that reportedly was considered infrequently, if at all, prior to the use of COACH. As one special education teacher observed, "Looking at the regular education curriculum, I think people were surprised...it made a big difference when people look at the elementary curriculum and say, 'Wow!' Boy, there's a lot here that we can be focusing on."

When professionals realized that the Breadth of Curriculum component provided a substantial opportunity for them to share their knowledge and perspectives, they reported that it made it easier for them to relinquish control for decision making to the parent through the Family Prioritization Interview. Some teachers found the General Supports (Part 2.3) a useful mechanism for distinguishing and documenting the difference between what they wanted a student to learn and what they needed to do for a student.

Traditionally, special education checklists and curriculum guides provided no mechanism for considering the content of the general education curriculum. The Breadth of Curriculum component explicitly includes fact finding and decision making about learning outcomes in the general education curriculum as a way to augment and extend the listings included in Part 1 (Family Prioritization Interview) of COACH. This expansion ensures that students' learning options are not artificially limited. The combination of the Family Prioritization Interview (Part 1), Breadth of Curriculum (Part 2.2), and General Supports (Part 2.3) is designed to offer breadth and balance to the education program unlikely to be achieved if using only Part 1 of COACH.

While acknowledging the time commitment involved with COACH, study participants commented that it was "worth it" and indicated that they were "really happy with the results." Use of COACH served as a motivating prompt for teams to work together. "I believe that COACH committed us to really working hard to see how we could fit those learning outcomes of COACH into her school day more." In some cases, COACH-identified priorities were observed being taught in classrooms as staff referred to the student's Program-at-a-Glance (Part 2.4), which is a one- or two-page summary of COACH results. As one general education classroom teacher said, "We use it everyday. There's a pretty discreet [sic] number [of priority learning outcomes] that we're trying to address; this has let everyone be able to remember what's being worked on."

One physical therapist summarized her perspectives about COACH use by saying,

> I firmly believe in the process and just thought it was extremely challenging and exciting and it made a much better educational program for the child. It was just a very satisfying way to work because you felt you had a road map of where you wanted to be and a way to get there. It was exciting to see....

COACH was used by some teams as one component of the annual transition planning from grade to grade as well as a component for major transitions such as those from early childhood programs to kindergarten and from high school to postsecondary experiences. In two cases, the use of COACH was reported to be instrumental in helping students make the transition from part-time special class placements to full-time general education placements when team members recognized that the Valued Life Outcomes and learning outcomes identified for the student could not be adequately pursued in separate environments. As one mother said, "COACH was instrumental in transition to regular class placement because we were able to say, 'Well gee, how do we do a large group in a self-contained class?' "

How Individualized Education Programs (IEPs) Changed Based on Use of COACH   Use of COACH often resulted in a smaller number of goals included on the IEP than has been typical. IEP goals, which have tended to be broad and general (e.g., improve communication skills), tended to be quite specific (e.g., makes requests to get out of his wheelchair) (Giangreco et al., 1995). For students placed full-time in general education, the shift was from functional skills traditionally associated with special classes (e.g., personal management/self-care) to communication and social skills that reflected the changing needs of students who are in environments with students without disability labels. One special educator stated, "This will be the first time that Kevin hasn't had an eating goal on his IEP, which is kind of interesting; that is something that will change as a result of having COACH done." Using COACH to consider potential priorities and other learning outcomes (i.e., Breadth of Curriculum) in general education settings also shifted some teams toward considering academic learning outcomes (e.g., literacy) for the first time.

COACH Positively Affected Relationships Between Families and Professionals   It was reported that COACH enhanced relationships between parents and professionals by providing a process for families to express their ideas and priorities, while the professional's primary role was to listen and seek to understand the perspectives of families (Giangreco et al., 1995). As one special educator said, "I think COACH really gave an opportunity for her parents to have an articulate way to contribute to her educational life, and for us as a team to hear from them."

For some families, using COACH was reported to be the first time they had actually been asked for their input rather than presented with professional recommendations for their approval or disapproval. Parents indicated that COACH gave them an acceptable way to say no to professionals that did not require them to explain or rationalize their decisions. COACH helped some families clarify their thoughts within the family unit. As one mother said, "I think it helped my husband and I because we did it [COACH] together, because sometimes we have different views on what Eddie should be doing or what our vision is for Eddie."

This change in the nature of interactions between parents and professionals was reported to increase the level of parent participation in educational planning and to open dialogue about previously undiscussed topics: "It helped us broaden our ideas...." For some teams, this developing relationship between parents and professionals established a sense of mutual support and interdependence. "People feel so much better about teaming; that you're not out there by yourself trying to work miracles on this kid.... Getting people to sit down and communicate and talk really helped."

Initially, some professionals in this study negatively characterized a student's parents (e.g., not knowledgeable, low expectations, unrealistic, demanding, poor judgment). Using COACH was reported to prompt several professionals to view parents in a more favorable light. Professionals reported being pleasantly surprised by the depth, quality, and realism of parental input elicited by the use of COACH. "They [the parents] are working so hard the whole time [during the Family Prioritization Interview]. It is like they are thinking and they have so much to say.... The comments the parents made were all very valuable." In reference to a set of parents who had originally been described as "very demanding," one service provider said, "Once we started working with them and really working with them as an integral part of the team they were exceptionally fine parents and a joy to work with."

Professionals said they misinterpreted low levels of parental participation in previous meetings as disinterest, lack of caring, or lack of ability to make appropriate decisions. These professionals said COACH offered a way to draw out important information and insights from parents who tended to be quiet during meetings. COACH provided opportunities for families to display their knowledge about their child. What professionals learned from listening to families helped them to better understand the families and work with their children. As one special educator said:

> I was impressed with how well this mother knows her child. I was very impressed with her present goals and expectations for the future and I didn't necessarily have that understanding of the mom up until going through COACH with her the first time. I felt her goals and expectations were very realistic. It exposed a side of the mom to me that I hadn't seen at that level before, and I was very pleased and I felt very comfortable with that.

When professionals act on the priorities established by parents, they have the potential to send a powerful message of respect for the family by backing written and spoken words with substantive actions.

COACH Shifted Control of Educational Decision Making   Use of COACH challenged traditional types and levels of professional control regarding educational decision making, shifting more control to parents, particularly through the Family Prioritization Interview (Giangreco et al., 1995). As one parent acknowledged, "We feel like we have more control." Some professionals reported that the prospect of losing some of their control was "scary" and "uncomfortable." As one special educator said, "I felt like I couldn't surrender the agenda that we [professionals] had…." Some of these same professionals indicated that COACH helped legitimize this shift of control. As one special educator mentioned, "COACH really surrendered that feeling of guilt for me [about not being in control of all educational planning decisions]." For other professionals, relinquishing some level of control was reported to provide a sense of relief:

> One thing that was nice for me was some of the letting go, that I could defer to somebody else. I didn't have to have all the answers. They [the parents] could say, "How about we try this?" and I would say, "Great idea!"

Whether professionals sensed relief or anxiety, several recognized the value of relinquishing some of their control. As one special educator said,

> Even though initially it was like, "Oh, this is hard for me," you know by the end of it because of the way I saw it follow through, the way it made the IEP much smoother, the way it made our team work so much better, it made me feel real good. It just made a big difference overall, and the whole relationship I've had with parents. I can honestly say that they are part of our team now.

Providing parents with a mechanism to assume greater control distinguishes COACH from many other planning processes. Greater control for parents has the potential for changing the relationship between family and professionals from adversarial to more collaborative, encouraging professionals to clearly see their roles in providing families with strategies for making sound educational decisions.

Impact of COACH on Valued Life Outcomes for Students Changes in valued life outcomes were facilitated by the use of COACH and were reflected in new programmatic and social opportunities (Giangreco et al., 1995). However, it is clear that the reported changes cannot be attributed to COACH exclusively. Contextual elements believed to enhance COACH use are 1) general education placement; 2) collaborative teamwork; 3) willingness of team members to learn new ideas and skills; 4) willingness to share control; 5) active participation of students in general education class activities, even if they have different learning outcomes; 6) peer and other natural supports; and 7) taking action on plans.

Therefore, Valued Life Outcomes discussed in this section are those that team members said were facilitated by using COACH in combination with other effective practices. The impact on students' Valued Life Outcomes began for some study participants with a basic awareness about what might make a student's life better. As one parent said, "I think probably if anything has benefited my thinking and the team's thinking about what is appropriate for Sam, it is the Valued Life Outcomes." Asking questions about Valued Life Outcomes as a context for educational planning did not necessarily yield immediate results; team members reported that this sometimes had a delayed impact, just like seeds planted that sprout at a later date.

For several students, use of COACH led to new opportunities and raised expectations, some of which were as basic as riding the school bus with classmates, having access to human touch, or actively communicating with peers. Parents talked about the routines of their families and the new opportunities their children had as a result of priorities established using COACH. For some families, this meant their children were now attending the ballgames of an older sibling, attending religious services with the family, going shopping, or participating in general education classes. As the mother of a high school student said, "Her repertoire of activities has expanded and a lot of those things that were identified [during the COACH interview] have been dealt with." New opportunities in school led to other opportunities after school. These new experiences were reported to have provided opportunities for students with disabilities to make friends. One mother said, "He went to dances, he went to games, he was just part of it. He was a kid in the sixth grade or seventh grade. It was just exciting to see that; things that people generally take for granted."

Often the Valued Life Outcomes identified in the COACH process are interrelated. For example, Tim's parents were concerned about his health; they selected fitness activities as priority learning outcomes for him. The team arranged for Tim to work out at the local YMCA. While there, Tim met new friends with whom he exercised on a regular basis. In this example, at least two other family-identified Valued Life Outcomes were also addressed: 1) having access to a variety of places and engaging in meaningful activities, and 2) having a social network of personally meaningful relationships. The ways in which the team chose to address improvements in Tim's health—at a community setting with other people—created additional opportunities to pursue additional Valued Life Outcomes.

New opportunities frequently prompted both professionals and parents to change, expand, and raise their expectations regarding the ways in which the students could participate in school, at home, and in the community. The mother of a high school student with deafness-blindness came to consider supported employment as a realistic and attainable outcome for her daughter, something she said she previously would not have even considered. This mother's optimism was rooted not in speculation, but in the reality of her daughter's high school experiences. As her mother said, "She's a teenager; she's got money; she's getting minimum wage."

Use of COACH prompted natural peer supports. When teachers created climates conducive to interaction among students, "They [peers] know when he needs somebody with him so the kids automatically go to be with him." As one mother explained,

> If she needs something, if she needs help opening the paint, she'll tap one of the other kids and hand them the jar like, "You know, I can't get this cover off." And they have gotten so they've been as excited as I have. "Hey, Holly wants me to open it! Holly asked me to do it! She's communicating!"

IMPLICATIONS FOR FUTURE USE

COACH has been continually evolving since its inception; in order for it to remain a viable planning tool, such change will need to continue. The original emphasis of COACH on students with significant disabilities should be extended to students with a wider range of characteristics by considering the similarities in Valued Life Outcomes sought for students, including curriculum individualization needs for students without disability labels. Therefore, COACH should move in the future toward generic process steps that are increasingly applicable to an ever-widening audience. To accomplish this extension, the Valued Life Outcomes and specific learning outcomes included in COACH will need further consideration and change so that they can be interpreted in individually meaningful ways by more families with diverse characteristics and needs. The process of COACH will also need to undergo continual reevaluation to retain its problem-solving attributes while simplifying and streamlining it so that it becomes more user friendly. Although these potential revisions should be facilitated through continued research, the greatest sources of ideas for potential improvements are the thoughtful adaptations to the process invented by professionals and family members who join together on behalf of the students they care about and seek to educate. Therefore, as stated in the COACH manual, "Consumers are reminded that COACH is a flexible tool. Its process is specifically intended to help teams develop educational plans that reflect valued life outcomes identified by the family and to encourage participation in a variety of inclusive settings. Your team is encouraged to modify COACH as necessary to be useful under unique circumstances" (Giangreco, Cloninger, & Iverson, 1993, p. 31).

REFERENCES

Banks, J.A. (1994). *Knowledge construction, curriculum transformation and multicultural education* [Cassette Recording No. 2-94145x99]. Alexandria, VA: Association for Supervision and Curriculum Development.

Capone, A., Ross-Allen, J., DiVernere, N., & Abernathy, N. (1991). *Characteristics of family-centered practitioners.* Burlington: University of Vermont, University Affiliated Program of Vermont.

Dennis, R., & Giangreco, M.F. (1994). *Creating conversation: Reflections on cultural sensitivity in family interviewing.* Burlington: University of Vermont, University Affiliated Program of Vermont. Manuscript submitted for publication.

Downing, J. (1988). Active versus passive programming: A critique of IEP objectives for students with the most severe disabilities. *Journal of The Association for Persons with Severe Handicaps, 13,* 197–210.

Fox, T., & Williams, W. (1991). *Best practice guidelines for meeting the needs of all students in local schools.* Burlington: University of Vermont, University Affiliated Program of Vermont.

Giangreco, M.F., Cloninger, C.J., Dennis, R.E., & Edelman, S.W. (1993). National expert validation of COACH: Congruence with exemplary practice and suggestions for improvement. *Journal of The Association for Persons with Severe Handicaps, 18*(2), 109–120.

Giangreco, M.F., Cloninger, C., & Iverson, V. (1993). *Choosing options and accommodations for children: A guide to planning inclusive education.* Baltimore: Paul H. Brookes Publishing Co.

Giangreco, M.F., Cloninger, C.J., Mueller, P., Yuan, S., & Ashworth, S. (1991). Perspectives of parents whose children have dual sensory impairments. *Journal of The Association for Persons with Severe Handicaps, 16,* 14–24.

Giangreco, M.F., Dennis, R., Edelman, S., & Cloninger, C. (1994). Dressing your IEPs for the general education climate: Analysis of IEP goals and objectives for students with multiple disabilities. *Remedial and Special Education, 15*(5), 288–296.

Giangreco, M.F., Edelman, S., Dennis, R., & Cloninger, C.J. (1995). Use and impact of COACH with students who are deaf-blind. *Journal of The Association for Persons with Severe Handicaps, 20*(2), 121–135.

Hansen, M. (1992). Ethnic, cultural and language diversity in intervention settings. In E. Lynch & M. Hansen (Eds.), *Developing cross cultural competence: A guide for working with young children and their families* (pp. 3–18). Baltimore: Paul H. Brookes Publishing Co.

Harry, B. (1992). *Cultural diversity, families, and the special education system: Communication and empowerment.* New York: Teachers College Press.

Parnes, S.J. (1985). *A facilitating style of leadership.* Buffalo, NY: The Creative Education Foundation, Inc.

Parnes, S.J. (1992). *Sourcebook for creative problem-solving: A fifty year digest of proven innovation processes.* Buffalo, NY: The Creative Education Foundation, Inc.

17

Celebrating Diversity, Creating Community

Curriculum that Honors and Builds on Differences

Mara Sapon-Shevin

CREATING AN INCLUSIVE school in which all students feel acknowledged, valued, and respected involves attending to what gets taught in addition to how the curriculum is delivered. Not only must teaching strategies be designed and curricular areas determined in order to respond to a broad range of student differences, but the curriculum itself must address the many ways in which students differ.

Inclusive communities are ones in which all members feel that they belong and feel that they can make a contribution; students cannot become a community, cannot be comfortable, if they feel that the price of belonging is ignoring their own differences and those of their classmates. Our goal as community members should not be to become oblivious to differences and not to notice the diversity around us. Encouraging students to ignore differences is neither a realistic goal nor a desirable one. The same child who notices that Rumpelstiltskin is wearing a hat on page 4 and not on page 5 certainly notices that she has classmates who are larger or smaller, use a wheelchair, have different skin color, speak different languages, celebrate different holidays, or come from nontraditional families. Not attending directly to differences, not acknowl-

This chapter is a revised version of Sapon-Shevin, M. (1992). Celebrating diversity, creating community: Curriculum that honors and builds on differences. In S. Stainback & W. Stainback (Eds.), *Curriculum considerations in inclusive classrooms: Facilitating learning for all students* (pp. 19–36). Baltimore: Paul H. Brookes Publishing Co. Used by permission.

edging the many ways in which we are different (as well as the many ways we are similar), gives children the message that differences are something that cannot or should not be talked about. If teachers do not address differences, children's discussions about how children differ go underground and become occasions for whispering and tittering, for exclusion and isolation.

Our goal as educators must be the honest exploration of differences, the chance for students to experience and understand diversity within a community that is safe and supportive.

THINKING INCLUSIVELY ABOUT INCLUSIVE TEACHING

Children differ along many dimensions, and each child's identity is shaped by memberships in many groups. To describe 6-year-old Jonas only as a child with "physical challenges" is to ignore the fact that he is also Jewish and an only child. To discuss Carmen only as a child who requires extensive enrichment materials because of her accelerated performance may mask the fact that she comes from a single-parent, Spanish-speaking family. Just as single labels for children are not relevant to providing adequate educational programming, making certain aspects of the curriculum inclusive without attending to the child's whole identity or whole life is also inadequate. Adapting a Christmas craft activity for Jonas so that he is able to make decorations with the other children does not address the fact that such a craft project may be inappropriate or insensitive to children's religious differences. Providing Carmen with a book at her reading level is important, but it should not keep us from noticing that all the classroom textbooks and reading materials show only white, middle-class, traditional families and do not address the reality of a Spanish-speaking child who lives with her mother in an apartment.

The increasing racial and ethnic diversity of our society and our schools has made it imperative that school programs and curricula be responsive to children's differences. Ramsey (1987) described eight goals for teaching from a multicultural perspective, and all of these are applicable to the concept of inclusion. The author listed these goals as follows:

1. To help children develop positive gender, racial, cultural, class and individual identities and to recognize and accept their membership in many different groups.
2. To enable children to see themselves as part of the larger society; to identify, empathize, and relate with individuals from other groups.
3. To foster respect and appreciation for the diverse ways in which other people live.
4. To encourage in young children's earliest social relationships an openness and interest in others, a willingness to include others, and a desire to cooperate.
5. To promote the development of a realistic awareness of contemporary society, a sense of social responsibility, and an active concern that extend beyond one's immediate family or group.
6. To empower children to become autonomous and critical analysts and activists in their social environment.
7. To support the development of educational and social skills that are needed for children to become full participants in the larger society in ways that are most appropriate to individual styles, cultural orientations and linguistic background.

8. To promote effective and reciprocal relationships between schools and families. (pp. 3–5)

As Sleeter and Grant (1988) have argued, education that is multicultural may not be adequate to creating a just society unless it directly addresses issues of structural social inequality, power, and oppression. They argued that we must move beyond simply "celebrating diversity" and must teach students to understand social inequalities and empower them to work actively to change society. Our teaching must be specifically antiracist and antisexist in order to overcome the predominant messages children receive elsewhere in society.

Teaching children to be knowledgeable about differences, supportive of others, and to be active change agents in challenging structures that are oppressive to various groups can all begin within inclusive classrooms. There is probably no better situation in which to help students experience the democratic structures that empower and support all participants than in a classroom that openly and directly addresses the interests, needs, and possibilities of all its members.

Our goal must be to create a community that embraces differences, uses children's differences as part of the curriculum, and respects children's differences throughout all aspects of the school program. This chapter explores some of the areas of diversity that teachers must address if they are to create classroom communities that reflect and respect the multicultural, multifaceted nature of their students and that teach students to respond effectively to injustice and inequality.

TRANSFORMING OUR CLASSROOMS

Learning About Racial Differences

Learning about different racial groups cannot be an activity separate from the rest of the curriculum; a 1-day multicultural fair may be an interesting learning experience for children, but it does little to communicate the message that there have been people of color throughout history and that the contributions of men and women of color are not a thing apart from the standard curriculum. A positive respect and acknowledgment of racial differences can permeate everything that happens in the classroom, including not only the social studies lessons but also the bulletin boards, the books in the book corner, and the songs learned in music class.

Depending on the racial differences represented in the classroom, teachers' goals in this area may differ. Derman-Sparks and the A.B.C. Task Force (1989) suggested that in classes made up mainly of children of color, the primary task is to build knowledge and pride in physical characteristics and to counter the influences of rac-ism, which have left some children believing that being white is better than having a darker skin color. In classrooms that are all white, children can be guided to see the many ways in which they *do* differ, including skin shade, hair color, or freckles. Teachers who teach in predominantly white communities have a particular responsibility for teaching about racial diversity and doing so in a way that is accurate and respectful. In classes where there are only a few children of color, it is important that teachers talk about the ways in which all children are different, rather than imply that "We're all the same except for Michael."

Derman-Sparks and the A.B.C. Task Force (1989) offered the following cautions and words of warning about promoting a "tourist curriculum," which presents diversity as something foreign, exotic, and isolated from the rest of the classroom. They urged teachers to avoid the following:

- Trivializing: Organizing activities only around holidays or only around food. Only involving parents for holidays and cooking activities.
- Practicing tokenism: One Black doll amidst many White dolls; a bulletin board of "ethnic" images as the only diversity in the room; only one book about any cultural group.
- Disconnecting cultural diversity from daily classroom life: Reading books about children of color only on special occasions. Teaching a unit on a different culture and then never addressing that culture again.
- Stereotyping: Images of Native Americans only from the past; people of color always shown as poor; people from outside the United States shown only in "traditional" dress and rural settings.
- Misrepresenting American ethnic groups: Pictures and books about Mexico to teach about Mexican Americans; of Japan to teach about Japanese Americans; of Africa to teach about Black Americans. (p. 63)

There are many excellent resources available for helping teachers think about including racial differences in everything they teach; these include curriculum guides on multicultural education, sources for children's books about children of color, and curricula for teaching about differences. (Some of these are included in a resource list at the end of this chapter.)

History presents an ideal opportunity to teach multiple perspectives. Behind the story of Columbus, for example, and his "discovery" of America, lie many stories about the destruction of native peoples, the slave trade Columbus initiated, and the effects of greed and colonialism on people and cultures. Inclusive history means talking about why many people consider Columbus Day to be a day of mourning, encouraging students to read standard textbooks critically, and not limiting our study of historical events to a single perspective. We can go beyond studying racial differences to helping students understand racism (prejudice plus power) and the ways in which we can be allies to people who are discriminated against on the basis of race.

Virtually every activity or curriculum project can be expanded or redefined so that it is inclusive. For example, an activity on American painters can be expanded to include the paintings of Ben Shan and Raphael Soyer, both white immigrants from Russia; Diego Rivera and Antonio Garcia, two Mexican artists who worked in the United States; and Allan Crite and Charles White, both African American artists (Grant & Sleeter, 1989). Students can be helped to see the diversity in American painting and the effects of various cultural influences on art. Music activities can also be inclusive: listening to music from all over the world and learning songs in sign language, authentic songs from other cultures, and family songs that relate to various rituals or holiday celebrations. Including one Chanukah song in the traditional Christmas program is an example of tokenism and may actually discourage children from understanding the cultural diversity of their classmates. Including a broad range of music activities throughout the year is a more convincing demonstration of inclusiveness and respect.

Learning About Cultural Differences

Everyone has a culture, a background, a history, and customs that inform his or her daily life, beliefs, attitudes, and behavior. Although it may be tempting to believe that only visible "minority" groups have a culture, it is not true. Even within a classroom that appears to be homogeneous, there are many differences in cultural backgrounds. Therefore, it is best to approach learning about cultural differences from the perspective that everyone has a culture, all cultures are valuable and deserving of respect, and that diversity enriches the classroom. Whaley and Swadener (1990) explained that "early multicultural education is not a curriculum; it is a perspective and a commitment to equity, sensitivity and empowerment" (p. 240).

One particularly useful way of beginning to talk about different backgrounds and cultures is through children's names. When children are asked to share the background of their full names, many exciting details of cultural background and history emerge: Rebecca is named after her Jewish great-grandmother Rivka who came to the United States from Russia at the turn of the century. Why would Rebecca's grandma have come then? What was happening in the world? What kind of a name is Rebecca? What does it mean? Richard Flying Bye is Native American. What tribe is he from? Who gave him his name and why? What are his tribe's customs related to names and naming? Jenna, who was adopted at age 2, is Korean. What is the meaning of her middle name, Mei-Wan, and how did she get it? Why do some people call Richard *Ricardo,* and which does he prefer? An exercise such as this makes it clear that all children have a culture and a unique background and allows children and adults to take pride in their own heritage and to see similarities and differences.

Language differences present another excellent way to learn about diversity. For example, some children in this class speak Spanish, LaMont has cerebral palsy and you must listen closely to understand him, two children are studying Hebrew after school, one child speaks Japanese to her mother at home and to her grandmother whom she visits in California, Carla uses sign language, and Dustin uses a talking computer. What these children all have in common is a need to communicate, to be understood, and to be connected to other people. Inclusive classrooms encourage children to become as multilingual as possible. All children can learn the rudiments of sign language, they can be taught the braille alphabet, and they can learn to say important phrases in other languages. The teacher can emphasize the value of such multiple repertoires by making some classroom signs in other languages, by telling stories in sign language, or by having a Spanish-speaking parent come and share a story in her own language. The message is important: There are many ways to communicate, and we can learn how to talk to each other if we really want to.

Teachers can also use children's direct experiences to discuss instances of prejudice, discrimination, and injustice related to cultural or racial differences. Carl Burk, a social studies teacher at Gompers Middle School in Madison, Wisconsin, used a local hunting rights/spear fishing controversy to engage his students in a discussion of Native-American rights and traditions. Students had seen ads reading, "Spear an Indian, Save a Fish," and some were aware that many hunters and sportsmen were complaining about the "Indians taking our fish, our deer, and our land," but many had never met or talked with a Native American. When Mr. Burk invited members of various tribes to talk to his class about their traditions and beliefs, students' prejudices and stereotypes were challenged (The Teachers' Workshop, 1989).

Learning About Family Differences

There are many kinds of families. Some children live with one parent; others live in extended families with cousins, aunts, and uncles in the same household; some live in blended families; some live with adoptive parents; and others live in foster families. How do we communicate to children that there are many ways to be a family, many ways in which people can give each other support and love?

Very young children can be helped to make posters or books about the people in their families. A teacher's response to diversity can provide a model of full and complete acceptance of various family arrangements: "Tara's father lives in California, but she put him in her picture because he's still part of her family," or "Zach drew two mothers in his picture because Mama Alice and Mama Kate are both part of his family—they both love him and take care of him."

Older children can engage in more sophisticated lessons on step-parents, half-brothers and -sisters, adoption and foster care, lesbian parenting, or joint custody arrangements, for example. Teachers must remember that they are not raising difficult or uncomfortable issues with students; they are acknowledging and validating the situations that students are already experiencing and making clear that is all right to talk about such differences.

Teachers must also be careful about implementing projects or activities that assume that all children come from traditional nuclear families. Father–son hockey games, mother–daughter teas, and even grandparent visiting days can all be painful for children whose parents or grandparents are not alive, available, willing, or able to be involved in such activities. Teachers can create more inclusive opportunities: Bring-someone-you-love-to-school day (who might be a member of a student's church, his or her little sister, or the next-door neighbor), and other creative opportunities will make it clear to all children that there are many kinds of families and many ways of being closely and warmly connected to people.

Teachers must also exercise caution in giving assignments related to family trees, baby pictures, and other activities that presume that children are living with their biological parents and have access to information about their early years. Alternative assignments can preserve the intent of the lesson and still honor children's various situations and experiences; for example, interview someone in the community who is over 60 and find out what things were like when he or she was a child, or bring in a picture of yourself at an earlier age or a picture of someone else in your family and let others guess who that person is.

Learning About Gender Differences

As with other areas of difference, our goal in this area should be for children to acknowledge and accept sex differences and, at the same time, not be limited by those characteristics. Two specific goals in this area might be 1) to free children from constraining, stereotypical views of what "girls can do" and of what "boys can be," thus opening up greater options for growth and development; and 2) to encourage children to interact with and understand children from what is, unfortunately, referred to as "the opposite sex."

In order to meet the first objective, teachers must be attentive to both their own language and behaviors in the classroom and the materials and activities they provide for students. Admonitions that "big boys don't cry" or attempts to redirect a boy away from the housekeeping corner and into the block area communicate clearly that there are certain things that boys just do not do. Similarly, studying only male authors, male inventors, and the history of "mankind" disenfranchises girls and boys from full understanding of or pride in women's accomplishments and potential.

Teachers must continually examine their materials and their activities to ensure that all children feel included and welcome. There are many children's books available that challenge stereotypical roles: Reading *William's Doll* (Zolotow, 1972), for example, can help all children explore the role that loving and nurturing can play in their lives. Older children can read books with female protagonists and can be encouraged to find out about the many women who have been omitted from history books. Children can also be encouraged to become critical consumers and challengers of sexism in their lives and their materials. Teachers can help even very young children explore the assumptions in the books they read: "In this book I noticed that only the women were doing the cooking....can men cook too? Do you know men who cook?" Storytime can then be followed by a cooking activity that involves all students. Children can also explore toy catalogs and notice how there is a "boys' section" and a "girls' section" and discuss which of the toys look interesting to them and why and how parents and other adults often make decisions about "who gets what" along gender lines.

If the teacher notices that girls rarely choose science projects, for example, he or she might want to address this issue directly, assigning girls to specific projects that will build their competence and confidence in the science area. If a boy is teased because he mentions that he is learning to crochet, the teacher can talk about the history of men in knitting and netmaking and can teach *all* children to crochet winter hats and scarfs.

Getting children to play and interact across gender lines can be approached in the same way as other integration strategies. Teachers must ask: How can I arrange my classroom and my activities so that boys and girls feel comfortable working together and choosing one another as partners? Again, teachers must be careful to avoid perpetuating such artificial distinctions by having a "girls' line" and a "boys' line," or by having a girl leader of the week and a boy leader. However, more intervention may be required in order to counteract the prevailing practices and attitudes that tend to separate girls and boys and keep them from forming meaningful relationships. Teachers can assign children to work with partners or in groups on a regular basis and can ensure that these groups are heterogeneous in gender as well as in race and ability. Truly random assignments of tasks and responsibilities can also make gender less of an issue in the classroom—if children's names are pulled out of a can for daily math partners, then some pairs will be boys, some girls, and some a boy and a girl. If a teacher notes teasing or ridicule based on gender issues, such as, "Ha, Michael chose pink for his drawing," "José's playing with the girls," or "Marina's reading a boy's book," the teacher can intervene and address the issue directly. At minimum, the teacher should explain that teasing is not allowed and will not be permitted; even better would be a discussion of why people think pink is a girl's color or why books about rockets are considered boys' books. Plentiful opportunities for children to engage in projects that cross traditional gender lines (cooking, woodcraft, science, arts and crafts) can be provided. One third-grade teacher taught all her students to do counted cross-stitch. She reported that none of the boys or their parents objected, and all were pleased with the beautiful samplers the children made. A fifth-grade teacher had all the students build and launch rockets; it was not presented as a boys' activity while, for example, girls built bird feeders.

Because cultural norms regarding sex roles differ considerably, Derman-Sparks and the A.B.C. Task Force (1989) cautioned that teachers must be careful not to be racist by trying to be antisexist. For example, insisting that girls wear pants for gym or outdoor play may violate cultural or religious principles for some children and their families. The authors proposed that teachers present gender roles as offering multiple choices rather than assign superior values to some roles and that teachers find ways of providing options that promote children's full development and still respect their backgrounds. They stated that, for example, if parents really object to their daughter wearing pants or to their son being encouraged to cry, the teacher should develop alternatives such as having certain periods of the day when pants are worn for large motor activities or encouraging the boy to write his feelings or dictate them in a story.

Learning About Religious Differences and Holidays

Although the U.S. Constitution mandates the separation of church and state, the reality is that many schools and teachers behave as if all children were Christian. Many teachers organize their classrooms and activities from holiday to holiday. October is Halloween, November is Thanksgiving, and December is Christmas. Bulletin board decorations, stories, music, art projects, and the general curriculum often revolve around these holidays. There are many reasons that teachers focus their classrooms and the curriculum around holidays: Holidays provide an excellent way to program across subject areas around a theme, the symbols are recognizable and known to many children, and many of the typical holiday activities (parties, plays, singing, and community-building projects) represent a welcome source of social and affective development opportunities (Sapon-Shevin, King, & Hanhan, 1988).

Children who are Jehovah's Witnesses, however, may not celebrate holidays at all, Native American children may be uncomfortable with traditional presentations of Thanksgiving, and Christmastime can be difficult for children whose families do not celebrate it at all or celebrate it religiously as opposed to materialistically. Learning about religious differences can be closely related to learning about cultural, racial, and family differences; teachers must find ways to teach about religious differences and honor the ways in which children differ without fragmenting their class or destroying the sense of community. As with other areas of difference, it is important for teachers to avoid the language of "us" and "them," for example, "While we're having our holiday, Naomi and her family are having their holiday." The message must not be that most of us are the same while some of us are different, but that we all have unique backgrounds and characteristics.

As a start, teachers can deemphasize traditional holidays so that they do not occupy the majority of school time and activity. Children have plentiful opportunities to celebrate Christmas with their families and in their churches; school time can be devoted to other areas of study and involvement. For those holidays that teachers do choose to celebrate, a serious commitment can be made to presenting multicultural perspectives. Davids and Gudinas (1979) of the Department of Human Relations, Madison Wisconsin School District, for example, prepared and disseminated a "Thanksgiving Holiday Packet" for use by elementary school teachers in the district. The packet included "Thanksgiving: A New Perspective," an article describing recent research on the first Thanksgiving and its implications for the classroom; "Indians and Pilgrims," a simulation story to help children experience what it would feel like to have been the indigenous people when the Europeans arrived and settled here; "Thanksgiving: A Multicultural Approach," an activity that emphasizes how the concept of gratitude is expressed by people around the world; and "Teaching About Hunger," a list of suggestions for helping children think about hunger and responses to hunger. Other states such as Oregon have also implemented statewide curricula regarding Thanksgiving and Columbus Day that present a variety of viewpoints and respect the history and traditions of indigenous people.

Teachers can also make a serious effort to learn and teach about other religious and nonreligious holidays: Kwanzaa, the different new year's celebrations around the world, Sukkot, and Buddha's birthday all present opportunities to talk about different religions, nationalities, and beliefs. One of the major barriers to teaching about other religions and customs is often the teachers' own inexperience and relative ignorance. Although parents and children can both provide wonderful resources, teachers must also take seriously their own responsibility to read, listen, and become informed so that they can talk comfortably about religious differences. It is also possible to organize instruction around nonholiday themes. One teacher organized an entire month's curriculum around bears: Children read stories about bears, learned bear songs, studied about bears in science, did plays and fairy tales about bears, and did art projects related to bears. The unit culminated with a bear party to which children brought stuffed bears and feasted on goodies made with honey! Another teacher organized a unit around oceans and implemented activities across the curriculum related to water, tides, the animal and plant life of the ocean, and myths and legends about the sea. Such units preserve the benefits of organizing instruction topically, are inclusive of all children, and stretch the limits of the curriculum past often-repeated songs, stories, and art projects.

Holiday celebrations are also popular because they are often the occasion for teachers to engage in community-building activities in their classroom and school. Secret Santas (children pick secret friends to do favors for) and schoolwide food drives provide important opportunities for children to think empathetically about their classmates and the greater community. Such opportunities, however, need not be limited to holiday time. Local food cupboards need food all year, not just in December, and environmental concerns like recycling are ongoing. A long-term commitment by a particular class to such a project would be a valuable demonstration of the importance of caring about other people all the time, not just at holidays. Singing, preparing food, doing favors for friends, making gifts, and being friendly can all be implemented on a year-round basis. Community-building activities are most effective when they are seen as important and valued throughout the school year and not just occasionally.

Learning About Skill and Ability Differences

Although some differences in skills and abilities may be more readily apparent in an inclusive classroom—Dalia has a hearing impairment and wears hearing aids, Everett gets his math finished before anyone else, Carlos cannot walk and uses a wheelchair—the reality is that all children have strengths and weaknesses, areas of competence, and areas in which they need help. In order to contradict and challenge some of the typical hierarchies that become established in classrooms based on children's performance in a particular area (the highest reading group, the fastest runner), teachers can see to it that children are engaged in a broad range of activities and projects throughout the year, thus enabling many kinds of excellence and expertise to be validated and shared. One teacher created a Classroom Yellow Pages, which listed children's names, their areas of "expertise," and the ways in which they were willing to provide assistance to classmates. The guide included entries such as

LaDonna Smith: Jump rope songs and jingles; willing to teach double-dutch jumping and crossing over to anyone interested.

Miguel Hernandez: Baseball card collector; can show interested people how to start a collection, how to look for special cards, and how to figure batting averages and statistics.

By encouraging students to look beyond the typical school subjects by which they rank and evaluate themselves and each other, this teacher created new areas of interest, promoted peer interaction, and broke existing stereotypes about who was "smart" and who was not.

Teachers can also engage students in a discussion of helping and can have students generate and practice appropriate ways of offering and receiving help such as, "Can I help you?" rather than, "Let me do that, you're too short/dumb/slow," and ways of accepting and declining help gracefully such as, "No thanks, I'm doing fine," rather than, "What do you think I am, dumb or something?" These are repertoires that all people need, not simply people whose skills are limited. Teachers can help students reflect on questions such as the following:

- What are three things I'm really good at?
- What are three things I have trouble with?
- What are some ways I can provide help to people?
- What are some things I need help with, and what kind of help would I like?

By generating answers in this way, students and the teacher can see that everyone has skills and abilities and that everyone needs help in certain areas. Karen may be a whiz as a reader, but she may need help fitting into playground games. Carmen may struggle with her math, but she is great at remembering things and getting people and activities organized. Classrooms can become communities of mutual support if teachers promote respect for differences and provide multiple opportunities for students to see each other in many ways.

Other chapters in this book explain the ways in which competitive teaching and evaluation structures are incompatible with creating accepting and inclusive school communities. Star charts on the wall that indicate to all who enter who is doing "well" and who is doing "badly," choosing the "best artist" or the quietest group, or rewarding children for finishing first are not practices conducive to creating classroom communities that respect diversity. Competition is damaging not only to the student who does poorly ("We don't want Miguel on our math team, we had him last week") but also to students who consistently do well ("She thinks she's so smart just 'cause she got done faster than everyone else").

In cooperative classrooms, children help one another, provide each other with instructional help and peer support, and discover that by working together they can accomplish far more than by working alone. Children with different strengths and repertoires can all be functioning, contributing members of groups because skills and expertise are shared. Cooperative classrooms prove the truth of the saying "None of us is as smart as all of us."

Teachers in inclusive classrooms who individualize instruction may be asked, at first, "How come LaVonne doesn't do the same math we do?" or "When will I get to work on the computer like Kari does?" Teachers' responses to these and similar questions set the tone of the classroom. Generally speaking, honest, forthright answers seem to be best: "LaVonne works in a different book because she's working on addition, and she's not ready for multiplication yet," or "Let's find a time when you can work with Kari on the computer." After a short period of time, most children accept the fact that just as children come in different shapes and sizes, they also may do different work. When needing help is not stigmatized but is seen as a common natural occurrence, and when giving help is regarded as a valuable natural occurrence, then children can be very accommodating of one another's challenges and appreciative of their accomplishments.

The resource list at the end of this chapter includes some excellent readings on teaching about differences. However, teachers must be careful not to stress differences at the cost of allowing students to see the many ways in which they are similar. In order for students to find their common ground, teachers must make sure that they demonstrate that all students are in school to learn, that all people have things they are good at and things they are not good at, and that all of us do better with encouragement and support. One teacher did a wonderful lesson in which children learned that some children had blue eyes, some children had pets, some children had little brothers, some children were good runners, some children liked spinach, some children knew another language, but all children had feelings that could be hurt, and all children wanted friends.

Learning About and Challenging Stereotyping and Discrimination

In order for us to create and maintain truly inclusive schools and communities, children and teachers must see themselves as active change agents, willing and able to confront and challenge stereotypes and oppressive, discriminatory behavior. Depending on the age of the students, different levels of social activism and response are appropriate, but even young children can come to recognize and respond to stereotypes and prejudices.

One first-grade teacher explained to her students the difference between a "dislike" and a "prejudice." She allowed students to dislike something, that is, to have a negative reaction to something (a food, an activity) after they had had extensive experience with it but not to prejudge people and things without sufficient experience. Children came to discriminate legitimate dislikes ("I tasted broccoli and I hate it," or "Jared hits children and I don't want to play with him") from prejudices ("I don't want to taste that, it looks yucky," or "Children with dark skin are mean"). A teacher of preschoolers taught her class about words that were "exclusive" and "pushed people away" such as, "You can't play with us," and "There's no room here for you" and words that were "inclusive" and "brought people together" such as, "Do you want to be in our group?" and "Move over and make room for Micah."

Children can also become critical consumers of their own environments and the materials they encounter. There are numerous checklists that enable readers (even young readers) to examine materials for evidence of discrimination, misinformation, and omission of people of color, women, people with disabilities, or nontraditional families, for example. Young children can come to recognize that there are no people of color in many children's books or that the mommies in the books all stay home and the daddies all go to work in suits, although their mommies are waitresses and their daddies are farm laborers. Older children can engage in more sophisticated analyses of classroom materials. In an article on sensitizing children to Native American stereotypes, Califf (1977) shared her experiences teaching children about Native American values and traditions and how to recognize misrepresentations and stereotypes of Native American people in the media. As the culmination, she shared a book about Christopher Columbus with the class and was delighted that the children detected many stereotypes and distortions. Thirteen of the children wrote letters to the editor of Scholastic Magazines (which published the book). Following are two of the children's letters:

Dear Editor, I read your book. It made the Indians look like dogs. Those people talked the way we do and you do but in their language.... When they wanted to give something, the book did not tell about what language they spoke. It just said they spoke Indian. Sincerely, Scott Dames

Dear Editor, I don't like your book called The Cruise of Mr. Christopher Columbus. I didn't like it because you said things about Indians that weren't true.... Another thing I didn't like was on page 69 it says that Christopher Columbus invited the Indians to Spain, but what really happened was that he stole them! censearly [sic], Raymond Miranda (Califf, 1977, p. 7)

When the editor wrote back to the students and responded that she agreed with the criticism and agreed to stop publishing the book, the children were able to experience the importance and effects of being allies and confronting racism.

Students can also learn to confront racism, sexism, and discrimination in their own environments. One seventh-grade social studies teacher assigned his students to complete an accessibility checklist of their school (Sapon-Shevin, 1988). Students set out with guidelines and tape measures in order to find out whether students in wheelchairs, those using braille, and those who could not hear would be able to have full access to the building and its programs. These students then wrote letters to the principal sharing what they had found. Their insights into inclusion ("The elevator goes up but doesn't go down, so students in wheelchairs could never take classes on the second floor") and their indignation about injustice ("How would you like it if your child couldn't come to this school?") were promising indicators of their growing ability to recognize and challenge discrimination and exclusion.

At the most basic level, children can also learn how to respond to name calling and exclusion of children based on differences. The Madison Public Schools (1989) articulated a specific policy in this area, which reads: "In accordance with the District's nondiscrimination policy, racial name-calling will not be tolerated. This includes all derogatory language, gestures and behaviors with racial overtones."

The district's handout goes on to state that children need to know that racial names and slurs represent a form of verbal abuse and are unacceptable. They suggest that when racist language is used, the following statements could be useful: "Racial name-calling is not allowed in this school. Racial name-calling is demeaning. I find that word offensive. We value all people in our room and in our school and we do not use that language."

Similarly, children can come to recognize and interrupt racist, sexist, and ethnic jokes. Teachers can explore with students the ways in which such jokes perpetuate stereotypes and are damaging to people, although they may be intended as humorous. Students can learn ways of interrupting such humor firmly ("I don't think that's funny") and can also be encouraged to find and share jokes and stories that are funny but not at the expense of another group. One teacher told her class that the first 5 minutes of class would be devoted to sharing jokes, with the provision that the joke not be offensive to any specific group. This offer challenged students to listen critically to the jokes they heard and to analyze humor for its potential negative overtones and consequences.

It is important that children feel that they can make a difference. Classrooms that are inclusive work to empower all children to improve their own situations and those of their classmates. Students who feel powerful and effective in elementary school are far more likely to grow up to be adults who feel that they can change things and make a difference. The typical school day or year provides multiple opportunities to problem-solve issues of inclusiveness. When one fifth-grade class that included a child who was a vegetarian, a child who kept kosher, and a child who was Muslim wanted to plan refreshments for their party, the children brainstormed food choices that would allow all of the children to eat comfortably. When a child who used a wheelchair was not strong enough to lift himself out of his chair, the whole class became involved in a fitness and muscle-building unit to improve upper body strength. The messages in these classrooms are consistent: We are a community, we are all in this together, we will take responsibility for one another, we will not abandon people because of their differences or difficulties.

CONCLUSION

Creating classrooms that honor and respect all children and all of their differences is an ongoing, time-consuming challenge. As teachers, we will need to continue to struggle with our own language, teaching, and curriculum in our attempts at inclusiveness, fairness, and respect. The most important thing teachers can do is explore their own understandings, values, and beliefs about diversity. For example, when and how did you first learn about racial differences and what was communicated? When you were growing up, what groups of people did you have ongoing contact with, and with whom did you never interact? How comfortable are you yourself with people of color? Lesbians? Single parents? African Americans? Hispanics? Jews? Latinos? Koreans? Only by exploring our own personal histories and experiences can we attempt to unravel the effects of our own upbringing, thus strengthening our adult commitments to create inclusive classrooms that model social justice and equality.

Swadener, Gudinas, and Kaiser (1988) asked teachers to respond with a statement beginning "I feel" to the following authentic quotes from parents:

Chinese American parent: "My four-year-old son asked me, When I grow up can I be blond? It's better to be blond, Dad!" I feel...

Adoptive parent of Korean child: "We had to remove our child from the day care when other children kept teasing her about 'not being a real American' and the teacher didn't take this seriously." I feel...

Hmong parent: "In our Hmong tradition, masks have spiritual significance. My child was expected to do an art project making scary masks and was very upset by this." I feel...

Low-income parent: "It is so hard to just tell my 6-year-old that we cannot afford the things that other kids at school take for granted—you know, the brand name jeans and Cabbage Patch stuff." I feel... (Swadener, Gudinas, & Kaiser, p. 5)

Discussing our own responses to such parental concerns and classroom dilemmas can help to sensitize us to the many kinds of diversity that our children present and to the need to develop caring, inclusive responses. The task is a difficult one, but it is critical to our ability to shape the kinds of schools we envision.

REFERENCES

Califf, J. (1977). Sensitizing nine-year-olds to Native American stereotypes. *Interracial Books for Children Bulletin, 8*(1), 3–7.

Davids, D.W., & Gudinas, R.A. (1979). *Student activities and teacher materials for use during the Thanksgiving season.* Madison: Department of Human Relations, Madison Wisconsin School District.

Department of Human Relations, Madison Wisconsin School District. (1989). *Racial name-calling: Strategies, activities and resources.* Madison: Author.

Derman-Sparks, L., & the A.B.C. Task Force. (1989). *Anti-bias curriculum: Tools for empowering young children.* Washington, DC: National Association for the Education of Young Children.

Grant, C.A., & Sleeter, C.A. (1989). *Turning on learning: Five approaches for multicultural teaching plans for race, class, gender and disability.* Columbus ,OH: Charles E. Merrill.

Ramsey, P.G. (1987). *Teaching and learning in a diverse world: Multicultural education for young children.* New York: Teachers College Press.

Sapon-Shevin, M. (1992). Ability differences in the classroom: Teaching and learning in inclusive classrooms. In D. Byrnes & G. Kiger (Eds.), *Common bonds: Anti-bias teaching in a diverse society.* Washington, DC: Association for Childhood Education International.

Sapon-Shevin, M., King, R., & Hanhan, S. (1988). The holiday-centered curriculum. *Education and Society, 1*(3), 26–31.

Sleeter, C.E., & Grant, C.A. (1988). *Making choices for multicultural education: Five approaches to race, class, and gender.* Columbus ,OH: Charles E. Merrill.

Swadener, E.B., Gudinas, R.A., & Kaiser, R.B. (1988). Parent perspectives: An activity to sensitize teachers to cultural, religious and class diversity. *Journal of School Social Work, 2*(2), 1–7.

The Teachers' Workshop. (1989, November). *The Teachers' Workshop Newsletter.* Madison, WI: Emerson Elementary School.

Whaley, K., & Swadener, E.B. (1990). Multicultural education in infant and toddler settings. *Childhood Education, 66*(4), 238–240.

Zolotow, C. (1972). *William's doll.* New York: Harper & Row.

RESOURCES

There are many excellent resources available for teaching children about differences; for implementing education that is multicultural; and for helping students and teachers to challenge racism, sexism, and other forms of oppression and discrimination.

Teachers are also encouraged to seek out and identify children's books that are inclusive and that represent diversity positively.

Barnes, E., Berrigan, C., & Biklen, D. (1978). *What's the difference: Teaching positive attitudes towards people with disabilities.* Syracuse, NY: Human Policy Press.

Byrnes, D. (1987). *Teacher, they called me a....* (Available from Anti-Defamation League, B'nai B'rith, Department JW, 823 United Nations Plaza, New York, 10017.)

Byrnes, D., & Kiger, G. (Eds.). (1992). *Common bonds: Anti-bias teaching in a diverse society.* Washington, DC: Association for Childhood Education International.

Children's Book Press, 1461 Ninth Avenue, San Francisco, CA, 94122. (Publishers of multicultural literature and audiocassettes for children.)

Council on Interracial Books for Children, 1841 Broadway, New York, NY 10023. (Publishers of book lists, film strips, and other media about unlearning racism.)

Cummings, M. (1977). *Individual differences: An experience in human relations for children.* (Available from Anti-Defamation League, B'nai B'rith, Department JW, 823 United Nations Plaza, New York, 10017.)

Derman-Sparks, L., & the A.B.C. Task Force (1989). *Anti-bias curriculum: Tools for empowering young children.* Washington, DC: National Association for the Education of Young Children.

Froeschl, M., & Sprung, B. (1989). *Resources for educational equity: A guide for grades pre-K–12.* New York: Garland Publishing.

Grant, C.A., & Sleeter, C.A. (1989). *Turning on learning: Five approaches for multicultural teaching plans for race, class, gender and disability.* Columbus, **OH**: Charles E. Merrill.

Kendall, F. (1983). *Diversity in the classroom: A multicultural approach to the education of young children.* New York: Teachers College Press.

Ramsey, P.G. (1987). *Teaching and learning in a diverse world: Multicultural education for young children.* New York: Teachers College Press.

Ramsey, P.G., Vold, E.B., & Williams, L.R. (1989). *Multicultural education: A sourcebook.* New York: Garland Publishing.

Schniedewind, N., & Davidson, E. (1983). *Open minds to equality: A sourcebook of learning activities to promote race, sex, class and age equity.* Englewood Cliffs, NJ: Prentice Hall.

18

Community Learning in Inclusive Schools

Michael Peterson

IN A SCHOOL district in a Midwestern state in one week in April, a group of 20 students was on a full-day canoeing expedition and sampled the water quality as part of their year-long project studying the effects of a new business on the community, environment, and economy. Three students who recently emigrated from other countries were learning English while sharing their knowledge. A student with mental retardation was co-director of materials and supplies for the group. The learning group also included a student with autistic disorder, whose talents for organization and memorization the group was using to help keep track of important information. The teacher helped to organize a management team for the expedition that facilitated the development and coordination of work teams. A student with quadriplegia was chairperson of the team on water quality. The management team met each morning and made decisions for the day's "learning work." In the afternoon, they attended classes in language, math, and other traditional subjects in which they focused their skill development in areas that were related to their learning project. Before they left for school, the group met with the teacher to debrief and share about personal and learning issues.

This scenario illustrates some important concepts for learning, curriculum, and community building in inclusive schools. Students learn skills and acquire knowledge by engaging in real-world, important problem-solving activities in heterogeneous groups in which people assume various roles. In the process, students learn how to deal with complexity and diversity as it is in the real world. Most important, they experience a sense of support, fun, and community in the process. A wide range of curriculum restructuring approaches that this scenario illustrates may be summarized in three simple, but powerful, themes:

- *What is learned:* Students learn to function as effective members of their communities in a democratic society.
- *How students learn:* Students learn by engaging in meaningful, real-world activities in which skills are learned through their application, in which inquiry, reflection, and critical thinking occur in interaction with and are supported by other learners, and in which multiple approaches and styles of learning are used.
- *Who learns with whom:* Students learn in diverse, heterogeneous groups where they develop supportive relationships, learn how to work as teams, and learn how to value and accommodate a wide range of diversity.

A range of curriculum approaches are based on these ideas—community-referenced learning; community-based instruction; authentic curriculum; interdisciplinary, thematic curricula; problem-based learning; and active learning. Although each of these is distinct, the basic idea is the same. The term that is used in this chapter is community learning. Community learning has multiple meanings that are mutually reinforcing and that together provide a comprehensive approach. What are these meanings? First, learning is *for* the community; that is, learning prepares students for active participation in community life and for leadership in community activities that range from holding a job to identifying and addressing key community and social issues. Second, community may also be a geographical location that is the center for groups of people or networks of individuals across locations. Finally, community refers to the psychological sense of belonging that occurs when people feel they have connections and mutual support. In this sense, students learn to value and help develop a sense of mutuality, teamwork, and caring among diverse groups of people. Learning is also *in* the community. Learning occurs through applied activities; learning and doing become linked.

THE JOURNEY TOWARD COMMUNITY
LEARNING FOR DIVERSE STUDENT LEARNERS

The concept of community learning is not new. Dewey (1943) espoused the use of experience as the foundation of education. He was concerned about the isolation of the school from typical community life and the routine nature of learning in the classroom and called for the utilization of work and community activities as the center for learning. Not only would such approaches help students learn skills and their applications in the community, but social learning and relationship building would occur as well.

> A society is a number of people held together because they are working along common lines, in a common spirit, and with reference to common aims.... In the schoolroom the motive and the cement of social organization are alike wanting.... The difference that appears when occupations are made the articulating centers of school life is not easy to describe in words; it is a difference in motive, of spirit and atmosphere. As one enters a busy kitchen in which a group of children are actively engaged in the preparation of food, the psychological difference, the change from more or less passive and inert recipiency and restraint to one of buoyant outgoing energy, is so obvious as fairly to strike one in the face. (Dewey, 1943, p. 18)

In the spirit of inclusive schooling, Dewey called for schools that bring children together and create opportunities for learning through doing in mutually supportive relationships. It is clear schools have not incorporated experience as the basis for cognitive and social learning. Rather, education in the United States took a path, based on the same paradigm as the factory and industrial processes, of separating increasing numbers of students from one another, teaching lessons in increasingly abstract and segmented ways, and increasing the distance between home, school, and community. Goodlad (1984), for example, in his classic study of high schools throughout the United States, verified that the typical classroom and school curriculum are based on rote learning of isolated skills through worksheets and drills. The results are that many students leave schools without knowing how to accomplish real-world work and community living tasks.

Concern about the nature of academic curricula in public schools has been particularly marked among many of us who deal with students with "special" learning needs. In response to this issue, since 1980, numerous projects, programs, and publications have attempted to develop "functional curricula" for special students—instruction in which the focus is less on academic skills than on those functional work, home, community, and leisure skills needed by students with disabilities. Initially, much of the focus was on *what* students should learn and on identifying *places* in the school or community where such learning could occur. Much of this work was concurrent with the career education movement. Brolin began work in the 1960s on the *Life-Centered Career Education* curriculum, which has, perhaps, been among the most recognized and utilized of the functional curricula (see Brolin, McKay, & West, 1993, for the most current of many versions). As the focus became more centered on students with significant disabilities, the field began to develop approaches and a technology for *how and where* to teach such functional skills. Thus, *community-based instruction* was developed and implemented by several researchers (Falvey, 1989; Ford et al., 1989; Wilcox & Bellamy, 1982). To some extent, special educators concerned about these issues worked in two groups—one associated with the Council for Exceptional Children (CEC) through the Division for Career Development, which focused primarily on students with learning disabilities; the other associated with The Association for Persons with Severe Handicaps (TASH), whose obvious emphasis has been individuals with significant disabilities.

At the same time, a number of people were working to include and support students with special needs in vocational education classes in high schools. The vocational education approach of teaching skills through direct instruction and involvement in work activities and utilization of on-the-job learning in "cooperative education" seemed to many of us to be a key in addressing the need for students with disabilities to learn real-world skills in real-world settings. Although much instruction was provided in separate vocational programs for special students, many effective support systems were set up to include such students in general vocational education classes. In many ways, such vocational education programs developed the technology for providing individualized learning goals and strategies of needed classroom supports that formed the foundation for what was later called "inclusive education."

More recently, several concurrent movements, some tenuously connected with one another but all part of an effort to facilitate significant reforms in public schools, have gained momentum. The move to restructure schools is now at the point at which school reform is being considered on a broad basis. Although previous efforts at school reform focused largely on decision-making and management processes, school restructuring has begun to focus on what children learn and where, how, and with whom. Some efforts have looked at methods of curriculum reform and at the negative impact of separate educational processes for learners with disabilities and learners who are disadvantaged or gifted (Ogle, Pink, & Jones, 1990). Subsequently, grants have been awarded for the design of "break the mold" schools, most of which have established truly interesting approaches that incorporate all students in learning by doing together.

A variety of initiatives have questioned the practice of separating students with special needs from the larger school community. Substantial controversy has been generated by research related to tracking of students and the impact on learning. Many have read the research results as supporting heterogeneous groupings of students, and literature and initiatives for "untracking" have occurred.

The movement toward inclusive education for students with disabilities occurred simultaneously with all these efforts, and the common links between many of these initiatives that originally proceeded along separate tracks are now recognized. Both practice and policy are moving toward integration of many of these themes and toward merging concepts of building inclusive schools and applied learning.

There is much yet to do, however. These movements confront special and general educators with some important choices and challenges as we strive to improve schooling. It is still true that most of our schools, and high schools particularly, utilize standardized rote methods of teaching and learning with little that involves learning or practicing through important work and community activities. Many special educators express concern that appropriate learning of functional skills cannot occur in these schools. Consequently, it is best, they feel, to engage in separate programs of functional life skills and community-based learning designed specifically for students with disabilities. The Mental Retardation Division of CEC took this position (1992). From this position, it is often stated that inclusive education is choosing increased social experiences and minimizing learning or skill development. Brown et al. (1991) suggested that the base placement for students with significant disabilities should be in the general education classroom but that students be engaged in community-based instruction outside the classroom as needed.

There are several issues that must be carefully considered. First, do existing separate functional-skill and community-based instructional programs achieve the intended results? Second, what is the actual impact on skill development and community participation when students with disabilities are included in general education classes, even at present levels? Third, and most important for this chapter, we must consider what we want our schools to be in the future and whether general and special education will merge to shape that future together or continue to go separate ways. We have the opportunity to shape schools to produce better outcomes for all students as we move to create schools that incorporate new technology and new learnings from the ideas developed by Dewey (1943) and others earlier in the 20th century. Special educators have developed much expertise in the design and implementation of functional curricula, community-based instruction, and transition from school to adult life. General educators have been engaged in developing related innovations in authentic instruction, problem-based learning, and similar strategies. We have much to learn from and to offer each other that will improve learning for all students. There are multiple opportunities at multiple levels for special and general educators to work together to improve the relevance and meaning of schools and to ensure that this is done in a way that supports a diversity of learning styles and abilities. The goal of this chapter is to provide some ideas and resources to assist in this process.

OUTCOMES-BASED EDUCATION

As we think about improving learning outcomes in inclusive schools, we must first consider *what* students are to learn. A major movement of school restructuring is toward *outcomes-based education,* that is, identifying what all students should learn and holding schools accountable for student learning outcomes. Ysseldyke, Thurlow, and Shriner (1992) encouraged special education personnel to be integrally involved in the process of identifying important learning outcomes for students. This presents both opportunities and challenges.

Schools have traditionally been concerned primarily with the ability to demonstrate skills as assessed on abstracted tests in artificial settings independent of future outcomes. Although this approach has been modified with the expansion of vocational education, a variety of elective courses, and extracurricular activities, schools focus primarily on teaching basic academic skills in contexts disconnected from how such skills are used in professional and everyday life. This continues to occur despite evidence of the lack of effectiveness of such approaches. However, as curriculum restructuring occurs through association with national reform networks (Coalition for Essential Schools and others), we are seeing schools and states clarify and focus the content, or standards, of learning. In almost all cases, these efforts result in learning goals that focus on real-world outcomes.

Some key constructs may be helpful in sorting out this complex of performance skills expected of learners. We can think about students acquiring sufficient *knowledge* and *basic skills* (reading, writing, psychomotor) to be able to engage in important community and living *activities* and have needed and valued *roles* (friends, committee chairperson, choir member, employee). We further expect that individuals will engage in critical thinking in order to grapple with important problems and that students will develop a network of supportive *relationships* and understand how to *work in teams* to get work done.

Skills for Adult and Community Living

Educators and communities typically believe that schools should equip students with skills to enable them to function as effective adults and community members (Berryman, 1988; Jones, 1990; Michigan Department of Education, 1994). Although the specific language varies, most studies have indicated that people believe schools should prepare students for the challenges of adult and community living. Such goals change the focus of education from isolated academic skills to skills in performing community activities. The Michigan Department of Education (1994), for example, has identified competencies that are expected to be integrated in more traditional "core curriculum" areas. These include skills for life management, vocation, avocation, employability, aesthetic appreciation, and technology. Earlier, Benjamin (1989) described education that focuses on the whole person as including affective skills, relationships, mental health, and physical health, as well as more traditional academic skills.

According to others, students should have opportunities to understand community, state, national, and world problems and engage in activities designed to affect such problems (Banks, 1988; Berryman, 1988; Boyer, 1984; Jones, 1990). This broadened curriculum naturally involves students in community life in an active manner.

Critical Thinking Skills

Central to reforms to restructure the school curriculum is a focus on critical thinking skills. Rather than providing students with predetermined content, teaching students to think involves them in active processes of identifying problems, gathering information, and identifying, testing, and evaluating potential solutions. Such critical thinking and problem-solving skills are intended to be at the base of all learning rather than available to students only after the basics have been learned (Berryman, 1988; Jones, 1990; Resnick & Klopfer, 1989). Problem solving is mastered only by engaging in actual problem-solving activities, not by treating it as a separate, abstract subject (Benjamin, 1989). From this perspective, the participation of students in support circles, life planning, curriculum adaptation, and other activities designed to aid students with disabilities provides excellent opportunities for the learning and use of critical thinking skills.

Teamwork and Interpersonal Relationships

Relationships clearly have to do with our interactions with others and the type and extent of connection with them. We seek to create communities in which all people have a network of supportive relationships of intimate friends, acquaintances, and helpers. Our society is increasingly dependent on complex interpersonal relationships in groups that work together to solve problems. Therefore, teamwork and interpersonal communication are increasingly important as educational goals (Berryman, 1988). Students need opportunities to engage in teamwork in a wide range of activities. Cooperative learning sees teamwork as an appropriate learning goal in itself while also being an effective learning strategy for acquiring other skills as well (Johnson & Johnson, 1989). Particularly important in the workplace is the ability to work as part of a team in order to design and test solutions to technical and social problems (Berryman, 1988).

PRINCIPLES OF PRACTICE FOR COMMUNITY LEARNING

What are the principles that undergird what we call community learning? Newmann and Wehlage (1993) described five standards of "authentic instruction" that capture many of the principles with which we are concerned. These include

- Higher-order thinking
- Depth of knowledge
- Connectedness to the world beyond the classroom
- Social support for student achievement

The following can be added standards or critical principles:

- Transdisciplinary or interdisciplinary learning
- Active learning
- Heterogeneous groups
- Diverse learning styles and abilities

These concepts provide practical guidelines or standards for developing and implementing community learning that enhances the learning of all students. Each standard is now described in more depth.

Higher-Order Thinking

Lower-order thinking occurs when students receive or recite factual information. In higher-order thinking, students use information to arrive at conclusions. Such critical thinking requires an element of uncertainty, as well as judgment and problem-solving skills. The typical assumption is that students with special learning needs use only lower-order thinking. This may be true for some individuals, but for most individuals, it is not. In either case, students with significant disabilities can often be part of learning teams using higher-order thinking skills in ways that contribute to their learning.

Depth of Knowledge

Knowledge may be considered "shallow" when it "does not deal with significant concepts of a topic or disciplines" (Newmann & Wehlage, 1993, p. 9). When students are involved in dealing with key ideas, developing arguments, or solving problems, they learn information at a more substantive level. Shallow learning often occurs when a large number of topics are covered in a fragmented way. Thus, depth of knowledge can more easily occur when fewer topics are covered.

Connectedness to the World Beyond the Classroom

Schools must be reconnected to the community in multiple ways for learning to be effective. This is perhaps the centerpiece of improving schools. This reconnection must occur in many ways. Students should engage in learning through meaningful activities related to the community in the community. Additionally, members of the community should be involved in the process of learning through mentoring, apprenticeships, lectures, or advising a class on community learning. Partnerships should be made with community organizations such as universities, hospitals, and businesses, and community members of all sorts to work collaboratively with schools to stimulate student learning. Older persons can mentor students and provide their expertise (Angelis & Wathen, 1994). People with disabilities can share their experiences and learning and present policy issues in classes on social issues. Seeking out such connections increases the resources for learning, reduces the isolation of the school, and makes learning real for all students.

Social Support for Student Achievement

Students learn most effectively in an atmosphere of support, cooperation, and encouragement in which all students are welcome rather than in an atmosphere of competition and exclusion. All students benefit when students provide peer support to others. Supervision of peer tutoring should ensure that such interaction meets the learning objectives of both tutor and tutee.

Transdisciplinary Learning

Transdisciplinary learning has also been espoused in school restructuring literature (Jones, 1990). In transdisciplinary learning, various school disciplines or subjects are jointly focused on related learning goals. Community problems often require the simultaneous application of language, math, science, and interpersonal skills. Therefore, as students learn to engage in community activities and apply skills, it is reasonable to expect that teachers from these various disciplines work together. For example, several teachers may join together to engage in a community project related to environmental problems. In such a project, students might apply skills related to math, science, technical language, and other skills.

Active Learning

Community learning strategies provide opportunities for students to be active shapers rather than passive recipients of the learning process. Under the guidance of teachers, students identify problems, develop learning teams, and direct the course of learning.

Heterogeneous Groups

All students learn most effectively when their education is individualized and they have opportunities to learn in a heterogeneous group. Most models of community learning intentionally move toward untracking the school and the instruction of diverse learners together. As community learning moves beyond the narrow confines of the walls of the classroom and the boundaries of subjects in order to improve substantive learning, the involvement of diverse students sharing various perceptions, working together across cultures and abilities, and engaging in mutual problem solving is seen as a critical component of learning. For example, students may provide assistance to others involved with higher-level learning tasks, students working on simple tasks may be taught these tasks by other students, and learning circles may be used that involve students of all levels in solving problems together. A diversified learning approach gives all students opportunities to pursue their individual learning goals while learning with a diverse group.

Diverse Learning Styles and Abilities

To effectively respond to heterogeneous groups of students, community learning must develop mechanisms for responding to the various learning styles, multiple intelligences (Armstrong, 1994; Gardner, 1983), and various learning and performance abilities. Gardner's (1983) concept and approach to teaching in ways that respond to the various intelligences of students provides one effective framework and set of strategies. Armstrong (1994) has provided information and examples that can be used by teachers to develop teaching strategies that respond to various individual strengths in learning and thinking.

COMMUNITY LEARNING AND INCLUSIVE SCHOOLS

Community learning provides opportunities for learning functional skills through simulations and community-based instruction and would appear to address concerns and recommended practices developed for special students. However, as with inclusive schooling in general, the question is, how can we manage the instruction of students with widely ranging learning goals, abilities, language, and culture? Some students may learn to ride buses, wash clothes, and work in a team. Other students may be engaged in solving a financial crisis of a simulated corporation. How does community learning then facilitate the process of inclusive schooling, or does it? Certainly, embracing inclusion does not happen automatically with community learning. However, community learning offers the opportunity for inclusion to occur to the benefit of all involved. Why and how might this occur?

Community learning strategies offer a much wider range of tasks, activities, and roles than the typical general education classroom offers. Let us use the example at the beginning of this chapter of the learning team on a canoe trip, conducting experiments and interviewing local people. All of these activities can include students of various levels of ability and with different learning styles because individuals are needed to provide emotional support, organize the group, carry supplies, and participate in team decision making.

As we identify learning goals and objectives for students with disabilities that focus on functional life outcomes in work, home, community, and relationships, we can identify ways in which to incorporate these goals into community learning activities. Additionally, community learning activities can be designed with the needs and interests of various students in mind. For example, if it is important that a student with a disability learn to use the city bus, community learning activities could simply include this. A learning group could take the bus to various destinations. Instruction could be given by the teacher to the student with a disability and a buddy. They could take the bus and then lead the other students in using the bus. While this helps the student with a disability and engenders a sense of community, the fact is that this is a skill that other students need as well. Additionally, such activities can often connect in more complex ways to issues being studied in the classroom. If the learning group is also interested in the impact of a new business, how does this affect transportation needs? Is transportation for potential workers adequate? The specific needs of a student with a disability can be the source of very interesting and complex analyses on the part of all students. Major social issues are involved in these questions: How do we manage diversity in our communities and workplaces? How do people with very different cultures, learning styles, and physical and mental abilities work together, and what resources—housing, transportation, employment—are available in the community to make this possible. As students grapple with such questions in community learning, creative educators can find many opportunities to link the needs of a range of students.

STRATEGIES FOR COMMUNITY LEARNING

A wide range of approaches can be used to center learning in meaningful community activities in which roles and relationships are also emphasized. *Single classroom-based strategies* are those that can be implemented by a single classroom teacher within the constraints of a traditional curriculum. For example, simulations and community-based projects may be designed by an individual teacher in any subject area. *Collaboration by two or more teachers* involves linking lessons across subjects around a common theme or project. For example, a math teacher and a political science teacher might collaborate on a project involving analysis of the state budget and its implications for the local community. *Special programs* are established specifically for the purpose of providing community learning. These may be integrated and coordinated with the rest of the curriculum or implemented in parallel fashion. Cooperative vocational education, service learning, and some methods of implementing mentor programs are examples of special programs. *Curriculum design involving the total school* utilizes strategies in which activity learning is at the center of the learning process. Typically, this involves a mix of traditionally organized subjects and interdisciplinary team teaching based on larger themes and community projects.

Another aspect of community learning is whether instruction occurs in the school, community, or in both. Some strategies tend to be used in the school—simulations, learning centers—either in an individual classroom or as a collaborative effort involving two or more teachers and subjects.

Class Simulations

In class simulations, essential elements of community activities are acted out or replicated in the school. These may involve relatively short activities with a few students or engage a total class (or even a school) in a project. Berryman (1988) described a fifth-grade teacher in Virginia who ran a simulation of a small economy in her classroom. As Berryman (1988) stated, "'Taxation' means much more when another seatmate who represented government has bought the classroom door, forcing everyone to pay taxes every time they need to go in or out of the room..." (p. 8).

One method of using simulations in the classroom is by structuring *applied learning* centers in an individual classroom or for a total school. Peterson, LeRoy, Field, and Wood (1992) described some examples. In a third-grade classroom, the math learning center focused on measurement for 2 weeks in the fall. At the learning center station, students were encouraged to complete at least five measurement activities. They had a checklist for recording their answers and responses to each activity. At the bottom of the checklist were two blanks encouraging students to create their own measurement activities and to "test" those activities with other students. All activities at the learning center required teamwork, and partners were assigned by the teacher. For each activity at the station, performance levels were individualized to enable students with diverse interests and abilities to participate. Examples of activities were measuring quantities of ingredients to make popcorn, salad, and cookies; measuring the temperature of various liquids and charting changes in them; guessing the weights of various objects and then measuring them; and calculating the mileage for a family trip using a map and scale measurement.

Role play and demonstrations are additional valuable techniques. Peterson et al. (1992) described several examples: A teacher incorporated cooperative grouping in a 10th-grade television production class, with demonstration techniques that actively engaged his students in learning television production. They worked in small groups to develop a format for teaching ninth-grade students to operate video cameras and recorders. In an elementary classroom, the fifth-grade class demonstrated how to structure a cooperative group activity for second-grade peers and then helped them make a pizza.

Using Community Resources

At the most basic level of community learning is the utilization of community resources for short-term projects. These projects may be centered in traditional subjects and assignments or focus on school-based community-referenced learning projects. Peterson et al. (1992) described some examples of this strategy. In a third-grade class, the students were divided into small groups for visits to the city library. Parents and local neighborhood volunteers assisted each group individually as it visited the library. Students learned to cross streets, identify landmarks, utilize the library resources, find books, and check out books on a specific topic and project each student was to complete. A student who required additional practice to master these skills accompanied several groups on library visits.

Schools within Schools

School buildings can be made into smaller, cohesive communities that facilitate design and implementation of community learning and that build a sense of mutual support among students and teachers. A core group of teachers and students join together for all instructional activities. These minischools may establish separate identities through choosing a name or mascot, going on retreats to build a sense of belonging and community, and planning schoolwide learning experiences around specific themes (e.g., ecology, civil war, a multicultural fair). Entire classrooms may assume various themes, and children mix throughout the school to engage in each learning activity (Peterson et al., 1992).

Problem-Based Learning

In problem-based learning, students are presented with real-world problems and are provided support for researching and developing proposed solutions. For example, in one school's summer program, students were challenged to understand and develop ideas regarding the health risks posed by low-level nuclear waste. They visited a waste site, surveyed the community, conducted experiments, and presented their solutions to government officials and community activists.

In problem-based learning, students "Learn how to use an iterative process of assessing what they know, identifying what they need to know, gathering information, and collaborating on the evaluation of hypotheses..." (Stepien & Gallagher, 1993). Students take on the real-world roles of scientists, historians, doctors, and others who have a real stake in issues and their solutions. The goal is to facilitate learning of critical thinking and problem-solving skills and collaboration and team-building. Teachers act as models, supporters, and mentors. They think out loud with the students, helping them ask questions and think through the problem-solving process. Over time, students work in self-directed teams with ongoing support from a teacher.

The Center for Problem-Based Learning at the Illinois Mathematics and Science Academy has developed a series of courses and projects in problem-based learning in the community. One course, "Science, Society, and the Future," is taught by a team of science and social science teachers and focuses on unresolved science-related social issues. Short-term projects, or "post-holes," can also be used in the classroom. For example, one simulation had students respond to a letter from the Nazi ministry of propaganda asking them as directors of art galleries to review their collections and discard degenerate art work. The teacher asks, "What must we know in order to respond to this situation?" The students then think about how to respond to this situation (Stepien & Gallagher, 1993).

Community Projects

Projects can turn routine learning into an active process for all students. Peterson et al. (1992) described a number of examples of community projects. In a seventh-grade social studies class, for example, students completed reports about various states. Two students worked as partners, and the project contained the following components: a written report, a travel poster, an oral report to the class and/or to another class in the building, and one of four optional activities—a play on an interesting historical event or person in that state, a food festival related to local cuisine, a video simulation of an interview with the governor of the state, or a student-generated activity. Each student team contracted a plan with the teacher for completing the project and developed a timeline for their activities.

In a high school law class, student teams served on juvenile juries in the local court system. Through this experience, they gained direct knowledge of the judicial process. They heard testimony on actual juvenile court cases (based on an agreement between the judge and the defendant), assigned verdicts, and recommended punishments. After their rotation on the court, the students returned to the classroom to share their experiences via reenactments and written briefs.

In a sixth-grade class, a partnership between a classroom and a branch of a local bank allowed students to practice several academic, community, and vocational interest activities during the year. Small groups of students traveled on the public bus to spend a day at the bank several times during the year. At the bank, the students learned about banking functions and personnel roles, and they developed social skills and money-handling skills. They ate lunch with bank personnel and followed their routines. Students engaged in learning based on individual need—one learned about loans, another helped a teller, while another student counted money in the vault. In a physics class, teams of students worked with a local bioengineering firm to develop adaptive equipment for a classmate. In a home economics class, teams of students rotated once a week at a local church to prepare food for the shelter's breakfast program.

Yager (1987) suggested that, in science, learning does not come from applying knowledge to solve problems; rather, if students identify real-world problems that they want to solve, they will seek knowledge. For example, in one ninth-grade biology class, a teacher engaged students in active learning about ecology, scientific inquiry, and scientific measurement. In this activity, the students formed learning teams who tested the water quality of a local river on a biweekly basis. The teams gathered samples of the water, cultured the organisms, and measured the levels of various chemicals in the water. One student with challenging needs in this classroom assisted in the experiments and worked on other individualized education program (IEP) goals, such as crossing the street at the crossing, becoming familiar with the community, and walking on uneven terrain.

Service Learning

Students may also be directly involved in community activities as part of the learning process. Benjamin (1989), for example, described service learning in which students engaged in actual problem-solving and work activities in their community. Toffler (1981) and Shuman (1984) suggested that learning should focus on real problems in which students provide services to the community. Such service commitments may be coupled with discussion and analysis in the school. Service experiences may include assistance in hospitals, museums, community agencies, schools, and other organizations via internships and mentorships. In one school, for example, students spent their mornings helping in the community through a "City as School" program. Students selected areas of interest to them such as working in the local parks, at the community-access television station, at city hall, in programs for older people, or in child care centers. One 15-year-old student described his work with children in the elementary school who were headed toward some of the same troubles he had (Richardson, 1994).

Service learning has gotten a substantial boost from passage of the National Community Service Trust Act of 1993, which provides funds for local schools and students to engage in community service as an integral part of their education. Although vocational education has implemented such cooperative vocational education for years, the difference is that such activities would become central to the educational process in the *total* curriculum of the school.

Mentoring and Apprenticeships

Students may be connected with individuals in the community who may agree to be mentors for student growth and support and/or an apprenticeship in a specific skill area in a wide range of settings. Rather than involving a total class, such approaches are individualized. For example, Peterson et al. (1992) described one Michigan high school program that created an open and cooperative campus with the community and the school. In each academic and nonacademic class, four to five community references for student skill enhancement have been developed. Each student is required to complete a community experience in at least 50% of his or her classes, and the choice is theirs. Students receive academic credit for each learning experience. For example, in English, students may complete community experiences in journalistic writing at the local newspaper, in radio writing at one of three radio stations, television script writing at the local television station, writing for a church newsletter, writing for nonprofit organization newsletters, writing advertising script at one of three advertising companies, or by learning editorial skills at a local book publishing company. Teams of students in art and business classes complete internships at one of four local art centers, developing practical knowledge and skills in marketing, selecting and booking art events, and in business management.

Transition from School to Work

With the passage of the School-to-Work Opportunities Act (PL 103-239), there is a heightened emphasis on developing partnerships between schools and businesses and connecting student learning with employment settings. In many ways, this builds on efforts in the 1970s related to career education and builds on the experience of vocational education in providing both school-based and employer-based learning of work skills as part of the school curriculum. Additionally, special educators have been working for a number of years to develop transition programs for students with disabilities that provide community-based instruction and on-the-job learning. Multiple strategies are used to incorporate learning for employment in the school curriculum. These include

- Cooperative education in which students work part time and studies at school are linked to on-the-job learning

- Mentorships in which employers or workers help students learn job skills and also develop relationships with them to assist them with life planning and provide emotional support
- Vocational and career exploration programs that utilize computer decision-making and exploration programs; "shadowing," in which students spend a day on the job with an employee seeing what he or she does; career fairs where students can talk to different employers; and career exploration information interviews.

Microsociety

Microsociety schools operate miniature civilizations with all the institutions that occur in the real world—legislatures, courts, banks, post offices, newspapers, businesses, and an internal revenue service. Some 30 microsociety schools are known to be operating throughout the country. In these schools, in the morning, students attend subject classes that are taught with a focus on real-world applications. For example, in the English class the emphasis might be on writing and publishing; in mathematics, personal and social economics; in social studies, governments. In the afternoon, students go to their jobs in student-run businesses, government agencies, newspapers, or other enterprises. A miniature marketplace, currency, and legal system are established and utilized in the course of events in the school year.

Expeditionary Learning

Expeditionary learning involves students in extended activities outside the school building in which the traditional school subjects are blended together. According to Richardson,

> School-based expeditions run about three to nine weeks…. Students spend about 25 percent of their time out of the classroom…. The rest of their time is spent on hands-on curriculum activities to make connections between their studies and draw their own conclusions. (1994, p. 25)

Portions of the curriculum, such as reading or science, may be given through traditional courses, and teachers work to connect district and state expectations regarding traditional curriculum goals (math, reading) with the expeditions.

Expeditions involve students in real-life challenges and are based on several key principles: self-discovery, responsibility for learning, intimacy and caring, diversity and inclusivity, success and failure, solitude and reflection, and service and compassion. These principles provide a foundation on which students learn through doing and from which relationships, mutual support, discovery, and skill development are blended.

Expeditions revolve around themes or activities. An elementary school spent several weeks, for example, focusing on transportation and space exploration. This set of studies involved a number of activities including demonstrations of a hot-air balloon, a helicopter landing at the school, and a visit to an air show. In LaCrosse, Wisconsin, a school district developed a "School on the River" program in which students are engaged throughout the year in learning on the Mississippi River. They make numerous trips to the river canoeing, fishing, sampling the ecosystem of the river, and to visit the sewage treatment plant (Pitsch, 1994). Outward Bound is an expeditionary learning strategy developed in England that involves wilderness expeditions to facilitate learning about teamwork, perseverance, and leadership. Trips last up to 3 weeks, and groups engage in activities such as rock climbing, rope exercises, and camping. Another school designed a physical education course, Metric Sports, to teach students practical applications of metrics through physical outings such as a fishing expedition (Richardson, 1994).

As projects are implemented, teachers work in teams with groups of students to facilitate "guided discovery." Students keep daily journals and are provided time to reflect on their learning experiences. Additionally, students are provided opportunities to direct the curriculum and revise learning activities. Teachers are typically matched with groups of students for a 2-year period. This is intended to facilitate building a sense of community, a variation of "schools within schools" (Richardson, 1994).

Extracurricular Activities

Increasingly, extracurricular activities such as olympics of the mind, drama clubs, service clubs, and other activities fulfill functions that the factory model in typical public schools has not fulfilled.

Curriculum Subject Resources

As those responsible for the school curriculum, design, implement, and test curriculum restructuring efforts, professionals in various traditional subject areas are working to connect the learning content of their disciplines to community activities. The following resources are useful in giving teachers ideas regarding the development of community learning projects and programs.

Reading Language and reading instruction is emphasizing the use of language in natural contexts through drawing on the life and language experiences of students and engaging students in active understanding of what they are reading rather than focusing on the mechanics of the reading process (Commission on Reading, 1990; Weber & Dyasi, 1985).

Math Math educators (National Council of Teachers of Mathematics, 1990) have greatly restructured the teaching of mathematics and recommend that students learn and apply math skills related to actual problem situations as part of learning teams. Romberg (1988) observed that "in various classrooms, one could expect to see students recording measurements of real objects, collecting information and describing the properties of objects using statistics, or exploring the properties of a function by examining its graph" (p. 16).

Science Yager (1987) has described the key elements of a science curriculum for elementary schools: 1) understanding and experiencing processes of discovery, 2) creativity, 3) positive attitudes toward science, and 4) connections and applications to daily life. An Iowa curriculum ("Science, Technology, and Society") involves students in active inquiry and problem solving related to real-world activities associated with their daily lives.

Social Studies   The National Council of Social Studies (Viadero, 1992) articulated similar approaches. The approaches taken by these standard-setting groups provide very natural opportunities for engaging students of all ranges of ability levels in learning simultaneously in actual community situations. These efforts are important because most schools are making curriculum reforms that maintain existing school subject areas. In the Michigan core curriculum, for example, life competencies are incorporated into core curriculum subject areas of art, health, language, mathematics, science, and world studies (Michigan Department of Education, 1994).

Hendrikson (1992) described a social studies curriculum for "community study" based on a four-dimensional model: the community as a source of content, the community as a source of learning experience, community service as a dimension of community study, and the community as a source of skill development. He argued that community studies improve student motivation and aid in developing "citizenship participation skills."

Civics   Nader (1993) stated that "civics cannot be properly taught without using the community as a natural laboratory so that students can learn by doing, by connecting with problem-definition and response where they live" (p. 40). According to Nader, there is an eagerness among young people to become connected to their communities and the world, with most favoring a community services requirement for graduation and the majority stating that volunteer service work should be awarded school credit. Toward this end, the Center for the Study of Responsive Law and Essential Information sponsored a publication with guidelines for community learning, *Civics for Democracy: A Journey for Teachers and Students* (Isaac, 1992). The book contains profiles and case studies of students in community learning, the history of major citizens' movements, techniques for democratic participation, and student projects that can be utilized as thematic lessons to connect the curriculum across two or more subjects.

Community-Based Instruction for Students with Special Needs

Special educators began developing "work–study" programs in the 1960s for students with disabilities. Since then, much school and community-based instruction has been developed that provides opportunities for community learning by students with special needs. Some excellent resources have also been developed and are briefly described below. These resources can be used in many ways. First, they provide overall curriculum structures that focus on the life needs of students. While the specific level of the activity may need to be individualized, these activities nevertheless provide a framework for organizing curricula that consider the whole life of students in the community. General education teachers may be able to adapt these materials to community learning activities or functional community learning around the specific needs of special students in more traditional classrooms. Second, these resources provide excellent frameworks for planning for individual students with disabilities. Care must be taken, however, to not use a curriculum guide rigidly. We are learning more all the time about how to create better outcomes through community learning for all students. The use of any resource needs to be approached as a learning experiment.

Life-Centered Career Education (LCCE)

Life-centered career education (Brolin et al., 1993) is designed around "competencies" for adult living in three areas (daily living skills, personal-social skills, and occupational guidance and preparation), 22 competencies, and 102 subcompetencies. Examples of competencies associated with daily living skills include managing family finances; selecting, managing, and maintaining a home; caring for personal needs; raising children; enriching family life; and buying and caring for clothes. Supporting materials include a comprehensive trainer's manual and a curriculum guide that provides suggested teaching strategies for each of the competencies and subcompetencies. Some schools have developed a matrix of life competencies and their potential relationship to the curricular offerings of the school.

The Syracuse Community-Referenced Curriculum Guide for Students with Moderate and Severe Disabilities

Ford and colleagues at Syracuse University and the Syracuse Public Schools developed and field tested a curriculum and school and community-based instructional procedures that focus on students with significant disabilities. This resource provides excellent detailed information regarding teaching procedures and activities and management of community-based instruction. The Syracuse curriculum combines strategies for developing various cognitive, social, and motor skills with the performance of activities and tasks in community settings (Ford et al., 1989).

The Activities Catalog

Wilcox and Bellamy (1987) developed a curriculum that identifies valued community activities, which are the things that people *do* in communities. The curriculum manual identifies activities and provides a simple task analysis of each activity and strategies, suggested materials, and locations for helping individuals with significant disabilities participate in activities of their choosing. For example, some activities related to food purchases include using fast-food restaurants, using a sit-down restaurant, using a cafeteria, and using vending machines. A card sort with pictures of the various activities is provided to help the student select activities of interest for learning and participation.

Community-Based Curriculum

The community-based curriculum and instructional process developed by Falvey (1989) are focused on students with significant disabilities. Instructional areas include community skills, domestic skills, recreational skills, employment skills, motor skills, communication skills, and developing and fostering friendships.

PLANNING COMMUNITY LEARNING CURRICULA

A school interested in implementing curriculum reform across a district or building typically organizes teachers to work in planning teams, with the assistance of a consultant, in order to develop the curriculum. Teachers report that the time spent engaging in such planning is substantial, but results appear worth the effort. Strategies to provide the necessary time include mini-sabbaticals, release days during the school year, and paid summer work time (Richardson, 1994).

If schools do not engage in such comprehensive approaches, however, teachers can begin to implement many of these same principles individually or in collaboration with other teachers in a building. Any of the planning strategies, approaches, and resources related to community learning can be utilized and adapted by one or more teachers working together. One key is to start small and build on successes.

Each school or each teacher working with other teachers will need to engage in collaborative planning. This involves collaboration between general and special education teachers and community resources. Collaboration is a key factor because a central goal is to reduce the fragmentation of knowledge and learning across typical school subjects and to reduce the isolation of learners in school and the community. As such, planning community learning may be an experience that many people have not had. Although the process is challenging, teachers typically report that the process of planning and learning to work in teams is most important and valuable. Planning and implementing community learning helps teachers themselves develop a sense of community, challenge, and learning. This cannot help but be passed on to their students.

From Multidisciplinary to Transdisciplinary

Drake (1993) provided a useful guide for helping teachers plan the integration of curriculum in which she distinguished three basic approaches. In a *multidisciplinary approach,* the focus is on obvious connections between particular disciplines or subjects. Teachers may work in teams, but learning is focused around the question, What is important to learn within my discipline? Efforts are then made to connect across the disciplines using strategies such as webbing and clustering/reclustering. In an *interdisciplinary skills approach,* the emphasis shifts to commonalities across the disciplines, most often with an emphasis on critical thinking skills. Content lessens in importance as teachers focus on learning how to learn.

The *transdisciplinary/real-world approach* organizes learning around the question, How can we teach students to be productive citizens in the future? This approach is most consistent with community learning as described in this chapter. As student outcomes are identified, planning teams identify the multiple interconnections of information. According to Drake (1993), "No matter what focus or issue starts the process, the same array of vast interconnections become immediately apparent. Each theme is embedded in its cultural or real-life context" (p. 42). Although the process of planning and discovering the complex nature of interconnections can be frightening and overwhelming to planning groups, struggling with this complexity and organizing flexible instruction in which disciplines transcend their typical boundaries result in instruction and curriculum that is challenging and exciting to both teachers and diverse learners.

Tools of Planning

Teachers and planning teams have found several process tools helpful in planning the curriculum and relating individual learning goals to the overall curriculum.

Curriculum Webbing Curriculum webbing is a simple but powerful way of brainstorming and organizing the relationships of ideas. "Trigger words," words that describe curriculum themes of interest, are placed at the center of the web. Then, related concepts are identified, each with other relationships. Webbing allows a graphic representation of subject content that helps teachers think about the relationships of complex subjects. Webbing may be done on various themes, and curriculum teams may then cluster and recluster subject content in ways that help them organize learning in which key concepts, rather than traditional disciplines, are at the center (Drake, 1993).

Curriculum Matrixing Curriculum matrixing is a process whereby the relationships of different methods for organizing instruction are identified. For example, learning goals may be identified for an individual student and a matrix completed that illustrates various classes and learning activities in which such learning goals can be achieved. A curriculum matrix can also be used for overall curriculum planning. For example, major themes may be matrixed against traditional class subjects in a multidisciplinary curriculum planning approach. In a transdisciplinary approach, with learning goals and themes as the organizers of instruction, skill areas of language, reading, and math can be matrixed against these themes. This allows a way to think about and show the relationship of community learning activities and projects, such as a microsociety or expeditionary learning, to academic skills.

Where to Start

Teachers can begin almost anywhere—with the needs of an individual student, with a particular project, or with a theme or problem focus that teachers want to use as the basis for applied learning projects throughout the year. The following approaches may be useful:

Starting with Discipline It may be easiest for many people to begin the process of designing community learning by focusing first on the subject as it exists and ask the question, "How can I teach these objectives in a more applied way and in the community?" It is helpful to look at the range of curriculum objectives. The next step is to identify projects that have the potential to achieve this goal. This is essentially a brainstorming process. If teachers keep up with issues in their communities through the media and involvement in community groups, these can always provide sources for focus ideas or issues that have local relevance. Teachers can first identify one or two issues and then use webbing to help expand the ideas as discussed above. This will help teachers think about how a topic links across the curriculum and also helps teachers identify ways to work with other teachers. Teachers can then proceed to sketch out what to actually do, identifying activities in the classroom using simulations, activities, and situations in the school and community that may be used for learning. The curriculum resources and community learning strategies described above may be helpful. Teachers can start with a simple, short-term project or use a theme to involve students in multiple projects throughout the year.

Starting with Learning Goals of Individual Students Students, their families, and educators may use MAPs (Making Action Plans; discussed in detail in Chapter 5) or other planning processes to identify learning goals. Initially, teachers can use a curriculum matrix to compare these learning goals to the existing curriculum. However, teachers may also consider how they may use interesting and unique learning goals, particularly those that are difficult to fit into the regular school curriculum, as the basis for designing a community learning activity for the entire class. Below is an example of a learning goal for a student as well as possible community learning activities related to the theme that involve a class or multiple teachers organized around it. An individual student may need to learn how to ride a bus. Such a learning activity could be incorporated into a unit on transportation that could include the following activities: Study community resources, availability of public transportation, and transportation needs; ride buses to get the experience; interview individuals with limited community mobility about their need; study how people learn how to use the bus system and problems they have; and interview passengers and drivers.

Starting with Outcomes and Learning Themes Teachers and schools can begin by thinking carefully about the kinds of outcomes wanted for all students *and* about the types and range of options needed for individually directed learning goals. This leads to a process of organizing the curriculum and instruction around major themes and areas of learning. The key in this approach is to pick a series of themes what will be effective in helping students achieve outcomes. The webbing process is used to help think out the multiple aspects of any one theme. The complexity of the world makes the selection of specific themes less an issue than one might think. The fact is that everything in the world is related in concrete ways to virtually everything else. Consequently, when the webbing process is used, content crosses over into multiple areas involving wide ranges of activities and skills. This process needs to involve the total school to be most effective. However, an individual teacher or a group of teachers can work together to center their own instructional process around themes.

CONCLUSION: LEARNING TO BUILD COMMUNITY

Dewey (1943) and Sarasson (1974) wrote about the isolation of the school from the community and the isolation of children and education from the family and community. As we build inclusive schools, it is critical to remember that the purpose of schools is to strengthen community among us all. It was perhaps predictable that as we separated learning processes from the community in which they occurred and created these segregated places of learning that we call schools, we would find that the separation process continued, separating types of learning (subjects, vocational education, special education) and types of students (gifted, with disabilities). We have separated our society in many ways. Our challenge is to create and support community—the common bond holding us together, which, in turn, is supported and maintained by our relationships. Relationships and connectedness, however, in a complex world cannot exist only between individuals or even only in our smallest group, the family. Relationships of mutual support are critical across organizations in our community life. Community learning provides the opportunity to reconnect schools with community life. It is not surprising that such approaches may also be our best hope to help the people in our communities reconnect with one another so that inclusive schools become contributors to and social incubators for the creation of communities and a society that values, is inclusive of, and celebrates the diverse cultures and abilities of its members. We have an opportunity to move together in an exciting journey, the end of which we will know only when we arrive.

REFERENCES

Angelis, J., & Wathen, L. (1994, November 9). Involving older adults in schools. *Education Week, 33.*

Armstrong, T. (1994). *Multiple intelligences in the classroom.* Alexandria, VA: Association for Supervision and Curriculum Development.

Banks, J. (1988). Education, citizenship, and cultural options. *Education and Society, 1*(1), 19–22.

Benjamin, S. (1989). An ideascape for education: What futurists recommend. *Educational Leadership, 7*(1), 8–14.

Berryman, S.E. (1988, October). *The educational challenge of the American economy.* Paper presented at a forum of the National Education Association, Washington, DC.

Boyer, E. (1984). A critical examination of American education. In J. Surwill (Ed.), *A critical examination of American education: A time for action.* Billings: Conference sponsored by Eastern Montana College (ERIC Document Reproduction Service No. 269 357)

Brolin, D., McKay, D., & West, L. (1993). *Trainers guide to life-centered career education.* Reston, VA: Council for Exceptional Children.

Brown, L., Schwarz, P., Udvari-Solner, A., Kampschroer, A., Johnson, F., Jorgensen, J., & Gruenwald, L. (1991). How much time should students with severe intellectual disabilities spend in regular education classrooms and elsewhere? *Journal of The Association for Persons with Severe Handicaps, 16*(1), 39–47.

Commission on Reading. (1990). What is reading? In D. Ogle, W. Pink, & B.F. Jones (Eds.), *Restructuring to promote learning in America's schools.* Columbus, OH: Zaner-Bloser.

Dewey, J. (1943). *The school and society.* Chicago: University of Chicago Press.

Division of Mental Retardation, Council for Exceptional Children. (1992, April 15). *Position statement on educational program design.* Reston, VA: Author.

Drake, S. (1993). *Planning integrated curriculum: The call to adventure.* Alexandria, VA: Association for Supervision and Curriculum Development.

Falvey, M. (1989). *Community-based curriculum: Instructional strategies for students with severe handicaps* (2nd ed.). Baltimore: Paul H. Brookes Publishing Co.

Ford, A., Schnorr, R., Meyer, L., Davern, L., Black, J., & Dempsey, P. (1989). *The Syracuse community-referenced curriculum guide for students with moderate and severe disabilities.* Baltimore: Paul H. Brookes Publishing Co.

Gardner, H. (1983). *Multiple intelligences: The theory in practice.* New York: Basic Books.

Goodlad, J. (1984). *A place called school: Prospects for the future.* New York: McGraw-Hill.

Hendrikson, L. (1992). *Community study.* ERIC Digest No. 28 ED268065.

Isaac, K. (1992). *Civics for democracy: A journey for teachers and students.* Washington, DC: Essential Books.

Johnson, D.W., & Johnson, R.T. (1989). *Leading the cooperative school.* Edira, MN: Interaction Books.

Jones, B.F. (1990). The importance of restructuring schools to promote learning. In D. Ogle, W. Pink, & B.F. Jones (Eds.), *Restructuring to promote learning in America's schools.* Columbus, OH: Zaner-Bloser.

Michigan Department of Education. (1994). *Core curriculum content standards.* Lansing, MI: Author.

Nader, R. (1993, April 7). Teaching the other half of democracy's story. *Education Week,* p. 40.

National Council of Teachers of Mathematics. (1990). *Curriculum and evaluation standards for school mathematics.* Reston, VA: Author.

Newmann, F., & Wehlage, G. (1993, April). Five standards of authentic instruction. *Educational Leadership,* 8–12.

Ogle, D., Pink, W., & Jones, B.F. (1990). *Restructuring to promote learning in America's schools.* Columbus, OH: Zaner-Bloser.

Peterson, M., LeRoy, B., Field, S., & Wood, P. (1992). Community-referenced learning in inclusive schools: Effective curriculum for all students. In S. Stainback & W. Stainback (Eds.), *Curriculum considerations in inclusive classrooms: Facilitating learning for all students* (pp. 207–227). Baltimore: Paul H. Brookes Publishing Co.

Pitsch, M. (1994, October 12). Mississippi learning. *Education Week,* 29–30.

Resnick, L.B., & Klopfer, L.E. (1989). Toward the thinking curriculum: An overview. In L.B. Resnick & L.E. Klopfer (Eds.), *Toward the thinking curriculum: Current cognitive research 1989 ASCD yearbook.* Washington, DC: Association for Supervision and Curriculum Development.

Richardson, J. (1994, November 9). Adventures in learning. *Education Week,* 25–28.

Romberg, T.A. (1988, November). *Principles for an elementary mathematics program for the 1990s.* Paper presented at the California Invitational Symposium on Elementary Mathematics Education, San Francisco.

School-to-Work Opportunities Act of 1994, PL 103-239. (May 4, 1994). Title 20, U.S.C. 6101 et seq: *U.S. Statutes at Large, 108,* 568–608.

Shuman, R. (1984). Education, society, and the second millennium. *NASSP Bulletin, 68*(474), 95–103.

Stepien, W., & Gallagher, S. (1993, April). Problem-based learning: As authentic as it gets. *Educational Leadership,* 25–28.

Toffler, A. (1981). Education and the future. *Social Education, 45*(6), 422–426.

Viadero, D. (1992). The gain unity council defines social studies. *Education Week, XII*(13), 12.

Weber, L., & Dyasi, H. (1985). Language development and observation of a local environment: First steps in providing primary-school science education for non-dominant groups. *Prospectus, XV*(4), 665–676.

Wilcox, B., & Bellamy, T. (1982). *Design of high school programs for severely handicapped students.* Baltimore: Paul H. Brookes Publishing Co.

Wilcox, B., & Bellamy, T. (1987). *The activities catalog: An alternative curriculum for youth and adults with severe disabilities.* Baltimore: Paul H. Brookes Publishing Co.

Yager, R. (1987). Assess all three domains of science. *The Science Teacher, 54*(7), 33–37.

Ysseldyke, J.E., Thurlow, M.L., & Shriner, J.G. (1992). *Teaching Exceptional Children, 25*(1), 36–50.

V

BEHAVIORAL
CONSIDERATIONS

19

Strategies for Managing an Inclusive Classroom

Annette M. Iverson

A KEY CHARACTERISTIC of an effective teacher is classroom management (Emmet & Evertson, 1981). The diversity in today's classroom is great (Rogers, 1993) and presents a variety of management challenges to teachers (Froyen, 1993). Rogers (1993) asserted that inclusion *typically* adds a child who has *more* needs than most other children in the classroom but those needs are not always different from those of other children in the class. Therefore, effective teacher/managers in noninclusive classrooms also can expect to be effective teacher/managers in inclusive classrooms (Rogers, 1993).

Effective classroom management has been found to contribute more to school learning than does curriculum design, classroom instruction, student demographics, motivation, home support, and school policy (Wang, Haertal, & Walberg, 1993). Classroom management strategies should not be neglected when planning practical strategies for inclusive schooling. In fact, they probably should be awarded priority status in the planning process. Planning is related to feelings of efficacy and success (Bandura, 1977; Ashton, 1984). The need for a classroom management plan, similar to the need for a lesson plan, has been suggested by Charles (1992) and Medland and Vitale (1984).

This chapter presents strategies that effective teachers of inclusive classrooms can use in their management plans, especially strategies that encourage student participation. This chapter is not intended to present foundational knowledge in schoolwide discipline and classroom management. There are many excellent comprehensive tests and instructional videos for those teachers who have received relatively little or no formal training in classroom management. The section that follows on staff development

late to
sta and physical
visual/physical activities

includes some resources that can assist in building foundational knowledge in class-room management.

STAFF DEVELOPMENT

Lee (1993) offered training in developing a flexible classroom management plan for the group and for individual students. The training is atheoretical and offers a large menu of strategies that are appropriate for addressing common difficult behaviors. Teachers select strategies with which they can work comfortably. Teachers who complete the training can expect to develop their own personal management plan that includes preventive approaches, general intervention approaches, motivational approaches, and supportive/communication approaches.

In addition to a classroom management plan, good managers possess a number of skills that are based on (Jones & Jones, 1990)

- Understanding research and theory on classroom management
- Understanding students' needs
- Knowing how to establish positive classroom relationships that help meet students' basic psychological needs
- Knowing how to use instructional methods that promote learning by individual students and the classroom group
- Knowing how to use instructional methods that maximize students' on-task behavior
- Knowing how to use a wide range of methods that involve students in examining and correcting their inappropriate behavior

It should be clear that good classroom managers are taught and not born. There are always those few teachers who appear to be natural classroom managers, who have had very little formal training, and who just seem to know what to do in most or all problem situations. However, most teachers need quality training in order to be effective managers. Teachers who are excited about using their vast store of knowledge and techniques to teach their subject, but who do not have quality training in management, often find themselves frustrated with their jobs, frustrated with their students, angry, raising their voices and nagging throughout the school day, prone to use punishment, and suffering from significant stress (Froyen, 1993).

An actual case illustration of management/discipline problems is presented as one example of what school personnel must be prepared to manage. Untrained and trained managers were asked to provide solutions to the problems. Their responses are described in order to underscore the importance of specific training in classroom management.

Case Illustration

A 1994 article from a Midwestern city newspaper illustrated how management problems can mushroom in the seeming absence of planning and skills for meeting the diverse needs of students. For the purposes of this example, it is assumed that the news release was accurate and that the paper did not distort the facts. The story began when a sixth-grade male student did not want to stay in his classroom. The male sixth-grade teacher grabbed the student when the student ran to get out of the room. The teacher stated that he held the student underneath his arm because the student was unruly and the teacher was trying to keep him "in line," keep the other students safe, and keep the student himself safe. The student was then taken to the vice principal's office to telephone his mother and explain what he had done.

The mother understood her son to say that the male teacher put his hands around his neck to restrain him. Immediately, she came to school with her boyfriend. Once at school, the mother thought that no one was listening to her son's complaints and that she was not being listened to as well. Apparently not a private encounter, students, secretaries, teachers, administrators, and others were on the scene to witness all events. When the mother decided that the female vice principal was taking the teacher's side, she punched the vice principal. The mother began throwing vases, precipitated by her fear of a teacher in the group who had a pair of scissors. Hair pulling was also reported. The mother and her boyfriend then exited the building. Several school personnel sustained minor injuries, and one person required medical attention at a local hospital.

The newspaper quoted the school spokesperson as stating that the student's mother started the fight and that the student was treated according to school policy. The insinuation was that the school personnel believed that they were in the right and had done nothing to cause the problems. The newspaper quoted the mother as stating that she was angry with the school before her son phoned home because older students had beaten her son just a couple of days before. She further stated that she was also angry because school officials had her son phone her. She believed that the call was the responsibility of school officials. She expressed sorrow that the incident had occurred and hoped that matters could be resolved.

What a fine mess for this school! The issues at stake are many, varied, and of considerable magnitude. They range from the image of the school in the community to restoring a healthy working relationship with the child and his mother. This is an example of management problems teachers and administrators encounter in both inclusive *and* noninclusive classrooms. Planning and skills could have prevented the escalation of the problem.

After the fact, a number of professional educators generated solutions to this scenario, both preventive and remedial. Obviously, professionals who had been trained in classroom management approached this scenario from a richer, broader knowledge base than did professionals who had not been trained in classroom management. Professionals untrained in classroom management responded as predicted by Swanson, O'Conner, and Cooney (1990); specifically, novices were much more simplistic in their analysis of the problem, did not account for all possible reasons for the student's or mother's behavior, and had a dearth of interventions to recommend. The untrained blamed the behaviors on socioeconomic status, race, and disabilities and decided that nothing could be done with "those people," that there were more and more of them in the schools, and that professional educators had a bleak future. Referrals for segregated special education placement were recommended. Professionals trained in classroom management believed that the problems could have been prevented or minimized. They offered the following suggestions for planning in the areas of home–school relationships, prevention, and comprehensive staff development:

- Have students participate in developing classroom rules and procedures during the first week of school.
- Inform guardians via letters at the beginning of the year about schoolwide and classroom discipline rules and procedures (see Figure 1).
- Give guardians the opportunity to disagree with procedures and negotiate alternatives.
- Build home–school partnerships through activities such as open houses that focus on alerting parents to differences (Silberman & Wheelan, 1980) between homes and schools (see Table 1).

Dear Parents/Guardians,

I want to let you know how welcome your child is in my room. We are going to have a challenging and interesting year. You as parents or guardians are important to your child's progress in my class and it is important for us to communicate. The best time to reach me is between 3:00 p.m. and 3:45 p.m. at 515-5555 or you can call the central office at 555-2168 for an appointment. I will return your call as soon as possible.

To have the best learning environment, the students and I selected five rules that students are expected to follow at school and in my classroom:

- Always do your best work.
- Work quietly and complete your assignments on time.
- Cooperate with your teacher and classmates.
- Listen and follow directions.
- Raise your hand for questions and comments.

The students and I have talked about the rules and practiced them in class. It would be very helpful to me if you would also discuss the rules to make sure your child understands them.

Special problems may call for consequences such as keeping your child after school or requiring your child to phone you to discuss a problem. Check the box to indicate your permission to use these rules and consequences with your child. If you have concerns, please write them in the spaces provided and I will work with you to decide on acceptable consequences.

___ Agree with rules and consequences   ___ Do not agree

Concerns: _____

_____

I am pleased to have your child in my room this year. I look forward to a year of growth.

Sincerely,

Figure 1.   Example of a letter to parents explaining school and classroom rules and procedures.

Table 1.   Open house presentation outline to inform parents of differences between home and school

1. Classrooms are crowded places.
2. Classrooms allow very little privacy.
3. Classroom relationships are not as intimate or close as relationships at home.
4. The menu of rewards and punishments is not as rich as at home.
5. Teacher authority is more easily undermined than parental authority.

Adapted from Silberman and Wheelan (1980).

- Train teachers in classroom management techniques that include management of academic content, student conduct, and teacher–student and student–student relationships.
- Develop procedures for managing students who leave the room and teach these to students in the first 2 weeks of school.
- Train educators in the use of appropriate restraint techniques.
- Train educators in rapport-building and listening skills, including those needed to deescalate angry students and parents.
- Train educators to use problem-solving steps, including the establishment of a calm atmosphere as the first step in problem solving (see Table 2).

The real-life scenario that was presented emphasizes the need for school districts to develop a high-quality staff development plan in schoolwide discipline and classroom management. More and more districts are conducting such staff development because school districts are faced with burgeoning discipline problems, and many educators have little or no training in classroom management.

Schendel (1994) noted that many people have opinions about staff development that are not complimentary. Workshops may be a social time, may be lifeless and boring, and may offer nothing new. Lecture-only formats, poor presentation techniques, and inappropriate content are certain indicators of ineffective staff development efforts (Schendel, 1994). Staff development need not be limited to formal training. It can be accomplished in a number of ways:

Table 2.   Problem-solving steps

1. Establish a calm atmosphere.
2. Identify the problem.
3. Gather information and then describe the problem.
4. Analyze all the forces contributing to the problem.
5. Brainstorm all possible solutions to the problem.
6. Select a solution and assign duties.
7. Implement the solution.
8. Evaluate the effects and cycle back through the steps if the solution did not work.

- Self-directed learning
- Peer coaching
- Workshops and in-services
- Coursework in higher education

However, to be effective, a staff development plan must have *all* of the following elements:

- Relevance to participants' needs
- Clear objectives
- Opportunities to practice skills and engage in active learning

Unless all of these elements are part of the staff development plan, teachers will not develop the expert skills that they need. Teachers should actively participate in planning their own training, ensuring that all three elements listed above are included. Teachers should ensure that the training plan allows opportunities for self-directed learning and peer coaching.

Staff development plans that focus on training teachers in foundational knowledge of classroom management should consider the following topics:

- Developing a classroom discipline and responsibility plan: rules and expectations, first weeks of school, procedures for correcting irresponsible and inappropriate behaviors and for acknowledging responsible behaviors, and procedures for transitions
- Teaching students to focus on positive expectations
- Establishing positive attitudes for the success of every student
- Designing the physical environment to support appropriate student behavior
- Scanning, monitoring, and proximity management
- Practicing content management: analyzing the daily schedule and planning lessons
- Practicing covenant management: communication skills, classroom climate, relationship building

Sprick, Sprick, and Garrison (1993) have developed excellent training materials for professionals seeking advanced knowledge and skills in planning and implementing management interventions that encourage responsibility and motivation of students at risk. The authors provide step-by-step instructions and rehearsal scripts for dozens of common and not-so-common classroom management problems. Forms to help in recording and carrying out interventions are provided and are generally exempt from copyright protection. One set of training materials could be purchased for a single building and kept in the office of the professional most likely to serve as a management consultant to others in the building. School building personnel could conduct their own staff development sessions using Sprick et al.'s (1993) materials and an in-house consultant as a facilitator/trainer. This is an inexpensive way to increase expertise of school staff via a staff development program. Who knows? Administrators might be willing to use funds, set aside for the usual staff development speakers, in order to give participants a stipend for practicing skills in their classrooms.

MANAGEMENT ISSUES IN INCLUSIVE CLASSROOMS

Experienced teachers in inclusive classrooms have indicated that priority issues in classroom management are 1) tailoring instruction to the level appropriate for each student, 2) facilitating peer acceptance of students with differences, and 3) coping effectively with physically dangerous and significantly disruptive behaviors (R.M. Iverson, personal communication, December 27, 1994). It is interesting to note that each one of these management issues corresponds to one of Froyen's (1993) key categories in planning classroom management strategies. The first point (tailoring instruction) corresponds to instructional or content management, the second point (facilitating peer acceptance) to covenant or relationship management, and the third point to conduct or behavior management.

Effective teachers already have management skills in each of these areas. Teachers in inclusive classrooms may need to apply their skills to problems that they have not encountered in the past. For example, many teachers may never have experienced a student turning desks over, throwing things, swearing, threatening to hit, or using a weapon. These can be very adrenaline-pumping experiences for teachers the first few times they occur, even if teachers have been prepared to deal with such behavioral outbursts. It should be emphasized here that this is *not* meant to imply that all or most students with disabilities have such problems. Clearly, the vast majority do not, but just like students without disabilities, a few unfortunately do present such behavioral concerns.

The following sections illustrate strategies in specific areas for coping with a variety of problems that teachers may encounter in a diverse group of students.

Issues in Content Management

There are three general behavior outcomes for a student during periods of instruction or academic engaged time: 1) on task and engaged in learning, 2) off task and engaged in sitting passively or withdrawing, or 3) off task and engaged in being disruptive. Many students with special needs are off task and either withdrawn or disruptive during periods of instruction. From a content management perspective, at least two concepts in the learning theory and research literature provide direction for decreasing off-task and increasing on-task behavior during instructional periods. Specifically, teachers need to plan lessons that take into account students' 1) prior knowledge and interests and 2) mastery orientation.

Prior Knowledge and Interests Lessons that are planned to accommodate students' prior knowledge and interests increase student engagement and comprehension. Recht and Leslie (1988) provided an example of the importance of prior knowledge in assisting *poor* readers' comprehension of a reading task. They tested good and poor readers in junior high on their knowledge of baseball and found that knowledge of baseball was not related to reading ability. Students then were identified as: good readers/high baseball knowledge, good readers/low baseball knowledge, poor readers/high baseball knowledge, and poor readers/low baseball knowledge. Following identification of each student's reading level and prior baseball knowledge, all students read a passage describing a baseball game and answered questions to see if they understood and remembered what they had read. The importance of prior knowledge was clearly demonstrated in that *poor* readers who knew baseball remembered *more* than good readers with little baseball knowledge and almost as much as good readers who knew baseball.

When the lesson is difficult to comprehend because students have little or no prior knowledge and little interest in the topic, off-task behaviors increase and comprehension decreases. Prior knowledge or interests of students with special needs, incorporated into lesson planning, improves academic engagement and achievement.

Teachers who are not aware of students' prior knowledge or interests have difficulty planning lessons that meet these criteria. To assist teachers in obtaining information about students' interests and prior knowledge, Figure 2 contains an inventory of questions for students to answer. Teachers can then adapt lessons to the prior knowledge and interests of their students. Obviously, it is not possible to plan lessons that address every student's knowledge or interests. Teachers are well-advised to plan lessons around the inventory results of students with special needs because they are more likely to be the students who are off-task and unengaged in learning.

Mastery Orientation   Content management through prior knowledge and interests is not a sufficient intervention to increase on-task behavior of off-task students who are not mastery oriented. Mastery-oriented students have a high need for achieve-

---

What Do You Like?

Name _____   Date _____   Grade _____

Please answer every item completely.

1. When I am not in school, I really enjoy (three things):
   _____

2. If you cannot watch television at home, what do you most like to do?
   _____

3. If you could do anything that you wanted to do this weekend, what would you choose?
   _____

4. If you could learn about anything that you wanted to learn about, what would it be?
   _____

5. What is your favorite television show? _____

6. Do you like to do your best work in groups or alone? _____

7. Which school subjects do you like best? _____

8. What three things do you like most to do in school? _____

9. If you had 30 minutes of free time at school each day to do what you really like, what would you do? _____

10. What three jobs would you enjoy doing in class? _____

Figure 2.   Student interest inventory.

ment and a low fear of failure. They set moderately difficult and challenging learning goals and believe that effort and use of the right strategy are the reasons for their success. Mastery-oriented students use adaptive strategies to solve educational problems (e.g., try another way, seek assistance, practice or study more).

Unfortunately, some students with special needs do not believe that they are capable of mastering academic tasks that involve new learning. These students exhibit failure-avoiding or failure-accepting behaviors. Students have learned to react to learning in failure-avoiding and failure-accepting ways because of prior home, school, or home/school management. For example, in school, students may have experienced many difficulties or failures as early as kindergarten. Perhaps they were not successful in prereading tasks (e.g., learning the alphabet, nursery rhymes) or prewriting tasks (e.g., could not color neatly, did not like to color or do artwork, could not draw shapes or print the alphabet neatly, did not like to draw). When teachers made many corrections or red marks on their papers, these children became discouraged and soon developed non–mastery-oriented, failure-avoiding or failure-accepting behaviors. Even if teachers are supportive, some children compare themselves to others in the class and become discouraged. Having students such as these in the classroom renders content management a more complex task.

Failure-avoiding students believe that they lack the ability to learn and that the ability to learn cannot be increased. Subsequently, they have a high fear of failure. You can recognize failure-avoiding students because they 1) set performance goals that are too high or too easy and 2) use self-defeating strategies (e.g., make feeble efforts, pretend not to care, make excuses for not completing work, make excuses for not seeking offered assistance).

Failure-accepting students expect to fail. They tend to set no learning goals and believe that their lack of ability to learn is the cause of their academic failures. If they attempt a task, they are likely to give up easily. To understand the concept of failure-acceptance, it is helpful to recall the illustrations in psychology texts of dogs kept in cages that were electrically wired on all sides. When the electricity was activated, dogs could not escape the punishment no matter how they hopped around. At first they moved around actively, trying to find a way to achieve success in getting away from the shock. But no matter what they tried, every part of the cage that they touched shocked them. The dogs eventually gave up and lay passively in the cage; their behavior was labeled learned helplessness. Once a dog took on the characteristics of learned helplessness, it was difficult to help the dog regain a sense of mastery orientation. Weiner, Russell, and Lerman (1978) reported that students also experience learned helplessness when they attribute their failures to stable and uncontrollable causes.

Failure-accepting students experience school as a punishing situation no matter what they do. These students suffer from learned helplessness and have given up, often experiencing feelings of depression. They tend to be those who sit passively in the classroom, doing little or nothing, and usually are not disruptive. Teachers are very busy people, and, "the squeaky wheel gets the grease" in classrooms as in other settings. Therefore, failure-accepting students are often overlooked and float through grade after grade producing very little work and learning very little. Failure-accepting students are likely to receive more attention and assistance if they are disruptive, which they rarely are. Remember, their behavior is not unlike that of the dogs who lay passively in the wire cage, doing nothing, not even trying to escape.

The following guidelines, adapted from Woolfolk (1993), are offered as ways to help a student regain a sense of mastery through encouraging self-worth.

• **Select Appropriate Learning Tasks**   Examples of strategies to help in selecting appropriate learning tasks are 1) Ask consultants to assist you in lesson planning and in obtaining materials. If the student was in a segregated setting before coming to your class, ask the special education staff to share curriculum and materials. Most are pleased when you request their expertise and 2) capitalize on the student's interests and prior knowledge by studying past IEPs and by conducting an interest inventory (see Figure 2).

• **Assist Students in Setting Learning Goals and Train Students in Mastery Orientation**   Examples of strategies to assist students in setting goals and train them in a mastery orientation are 1) offer a menu of appropriate learning goals and have the students choose from them, 2) assist students in setting an appropriate level of difficulty in order to achieve their goals, 3) recognize progress and improvement by helping the student graph it, 4) read stories about students who overcame similar challenges, 5) share examples of how you developed in a particular area, and 6) help the student succeed in school in spite of failures outside school.

Emphasize Students' Progress   Examples of strategies to emphasize student progress are 1) Return to earlier material and show the student how easy it now is. Ask the student, "Remember how hard this was for you before? Look how your hard work paid off. Now you do it so easily." 2) Keep a portfolio of the student's best work that both of you refer to on a regular basis. 3) Have the student learn more before returning to improve earlier work.

Offer Specific Suggestions for Improvement Before Calling for and Grading Final Drafts   Examples of strategies that offer specific suggestions for improvement are as follows: 1) Make comments on what the student did right, what the student did wrong, and why the student made mistakes. 2) Use peer feedback/editing before the student submits the first draft. 3) Graph grades to show that revised higher grades reflect student learning and competence.

Point Out Connections between Effort and Accomplishment   Examples of strategies that point out connections between effort and accomplishment are as follows: 1) State to the student that his or her effort resulted in a successful project, every time effort leads to success. 2) Coach the student to be able to state that his or her effort resulted in a successful project: "My project is good because I worked hard and used the right strategies." 3) Confront self-defeating strategies directly: "You are acting as if you do not care. Is that how you are really feeling?" 4) Confront failure-avoiding strategies directly: "You are giving up because you think that no matter what you do it won't be right. What are you supposed to do when you feel like that?" Cue the student to state, "I need to set a goal and work toward it. After my first attempts, I can lay it aside and improve it later."

It is easier and less time-consuming to intervene with failure-avoiding students and to help them become mastery-oriented than it is to intervene with and help failure-accepting students. Teachers who make a commitment to helping either type of failure-oriented student become mastery oriented should be aware that intervention will be required throughout the school year. Students will probably make small degrees of progress over long periods of time toward mastery orientation. If the following year the teacher continues the interventions, more progress will be made, and so it can continue.

Issues in Covenant or Relationship Management

Teachers in inclusive classrooms may need to increase their skills in managing student–teacher relationships. For example, communication skills can build relationships that prevent conduct problems from developing and assist in deescalating problems when they have started. Examples of communication approaches (Lee, 1993) that teachers may need to develop are provided in Table 3. Communication skills are not easy to develop solely through self-directed learning. Peer coaching and formal training are recommended for those teachers who are serious about acquiring skills to build student–teacher relationships through communication approaches.

Student–student relationships represent an additional area that teachers in inclusive classrooms may need to facilitate. Children's cognitive development influences the development of friendships. Developmental psychologists offer some helpful insights into friendship formation across the age span. Preschool and early elementary children are not very discriminating about whom they call a friend. For example, a friend is whomever they are playing with at the moment. "Precrowds" begin to form in preadolescence and are informal aggregations of same gender members. Friendships in this age group are based upon the activities that friends share (e.g., we are friends because we do things together) and are more stable than the friendships of younger children. "Crowds" form in early adolescence and are groups of individuals (usually larger than nine) who get together regularly on the basis of mutual interests. Cliques develop within crowds. Cliques have fewer than nine members, all of whom share psychological intimacies.

Teachers in inclusive classrooms have noted that some students with special needs at about preadolescence may not enjoy the same level of peer acceptance that they did in the past. Teachers should interpret this as a normal developmental progression and not force students to accept each other. Instead, teachers can implement interventions that focus on sharing activities and doing things together in order to facilitate student–student relationships (see Table 3).

Issues in Conduct Management

An ounce of prevention is worth a pound of cure, as the saying goes. Content and covenant management prevent many difficult behaviors from occurring in classrooms

Table 3. Communication approaches

Communication approaches that build student–teacher relationships

"I Messages" are confrontational messages delivered without emotion or blame. Through these, the teacher lets the student know how he or she feels about the student's behavior.

"Active Listening" includes paraphrasing or restating what the student has said and results in the student's feeling understood.

"Interviews" are used to talk to students about their out-of-school activities. They result in students feeling closer to teachers and decrease misbehavior.

"Send Notes" when students experience success, difficult times, or sickness. Excellent for developing rapport with students.

Communication approaches that facilitate student–student relationships

"Dyads" are pairs of students who do not know each other well whom teachers put together to talk about interests.

"Social Skills Training" occurs after the teacher pinpoints students' needs (i.e., play with others, start a conversation). The best approaches train students in natural settings with peers.

"Anger Control" teaches students to monitor their anger, teaches reduction techniques, and teaches strategies to self-reinforce (Sprick, Sprick, & Garrison, 1993).

"Cooperative Learning" brings small groups of students together to use critical thinking and creativity to problem-solve in a shared activity. The teacher assigns a role to each group member. Social skills are necessary in order to be a successful group member.

Communication approaches that build home–school relationships

"Get Acquainted Call" is an opportunity for teachers to build rapport with parents during the first week of school. The following is an example of a script for a call:

"Hi, I am Mrs. Brown, your daughter's teacher. I have only had Shawna in my class for a few days, but I really appreciate how helpful to others she is. I hope you don't mind me calling you and I want you to feel free to contact me here at school anytime regarding Shawna's progress. You will be receiving a letter if you haven't already regarding the rules of the classroom. I just wanted to remind you of our Open House, too. I hope to see you and Mr. Smith there."

---

but does not prevent all of them. Wise teachers anticipate worst-case scenarios and plan their solutions accordingly. Planning involves establishing rules and procedures for the classroom and teaching students and staff how to follow the rules and procedures.

For example, some students with special needs may exhibit physically dangerous or severely disruptive behaviors, and teachers must always be prepared with a plan to manage whatever occurs. Planning is done for the safety of the disruptive student, of peers, and of the teacher. Examples of these behaviors include fighting, head banging, breaking windows, self-biting, self-pinching, assault, out-of-control behaviors, verbal threats, carrying weapons, overt defiance or flagrant disrespect of adults, hitting, hair pulling, grabbing, biting, screaming, and other loud sustained disruptions (Sprick et al., 1993).

School psychologists, special education teachers and consultants, school guidance counselors, and other school personnel with advanced training and expertise in managing difficult behaviors can be used as resources in developing classroom and schoolwide plans. Intervention plans should include procedures to immediately ensure the safety of everyone, involvement of parents/guardians, keeping records, determining need for interagency support, and teaching the student to manage his or her own behavior (Sprick et al., 1993). Staff development training may be necessary in order to train teachers to manage some extreme situations.

Teachers need to have a plan for each contingency in their classrooms. Following is an example of a comprehensive plan developed to manage the behavior of a student with a history of occasionally being out of control (e.g., throwing books, turning over desks, yelling, swearing) in a classroom full of sixth-grade peers.

First, school personnel have taken steps to ensure the safety of everyone through a well-articulated and well-understood crisis management system. Do not confuse school rules and policies about violent behavior with a plan and procedures of designated action to be implemented when a student is out of control. Beginning in the first week of school, teachers typically assist students in drill and practice of safety routines for fires, earthquakes, and tornados. The same sort of procedures must be practiced to ensure safety from other threats, such as the out-of-control behavior of a peer. Teachers periodically repeat drill and practice throughout the school year, and once per month is not too often to rehearse safety routines if threats occur frequently and students have difficulty remembering or following procedures. If one practice of the routine does not go smoothly, immediately try it again.

An example of a script that teachers can use to introduce safety instruction is provided in Figure 3. The script includes instruction in the important prompt, "Room clear." Teachers use this prompt to cue students to complete the prescribed safety routine. The prompt can be written on a sign and displayed on classroom walls, along with the prompts for tornado and fire drills. Teachers may find it appropriate to use variations of this prompt. For example, the prompt "Students, move away" may direct students away from a danger zone if the path to the door and the hall is obstructed or the threat is great enough to necessitate moving students out of the way but not so great that students need to exit the room. If someone is brandishing a weapon, students may not be able to escape from the room. Students can be instructed that a prompt means to calmly and quickly drop to the floor and stay down and out of sight.

The script in Figure 3 should be followed by role play or drill and practice of the actions students are to take in case of a threat. For example, the teacher introduces the safety lesson in the script, states the prompt "Room clear," tells students to imagine that someone in the middle of the class is angry and is going to throw something, and then has students practice moving away from the middle of the room into the hallway. It is important to note the final paragraph of the script in Figure 3. Teachers should always present this portion of the lesson in order to facilitate peer acceptance and support for the student who demonstrated the out-of-control behavior.

In such situations, teachers are often busy with the out-of-control student or with assisting other students. Therefore, teachers should train three responsible and dependable students in how to get help. Options for getting help include a student assistant contacting the principal's office via the intercom, telephone, or beeper system in the school.

> There may be times when it is not safe in school, not because of a fire or a tornado, but because somebody is upset and doing unsafe things such as fighting and hitting. Can you think of some other unsafe things that somebody might do when they are upset? [Discuss student responses.]
>
> When someone is doing things that are not safe, it is very important that the rest of us act very quickly to keep everybody safe. I am going to tell you the steps to keep safe and then we will practice them. When I notice that somebody is upset and doing dangerous things, I will say. "Room clear." When you hear me say "Room clear," each of you will stay calm and move away from the danger. What does staying calm mean? [Discuss student responses.]
>
> To move away from the danger, you are to leave the room and wait in the hallway for an adult to come. The two steps are 1) the teacher will see the danger and will say "Room clear"; and 2) students will stay calm and quickly move away from the danger, go out of the room, and wait in the hall.
>
> Let's practice the Room clear drill. Not everybody can get out of the door at the same time, and I will show you how to take your turn leaving the room. When we have finished our first practice, I will answer any questions that you have.
>
> [Drill is completed, and students return to their seats.] Shawna has had a very difficult time. Everyone of us will need to continue working as a community/group. Shawna will probably feel very uncomfortable about what has happened and it will be important for all of us to help her feel like a regular sixth grader. Everyone in here has a special goal to work on, not just Shawna. For example, I have to work on being more patient. Shawna will be working on handling her angry feelings.

Figure 3.   Script for a sixth-grade lesson on safety threats.

After the room is cleared, teachers often can step into the hall right outside the door and monitor the disruptive student until help arrives. Sometimes teachers may be able to use their communication skills to calm the student. Physical intervention is used only if necessary to prevent physical harm. Teachers who anticipate having students with physically dangerous and severely disruptive behaviors in their classrooms should insist on training in skills to restore calm and deescalate behaviors and in physical restraint.

Second, the student needs to learn anger management and impulse control. Academic assistance, restructuring self-talk, signal interference cueing, mentoring, goal setting and contracting, self-monitoring, structured reinforcement systems, managing stress, and increasing positive interactions may be helpful interventions in this task and are thoroughly described and scripted by Sprick et al. (1993).

Third, an additional component of the planning process is establishing a menu of positive and negative consequences that students can expect to encounter when they follow or do not follow rules and procedures. Table 4 presents such a menu, and teachers can use it to develop their own hierarchy of consequences.

CONCLUSION

Effective classroom management is a necessary ingredient in effective teaching. Teachers of inclusive classrooms may profit from increasing their repertoire of mar agement skills in content, covenant, and conduct management and strengthening these skills to more effectively teach all children. This chapter has presented knowledge, procedures, and conditions (when and why) in each of the three management categories. References have been cited that can assist teachers in planning staff development training at foundational and advanced levels of classroom management.

Other chapters in this book focus specifically on one of the three management categories: content or curriculum management or planning for instruction, covenant management or planning for relationships, and conduct management or planning for

Table 4. Hierarchy of positive and negative consequences in classrooms

Positive consequences
> Verbal and written feedback to students and guardians:
>> Tell the student what he or she did well
>> Send a special note to the student or give the student a certificate of merit
>> Call the parent or guardian and tell him or her what the student did well
>> Send a positive note to the parent or guardian
> Social responsibility
>> Give the student special jobs—student helper, peer tutor
>> Give the student privileges
>> Let the student teach a portion of the lesson
> Freedoms
>> Give class 5 minutes of free time
>> Provide extra computer time
>> Allow a few extra minutes of recess
>> Hold class outside
>> Have a short class party
>> Play music during seatwork
>> Arrange dress up/down day
>> Let student choose activity
> Public attention
>> Compliment the student in front of another staff member
>> Ask another staff member to acknowledge the student's accomplishments
>> Post the student's work in a public place
>> Read the student's work to the class
>> Shake the student's hand
>> Give the student extra time with an adult

Negative consequences
> Ignore
> Deliver gentle verbal reprimands
> Deliver verbal cues and warnings
> Implement delaying
> Contact parent
> Implement time owed
> Implement in-class time-out
> Complete the behavior improvement form

behaviors. Everything teachers do in their classrooms constitutes a management action. Management planning is necessary to assist in creating productive, safe, and respectful learning environments. Individual classroom teachers should not be expected to create such environments alone. Schools must provide support and collegiality so that educators and students participate together in management planning.

REFERENCES

Ashton, P. (1984). Teacher efficacy: A motivational paradigm for effective teacher education. *Journal of Teacher Education, 35,* 28–32.

Bandura, A. (1977). Self-efficacy: Toward a unifying theory of behavioral change. *Psychological Review, 84,* 191–215.

Charles, C.M. (1992). *Building classroom discipline* (4th ed.). New York: Longman.

Emmer, E.T., & Evertson, C.M. (1981). Synthesis of research on classroom management. *Educational Leadership, 38,* 342–345.

Froyen, L.A. (1993). *Classroom management: The reflective teacher-leader.* New York: Macmillan.

Jones, V., & Jones, L.S. (1990). *Comprehensive classroom management* (3rd ed.). Boston: Allyn & Bacon.

Lee, S.W. (1993). *The flex model classroom management planning system.* Lawrence, KS: Child Research Institute.

Medland, M., & Vitale, M. (1984). *Management of classrooms.* New York: Holt, Rinehart & Winston.

Recht, D.R., & Leslie, L. (1988). Effect of prior knowledge on good and poor readers' memory of text. *Journal of Educational Psychology, 80,* 16–20.

Rogers, J. (1993). The inclusion revolution. *Research Bulletin, 11.* Bloomington, IN: Center for Evaluation, Development, and Research.

Schendel, J. (1994, October). *Staff development: A tool for change.* Presentation at the annual convention of Iowa School Psychologists Association, Des Moines, IA.

Silberman, M.L., & Wheelan, S.A. (1980). *How to discipline without feeling guilty.* Champaign, IL: Research Press.

Sprick, R., Sprick, M., & Garrison, M. (1993). *Interventions: Collaborative planning for students at risk.* Longmont, CO: Sopris West.

Swanson, H., O'Conner, J.E., & Cooney, J.B. (1990). An information processing analysis of expert and novice teachers' problem solving. *American Educational Research Journal, 27,* 533–556.

Wang, M.C., Haertel, G.D., & Walberg, H.J. (1993). Toward a knowledge base for school learning. *Review of Educational Research, 63,* 249–294.

Weiner, B., Russell, D., & Lerman, D. (1978). Affective consequences of causal ascriptions. In J.H. Harvey, W.J. Ickes, & R.F. Kidd (Eds.), *New directions in attribution research* (Vol. 2). Hillsdale, NJ: Lawrence Erlbaum Associates.

Woolfolk, A.E. (1993). *Educational psychology* (5th ed.). Boston: Allyn & Bacon.

20

Support and Positive
Teaching Strategies

Wade Hitzing

MOST BUSINESSES DO not hire behavior specialists to work with their customers!
They do not because they operate on a premise different from that of most human services and educational programs. Their premise is that the customer is always right.
When a product does not sell or a service is not being used, they do not hire staff to go
"fix" the customer. They listen to the customers and change services and products to
better meet the customers' needs and wishes. Imagine the uproar that would be created if, after looking carefully at a product and deciding not to buy it, a customer walked
away, only to have a behavior specialist suddenly appear, shout "No!" and then gently
but firmly redirect the customer back to the product—providing hand-over-hand assistance if needed. If a teenager decides not to buy anything at the music store, the staff
do not attempt to send a note home with him or her indicating that dessert be withheld
to ensure that the inappropriate buying behavior is not rewarded. No time-out rooms
are needed because most businesses respect customers' decisions and do not require
them to become disruptive, even dangerous, before their wishes are honored. Like
schools and other human services programs, businesses are vitally interested in changing the customer's behavior, but instead of assuming the customer is wrong and must
be fixed or changed, most businesses, especially those that succeed, solve the behavior
problems they face by changing their products or the way their services are delivered
(i.e, their behavior). Granted, the situation in schools is different. A basic assumption
of all education programs is that the student (the customer) will be changed in some

The author acknowledges Lysa Jeanchild, Larry Douglass, and Kathy Hulgin, whose work in the Society
for Community Support's school projects contributed to this chapter. This chapter is based on Hitzing, W.
(1992). Support and positive teaching strategies. In *Curriculum considerations in inclusive classrooms:
Facilitating learning for all students*. Baltimore: Paul H. Brookes Publishing Co.; used by permission.

313

way—the student's knowledge will be increased or his or her skills will be improved. If a school program operated only on the customer is always right premise, students would not change and important educational goals would not be achieved. However, those of us who work in educational programs need to learn that meeting the educational needs of all students, especially those with challenging behavior, requires that we listen to their feedback and respect their role as customers and critics of the programs we offer.

Although significant progress has been made in the inclusion of minority groups, including students with significant disabilities, in public school programs, schools have a long history of expelling and excluding students because of their disruptive, dangerous, or otherwise challenging behavior (Gliedman & Roth, 1980; Wooden, 1976). This chapter focuses on understanding the causes of challenging behavior and applying this understanding to the design of school programs that are more supportive of the inclusion of all students, including those with challenging behavior.

UNDERSTANDING AND SUPPORTING
STUDENTS WITH CHALLENGING BEHAVIOR

Traditional Behavior Management Approach

Before making decisions about how to best approach a student with challenging behavior, it is important first to look carefully at how we think and talk about challenging behavior. This is very important because the way we look at the student's behavior determines how we

- "Frame" or define the problem
- Select goals
- Choose appropriate intervention procedures
- Define success

Frame or Define the Problem A traditional approach to a student with challenging behavior is to label or categorize the behavior as inappropriate or a "problem" and as behavior that must be greatly decreased or eliminated. In fact, the case is often made that, until the student's challenging behavior is decreased or eliminated, other "positive" goals cannot be achieved. Although there may be some acknowledgment that inadequate instructional practices may contribute to the behavior, there is a strong presumption that the student's inappropriate behavior is the problem that must be directly addressed, and it is the student who must change.

Select Goals The teaching or behavior plans that are developed in this approach focus on the elimination of the student's disruptive or dangerous behavior (Bailey & Bostow, 1969; Foxx, 1982). Alternative, appropriate behaviors may also be identified, and teaching procedures developed to strengthen them, but the major focus of the teacher's energy and time is devoted to attempts to decrease the challenging behavior (Rose 1979).

Choose Appropriate Intervention Procedures Most intervention procedures or behavior plans developed to address challenging behavior focus on altering the contingencies of reinforcement and punishment in the school setting. The typical behavior plan usually calls for school staff to change their reaction to inappropriate target behavior by ignoring, not rewarding, or in some cases punishing the student when the target behavior occurs. The play may also call for the staff to "catch the student being good" and to provide a schedule of positive reinforcement for the teaching staff to follow in rewarding the student's appropriate behavior.

Define Success Success is defined as meeting the goals for reduction or elimination of the target behavior. Given that there has been success in decreasing or eliminating the target behavior, the process is justified in that 1) a seriously disruptive and possibly even dangerous behavior has been eliminated or at least decreased, and 2) the decrease in the behavior now allows staff to move on to accomplishing more positive teaching goals with the student.

Disruptive and Challenging Behavior as Communication

A fundamentally different way to look at a student with challenging behavior is to view the disruptive and sometimes dangerous behavior of the student as communication or feedback about the needs and wishes of the student or the quality or appropriateness of the instructional strategies, at least as perceived by the student (Carr & Durand, 1985b; Donnellan, Mirenda, Mesaros, & Fassbender, 1984; Prizant & Wetherby, 1987). Some students learn to communicate "Leave me alone," "Pay attention to me!", "Give me that," "I don't want to do this," or "I don't understand this—I need help" by engaging in disruptive and sometimes even dangerous behavior. The following description provides a brief explanation of how such learning takes place (the learning cycle), and Figure 1 illustrates this as a vicious cycle. The learning cycle can be described in four steps:

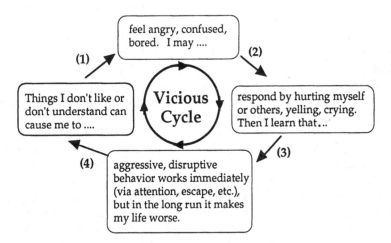

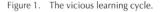

Figure 1.   The vicious learning cycle.

1. Students may be presented with school tasks and assignments that they do not value, understand, or know how to complete.
2. Students might then *feel* confused, frightened, angry, or in pain.
3. Students might then *behave* in ways that are disruptive and even sometimes dangerous. If their school assignments result in boredom or confusion, then their behavior often becomes more erratic and less predictable.
4. Students *learn* from their experiences and tend to repeat those actions that work for them. Disruptive or dangerous behaviors often work immediately for the student in that the student is able to escape from tasks and gain attention from the teacher. However, although the disruptive behavior often results in immediate rewards, in the long run more problems such as alienation, exclusion, and isolation are created. These usually increase the discomfort and confusion in the student's school life, which can result in even more disruptive behavior. This vicious learning cycle is clearly evident in the lives of many students with challenging behavior.

Many challenging behaviors are learned because they serve a very powerful, and usually immediate, communicative function. For example, a student may be presented with a task he or she finds confusing and frustrating. If the student does not have effective vocal or sign language skills, it may be hard for the teacher to understand that the student is confused and that a more appropriate task should be assigned. If, as is more often the case, the teacher *does* understand, by listening to the student or observing relevant body language and other signs, he or she still proceeds with the task anyway because of a focus on behavioral compliance or task completion. In fact, many behavior programs call for the teacher to ignore all inappropriate requests to stop or take a break. The teacher is advised to act as if he or she cannot hear the student if the student is behaving inappropriately. However, few, if any, teachers can continue to ignore a punch in the stomach, a slap in the face, or loud yelling and screaming. If the teacher waits until the student's behavior escalates to the point of disruption or danger before backing off or allowing the student to stop the task, the student is taught, in effect, to engage in disruptive behavior to escape from the task or situation (Carr, Newsom, & Binkoff, 1980; Weeks & Gaylord-Ross, 1981). A formal behavior plan may call for the teacher to ignore or not reward less disruptive or dangerous attempts at communication, but in the real world of the classroom the most disruptive, especially dangerous behavior is in fact listened to and rewarded.

To gain a better understanding of the causes of a student's behavior, it is usually necessary to complete a functional analysis, which results in a comprehensive description of the student's curriculum, the school environment, and how the student's behavior is effective for him or her. Special attention must be paid to the settings, events, and actions (antecedents) that are present or typically precede occurrences of the disruptive behavior and the consequences that follow, especially the reactions of fellow students and teaching staff (Durand & Crimmins, 1988; LaVigna & Donnellan, 1986). This analysis leads to an understanding that the student's disruptive and dangerous acts are not simply target behaviors to be eliminated and allows us to frame the issue in a way that recognizes the functional, adaptive role of the behavior and our responsibility in contributing to its development.

Use of Supports and Positive Teaching Strategies for Students with Challenging Behaviors

Frame the Problem   Recognizing that disruptive, even dangerous, behavior serves a communicative function does not mean that we must accept the behavior and do nothing to help the student learn to make better choices. However, this recognition does require that we acknowledge the legitimacy of the student's communication and that the problem faced by the school staff is much more complicated than simply decreasing or eliminating the student's challenging behavior. The following example of Cathy shows how important it is to frame the problem in a way that meets both the interests of the school and those of the student.

Cathy, who was labeled as having mental retardation, had much difficulty adjusting to her new school program. During the first few months she often cried and tried to run out of the classroom. Her teacher handled these situations by ignoring her crying, as much as possible, and redirecting her back to her desk if she attempted to run from the classroom. These procedures were successful in reducing Cathy's crying and running away, but her teacher became concerned about a new behavior that presented even more serious problems: Cathy had begun to vomit while at school. At first, this occurred infrequently, but the behavior gradually increased until she was vomiting in the classroom every day.

A behavior specialist was called in to consult with Cathy's teacher. The specialist asked what typically happened when Cathy vomited at school. Cathy's teacher said that almost every time she had to be sent home and that often she did not return to school until the next day. Based on this evidence, a behavior plan was developed to eliminate the vomiting behavior. The plan was simple: The teacher was instructed to ignore, as much as possible, Cathy's vomiting behavior, clean her up if necessary, but otherwise act as if nothing had happened. She also praised Cathy and rewarded her if she went short periods of time without vomiting.

At first, it looked as if the plan might not work. Cathy vomited repeatedly during the first few days. In fact, on the third day she vomited, or at least tried to, 23 times. However, after the third day the situation began to improve. The frequency of the vomiting steadily decreased over the next 27 days, and by the 30th day of the new procedures, she went the entire day without vomiting. She never vomited in class again.

The teacher and the behavior specialist had clearly accomplished *their* goal— Cathy's vomiting behavior was completely eliminated. But is this really a success story? It is important to look at the success of the behavior plan from the point of view of *all* of the individuals concerned. Given the way the teacher and the behavior specialist framed the problem, they judged their efforts a success. The other students in the class probably appreciated the change in Cathy's behavior. But what about Cathy? How might she answer the question of success? If she had been interviewed on the 30th day of the behavior plan, the first day she did not vomit, what would she have said? "I just love it here! My school work is very interesting and I am learning a lot"?

Or might she have said, "I still don't like it here. I'd rather leave. I just don't tell anyone about it anymore"?

Cathy was not very likely to see the results of the behavior plan as a success because nothing was done to help her with *her* problem. A reasonable functional analysis would probably have shown that her problem was either 1) she disliked or was afraid of the classroom setting or 2) she found nothing at school more interesting or engaging than being back home. The behavior plan did nothing to help or improve these concerns. The behavior plan was just that—a *behavior* plan. It was successful in improving Cathy's behavior but did nothing to help the basic reasons for the problem behavior.

Select Goals   The first step in developing a more effective educational plan might be to better support the student by changing the goals of the plan. The need for rethinking basic goals can be seen in the following example.

Betty worked as an aide in a third-grade classroom. Although she helped the teacher in many different ways, her main responsibility was to provide special assistance for Robbie. Robbie was the only student in the classroom with significant disabilities—both mental and physical—and a history of hurting himself and others. Betty and the teacher met with the school psychologist in an attempt to develop more effective ways of working with Robbie. They explained that if either of them sat by Robbie and attempted to engage him in a task, he tried to escape by rolling his wheelchair away from the table. If Betty prevented his escape by holding his wheelchair, he began to yell and refused to cooperate in the task. If she tried to manually guide him through the task, he tried to bite and scratch her. Betty indicated that she usually attempted to work through these episodes by ignoring his aggressive behavior, as much as possible, and redirecting him to the task. Both agreed that if Robbie appeared to be really upset, they would leave him alone for a while and introduce the task later. Betty's major concern was that this strategy was not working—in fact, the frequency and severity of Robbie's disruptive behavior seemed to be increasing.

Betty did not have a clear answer when the psychologist asked her *what* she was trying to accomplish with Robbie. She tended to think more in terms of *how* she was teaching and whether she was using the right instructional procedure rather than in terms of *what* she was attempting to teach. However, as the discussion progressed, the teacher pulled out Robbie's individualized education program (IEP) and showed the psychologist an example of one of the goals Betty tried to help Robbie achieve. The task criterion was that "the student will sort 20 objects, of four different colors, within 10 minutes with at least 90% accuracy, using only verbal prompts." The goal was that Robbie achieve this criterion 3 days consecutively and then move on to the next goal in the teaching sequence. Neither the classroom teacher nor Betty had seriously considered whether at least one of the factors contributing to Robbie's behavior was the lack of a good match between the instructional goals the team had selected and Robbie's *interests*. The goals in Robbie's IEP, like those for most students, focused primarily on skill acquisition (mainly self-help, academic, and social skills) and decreasing or eliminating behaviors seen as inappropriate. These goals were seen as most relevant to his current educational *needs*. These might seem to be reasonable goals until you remember that 1) if the teacher or aide sat by Robbie to work with him, he attempted to escape; 2) if the staff did not let him escape, he yelled and refused to cooperate; and 3) if they attempted to physically assist him in completing the task, he tried to bite, hit, and scratch them.

Given Robbie's long history of disturbing behavior, it would probably have been more appropriate first to help him learn that 1) the classroom is a safe place and that he can trust his teachers and 2) it will be interesting, fun, engaging, and somehow worth it if he does cooperate and work with the teaching staff. His behavior in the classroom suggested that, from *his point of view,* there was little reason to cooperate and that he was willing to "work" (yell, hit, bite) very hard to escape the situation. It is difficult to believe that the most effective way to help Robbie learn to trust his teachers and learn that cooperation would somehow pay off was to teach him to complete a task he did not understand and clearly saw no reward for doing, and was almost certain to lead to negative interactions with his teachers. Although this seems obvious, similar situations can be observed many times each day in classrooms across the country. School staff attempt to make significant changes in a student's behavior before first achieving a reasonable working relationship through establishing a sense of safety, trust, and cooperation.

Guidelines for Establishing a Sense of Safety, Trust, and Cooperation At first, it may seem unusual to think of developing formal teaching strategies to help a student learn that it is safe to be in the classroom and that the teaching staff can be trusted. Educators surely never intentionally try to teach the student that the classroom is a place to be feared or that staff cannot be trusted. However, many staff have been involved in the implementation of behavior plans that contributed to such feelings and beliefs on the part of a student. Many behavior plans call for rewarding or reinforcing behavior that is seen as appropriate and punishing behavior that is disruptive or dangerous. One minute students are rewarded with M&Ms, tokens, and praise for on-task behavior and cooperation, and the next minute they are punished by being restrained or placed in time-out for their inappropriate behavior. There is ample research and common experience to prove that such a combination of rewards and punishment can result in decreased disruptive or dangerous behavior. However, there can be other unintended negative effects of these procedures such as: "What is the teacher going to do next? First he patted me on the shoulder and said 'good job'…2 minutes later he squirted hot sauce in my mouth when I was biting my hand—it tasted awful—what's next?" Even if the student has no experience with such practices in his or her current educational placement, staff may still have to deal with past school experiences. The student may view the teacher as simply a clone of past instructors, responding as if the teacher is "one of them" until he or she proves otherwise. It may help to think in terms of a hierarchy of goals that the teacher wants the student to learn. For example,

- Level 1: It is safe to be with me and I can be trusted.
- Level 2: It will be fun, interesting, engaging, or somehow pay off to cooperate and work with me.
- Level 3: It will be beneficial to make a change in behavior, learn a new skill, gain competence, or decrease problem behavior.

The selection of this specific hierarchy is arbitrary, and there are a number of different ways to describe this analysis. The intent here is simply to emphasize the sequence of goal selection.

There are a variety of strategies that can be used to help achieve the goals at level 1 and level 2, both of which can usually be addressed at the same time. First, and most important, maintain a clear focus on trying to achieve these two goals. Most teachers have been trained to emphasize behavior change and skill acquisition, and it is often difficult for them to set these goals aside for the moment and focus on safety, trust, cooperation, and building a strong positive working relationship.

For example, a teacher who had just experienced a rough morning with a new student decided that she would stop trying to get him to follow the educational objectives in his IEP and just sit and have a glass of juice with him. The student had hit himself in the head many times. The teacher wanted to spend a few minutes with him that were as calm and as pleasant as possible. She began by pouring them both a small glass of juice. He drank only a little and then spilled the rest of it. She did not make a big deal about the spilling but did attempt to show him how to handle the glass more carefully. He resisted her efforts and refused to cooperate by pouring more juice. She poured the juice herself and then offered it to him. He refused to drink the juice even when she held it to his mouth and eventually knocked the glass from her hand. (It was clear that the teacher was gradually, but significantly, making a major change in her goals for this interaction.) Again, she did not overreact but simply picked up the glass and attempted to help him pour more juice. When he refused to cooperate, she poured the juice and held it up for him to drink. At this point, anyone observing their interaction would have concluded that, no matter what the teacher might have said or intended, she was in fact trying to get the student to comply with a drinking program. The focus and energy of the teacher had clearly shifted to one of promoting behavior change, and the situation was neither calm nor pleasant.

If the teacher had kept to her original goal she would not have cared whether the student spilled the juice or cooperated in pouring. As soon as she saw that she had probably made a mistake in selecting this particular situation as the way to relax and share a few pleasant moments, she could have said something to the effect, "I'm sorry, I thought you would like some juice, what else can we do?" She would not have taken this as an opportunity to teach juice pouring or work on compliance training. The focus of her efforts instead would have been to engage the student in something that he might find interesting and rewarding, which would allow them to experience time together with few, if any, demands on either of them.

Although it is usually possible and appropriate to address goals on the first two levels simultaneously, it is important to keep the distinction between the two levels in mind. For example, it is likely that a sense of safety and trust has already been established, but the student may not have had classroom experiences that resulted in interest, engagement, and cooperation. The student may trust the staff and feel safe in the classroom but have no reason, from his or her point of view, to cooperate or work with the staff, especially on *school* work. Of course, most students enter class willingly. They cause very few problems until the teacher says, "Time for work, let's all sit down and begin our work." Then the fireworks begin. The school day seems to cycle between disruptions and problems when attempts are made to engage the student in school work and relative quiet when the student is allowed to do preferred tasks and few instructions or demands are made.

Such students require a great deal of energy and creativity from the staff. At first, it may not be easy to identify or schedule a wide variety of available activities that interest the student, especially if staff limit themselves to traditional *educational* activities. At this first stage, it is important to keep in mind that the primary objective is for both the student and staff to survive the school day. Far too often, rigid behavioral criteria are imposed and strict intensive behavior management procedures are instituted to increase on-task performance and decrease problem behavior. Usually, because school staff is bigger and stronger than the student, they can "win" such power struggles. However, when such behavioral management procedures do not succeed it is the student who suffers the most. Exposed to the standard instructional curriculum and held accountable to general standards of behavior, the student is seen as having failed and may be moved to a more restrictive or segregated school program, assigned to home instruction, or expelled. Instead, following a "survival-first" strategy, staff could implement a curriculum and use teaching strategies that have the best chance of interesting or engaging the student, *whether or not these activities can be justified as educationally appropriate by traditional standards.* After establishing a history of interest and success in the classroom, it would be possible to negotiate with the student and gradually phase in more traditional activities that focus on building competencies and strengths.

Adopting the above approach to goal setting does not imply a lack of commitment to helping the student make major changes in his or her behavior (i.e., enhancing competence and decreasing challenging behavior). In fact, for many students with long histories of challenging behavior, it may be the only really effective way of *beginning* to make such changes. Far too often, the imposition of predetermined curriculum packages and disciplinary rules that apply to all students result in such a high rate of disruptive behavior that the student with challenging behavior is expelled or excluded from the school or classroom. This is justified as necessary because the assumption is that the student must have certain objectives in his or her IEP and that all students must obey the general rules of behavior. Teachers must not be misled by the fact that the lack of individualization in curriculum design and teaching strategies does not result in challenging behavior by most students. Many students are just as dissatisfied as those labeled with challenging behavior. They have simply given up telling us about it or have not yet learned that yelling, property destruction, aggression, and self-injury are forms of a sign language that work well at school.

Decide on Appropriate Intervention Procedures Recognizing the student's disruptive and dangerous behavior as communicative also has a significant impact on the selection of intervention strategies that can be developed to improve the situation. Four intervention alternatives that might be used individually or more likely in combination are now discussed.

Institute Support Strategies   Support strategies should be initiated because they contribute to the development of a positive working relationship between teacher and student and make it easier for the student to learn less destructive, alternative forms of communication by removing at least some of the sources of frustration and confusion.

The typical educational planning process does not lend itself well to the development of truly comprehensive support plans. Far too often, a number of important environmental influences, such as a student's school placement, class size and composition, and staffing arrangements, are taken as a given and not considered to be adaptable in order to better meet the student's needs. For many students with long histories of challenging behaviors, especially those students whose needs are not being met by existing educational strategies (i.e., more of the same is probably not the solution), a more comprehensive student-driven planning approach, such as Personal Futures Planning, may prove necessary (Mount & Zwernik, 1988; O'Brien, 1987).

It is consistent with the goal hierarchy described earlier in this chapter to focus first on removing as many of the negative aspects (judged from the student's point of view) of the instructional environment as possible. There are a number of studies that show that decreasing the difficulty of school tasks and changing the frequency and form of instructional directives can have a significant impact in decreasing disruptive behavior (i.e., the student has less to complain about) (Carr et al., 1980; Gaylord-Ross, Weeks, & Lipner, 1980).

In order to design a curriculum that is more supportive of the student and facilitates learning that cooperation in the classroom might be fun, interesting, or in some way pay off, the teacher should ask the following questions:

- Would the student ever choose to do this task?
- Will the acquired skill be functional in ways that have meaning to the student or directly benefit him or her?
- Would the student be willing to pay staff for helping him or her achieve this instructional objective?
- If we delete this goal, will the student miss it and ask that it be reinstated?

It is not likely that a teacher can develop an educational plan that would elicit a yes answer to all of the above questions. For example, most people probably benefited from learning the multiplication tables, but it was hard to see the benefit or be interested in the process at the time. Similarly, teachers probably have to include some instructional objectives that the student might never choose. However, this rationale cannot be used as an excuse for implementing an educational plan that contains few or no instructional activities that the student finds interesting, engaging, or would choose. The ratio often seems to be reversed: The *more* difficulties that exist in teaching the student, the *less* likely it is that he or she will have preferred goals. The plans of these students seem to be largely a collection of compliance training activities.

Developing really effective support plans is difficult. Perhaps as a result of teacher training that focuses on student behavior, most educators are more skilled and comfortable in teaching students to handle frustration than they are at devising strategies to remove some of the significant sources of frustration from a student's school program.

Teaching Alternative Ways to Communicate   For a variety of reasons, a student may never have learned standard ways to communicate or may, because of disabilities, be unable to communicate effectively in a typical (vocal) manner. This inability is especially significant because researchers have reported an inverse relationship between the ability to effectively use some form of sign or verbal communication system and the presence of challenging behavior (Cantwell, Baker, & Mattison, 1981; Carr, 1979; Durand, 1987). Therefore, it is not surprising that teaching the student to, in effect, substitute a less destructive yet still effective form of communication can result in a significant decrease in challenging behavior (Carr & Durand, 1985a, 1985b; Carr et al., 1980; Eason, White, & Newsom, 1982). Recognizing that much of a student's disruptive and dangerous behavior often serves a communicative function, the major goal of most intervention or behavior plans would necessarily focus on helping the student learn to communicate in ways that are equally effective and adaptive but are not disruptive or dangerous. Donnellan et al. (1984) pointed out

> There is a growing awareness among educators that the long-term successful functioning of persons with severe handicaps depends on expanding their limited response repertoires rather than simply limiting their inappropriate behaviors. Interventions designed to teach functionally related behaviors in place of aberrant responses make good educational sense in this regard. Further, such an approach explicitly acknowledges the functional legitimacy of even aberrant behavior and, in so doing, communicates a respectful attitude concerning the individual exhibiting the behavior. (p. 209)

Help the Student Learn to Tolerate School Conditions   Helping a student learn how to tolerate certain school conditions is a strategy that should be used only when those conditions cannot or should not be changed (i.e., it is clearly in the best interest of the student to learn to adapt to or tolerate the condition). Strategies can range from formal desensitization or relaxation procedures to help the student overcome phobias and fears (Morris & Kratochwill, 1983; Workman & Williams, 1980) to simply empathizing with the student's concerns and clearly letting him or her know that the teacher is there to help.

Teaching the Student to "Be Quiet," Stop Communicating   Careful efforts to understand the cause(s) of a student's disruptive and dangerous behavior almost always result in information that can be used to implement support and positive teaching strategies based on the three alternatives just mentioned: support, instruction, and toleration. However, there may be times when even the best analysis efforts do not result in the information necessary to make changes or do not make it possible to effect needed changes in setting, staffing, and curriculum, at least immediately. Under these circumstances (i.e., in the absence of a better idea), staff may have to implement behavior *management* procedures to directly decrease a student's challenging behavior, especially if it is highly disruptive or dangerous. If forced to make this compromise, it is important to use the least intrusive and least aversive teaching procedures possible. It may be enough to simply ensure that the disruptive behavior is not reward-ed. However, if that is not effective, staff may have to also reward a student for not engaging in the disruptive behavior. There should never be a need to go further than mild disciplinary procedures such as restrictions on rewarding activities. There is noth-ing inherently abusive or stigmatizing involved in teaching a student that one conse-quence of his or her aggressive and dangerous behavior on the playground is that he or she is required to return to the classroom. However, it is always preferable in such a sit-uation to try to understand the conditions that led to the anger and aggression and also help the student learn that there are other equally effective ways of handling the situa-tion. An array of positive programming strategies are described in a number of books (Donnellan, LaVigna, Negri-Shoultz, & Fassbender, 1988; Evans & Meyer, 1985; LaVigna & Donnellan, 1986; Meyer & Evans, 1989).

Some teaching strategies labeled as positive may still have unpleasant compo-nents from the point of view of the student. For example, students do not enjoy being put "on extinction"; most students who refuse to do a school task would prefer to be left alone rather than redirected. They would rather have free access to rewarding activ-ities than have to earn access by *not* behaving disruptively. However, there is never jus-tification for the use of pain, either emotional or physical, to control student behavior.

Define Success   Most of a student's disruptive and dangerous behavior can pro-vide staff with valuable feedback about what he or she is thinking and feeling, espe-cially about the quality of educational strategies. This feedback makes it clear that educators cannot settle for teaching students to simply stop communicating or to be quiet. The example of Cathy points out the need for defining success in terms of both the staff and the students.

CONCLUSION

Much of this chapter has been concerned with the need to implement educational plans that attempt both to decrease a student's challenging behavior and improve the stu-dent's quality of life at school. Students, especially those with challenging behaviors, are often subjected to behavior management plans that focus on decreasing specific target behaviors before support plans have been implemented that ensure the best pos-sible match between a student's current wishes and needs and what is offered in the educational program. Furthermore, a student's educational plan may call for major changes in behavior without providing reasons for the change that make sense to the student. This point was vividly described in a conference presentation by the mother of a young man with significant disabilities. Toward the end of her talk, she pointed out that over the years she had collected reams of data, provided by the many staff who had worked with her son. She showed the audience a thick folder that contained only data on her son's ability to control his head movements. The young man had cerebral palsy and for many years had been involved in various head control training programs. She said that in reviewing the data it was clear that, even after many years of training, her son still did not have "good head control." Some of the members of the audience became defensive, so his mother quickly pointed out she did not mean to be critical of the staff's training efforts. She understood that his cerebral palsy was a major barrier to the success of their teaching efforts. However, she added, last summer they had discovered that he could hold up his head, that he could be successful—you just had to surround him with pretty young women! As the laughter in the meeting room subsided, she made her most important point. She held up the folder to give an idea of the many hours of her son's life that were represented by the data in the folder. She pointed out that while she understood why hundreds, possibly thousands, of hours of staff time had been spent in training her son to hold up his head, she could not understand and could not accept that almost no time had been spent involving her son in situations and activities that ensured that, if he did look up, there would be something to see.

Sadly, this young man is not alone. Thousands of students each day are asked to follow teaching plans that call for "increased attention span" and "increased time on task." Many of these plans do not even specify what the task is—it is left as a blank to be filled in later. Even more plans provide no rationale for why a student should change his or her behavior other than to receive an immediate reward or to please the teacher. We must learn to implement educational plans that clearly reflect our responsibility to change, to listen to the critical feedback provided by students, and to adapt our instructional practices to meet their wishes and needs.

REFERENCES

Bailey, J.S., & Bostow, D.E. (1969). Modification of severe disruptive and aggressive behavior using brief time out and reinforcement procedures. *Journal of Applied Behavior Analysis, 2,* 31–37.

Cantwell, D.P., Baker, L., & Mattison, R.E. (1981). Prevalence, type and correlates of psychiatric diagnoses in 200 children with communication disorders. *Developmental and Behavioral Pediatrics, 2,* 131–136.

Carr, E.G. (1979). Teaching autistic children to use sign language: Some research issues. *Journal of Autism and Developmental Disorders, 9,* 345–359.

Carr, E.G., & Durand, V.M. (1985a). Reducing behavior problems through functional communication training. *Journal of Applied Behavior Analysis, 18,* 111–126.

Carr, E.G., & Durand, V.M. (1985b). The social-communicative basis of severe behavior problems in children. In S. Reiss & R. Bootzin (Eds.), *Theoretical issues in behavior therapy* (pp. 219–254). New York: Academic Press.

Carr, E.G., Newsom, C.D., & Binkoff, J.A. (1980). Escape as a factor in the behavior of two retarded children. *Journal of Applied Behavior Analysis, 13,* 113–129.

Donnellan, A.M., LaVigna, G.W., Negri-Shoultz, N., & Fassbender, L.L. (1988). *Progress without punishment.* New York: Teachers College Press.

Donnellan, A.M., Mirenda, P.L., Mesaros, R.A., & Fassbender, L.L. (1984). Analyzing the communicative functions of aberrant behavior. *Journal of The Association for Persons with Severe Handicaps, 9,* 201–212.

Durand, V.M. (1987). Assessment and treatment of psychotic speech in an autistic child. *Journal of Autism and Developmental Disorders, 17,* 17–28.

Durand, V.M., & Crimmins, D.M. (1988). Identifying the variables maintaining self-injurious behavior. *Journal of Autism and Developmental Disorders, 18*(1), 17–28.

Eason, L.J., White, M.J., & Newsom, C. (1982). Generalized reduction of self-stimulatory behavior: An effect of teaching appropriate play to autistic children. *Analysis and Intervention in Developmental Disabilities, 2,* 157–169.

Evans, I.M., & Meyer, L.H. (1985). *An educative approach to behavior problems: A practical decision model for interventions with severely handicapped learners.* Baltimore: Paul H. Brookes Publishing Co.

Foxx, R.M. (1982). *Decreasing behaviors of severely retarded and autistic persons.* Champaign, IL: Research Press.

Gaylord-Ross, R.J., Weeks, M., & Lipner, C. (1980). Analysis of antecedent, response, and consequence events in the treatment of self-injurious behavior. *Education and Training of the Mentally Retarded, 15,* 35–42.

Gliedman, J., & Roth, W. (1980). *The unexpected minority: Handicapped children in America.* New York: Harcourt Brace Jovanovich.

LaVigna, G.W., & Donnellan, A.M. (1986). *Alternatives to punishment: Solving behavior problems with non-aversive strategies.* New York: Irvington.

Meyer, L.H., & Evans, I.M. (1989). *Nonaversive intervention for behavior problems: A manual for home and community.* Baltimore: Paul H. Brookes Publishing Co.

Morris, R.J., & Kratochwill, T.R. (1983). *Treating children's fears and phobias: A behavioral approach.* Elmsford, NY: Pergamon.

Mount, B., & Zwernik, K. (1988). *It's never too early, it's never too late.* St. Paul, MN: Metropolitan Council.

O'Brien, J. (1987). A guide to lifestyle planning: *Using* The Activities Catalog *to integrate services and natural support systems.* In B. Wilcox & G.T. Bellamy (Eds.), *A comprehensive guide to* The Activities Catalog: *An alternative curriculum for youth and adults with severe disabilities* (pp. 175–189). Baltimore: Paul H. Brookes Publishing Co.

Prizant, B.M., & Wetherby, A.M. (1987). Communicative intent: A framework for understanding social communicative behavior in autism. *Journal of the American Academy of Child and Adolescent Psychiatry, 26,* 472–479.

Rose, T.L. (1979). Reducing self-injurious behavior by differentially reinforcing other behaviors. *The American Association for the Education of the Severely/Profoundly Handicapped, 4,* 179–186.

Weeks, M., & Gaylord-Ross, R. (1981). Task difficulty and aberrant behavior in severely handicapped students. *Journal of Applied Behavior Analysis, 14,* 449–463.

Wooden, K. (1976). *Weeping in the playtime of others: America's incarcerated children.* New York: McGraw-Hill.

Workman, E.A., & Williams, R.L. (1980). Self-cued relaxation in the control of an adolescent's violent arguments and debilitating somatic complaints. *Education and Treatment of Children, 3,* 315–322.

21

A Functional Approach to Dealing with Severe Challenging Behavior

David P. Wacker, Wendy K. Berg,
Jay Harding, and Jennifer Asmus

IN CONSIDERING SEVERE challenging behavior, it is tempting to focus almost exclusively on the form of those behaviors. For example, it is common to categorize behavior as aggressive, self-injurious, or destructive, among other terms. Given this focus on form, a chapter such as this would then contain separate subsections for each behavior noted, with a straightforward "cookbook approach" of discussing current recommended practices for assessing and treating each behavior by category. This approach to categorizing behavior by form (or topography) is appealing because it makes intuitive sense to respond to different forms of behavior with different interventions. The drawback is that the reasons for the occurrence of difficult behavior, regardless of form, are seldom identified except in a very general way. For example, the occurrence of aggression might be attributed to a student's functioning level, diagnostic group, or home situation. However, we know from observing children who exhibit these behaviors that most children are not self-injurious, aggressive, or destructive across all situations. In fact, for almost every child, we can identify situations in which the child seldom displays difficult behavior but engages in very appropriate, desirable behaviors. The changes in a child's behavior that occur across different contexts indicate that the child's behavior is influenced or controlled by events in the child's environment. By carefully observing the child across a variety of contexts, we can usually identify specific environmental events that are associated with appropriate behavior and specific environmental events that are associated with challenging behavior. When we identify the effects that different events have on a child's behavior, we can hypothesize about the reasons the behavior occurs. Therefore, rather than attributing the behavior to the child's mental retardation, diagnostic group, or home life, we define behavior as occurring in response to specific events in the child's environment; that is, the behavior serves a purpose or has a function for the child.

Identifying the purpose or function of a behavior is the basis for a functional approach toward difficult behavior. Regardless of its form, a functional approach to behavior focuses on identifying the events in the environment that prompt the behavior and the consequences that reinforce the behavior when it occurs. For example, group activities such as circle time may prompt aggressive behavior for two students in separate classrooms. The child in the first classroom might be removed from the group activity and be placed in a quiet area of the classroom with nothing to do (i.e., timeout). For this child, aggressive behavior resulted in the termination of any requirement to participate in the group setting. For the child in the second classroom, aggressive behavior during group time might result in a classroom aide sitting next to the child and prompting participation in the activity. For this child, aggression resulted in one-on-one attention and assistance for the remainder of the group activity. The context that prompted aggressive behavior was the same for both children. However, aggressive behavior produced a different outcome or served a different function for each child.

Carr and Durand (1985) proposed that the effects of behavior can be categorized into three functions: to gain desired events, such as attention or tangible items; to escape or avoid undesirable events; and to gain internal or automatic effects, such as self-stimulation, that we cannot observe directly. From an intervention standpoint, the critical issue is to determine what function the challenging behavior serves for the individual. If the function is identified, then intervention can be based directly on that function. For example, consider the student in the first classroom whose aggressive behavior resulted in an escape from the group activity. A number of intervention options are available, including reducing or changing the activity and teaching the student to request assistance or breaks. Depending on the student and his or her individualized education program (IEP) goals, any of these options might be considered. However, the use of time-out would probably not be appropriate because placing the student in time-out removes the demands contingent on aggression and thus reinforces aggressive behavior. Until we have identified the function of problematic behavior, we cannot determine an effective intervention.

In the following sections, we describe a functional assessment and intervention model that we have used successfully with children in school and home settings (Wacker & Berg, 1992a, 1992b). It is based on the functional analysis methodology described by Carr and Durand (1985) and Iwata, Dorsey, Slifer, Bauman, and Richman (1982). We first describe a comprehensive approach to behavioral assessment and then describe how intervention can be matched to the results of assessment. Three examples of specific intervention procedures are provided along with some considerations for their long-term use.

THE ROLE OF ASSESSMENT

The specific purpose of behavioral assessment is to identify why behavior occurs within a specific context in order to develop appropriate intervention (Wacker, Northup, & Cooper, 1992). A number of procedures are useful for identifying the function of behavior, each of which involves direct observation of the child. We have found the assessment techniques in Table 1 to be a useful and comprehensive approach to assessment.

DESCRIPTIVE ASSESSMENT

The first two assessment methods listed in Table 1, scatterplot and A–B–C, provide descriptive assessments. Descriptive assessment refers to procedures that describe interactions between the child's behavior and naturally occurring events in the child's regular routine (Bijou, Peterson, & Ault, 1968). To identify the function of the behavior, we first need to determine the time of day, the activities, and the people associated with its occurrence. The scatterplot analysis described by Touchette, MacDonald, and Langer (1985) is used to identify the times of day (by 30-minute segments) in which challenging behavior usually occurs. If high frequencies of the behavior occur during specific times of the day, it is important first to identify those times. Next, it is helpful to record the environmental events that surround the behavior. This procedure is sometimes called an A–B–C assessment because it describes antecedents (A) to the behavior (i.e., events that occur prior to or with the behavior), the specific behavior (B) associated with the event, and the consequences (C) of the behavior (i.e., events that immediately follow the behavior, which may serve to reinforce it). For example, a teacher may observe that a child frequently engages in hand biting when he or she is presented with a work task (antecedent), which in turn often results in the removal of the task (consequence). This sequence suggests that the presentation of a work task (demand) sets the occasion for challenging behavior and that the removal of the tasks reinforces the behavior. In the group–time example described previously, aggression for the first child occurred during group time and appeared to function as a way to avoid that activity.

Descriptive assessments are useful preliminary methods for gathering information regarding the naturally occurring events that are associated with the behavior.

Table 1. Summary of assessment procedures

Method	Purpose
Scatterplot (descriptive)	Identify the times of the day associated with behavior
Antecedent-Behavior-Consequence (A-B-C) assessment (descriptive)	Identify naturally occurring events associated with behavior
Structural analysis (experimental)	Identify antecedent events that set the occasion for behavior
Functional analysis (experimental)	Identify maintaining events for behavior

However, they are only preliminary assessments and are used to identify times and activities related to difficult behavior. Because naturally occurring events are not controlled, multiple hypotheses are often possible regarding why these events seem to be controlling an individual's behavior (Mace & Lalli, 1991). For example, if a student engaged in preferred activities when he or she left the group, then both escape (from the group) and gain (access to preferred activities) are equally plausible hypotheses. To determine which of these hypotheses is most likely, the next step in assessment is to conduct analyses that more precisely show the causal relation between behavior and variables in the environment. These next assessments are called experimental analyses (Iwata, Vollmer, & Zarcone, 1990) because they systematically assess environmental variables in single-case designs. There are two versions of these assessments: structural analyses, which evaluate antecedent variables, and functional analyses, which evaluate consequence variables.

STRUCTURAL ANALYSIS

Structural analysis (Axelrod, 1987; Carr & Durand, 1985) is a procedure for identifying the antecedent events that set the occasion for challenging behavior. In this procedure, the teacher or consultant uses information from the descriptive assessment to determine if specific antecedent variables correlate with the occurrence of the behavior. This is accomplished by comparing the child's behavior across a series of alternating conditions in which the hypothesized variable (e.g, social attention, task demands) is present and when it is absent. If, for example, the descriptive assessment reveals that attention is the variable of interest, the teacher might present a task and either provide continuous attention (high-attention condition) or require the student to work independently (low-attention condition). These two conditions would be repeated several times to see if a stable pattern of behavior emerged. If the child engaged in challenging behavior most often during conditions in which little attention was provided, then attention would be the likely function of the behavior. If we suspect that challenging behavior occurs when difficult or nonpreferred tasks are presented to the child, we would alternate tasks that are demanding (e.g., difficult academic tasks) with nondemanding tasks (e.g., playing with preferred toys). Similar levels of social attention would be provided for both tasks.

The benefit of a structural analysis is that we can identify the function of difficult behavior without reinforcing it. Thus, if challenging behavior occurs most often with high demands or low attention, then escape or attention functions can be inferred, respectively. However, the role of these functions has not yet been tested directly; we have to infer what consequence is reinforcing the behavior. To directly test the effects of a consequence on behavior, a functional analysis is needed.

FUNCTIONAL ANALYSIS

Functional analysis (Iwata et al., 1982) is a procedure in which hypotheses regarding the consequences (reinforcers) that maintain the difficult behavior are tested directly.

We might directly assess an escape function (negative reinforcement) by alternating two situations several times across days. In the first situation, the student is presented with a demanding task but is permitted to terminate the task briefly when displaying challenging behavior. For example, the teacher might turn away from the student and remove the demand for several seconds each time the student "acts up." In the second situation, the teacher might ignore the student as long as the student does not engage in challenging behavior but attend to (reprimand, discuss, redirect) the student briefly each time challenging behavior occurs. If challenging behavior occurs most often when it results in a break from the task, an escape function is identified. Conversely, if it occurs most often when it results in attention, an attention function is identified.

It is quite possible that a student's behavior is maintained by both attention and escape functions. In this case, problems occur in both situations described above. To show that the behavior occurs for both functions and not for other reasons such as automatic reinforcement, we include a control situation. For example, the above two situations might be alternated with a free-play situation, in which the student receives continuous attention but can engage in any activity that is preferred. In this situation, no demands are placed on the student, and constant attention is available. If no challenging behavior occurs during free play, then we know that the behavior is maintained by both escape and attention. If behavior occurs approximately equally across all three conditions, then we need to consider an alternative hypothesis.

There is no rule of thumb in determining how many times an assessment condition should be conducted. However, it is best to conduct as many as possible to make sure the results are consistent. Even very brief versions of functional analysis can have utility (Northup et al., 1991). Overall, we recommend the following sequence: We begin with a descriptive assessment that occurs over a 1- to 2-week period or until predictable times or activities are identified that correlate with challenging behavior. We then conduct a structural analysis of the most likely environmental variables and extend this analysis for at least 1 week. When a pattern is observed, we conduct only a few brief (e.g., 10-minute) conditions of the functional analysis, because we want to reduce the number of times we reinforce the behavior. For example, we might conduct two escape, two attention, and two free-play conditions in counterbalanced order.

MATCHING INTERVENTIONS TO THE FUNCTIONS OF PROBLEMATIC BEHAVIOR

In general, we can evaluate three functions of difficult behavior with the structural or functional analyses just described. These functions and the general intervention procedures matched to each function are provided in Table 2. As shown in this table, when the function is identified, we can initiate an intervention that is matched to the function of challenging behavior (Iwata et al., 1990). Conceptually this is rather simple, but it can be very challenging from a pragmatic standpoint. As you initiate an intervention, remember that you are going to teach the student a new skill and training will take at least as long as for any other skill that you might teach. In fact, this type of teaching will probably take even longer because the challenging behavior will interfere with

Table 2. Environmental functions and general interventions matched to function

Function	Type of reinforcement	Intervention approach
Attention	Positive	Provide attention contingent on appropriate or neutral behavior; withhold attention for challenging behavior; avoid reprimands, discussion, or other form of attention for challenging behavior
Tangible/preferred activities	Positive	Make access to preferred activities or toys contingent on appropriate behavior; restrict access at all other times; avoid changing activities or providing toys to "comfort" child or in response to challenging behavior
Escape/avoidance	Negative	Provide breaks and assistance only for appropriate behavior; reduce demands or change activities if possible, but never immediately after challenging behavior

learning, at least initially. As a final point, when you begin intervention, it is important not to give up. If the intervention is not successful, the challenging behavior may be even more resistant to subsequent intervention attempts. Thus, be sure you follow through with the intervention when you begin it.

For reasons that will probably never be totally known, the student has learned to engage in challenging behavior to receive reinforcement (to gain access to preferred situations or to escape nonpreferred situations). This does not necessarily mean that the student is aware of why he or she engages in these behaviors. It simply means that the student has been reinforced for these behaviors. The goal now is to replace the challenging behavior with more acceptable behavior (Carr, 1988). To accomplish this goal, we must remove all reinforcement for the challenging behavior and, instead, provide reinforcement for desired behavior.

Unfortunately, it often takes quite a bit of time initially to teach the student that a new set of rules is now in place. From the student's standpoint, you are taking away behavior that has worked in the past and are replacing it with new behaviors. When you consider the situation in this way, it makes sense that the student will continue to resist until the new behavior is learned. On a practical level, this means that difficult behavior will often get worse before it gets better (i.e., an extinction burst occurs). Even after the student has made progress and his or her behavior is improving, challenging behaviors often reappear on a periodic basis over time (i.e., spontaneous recovery occurs). These are normal events, and, if you anticipate them, the overall intervention may go more smoothly.

The main factor for success is to have confidence in the intervention. That is why we recommend conducting a structural or, if possible, a functional analysis prior to intervention. We have found that an experimental analysis gives us more confidence in our intervention than if we base intervention only on a descriptive assessment or on no assessment at all.

After the function of the challenging behavior is identified, there are two critical components to every successful intervention program. First, provide reinforcement *only* for desired behavior. Second, remove *all* reinforcement for challenging behavior. If either component is lacking, the probability of success is greatly reduced. The following steps are essential to successful intervention:

1. Identify as conclusively as possible the function of challenging behavior.
2. Determine as clearly as possible the alternative behavior you will reinforce.
3. Remove all reinforcement for challenging behavior.
4. Provide as much reinforcement as possible for desired behavior.

The most straightforward approach in intervention is to use differential reinforcement procedures plus extinction (Iwata et al., 1990). For attention-maintained behavior, this requires that you precisely and specifically show the student how to gain attention (e.g., show completed work, raise hand) and that you do not attend to instances of challenging behavior (planned ignoring). If it is needed, time-out may be used to augment ignoring. In other situations, you may want to position the student in the classroom to maximize the amount of attention received and then gradually increase the time that he or she works independently. For escape-maintained behavior, the student should be provided with breaks and assistance for working or staying on task, but the task should be continued for challenging behavior. Guided compliance may be needed for the student to continue the task. Initially, you may also want to reduce the demands until the student is successful and then gradually increase the demands over time.

SPECIFIC INTERVENTION OPTIONS

All behavioral interventions involve differential reinforcement procedures or variations of those procedures. This section describes three options that augment the standard differential reinforcement procedures summarized above.

Functional Communication Training

Functional communication training (FCT) was developed by Carr and Durand (1985), and an excellent summary of this procedure is provided by Durand and Carr (1991). (See also Carr et al., 1994; Durand, 1990; and Reichle & Wacker, 1993, for books on this approach.) Overall, we view FCT as a first step in effective intervention because other forms of differential reinforcement-based interventions will be needed after FCT has been successful

As described by Carr (1988), the goal of FCT is to replace challenging behavior with an alternative mand. A *mand* is a recognizable communicative response that requests, appropriately, a desired outcome. For example, if challenging behavior is maintained by attention, the student is taught to ask for, sign, gesture, or use an external device to gain attention. At the same time, the challenging behavior is ignored. For escape-maintained behavior, the student is taught to request a break, help, or a different activity (e.g., play). When the function of the challenging behavior has been identified, then the mand can serve the same function; and if only the mand is reinforced, then it makes intuitive sense that the student will learn the mand and to replace the challenging behavior with the mand.

To make this process go more smoothly, it is important that the mand be easy for the student to produce and be easily recognized by others. If complex or difficult-to-emit mands take more effort than the challenging behavior, then intervention will be more difficult. As discussed by Mace and Roberts (1993), four factors must be considered in the selection of alternative responses such as mands: 1) the efficiency of the response, 2) the delay between response and reinforcement, 3) the amount of reinforcement, and 4) the quality of reinforcement. If at all possible, make the mands easier to use than the challenging behavior—make the mand be more efficient, be more expedient, result in greater amounts of reinforcement, and produce a higher quality of reinforcement than the challenging behavior. An example of an FCT program conducted in relation to these four factors is provided in Table 3. As shown, three of four factors have been biased toward manding.

As stated previously, we view FCT as a first step because it is often not sufficient to require that the student only mand. Eventually, the student must also comply briefly before being permitted to receive reinforcement. We suggest that, initially, the goal is to reduce the occurrence of challenging behavior to zero or near zero for as long as possible. The longer difficult behavior is suppressed, the better the probability that increased demands can be placed on the student. If this initial objective is achieved, then you can begin to build in delays or increase the requirements for providing reinforcement.

For attention-maintained behavior, use a time-delay approach. Signal the student that you will attend to him or her (look at student and nod or place index finger in the air) and, initially, delay for only about 1 second. When this is successful, continue to signal the student but gradually increase the interval of delay. For escape-maintained behavior, initially require only that the student mand appropriately before providing a break from the task. Make the breaks longer than the time on task. Over time, gradually require more work ("You can take a break after you finish the next one") before the break is delivered and gradually reduce the length of the break.

Table 3. Example of functional communication training (FCT) program for attention-maintained behavior

Behavior	Factors			
	Efficiency	Delay	Amount	Quality
Mand (signing PLEASE)	Touch chest	Immediate (within 5 seconds)	30–60 seconds of attention	Enthusiastic, eye contact, touch student
Challenging behavior (self-injury)	Hit head	Delay as long as possible before blocking/ redirecting	Brief contact	Neutral, no eye contact
Bias comparison	Similar	Mand	Mand	Mand

Task Interspersal Procedures

This procedure is often useful when challenging behavior is used to escape task demands or nonpreferred tasks. Being able to follow directions is a critical skill for young children (Singer, Singer, & Horner, 1987), and they should not be allowed to avoid challenging tasks for long periods in their development. When a child engages in difficult behavior in response to an instruction or a task request, parents or teachers may begin to modify the type or content of their requests to decrease the likelihood that the child will engage in difficult behavior (Horner, Day, Sprague, O'Brien, & Heathfield, 1991). In essence, the child may no longer be asked to complete difficult, challenging, instructional, or functional tasks that are necessary to develop social, adaptive, and academic skills. A possible drawback to the use of FCT for children whose behavior functions to escape task demands is that FCT still allows the child to escape task completion.

Since the late 1970s, task interspersal procedures have been used to increase compliance (Dunlap, 1984). Task interspersal procedures deliver short and familiar tasks that are likely to be performed correctly and that have a high probability of being followed by reinforcement. In this way, the child is able to experience success and receive positive social reactions before engaging in a more difficult or less preferred task that typically is associated with increased effort.

Horner and colleagues (1991) demonstrated that interspersed requests are simple, effective, and efficient procedures that can produce decreased frequencies of challenging behavior and increased compliance to instruction on new or difficult tasks. For example, if the difficult or nonpreferred task is for the child to brush his or her teeth, toothbrushing would be interspersed with a "fun" task, such as pointing to different body parts or blowing bubbles (see Table 4). The amount of time engaged in the difficult or less preferred tasks is increased gradually until the fun task occurs only at the completion of the difficult task.

We have used interspersed requests with good success when working with young children in their homes with parents conducting the intervention (see second example in Table 4). We have always interspersed the nonpreferred task in the context of a pre-

Table 4. Task interspersal procedures

Hard task demand	Fun task	Intervention components
Toothbrushing	Blowing bubbles	1) Child is allowed to blow bubbles, and parental requests to brush teeth are interspersed.
		2) Positive attention and praise are provided during bubble blowing and toothbrushing.
Putting neutral toys away	Playing with preferred toys	1) Child is allowed to play with toys, and parental requests to put specific toys away are interspersed.
		2) Positive attention and praise are provided during toy play and toy pick-up activities.
		3) Child is redirected to pick up toys for challenging behavior.

ferred (low-demand) play situation. For example, Luke, a 3-year-old boy, engaged in aggressive, destructive, and self-injurious behavior when presented with task demands. During the structural analysis, we noted that Luke often chose to play with a set of connecting blocks but only if he could play "his way." The difficult task demand was that Luke's mother request that he place one block on top of another (e.g., "Luke, put this red block on top of the green block"). Initially, Luke ran from the task, threw the block, attempted to aggress toward his mother, destroyed items within the home, or engaged in head banging in response to her request. The intervention interspersed parental requests 1) for Luke to take a block presented to him by his mother and place the block anywhere on the building structure (a high-probability response), and 2) for Luke to place one block in a specific location indicated by the parent (e.g., "Luke, put this red block on top of the green one, right here") (a low-probability response). We always began with the high-probability response. As a result of interspersing high-probability with low-probability task requests, we were able to decrease Luke's resistance to task completion, increase his task compliance, and increase positive parent–child social interactions.

The process of using interspersed requests, then, includes identifying either a variation of the task (parent- vs. child-directed play) or a compatible response (blowing bubbles while being requested to brush teeth) that the child typically will do. Begin with the high-probability task and intersperse it with the original low-probability task. This process increases the overall amount of reinforcement the child receives. Initially, spend much more time doing the fun task than the challenging task, and then gradually increase the time spent on the challenging task. Finally, escape extinction is likely to be needed. This means that when the challenging task is presented or requested, compliance is needed before returning to the fun task. Remember not to reinforce challenging behavior by, in this case, permitting the child to avoid the challenging task.

Choice Making

A choice-making program is a good intervention option for students whose difficult behavior is maintained by preference or tangible reinforcement. The first step in a choice-making program is to identify clearly what is preferred or reinforcing to the student. Researchers have used a variety of methods to identify preferred stimuli that can be used to reinforce desired behavior. These methods have included training students with mental retardation to use a microswitch to indicate reinforcer preferences (Wacker, Berg, Wiggins, Muldoon, & Cavanaugh, 1985), measuring the percentage of approach responses to particular items (Pace, Ivancic, Edwards, Iwata, & Page, 1985), and having students choose between two available items (Fisher et al., 1992).

When both preferred and nonpreferred activities or items have been identified, choice making can be incorporated into intervention (Cooper et al., 1992; Dunlap, Kern-Dunlap, Clarke, & Robbins, 1991). For example, Dunlap et al. (1991) used choices with an adolescent girl with multiple disabilities and a long history of disruptive behavior (e.g., aggression, destruction). When the student was allowed to choose the academic tasks to be completed, substantial reductions in challenging behavior occurred. Similarly, Cooper and colleagues (1992) used a choice-making procedure with a 9-year-old boy with a disability who was frequently noncompliant with his teacher's requests. The student was allowed to choose between preferred and nonpreferred academic tasks as opposed to having the teacher simply assign him the preferred task. The results showed that the student performed best during the choice sessions, even though he was provided with preferred activities during the no-choice sessions. This suggested that providing a choice of activities was as important as the relative preference of the activities. In these two examples, choice was the primary intervention variable and, given the pragmatic benefits, it should be considered whenever possible.

In most cases, however, we have found that choice making works because one option is preferred over the other. The child complies initially because he or she has a preference for one of the tasks presented. This is important because the child is learning to follow the teacher's requests. Gradually, over time, the choices offered can be less related to the child's preferences. Because the child has learned to make a choice and then to comply, the degree of preference between the available options can be reduced over time. Basically, the child has learned a rule: Make a choice and then complete the assignment. Eventually, this is modified to a more common practice: Complete the less preferred task and then you can have the more preferred task.

In home settings with young children, we have used choice procedures in a slightly different way. Rob, a 4-year-old boy diagnosed with fragile X syndrome and mental retardation, engaged in destruction, noncompliance, and self-injury (face slapping, finger biting) when his mother asked him to do something that was nonpreferred. Choice-making sessions were conducted in the family living room, which was divided by placing a strip of masking tape down the center of the room. At the beginning of each session, Rob's mother directed him to the masking tape and described the available choices. Rob was allowed to move freely between the two areas, and we measured the percentage of time he spent in each area. His choice initially was between playing with his mother with preferred items or playing alone with neutral items. He chose to play with his mother and the preferred toys. This choice was, of course, expected, but it taught him the rule: Make a choice. His next choice was to play with his mother with neutral toys or to play alone with preferred toys. He chose to play with his mother. Finally, his choice was between directed play with his mother (a problem situation in the past) or playing alone with low-preference toys. In addition, if Rob did not comply with his mother's request after choosing to play with her, she used hand-on-hand guidance to assist him. After some resistance, he consistently chose to play with his mother and to play "Mom's way." Thus, at the end of the intervention, Rob was voluntarily complying to his mother's requests based on a choice-making intervention approach. We gradually increased the amount of effort required of him until he was completing less preferred activities for longer periods of time.

FURTHER CONSIDERATIONS

Thus far, we have described several alternative interventions that can be matched to the function of the challenging behavior. These interventions are useful for initiating the intervention process and can have excellent long-term results (Durand & Carr, 1991).

However, to increase the probability that intervention will result in durable, positive effects over time, it is important to consider 1) stimulus generalization and 2) response generalization. Stimulus generalization, in this case, refers to the display of acceptable behavior across people, settings, and tasks. Our goal is ultimately for the child to display the newly acquired behavior across situations. Using FCT as an example, the goal is for the child to generalize the use of mands from home to school and from classroom to classroom. Response generalization refers to the development of an increased number of acceptable behaviors. Thus, in addition to signing PLEASE to request attention, it would be desirable if the child also learned to engage in other appropriate behaviors to gain attention (e.g., hold up completed work, smile at the teacher). This section briefly describes procedures for programming these types of generalized responses.

Stimulus Generalization

Typically, intervention is initiated within one setting, using one adult, and working with one specific type of task demand or activity with the child. Through consistency and practice, decreases in challenging behavior are often achieved but only in the intervention context. Generalization is the demonstration of a desired behavior (e.g., use of the sign for BREAK to obtain a brief break from a task demand) under conditions that are different from the training situation and in which no specific training or very limited training has occurred (Stokes & Baer, 1977). Using this definition, generalization has occurred when either 1) a specific task (e.g., picking up toys) is completed in an untrained situation (e.g., at Grandma's house) or 2) the amount of training needed to perform subsequent variations of the task (e.g., picking up clothing instead of toys) is substantially reduced. Most people, whether they are individuals with or without developmental disabilities, need at least a minimal amount of direct instruction when presented with new versions of a task (e.g., placing toys on a shelf instead of into a bucket). We describe two strategies for producing generalization: sufficient exemplars and general case instruction.

One way to promote generalization of specific behaviors to novel situations is to provide the child with training on multiple (sufficient) exemplars of relevant settings, persons conducting training, and tasks used to conduct training (Stokes & Baer, 1977). By providing training across a variety of settings, with a variety of people, and with a variety of tasks and activities, you increase the likelihood that the child will continue to demonstrate desired responses in spite of changes in setting, task requests, or the people making the request. Training is considered sufficient when the child generalizes across changes in antecedent stimuli. For example, when training is conducted to teach a child to say help in order to obtain assistance in picking up toys, initial training might be conducted in the home by the parent. With sufficient exemplar training, the focus of training would then include expansion of the number of people who prompt the child to ask for assistance (e.g., Dad, Grandma, Grandpa, a neighbor), the situations in which the child is prompted to ask for help (e.g., getting dressed, brushing teeth, obtaining access to food items), and the places in which the child is prompted to ask for help (e.g., other people's homes, library, school). In general, sufficient exemplars training is used to promote generalization across variations in the situation, and training continues until the child is presented with a new situation and performs in the desired manner.

General case instruction is an extension of sufficient exemplars training (O'Neill & Reichle, 1993). Potential variations of the task are analyzed according to the specific stimulus features, and response demands are selected for training (Berg, Wacker, & Flynn, 1990). For example, if we are teaching a child to recognize the color red, we would include a variety of examples (red toy, red clothing item, red triangle, large red objects, small red objects). In this way, training ensures that the defining characteristic has to do with the color red, not the shape, size, texture, or location of the training materials. Teaching the general case to children with challenging behavior means that instruction must include different situations that vary in some way (asking for attention in one-to-one, small-group, and unstructured play situations). Rather than simply training multiple examples, the teacher or parent determines prior to training what variations are likely in the people (adults, children), settings, and tasks that the child will encounter. Training is conducted to encompass as many of these variations as possible.

Equally important, children are taught when to display their newly acquired behavior. For example, requesting a break via signing is not always relevant. Thus, during training, it is important to include both relevant and irrelevant situations and teach the child to discriminate between those situations. Relative to FCT programs, we most often teach both a break and an attention mand and set up training situations in which the child must select the appropriate mand.

Response Generalization

Response generalization refers to increases in other appropriate behaviors when a target behavior is reinforced. For example, when the child has learned to gain attention via signing, it is likely that a variety of other socially acceptable behaviors will occur. The child may smile, use other words or signs, or display physical affection. These behaviors are likely to be pleasing to the care provider and thus also to result in reinforcement. It is critical that these behaviors are noticed and reinforced as they occur. In this way, intervention can result in the acquisition of a broad array of appropriate responses and not be limited to only one or two target responses. Relative to FCT programs, as an example, the development of collateral behaviors can have important implications for maintenance. Initially, the mand serves as a one-to-one replacement for the problem behavior (Carr, 1988). However, as new positive behaviors occur, the opportunities for increases in overall reinforcement to the child increase because the child now has numerous behaviors, not just a mand, that are reinforced.

Billy's situation illustrates this process. Billy, a 2½-year-old-boy, was diagnosed with developmental delay. According to Billy's mother, she carried him around for most of the day because attempts to set him down resulted in severe tantrums and self-injurious behavior (head banging). The results of a functional analysis confirmed the hypothesis that parent attention maintained Billy's difficult behavior. Based on this assessment, Billy's mother implemented functional communication training in which

Billy was taught to sign PLEASE to obtain his mother's attention. Throughout the intervention, preferred toys were paired with his mother's attention. Each time he touched a toy, he received attention, and, after several weeks, he played by himself and only occasionally signed for attention. His mother taught him to play as a collateral effect of the FCT program. Thus, when his mother was busy, he often played. As Billy spent more time in appropriate play, he displayed many new play and social behaviors. These new behaviors also were reinforced by his mother, and eventually he often ignored his mother because he was busy playing. Through incidental instruction, his mother taught him a number of desirable behaviors, all connected with toy play, that further suppressed displays of self-injury.

CONCLUSION

This chapter presented a functional approach to the assessment of and intervention with challenging behavior. The process is complex and involves multiple phases and methodologies. However, the essential critical properties of this approach are to 1) identify the function of or reinforcer for the challenging behavior, 2) provide reinforcement for desired behavior only, 3) train in novel situations to produce stimulus generalization, and 4) take advantage of teaching opportunities to reinforce novel behavior that also competes with challenging behavior.

REFERENCES

Axelrod, S. (1987). Functional and structural analyses of behavior: Approaches leading to reduced use of punishment procedures? *Research in Developmental Disabilities, 8,* 165–178.

Berg, W., Wacker, D., & Flynn, T. (1990). Teaching generalization and maintenance of work behavior. In F. Rusch (Ed.), *Supported employment: Models, methods, and issues* (pp. 140–160). Sycamore, IL: Sycamore Press.

Bijou, S.W., Peterson, R.F., & Ault, M.H. (1968). A method to integrate descriptive and experimental field studies at the level of data and empirical concepts. *Journal of Applied Behavior Analysis, 1,* 175–191.

Carr, E.G. (1988). Functional equivalence as a mechanism of response generalization. In R. Horner, G. Dunlap, & R.L. Koegel (Eds.), *Generalization and maintenance: Life-style changes in applied settings* (pp. 221–241). Baltimore: Paul H. Brookes Publishing Co.

Carr, E.G., & Durand, V.M. (1985). Reducing behavior problems through functional communication training. *Journal of Applied Behavior Analysis, 18,* 111–126.

Carr, E.G., Levin, L., McConnachie, G., Carlson, J., Kemp, D., & Smith, C. (1994). *Communication-based intervention for problem behavior: A user's guide for producing positive change.* Baltimore: Paul H. Brookes Publishing Co.

Cooper, L.J., Wacker, D.P., Thursby, D., Plagmann, L.A., Harding, J., & Derby, K.M. (1992). Analysis of the role of task preferences, task demands, and adult attention on child behavior in outpatient and classroom settings. *Journal of Applied Behavior Analysis, 25,* 823–840.

Dunlap, G. (1984). The influence of task variation and maintenance tasks on the learning and affect of autistic children. *Journal of Experimental Child Psychology, 37,* 41–64.

Dunlap, G., Kern-Dunlap, L., Clarke, S., & Robbins, F.R. (1991). Functional assessment, curricular revision, and severe behavior problems. *Journal of Applied Behavior Analysis, 24,* 387–397.

Durand, V.M. (1990). *Severe behavior problems: A functional communication training approach.* New York: Guilford Press.

Durand, V.M., & Carr, E.G. (1991). Functional communication training to reduce challenging behavior: Maintenance and application in new settings. *Journal of Applied Behavior Analysis, 24,* 251–264.

Fisher, W., Piazza, C., Bowman, L., Hagopian, L., Owens, J., & Slevin, I. (1992). A comparison of two approaches for identifying reinforcers for persons with severe and profound disabilities. *Journal of Applied Behavior Analysis, 25,* 491–498.

Horner, R., Day, H., Sprague, J., O'Brien, M., & Heathfield, L. (1991). Interspersed requests: A nonaversive procedure for reducing aggression and self-injury during instruction. *Journal of Applied Behavior Analysis, 24,* 265–278.

Iwata, B.A., Dorsey, M.F., Slifer, K.J., Bauman, K.D., & Richman, G.S. (1982). Toward a functional analysis of self-injury. *Analysis and Intervention in Developmental Disabilities, 2,* 3–20.

Iwata, B., Vollmer, T., & Zarcone, J. (1990). The experimental (functional) analysis of behavior disorders: Methodology, applications, and limitations. In A. Repp & N. Singh (Eds.), *Perspectives on the use of nonaversive and aversive interventions for persons with developmental disabilities* (pp. 301–330). Sycamore, IL: Sycamore Press.

Mace, F.C., & Lalli, J.S. (1991). Linking descriptive and experimental analyses in the treatment of bizarre speech. *Journal of Applied Behavior Analysis, 24,* 553–562.

Mace, F.C., & Roberts, M.L. (1993). Factors affecting selection of behavioral interventions. In J. Reichle & D. Wacker (Eds.), *Communication and language intervention: Vol. 3. Communicative alternatives to challenging behavior: Integrating functional assessment and intervention strategies* (pp. 113–133). Baltimore: Paul H. Brookes Publishing Co.

Northup, J., Wacker, D., Sasso, G., Steege, M., Cigrand, K., Cook, J., & DeRaad, A. (1991). A brief functional analysis of aggressive and alternative behavior in an outclinic setting. *Journal of Applied Behavior Analysis, 24,* 509–522.

O'Neill, R., & Reichle, J. (1993). Addressing socially motivated challenging behaviors by establishing communicative alternatives: Basics of a general-case approach. In J. Reichle & D. Wacker (Eds.), *Communication and language intervention: Vol. 3. Communicative alternatives to challenging behavior: Integrating functional assessment and intervention strategies* (pp. 205–235). Baltimore: Paul H. Brookes Publishing Co.

Pace, G., Ivancic, M., Edwards, G., Iwata, B., & Page, T. (1985). Assessment of stimulus preference and reinforcer value with profoundly retarded individuals. *Journal of Applied Behavior Analysis, 18,* 249–255.

Reichle, J., & Wacker, D. (Eds.). (1993). *Communication and language intervention series: Vol. 3. Communicative alternatives to challenging behavior: Integrating functional assessment and intervention strategies.* Baltimore: Paul H. Brookes Publishing Co.

Singer, D., Singer, J., & Horner, R. (1987). Using pretask requests to increase the probability of compliance for students with severe disabilities. *Journal of The Association for Persons with Severe Handicaps, 12,* 287–291.

Stokes, T., & Baer, D. (1977). An implicit technology of generalization. *Journal of Applied Behavior Analysis, 10,* 349–367.

Touchette, P.E., MacDonald, R.F., & Langer, S.N. (1985). A scatter plot for identifying stimulus control of problem behavior. *Journal of Applied Behavior Analysis, 18,* 343–351.

Wacker, D.P., & Berg, W.K. (1992a). *Functional analysis of feeding and interaction disorders with young children who are profoundly disabled.* Washington, DC: U.S. Department of Education, National Institute on Disability and Rehabilitation Research.

Wacker, D.P., Berg, W.K. (1992b). *Inducing reciprocal parent/child interactions.* Washington, DC: Department of Health and Human Services, National Institute of Child Health and Human Development.

Wacker, D., Berg, W., Wiggins, B., Muldoon, M., & Cavanaugh, J. (1985). Evaluation of rein-
    forcer preferences for profoundly handicapped students. *Journal of Applied Behavior Analy-
    sis, 18,* 173–178.
Wacker, D., Northup, J., & Cooper, L. (1992). Behavioral assessment. In D. Greydanus &
    M. Wolraich (Eds.), *Behavioral pediatrics* (pp. 57–69). New York: Springer-Verlag.

22

Structuring the Classroom to Prevent Disruptive Behaviors

William Stainback and Susan Stainback

THE PRECEDING CHAPTERS in this section on behavioral concerns have introduced important practical considerations for addressing disruptive behaviors. The focus of this chapter is on structuring the classroom to prevent discipline problems from occurring in the first place. The ideas and strategies presented are not particularly new or innovative, but are simple, well-known, common-sense strategies that teachers have used for years to prevent discipline problems by students with a wide range of abilities and characteristics. They arose from the authors' experiences in classroom settings, reviews of research on preventing disruptive behaviors (e.g., Anderson & Prawat, 1983; Brophy, 1981; Evertson, 1982; Jones & Jones, 1994; Stainback & Stainback, 1980), and interviews and informal conversations with practicing classroom teachers who have been successful in preventing discipline problems.

PHYSICAL ARRANGEMENT AND TRAFFIC RULES

To prevent discipline problems, the teacher needs to be aware of what is actually going on in the classroom. One way to facilitate this awareness is to arrange classroom furniture and equipment to permit visual monitoring of students from either a sitting or standing position. The teacher should be able to make a visual sweep of the room and detect when students need assistance and what social interaction patterns are occurring.

It also is important to consider how students travel in the classroom. Heavily traveled classroom areas should be free of obstacles and wide enough to accommodate the traffic flow. In narrow, cluttered, and congested travel lanes, students often bump into furniture and one another, which can provoke outbreaks of laughing and shoving. Clear, uncongested traffic areas can reduce the probability of such disruptive behaviors.

Teachers can identify major traffic routes by "walking through" the activities that are likely to occur during the course of a school day. They may find that furniture and equipment placed in close proximity to storage areas, the coatroom, or the classroom door must be relocated to allow for smooth, unobstructed travel. Likewise, traffic pattern testing may suggest a classroom plan or rule that can eliminate some congestion or disruption; for example, no more than three students are allowed in the coatroom at one time; enter the coatroom from the left and exit to the right.

TIME MANAGEMENT

A major objective of time management is to increase student time on task. This not only increases learning opportunities but also prevents discipline problems by keeping attention focused on productive school activities. The more time students spend on task, the greater the probability of increased learning as well as less idle or "down" time available for them to engage in mischievous or other inappropriate school behaviors. Time on task may include teacher- and student-planned activities not only in academic areas but also in areas such as peer social interaction, play, and free time. Time on task need not be consistently teacher directed. Students need to be given the responsibility to become actively involved in developing, directing, and carrying out their own learning activities if they are to develop independent, goal-directed learning skills.

Effective time management in the classroom is facilitated by the teacher's and students' preparedness for daily lessons and activities and the ready accessibility of materials and equipment. Some interruptions or delays are unavoidable; for example, a student becomes ill or the principal needs immediate information about a student. However, the teacher should be careful not to add to these interruptions by taking class time to plan what comes next in math or to find the materials needed for art class. Any time students are idle, one or two will inevitably try to disrupt the classroom.

ASSIGNMENTS

The manner in which assignments are developed and presented is critical to facilitating learning and preventing discipline problems. Relating the assignments to the needs and interests of the students and carefully choosing the methods used to present assignments can influence their effectiveness, particularly for students who experience learning difficulties. The following suggestions are aimed at enhancing the effectiveness of classroom assignments.

Assignments should be clear and easily understood by the students. Ambiguity can lead to frustration and may cause some students to avoid or withdraw from the assigned task and engage in unacceptable behavior. Instructions should be stated so that students know exactly what is expected of them.

Assignments should be geared to the ability level of each student. If an assignment is too easy, some students may become bored. If the assignment is too difficult for others, they may become frustrated. In either case, they will tend to engage in other activities that are more reinforcing for them.

Assignments should be structured so that each student is provided with an opportunity to succeed. A student who is experiencing success is less likely to be in a rebellious frame of mind and can gain attention of the teacher and peers without acting out. The experience of success also builds the students' own expectations of success so that they are less likely to become apathetic about the classroom situation or uncaring about the events that occur in the classroom, either good or bad. This type of student involvement can be a key factor in preventing classroom discipline problems.

Materials and assignments should be presented in such a way that the students look forward to each school day. Although there are materials, topics, and assignments that are not, by their very nature, particularly exciting and others that require a great deal of repetition, much can be done to enhance the attractiveness of such activities. For example, probing questions, games, discussions, special projects, debates, films, guest speakers, and field trips can make almost any subject area more interesting and exciting.

The attitude of the teacher in presenting assignments also is vitally important. Enthusiasm is contagious. The teacher should treat assignments and new materials as something special and get students actively involved by letting them tell about any experiences they have had with the subject. Tasks should be related to things that are of interest and are familiar to the students. They should be allowed to discover new information, ideas, and concepts on their own in a structured way and to share their information with their classmates. Less interesting subject areas can be paired with more interesting material. For example, during math class the teacher can let the students determine how much money will be needed to grow a flower garden to beautify the school grounds. Then, if possible, they can carry out the project.

Finally, the teacher should provide immediate feedback and recognition for accomplishments made by each student, regardless of how small. Feedback on even a weekly basis is generally too infrequent to ignite interest and elevate motivation, especially for students who experience learning and behavior difficulties. One way to provide immediate feedback is for students to exchange their work or for a teacher assistant to check the students' work. Remember, a student who does not understand what is expected of him or her and who is unchallenged, unsuccessful, disinterested, or uninformed regarding progress can be disruptive. However, if assignments are appropriately selected and presented, such problems can be reduced substantially.

GROUPING PRACTICES

How students are grouped in a classroom can influence the amount of disruptive behavior that occurs. Unfortunately, disruptive students tend to gravitate toward each other. When disruptive students are grouped together, they tend to model, encourage, and reinforce each other's disruptive behaviors. As a consequence, the whole group displays an increase in disruptive behaviors.

However, disruptive students who are grouped with well-behaved students display fewer disruptive behaviors, and the group as a whole tends to remain well-behaved (Stainback, Stainback, Etscheidt, & Doud, 1986). This decrease in disruptive behavior appears to be a function not only of appropriate behavioral models but also of peer pressure by which the well-behaved students tend to ignore the disruptive students' inappropriate behaviors while encouraging and rewarding desirable behaviors.

Another consideration in grouping students to prevent the occurrence of inappropriate behavior is to organize group activities in a cooperative rather than competitive or individualistic manner. Cooperative group structuring, in which the group as a whole is assigned a common goal, tends to promote more goal-oriented student behavior than structures in which students are encouraged to work alone with the purpose of either outperforming each other (competition) or meeting a set criterion (individualistic learning) (Johnson & Johnson, 1980, 1986). In cooperative goal structuring, all students must remain task oriented and coordinate their efforts to achieve the group's goal. (See Chapter 11 of this book for more information about cooperative learning.)

CLASSROOM ATMOSPHERE

The consistent themes or attitudes that are conveyed when presenting classroom rules, materials, activities, and assignments contribute to the development of a general classroom atmosphere or orientation. There are a number of themes that tend to foster positive, productive behavior in the classroom.

Expectations and plans for success, rather than for failure, can help foster positive attitudes in students regarding their own classroom behavior and the behavior of their peers. Students enjoy being around teachers who are positive and pleasant and who convey the attitude that they enjoy their students as worthwhile and successful members of the group.

Teacher recognition of appropriate, rather than inappropriate, behaviors and of achievements, rather than deficits, can also promote a positive classroom atmosphere. One approach that many teachers have adopted to help them focus on the appropriate behaviors of a particular student is to record the number of times the student displays certain desired appropriate behaviors and how many times the behaviors were recognized and praised.

Recognition and understanding of each classroom member as an individual with his or her own unique set of characteristics, needs, past experiences, and home environment is another classroom theme that can reduce the potential for discipline problems. By recognizing each student as an individual, the teacher can foster classroom communication on a more personal and meaningful level. Students' self-concept can be enhanced if teachers indicate that they consider their students important enough to learn about and know personally.

A classroom theme or attitude that communicates the expectation of productive work habits can also prevent discipline problems. For example, a bulletin board can display the good work of *all* students, with the name of every class member listed and a corresponding space for each student to place the work of his or her choice. The best work of every student is displayed every week, thereby communicating the expectation that every child in the class will do good work every week. In addition, classroom models, rules, procedures, and materials can be presented that reflect standards of preparedness, neatness, and organization in assigned activities.

Students can be supported in their development of greater self-direction and independence by adhering to consistent routines and structured procedures in the classroom on a daily basis. For example, posting a schedule of daily activities and reviewing the schedule each morning lets students know when and what materials will need to be put away or taken out at various times throughout the day.

Similarly, rules can be developed, reviewed, and posted that inform students how to carry out routine classroom activities such as sharpening pencils, getting supplies, or going to the lavatory or what to do when a task is completed. Individual daily student checklists of classroom activities and duties or individual student folders outlining tasks to be completed can also help to guide them through a class session or day with minimal teacher assistance. Such procedures can be used to at least some extent with most, if not all, students if care is taken to adjust the presentation of the directions to meet individual student needs, whether in written, pictorial, or audio- or videotaped form.

Fostering a classroom theme or attitude that each student shares responsibility with the teacher for achieving his or her own learning objectives also can do much to focus student attention on learning and reduce potential discipline problems. Promoting such an attitude can be enhanced by working with each student to select appropriate learning objectives that will encourage a task or goal orientation in the classroom.

PROFESSIONAL DEMEANOR

Adopting a professional demeanor with students can reduce the chance of having minor classroom infractions develop into major discipline problems. A professional demeanor can be fostered by maintaining a calm perspective in the face of inappropriate behaviors. Teachers should draw as little attention as possible to inappropriate behavior and focus on helping the students exhibit appropriate behavior. In addition, teachers can build trust and understanding by handling classroom problems in private whenever possible. Public reprimands often lead to unnecessary embarrassment and humiliation. Teachers should be consistent in their responses to behaviors so students know what to expect. Finally, as much as possible, classroom problems should be handled by teachers themselves, rather than by other school personnel, to indicate that they have the knowledge and authority to handle decisions regarding infractions.

CONCLUSION

All students, regardless of whether or not they have been classified as having disabilities, need to learn to behave to the best of their abilities. It is important that inclusive classrooms be places where students feel safe and have opportunities to learn without being unduly disrupted by other students.

The best way to handle discipline problems is to prevent them from occurring in the first place. Although there is no foolproof way to prevent all discipline problems, proper organization and structuring of physical arrangements, time management, assignments, grouping practices, and the atmosphere in a classroom can help reduce the number of such occurrences.

REFERENCES

Anderson, L., & Prawat, R. (1983). Responsibility in the classroom: A synthesis of research on teaching self-control. *Educational Leadership, 40,* 62–66.

Brophy, J. (1981). Teacher praise: A functional analysis. *Review of Educational Research, 51,* 301–318.

Evertson, C. (1982). *What research tells us about managing classroom instruction effectively.* Palo Alto, CA: Teaching and Learning Institute.

Johnson, D., & Johnson, R. (1980). Integrating handicapped students into the mainstream. *Exceptional Children, 47,* 90–98.

Johnson, D., & Johnson, R. (1986). Mainstreaming and cooperative learning strategies. *Exceptional Children, 52,* 553–561.

Jones, V., & Jones, L. (1994). *Comprehensive classroom management.* Boston: Allyn & Bacon.

Stainback, S., & Stainback, W. (1980). *Educating children with severe maladaptive behavior.* New York: Grune & Stratton.

Stainback, W., Stainback, S., Etscheidt, S., & Doud, J. (1986). A nonintrusive intervention for acting out behavior. *Teaching Exceptional Children, 19*(1), 38–41.

23

Some Notes on Positive Approaches for Students with Difficult Behavior

Herbert Lovett

THE "TRUE" NATURE of education has been the source of reiterative and rebarbative debate since the advent of written language, with no end in sight. Camps tend to form based on two underlying systems of belief about people, including learners: One arises out of a basic faith in human nature, and one arises out of fear and distrust of human nature. To take a few examples: The learner already knows and the teacher helps primarily with remembering (e.g., Plato); The learner is ignorant and the teacher's job is to instill the information necessary to be considered "educated" (e.g., Locke). Burgess (1973) presented a similar dichotomy in *The Wanting Seed,* which is set in a futuristic Britain where the prevailing ideology of government oscillates between the Pelphase, named for the Gaelic heresiarch, Pelagius, who believed that people are capable of procuring their own salvation, and the Gusphase, named for Augustine Bishop of Hippo, whose theology held that humanity is born in original sin and salvation is possible only through the church.

A third variant of this dichotomy was offered by the English poet Matthew Arnold (1869/1962), whose father was the eminent liberal educator Thomas Arnold and who himself was an inspector of schools. Arnold suggested an essential division in European history between two world views that he labeled Hellenism and Hebraism:

> The uppermost idea with Hellenism is to see things as they really are; the uppermost idea with Hebraism is conduct and obedience. Nothing can do away with this inef-

The author wishes to thank Susannah Joyce, Jill Long, and Teresa Sotelo for suggestions and helpful comments made along the way.

faceable difference.... While Hebraism seizes upon certain plain, capital intimations of universal order, and rivets itself, one may say, with unequaled grandeur of earnestness and intensity on the study and observance of them, the bent of Hellenism is to follow, with flexible activity, the whole play of the universal order, to be apprehensive of missing any part of it, of sacrificing one part to another, to slip away from resting in this or that intimation of it, however capital. An unclouded clearness of mind, an unimpeded play of thought, is what this bent drives at. The governing idea of Hellenism is *spontaneity of consciousness;* that of Hebraism, *strictness of conscience.* (Arnold 1869/1962, pp. 132–133)

It is possible to consider some of Arnold's points in terms of people with disabilities generally and for those with "difficult behavior" specifically: The uppermost idea in Hellenism is to see things as they really are, while the uppermost idea in Hebraism is conduct and obedience.

American culture and its attendant educational policy has a long history of struggling with education as enlightenment and education as training for civic conduct and obedience. The Jeffersonian ideal of a literate, well-informed, population (presumably capable of seeing things as they really are) was co-opted in the 19th century by the need for a compliant industrial work force. American education, a profoundly conservative and slow-changing enterprise, still sees one of its prime tasks as providing good workers to the world of business.

Production lines intentionally employed each individual as a part of a large production machine. The model of the factory owner at the top of the pyramid giving orders to the bottom was, at one time, an efficient way to manufacture goods. It also presumes a bottom layer that will give up individuality and ownership in return for a wage. That America is, for the most part, no more.

VIEWS OF PEOPLE WITH DISABILITIES

Schools are routinely challenged to discover what proper conduct is and how to promote it. Given that students with disabilities are still often seen as receiving an education by virtue of the public's fond indulgence, any deviation from behavioral norms on their part is more quickly noticed. In addition, many learners with disabilities need accommodation in both instruction and in understanding, and, when their behaviors annoy or alarm, they are seen as "too much." It might be just as accurate to describe the capacities of the school as being "too little."

The Greeks valued youth and physical beauty as reflective of a moral state of goodness. A person with a disability could not, by definition, be good. True, Socrates, who was notoriously unhandsome, was seen as the wisest of the Greeks even in his own lifetime, but a person with a significant physical or mental disability would have been seen as an inferior person. This prejudice lingers.

In contemporary thinking, this bias has a more positive potential and can be seen in those who would attribute difficult behavior to neurological or physiological conditions: Donnellan and Leary's (1993) work showing pervasive developmental disorders (PDD) (e.g., autistic disorder, Tourette syndrome, and attention-deficit/hyperactivity disorder) as manifestations of motor disorders or Mesulam's (1985) discussion of aggression as secondary to temporolimbic disorders. This thinking moves misconduct from personal intention to involuntary movements of a body that does not accurately conform to will.

The Old Testament view of the body is that it distracts from the contemplation of God's will. The highest passion is to delight greatly in his commandments (Arnold, 1962). This view works against people with disabilities in that they cannot conform to norms of those without disabilities. If a culture puts an emphasis on right conduct over right thinking (a variant on the running argument of content vs. process), then those who can conform behaviorally have a higher value than those who cannot. Many people with disabilities, for whatever reasons, do not conform to social norms. This is not surprising because norms are set by the most powerful people, and people with disabilities (with some rare exceptions) are not usually found in positions of power.

Obviously, in a world view that sees children as blank slates, none of them can be seen to think properly. The image of people with mental disabilities as perpetual children comes, in part, from this general idea of children. Because there can be no rationally derived happiness by individuals who cannot, by definition, think rationally, then the only recourse is to govern their every impulse and every action. Rational thought is a network of prescriptions to govern every moment, every impulse, and every action of the life of an individual with disabilities. This stereotype persists in all forms of education for young learners and extends to people of all ages with intellectual disabilities.

TRUST VERSUS MISTRUST

Teachers facilitate learning and react to or think about difficult behaviors based on their trust or mistrust of students. Implications of this situation on educational practices are outlined in Table 1.

IMPLICATIONS FOR RESPONDING TO PEOPLE WITH DIFFICULT BEHAVIOR

The power of any relationship is in its mutuality—not mutuality at the level of money or status, necessarily, but at the level of empathy and concern. This mutuality has been classically difficult to articulate because it is almost entirely nonverbal. Our first experience of empathy and complete focus happens when we are infants and the center of adult concern, often for no other reason than that we exist. As we learn to return this empathy and focus, we may learn social forms for them, but the genuine feelings are nonverbal and difficult to quantify.

All relationships, of whatever emotional intensity or with whatever external demands—friendship, marriage, or other partnerships—are at risk of becoming authoritarian, arbitrary, or abusive. By the same token, even inherently unequal relationships—physician–patient, supervisor–employee—can become mutually supportive. The difference is that the controlling factors of the relationship are internal to the

Table 1. The dichotomy of trust and mistrust of students

Trust	Mistrust
Guidelines	
Classrooms that establish their own codes of conduct	The policy of zero tolerance for violence in schools and automatic expulsion for aggression
Trusting teachers and learners to choose content	Imposition of an antique and irrelevant (but nonetheless uniform) national curriculum
Abolishing grades in favor of individual progress reports	Efforts to impose conformity through school uniforms and the scheduling of prayers in school
Consumer satisfaction	Standardized tests and publicizing results
	External review and standards
Collaboration	
Negotiated cooperation among learners and the teacher	Students following the teacher's leadership efficiency
Because students generally love to learn, the sense that the teacher's job primarily is to support them in what they want to learn first	Because education is accompanied by some pain, the sense that students tend to avoid learning (the teacher's job is to model and provide discipline through a system of rewards and punishments)
Content	
Something the student finds worth learning	Something the teacher (or school board) has determined is worth learning
Choice	
Autonomy for each person in the classroom	Autonomy for the local authority to establish curriculum

relationship and to how the people involved perceive their responsibilities to and capacities for one another and themselves. An indispensable resource for further discussion on this topic is Kohn's (1993) *Punished by Rewards.*

The prejudice against children with disabilities is that they cannot negotiate cooperation with other learners or teachers, that they are not capable of knowing what is worth learning for themselves, and that without external controls they will make bad choices and run into difficulty. To the extent that these are characteristic of the human condition, they are true for people with disabilities—we all make mistakes in collaborating and in choosing what to do and how to do it. Unfortunately, this prejudice often accompanies the arrogance that comes from unchallenged power. Part of the absolute corruption that comes with absolute power is the arrogance of knowing what others need or should need, do, or be.

The factors listed under Mistrust in Table 1 can, in fact, promote a type of educational excellence. When students comply with their elders, they can assimilate good ideas and sound values. The problem is that this only works when learners themselves feel part of the school culture and connected with their teachers and thus submit to their instruction. When these elements are missing, students become restive and rebellious, and administrators, typically, become controlling. This only worsens the situation in that control tends to alienate people, and then the whole premise of shared values and relationships falls apart. For people with disabilities, this breakdown in understanding has led to long-term abuse and death in the name of therapy. There are still accounts of teachers using time-out closets for students, and, unfortunately, some states still subsidize the torture of learners with disabilities with electric shock or with other painful consequences of their failure to comply with the standards of their managers.

In general, the factors listed under Trust in Table 1 tend to promote mutually prosocial behavior. If we respect an individual's autonomy, then it creates a climate in which one is respected in return. Similarly, when people choose when, what, and how to learn, rebelliousness becomes an irrelevant communication strategy. If a person's simple protests result in a change, then it is unlikely he or she will need to escalate to more troublesome behavior. Too often when a learner resists instruction, the question becomes, "How do we motivate this person?" This often leads to an escalating and painful struggle for all involved. The more sensible question might be, "What does this person want to do?" and connect that enthusiasm with a socially valued skill or accomplishment.

The implications of trust versus mistrust for positive and control approaches to difficult behaviors are outlined in Table 2.

IMPLICATIONS

It is hoped that reflecting on the purposes of education will lead to better education and better behavior. My concern about the preferences and individualities of children is out of a concern for their well-being. However, this impulse also comes from my wish to be a whole and self-respecting person. It is hard to maintain that state as an adult while driving down the self-respect of children. In those moments when I find myself wanting to be controlling or hurtful, I know something is happening that I need to learn about myself.

What Can Teachers Do in Real Classroom Situations?

Some ideas about how a teacher might begin to think before acting follow. These are not recipes or step-by-step plans but are recurring concerns I have found in my own work.

Who Loves This Child? Whom Does This Child Love?

If the answer is "no one" on both counts, then it is obvious where our work needs to begin. A child living in this kind of isolation is in no position to be enthusiastic about learning much of anything, least of all "socially appropriate behavior." Just because children might have parents who obviously love them does not mean that child feels loved. It would be simple to make assumptions that what appears to be loving is loving. Often, though, no one knows the child well enough to answer these questions accurately, or the child does not have a close enough relationship with anyone so that the answer is true.

Table 2. Positive approaches and controlling approaches to difficult behavior

Positive approaches	Controlling approaches
Support people to grow and develop, to make their own decisions, to achieve their personal goals, to develop relationships, and to enjoy life as full participating members of their community.	Assess the learner's deficiencies, establish goals and criteria for progress and success, use remediation and rehabilitation to meet those goals, reassess progress in terms of the learner's compliance with the program.
Require an examination of all aspects of life including each person's living environment, relationships, activities, and personal dreams. Focus on the whole person, not merely on segments of the person's life. If a person resists service providers (e.g., teachers), reexamine their initial understanding to see what aspects of the person were missed.	Examine the person's environment, relationships, and activities and make access to them contingent on the person's compliance with a behavior program. If the person protests or resists, controls are typically increased.
Listen to each person and get to know his or her unique qualities as well as personal history. In this way, activities and techniques follow the person's preferences and style.	Require an ecological assessment, which is often "value free" in that it is used in special schools in which students have no basic civil liberties or rights, as well as in general education classrooms.
Assume that all behavior has meaning and that an individual's behavior can be a method to communicate needs and wants.	Assume that behavior may be communicative, but the main effort is to eliminate behavior unwanted by the teacher (or whoever is more powerful) and to increase behaviors valued by the power holders.
Measure success by the satisfaction of the person being supported.	Measure success by data showing conformity with goals set by others.
Do not focus on "fixing" a person, but on building competencies, creating opportunities, and offering choices that help each person live a fulfilling life.	Attempt to effect rapid behavior change, irrespective of what the person with the difficulty thinks or feels. The goal ideally is to make life better for the object of these interventions but, in practice, more often makes life more comfortable for those in charge.
Provide viable alternatives and eliminate the need to rely on aversive and coercive methods.	Rely on increasing levels of control until the person submits. If mild measures don't obtain the desired results, the history of these technologies shows that coercion and aversion can be escalated until the person is seriously injured or dies.

Adapted from Department of Public Welfare (1991).

Loving the Child

If it is you who loves and is loved by the child, then what can be done that does not involve personal judgment ("He is just a rotten kid!") or blame ("It's his mother's/father's/teacher's/the system's fault!"). Coercive-abusive systems "solve" problems by shifting and reassigning blame. If that is the best people can do, then some care has to be given to how they must be hurt and confused themselves. Blaming "a system" or "teachers" is no more logical than blaming "kids" or "parents."

Getting Past the Impasse

What would help all parties involved to get past this impasse? Who has the power or capacity to make that happen? If the people in this situation were all doing what they wanted to do (instead of what they were "supposed" to be doing), where would they meet? When and where would their separate interests overlap? The motivation is not so much intrinsically rewarding, although it might be, but it is about connection between the student's desire and the material at hand. I am less interested in rewards than I am in supporting people to follow their inner sense of pleasure.

For some reason, the presumption about learning is that people desire the least, when my experience has been that people desire the most. If we present education as an opportunity for you to learn what most engages you about the world, then you are probably going to strive for the greatest excellence you can achieve rather than the least. However, if education is presented as an obligation and a set of tasks you must perform for me, then you are indeed likely to find ways around me and to do the least amount of work you can. The nature of desire—which is neither good nor bad in itself—is for more. The blessing or curse of that comes from the focus of that desire, not from the wanting itself.

"Imagine Reality"

"To say that you and I share a common humanity, however, is not to say we are the same. On the contrary, I must encounter you as an other rather than as a mirror of myself or an object of my own experience. Empathy, in the sense of picturing myself in your situation, is not enough: The point is to see your situation from your perspective, which is not identical to mine. I must 'imagine the real'—see the world as you do, experiencing your inner life." This, according to Buber, is "a bold swinging— demanding the most intensive stirring of one's being—into the life of the other" (Buber, 1966, p. 81).

> When I both regard you as a subject and recognize your otherness, there is the making of human relationship at its fullest. All of us can strive to receive others in this way, and in so doing we prepare the ground for genuine dialogue, a reciprocal sharing by which both participants are enriched. (Kohn, 1993, pp. 137–138)

The concept of "disability" alone brings little clarity to the larger problem of difficult behavior in schools. The confusion around how to respond to children with disabilities and "challenging behavior" is mostly an expansion on the general cultural uncertainty of how to respond to this conundrum in *any* child.

Behavior Change as a Mutual Interaction: "Our Antagonist Is Our Helper"

Typically, children with difficult behavior have been seen as needing to learn something. This might be true, but they often do not have to learn things unilaterally. We cannot really teach without learning; neither can we impose on others without ultimately injuring ourselves.

Many children with difficult behavior have undiagnosed medical conditions, or emotional difficulties, or histories of abuse or neglect. We sometimes forget, however, that teachers do, too. Teachers who see learners with difficult behavior as opportunities to deepen their own healing may find it easier to act responsively than teachers who define their role as confined to teaching the subject.

How do we as adults pay attention to our own reality and the child's as an interaction rather than to just one or the other? How do we pay attention to our own present—and presence—rather than controlling and becoming anxious about the child's future. As we learn to see difficult situations as revealing us to ourselves, we find that good teaching is also a matter of lifelong learning.

If things are going to work well, there has to be lots of room for them to work badly. The quest for perfection drives out reality, whereas a respect for reality has within it the capacity for some shining but brief moments of perfection.

The failure of psychology-as-technology as a solution to human problems: The dream that someone has—or soon will have—a program to "cure" behavioral difficulty is gone. Rehabilitative-therapeutic programs are fundamentally a failure, except where they can foster the relationships necessary for people to grow, in which case the relationships are the significant variable and not the therapeutic swaddling in which they are delivered.

The "severely emotionally disturbed teachers" in a large urban school system explained how they understood their work: "To help kids get enough emotional and cognitive skills to be able to return to their ordinary classrooms." In this school, 250 students are currently enrolled, but only 3 graduated from this therapy last year.

Being Cruel To Be Kind Is Still Being Cruel

> The first thing therefore to be aimed at, is to bring your child under perfect subjection. Teach him that he must obey you. Sometimes give him your reasons; again, withhold them. But let him perfectly understand that he is to do as he is bidden. Accustom him to immediate and cheerful acquiescence in your will. This is obedience. And this is absolutely essential to good family government. Without this, your family will present one continued scene of noise and confusion; the toil of rearing up your children will be almost insupportable; and, in all probability, your heart will be broken by their future licentiousness and ingratitude.
>
> But the conduct of that matter is far more cruel who will allow the mind's inflammation to increase and extend unchecked; who, rather than inflict the momentary pain which is necessary to subdue the stubborn will, and allay irritation, will allow the moral disorder to gain such strength as to be incurable. The consequences thus resulting are far more disastrous. They affect man's immortal nature, and go on through eternity. There is no cruelty so destructive as this. (Abbott, 1834/1972, p. 76)

This antique of child-rearing advice has a camp hilarity now, but it still has the stamp of currency among some of the technologies fobbed off on children with disabilities. Where effective government or strong parent action has managed to outlaw the use of pain to control behavior, psychologists who formerly used corporal punishment and other aversives have titivated their vicious technologies by calling them teaching strategies and rehabilitative interventions. People with autism seem particularly attractive to this sort of practitioner; new "cures" for autism springing up at the same rate as the use of aversives fall. Few parents expect that they will have to become experienced clinicians within months of having a child; but unless they do, they are prey to all manner of professional presumption.

Interestingly, most programs that will "cure" whatever the disability entails require early intervention. This makes sense developmentally, but it also works out conveniently for charlatans who can make parents anxious that by not intervening in counterintuitive and noxious ways, they will "hurt" their child by withholding a vital and life-changing therapy from them. Since most parents will do anything to help their child, they end up doing many things to help everyone but their child.

Abbott's dated language, however, is always used by the powerful about the less powerful. It is not hard to see the same recipe for a "model child" being used at various times in history on slaves, peasants, women, dogs, disabled people. It is always offered as a commentary on the slave or peasant, but it is really a gloss on the arrogance of those who see others in this manner. Quick fix behavior programs (which are only quick to turn nasty if they don't fix fast enough) and other impersonal interventions for difficult behavior are more about the lack of power of the person with the difference and the lack of imagination of their helpers than anything else.

Inclusion

Inclusion, for the moment, is a political process and a liberation movement. Like most liberation movements, it is really the opposite of what it appears to be. The "problem" of "black people" in American society was really a problem with white people. Similarly, the needs people with disabilities have for adaptation are relatively smaller than the needs of those temporarily without disabilities. Seeing everyday reality (with its stairs, curbs, narrow toilet stalls, and the perversely narrow appreciation of what constitutes "intelligence") as needing rehabilitation and seeing people with disabilities as political equals radically reverses the old assumption that such people were broken and as a result badly suited for the real world.

The real world is badly suited for just about all of us. Adaptations that make every day life more accessible for a small group of people make it more convenient for many others. It is not just people who use chairs that benefit from accessible architecture—lots of people who *can* use stairs find them painful and awkward. The classroom that manages to adapt for one student's obvious needs invariably benefits people whose needs are not so obvious. If nothing else, adapting schools and classrooms to include everyone implicitly says "everyone belongs." Any culture that says "you are important" increases the probability that its members will be able to say that to one another and themselves.

REFERENCES

Abbott, J.S.C. (1972). *The mother at home; or, the principles of maternal duty.* New York: Arno Press and The New York Times. (Original work published 1834)

Arnold, M. (1962). Hellenism and Hebraism. In R.H. Super (Ed.), *Culture and anarchy: Vol. V The complete prose works of Matthew Arnold* (pp. 116–175). Ann Arbor: University of Michigan Press. (Original work published 1869)

Buber, M. (1966). *The knowledge of man: A philosophy of the interhuman.* New York: Harper Torchbooks.

Burgess, A. (1973). *The wanting seed.* London: Heinemann.

Department of Public Welfare, Commonwealth of Pennsylvania (1991, February 8). *Mental Retardation Bulletin,* Number 00-91-05, pp. 2–3.

Donnellan, A., & Leary, M. (1993). *Movement disorders.* Madison, WI: DRI Press.

Erikson, E. (1963). *Childhood and society* (2nd ed.). New York: Norton & Co.

Kohn, A. (1993). *Punished by rewards: The trouble with gold stars, incentive plans, A's, praise, and other bribes.* Boston: Houghton Mifflin.

Mesulam, M. (1985). *Principles of behavioral neurology.* Philadelphia: F.A. Davis Co.

VI

OTHER CONSIDERATIONS

24

Inclusion and the Development of a Positive Self-Identity by Persons with Disabilities

Susan Stainback, William Stainback,
Katheryn East, and Mara Sapon-Shevin

THE ISSUE OF educational integration or inclusion has been the focus of much debate, but there has been little or no attention focused on how inclusion into the educational mainstream influences the development of positive self-identity among students with disabilities. There is some research (Branthwaite, 1985) to support the contention that an individual's self-identity—feelings of confidence and worth—influences the way he or she interacts with the environment. Gliedman and Roth (1980) provided evidence that it is important for individuals with disabilities to develop a positive self-identity incorporating their disability. Ferguson and Asch (1989) described the issue as follows:

> How do disabled people come to think of themselves in ways that incorporate their disability as an important part of their personal and social identity? It is a theme that complicates the call for educational integration. In both the literature and our personal reflections we find an undeniable recognition that a well-developed sense of identity as a disabled adult needs some significant involvement as a child with other people (children and adults) who have similar disabilities. (p. 131)

Although the goal of inclusion is to create a community in which all children work and learn together and develop mutually supportive repertoires of peer support

361

and help, the goal of inclusion is not to be oblivious to children's individual differences. Within the field of multicultural education, the goal of color blindness (all people are the same and we do not notice differences) has been discredited and replaced by models that acknowledge and support the development of positive self-identity for individual groups. Similarly, the goal of inclusion in schools is to create a world in which all people are knowledgeable about and supportive of other people, and that goal is not achieved by some false image of homogeneity in the name of inclusion. Rather, we must look carefully at the ways schools have typically organized around individual differences and develop other alternatives. Typical models of special education services have involved identifying individual differences, labeling them, and then providing segregated services for people similarly labeled. However, the alternative is not dumping students in heterogeneous groups and ignoring their individual differences. This is the expressed fear of many who oppose inclusion—that students' individual needs will get lost in the process. We must find ways to build inclusive school communities that acknowledge student differences and their needs and yet do so within a common context.

Given the importance of this issue, we as professionals need to examine how we might enhance the development of such self-identity in the context of the integrated/inclusive school movement. This chapter outlines why there is an issue regarding the development of a positive self-identity and provides one perspective on addressing the concern.

THE MOVEMENT TOWARD INTEGRATION AND THE PROBLEM IT CREATES IN DEVELOPING POSITIVE SELF-IDENTITY

The educational practice of homogeneous grouping or clustering of individuals based on a common characteristic has been considered by many to be inappropriate, as earlier chapters in this book have detailed. Such homogeneous grouping also has been recognized as less than optimal for people with disabilities who are learning to live and work in integrated communities (Disability Rights, Education, & Defense Fund, 1983).

However, in integrated classrooms, there can be individuals with a disability that has a relatively low incidence in the general population, such as blindness or spina bifida, who are at risk of being restricted in opportunities to get to know and interact with other individuals with similar characteristics. To prevent this isolation, ways for these students to positively identify with others with similar characteristics may be needed. One way such access could be provided is through planned opportunities for people who share common characteristics to get together in school and community settings.

ACKNOWLEDGING INDIVIDUAL CHARACTERISTICS THROUGH PURPOSEFUL ACCESS

One way of acknowledging students' individual characteristics or differences is to provide them with opportunities to meet with others in groups that form around specific characteristics or issues and allow those students to share information, support, and strategies for transforming prejudice, discrimination, and practices. In the same way that the women's movement empowered women through consciousness-raising groups in which members felt safe and could then deal with the broader society, other people, specifically students, may have similar needs.

Purposeful access is a prominent characteristic of such support groups. Purposeful access (i.e., planned opportunities that allow people who share a common characteristic to get together) provides opportunities for voluntary affiliations among individuals sharing common characteristics, yet allows them to retain membership in the community as a whole. Asch, a colleague who is blind, pointed out that, while it was important for her educational and social development that she attend the neighborhood public school, having the opportunity to compare notes and share experiences with peers who also were blind was equally helpful to her. She stated (Ferguson & Asch, 1989):

> We talked about how our parents, teachers, and the kids in our schools treated us because we were blind. Sometimes someone who solved a problem told the rest of us what s/he figured out. Sometimes we complained together about those problems none of us had managed to solve. It was important to compare notes, have solid friendships where sight or lack of it did not affect the terms of the interaction, and just in general not feel alone. (pp. 132–133)

The benefits of formal and informal support or interest groups have been cited for students of divorced parents, students who are deaf, victims of abuse or rape, future farmers, religious groups, wheelchair sports enthusiasts, and teenage girls, among others (Hahn, 1985). Such groups have several important components. One component is that membership and participation are neither imposed (individuals can choose to participate or not) nor exclusionary (anyone who wants to be part of the group is accepted). Group membership is based on an individual's expressed needs and interests, not an adult's or authority figure's perception of an individual's identifying characteristic (e.g., blindness, deafness). In this way, individuals truly have free access to form friendships and identify with whomever they choose. As an illustration, in a work situation in which a number of individuals with mental retardation were learning job skills, staff members expressed concern over a young woman who chose to interact socially with the staff rather than with the other labeled workers. When asked why, the woman explained, "I am normal inside and I can't seem to get that out" (Kauffman, 1984, p. 89). All people are "normal" inside and must be allowed ample opportunities to express their normalcy through their talents, characteristics, friendships, and interests if they are to develop a healthy sense of personal identity. If a group of individuals who share a common characteristic such as having a disability or being African American, female, or Catholic want to get together, share experiences, or form an advocacy group, that is their personal choice. Although group formation may be assisted by those in authority, mandated participation may be counterproductive, particularly if the goal is to enhance positive self-identity.

There is a danger when those in authority make assumptions about who should be grouped together and around what characteristic or issue. In other words, if the principal decided that all bilingual students should be grouped together because their primary language is not English, or the special education coordinator decided that all students with mobility impairments should meet with one another, the potential for each group to achieve individual and group empowerment is automatically limited because the group was formed not out of common concern or mutual identification but because of a definition imposed by someone outside the group.

Another related consideration is that groups need to be started and defined by the members to avoid violating their interests, needs, and basic rights (Stainback, Stainback, & Forest, 1989). There are hazards when people in authority, including educators and parents, focus on any one of an individual's characteristics (e.g., disability, race, religion) and organize his or her life around that characteristic. According to Strully and Strully (1985), parents and educators who encourage children with disabilities to have only friends who have disabilities and to participate only in social events for people with disabilities perpetuate the segregation of years past. The real danger is that such groups become the only safe haven for people who have been defined as "different" and thereby remove from those in the mainstream the responsibility to make the broader community accessible and welcoming.

THE ROLE OF SCHOOL PERSONNEL

There is growing evidence from the experiences of people with disabilities that developing a positive self-identity that incorporates disability does not necessarily conflict with achieving school and community integration (see Ferguson & Asch, 1989; Hahn, 1985; People First, 1987). These experiences indicate that integration/inclusion in schools and communities can be achieved without restricting the rights of any person or group to freely form friendships and bonds or to identify with whomever they choose. However, school personnel may need to be sensitive to the desires of some students to identify with others who have similar characteristics and interests.

Schools can provide the framework necessary to allow students to form such groups, just as they have enabled students to initiate other student-centered groups such as pep clubs, circles of friends (Snow & Forest, 1987), or photography clubs. Some schools, for example, sponsor special support groups for students whose parents are divorcing so that students can overcome their sense of isolation and alienation about what is happening in their lives.

Opportunities for such student-initiated interest groups could be available at all levels of schooling, from preschool through high school. Facilitation by adults in various ways may be required. Schools supporting flexible groups guided by student interest and made up of members choosing to be there allow the benefits of positive self-identity to accrue. In this context, the school assumes the role of providing ways for students to become acquainted with and interact with other individuals who have characteristics similar to theirs should they choose to do so.

As noted earlier in this chapter, such groups are usually self-chosen—that is, initiated by the members. Although an adult or authority figure can certainly facilitate the formation of the group when there is expressed interest, any member of the school community should have the opportunity to initiate a group, including any student. For example, if one student decides that he would like to meet with others who are having problems with older siblings, or with those concerned about fights on the playground, that is how the group will be defined. By structuring groups in such a way, they are not necessarily disability-oriented groups, but special-interest groups related to a specific area or topic. If several students with hearing impairments decide to meet together to discuss their experiences in Jefferson Middle School as students with hearing impairments, they can seek others who are so identified or interested and form a group. These groups can also involve students who wish to identify themselves as allies of this group—people who will help to counteract any discrimination that these students are experiencing and who will commit to being there with them and for them in their struggles to achieve their goals. By having groups choose to form themselves in this way, the concern that resegregation of people with disabilities will occur is minimized.

As mentioned earlier in this chapter, school personnel should facilitate groups that are self defined. Self-defined groups are those that decide not only who is in them but also what their focus and purpose are. A group of students with visual impairments might decide that their goal is only mutual support and sharing issues and concerns in a safe setting. They might also decide that their goal is self-advocacy, educating students and teachers about ways their needs might be better met.

Finally, the emerging professional literature on mutual support groups (Vaux, 1988) indicates that they should be flexible. Flexible groups are those that remain intact only as long as they are useful and meet the needs of the individual members. Just as newly divorced or widowed people might seek out a transitional support group and leave that group when they no longer feel the need for that particular kind of support, groups should not be initiated with a fixed or inflexible duration. Joining the group and deciding how long the group will operate should be the decision of the group members.

A CALL FOR RESEARCH

At this point, there is little or no research in special education on issues surrounding the development of self-identity. An understanding of this issue for all students could be furthered by research. One route such research might take is to ask students how their sense of self-identity at school is being enhanced or could be enhanced. Another research route could be to ask students who have moved beyond school what changes could have made their educational experience more positive. Using the data gathered from students, combined with the understanding of how interest/support groups in schools and community organizations are developed and facilitated, a process for ensuring purposeful or meaningful access to interest/support groups for all individuals could be developed. After implementation, the impact of involvement in these support groups on the individuals, their peers, family, and teachers could be investigated.

CONCLUSION

To develop a positive self-identity, an individual needs opportunities to exercise and express his or her choices. Individuals need to exercise choice about their friendships and their group affiliations. To allow such choices, schools and the community in general are required to be flexible, adaptive, and sensitive to the unique needs of all members. Purposeful or meaningful access to support or interest groups can introduce these qualities into the mainstream by allowing each individual an opportunity to develop a positive sense of identity. The school must become a place where purposeful access groups are facilitated and where each student is given the opportunity to develop positive feelings about the unique qualities he or she brings to the educational community. After all, the goal of inclusion is not to erase differences, but for all students to belong to an educational community that validates and values their individuality.

Finally, as inclusion continues to be debated, it is critical that the voices of students be heard. One way of ensuring that students have a voice is by providing them opportunities to meet together, form friendships, generate allies across groups, and learn to take charge of their own education and lives.

REFERENCES

Branthwaite, A. (1985). The development of social identity and self-concept. In A. Branthwaite & D. Rogers (Eds.), *Children growing up*. Philadelphia: Open University Press.

Disability Rights, Education, and Defense Fund. (1983). *The disabled women's education project: Report of survey results: Executive summary*. Berkeley, CA: Author.

Ferguson, P., & Asch, A. (1989). Lessons from life: Personal and parental perspectives on school, childhood, and disability. In D. Biklen, A. Ford, & D. Ferguson (Eds.), *Disability and society* (pp. 108–140). Chicago: National Society for the Study of Education.

Fullwood, D. (1990). *Chances and choices: Making integration work*. Baltimore: Paul H. Brookes Publishing Co.

Gliedman, J., & Roth, W. (1980). *The unexpected minority: Handicapped children in America*. New York: Harcourt Brace Jovanovich.

Hahn, H. (1985). Toward a politics of disability: Definitions, disciplines, and policies. *The Social Science Journal, 22*, 87–105.

Kauffman, S. (1984). Socialization in sheltered workshop settings. In R. Edgerton & S. Bercovici (Eds.), *Mental retardation*. Washington, DC: American Association for Mental Deficiency.

People First. (1987). *People First* [video]. Downsview, Ontario: Canadian Association for Community Living.

Snow, J., & Forest, M. (1987). Circles. In M. Forest (Ed.), *More education integration*. Downsview, Ontario: G. Allan Roeher Institute.

Stainback, S., Stainback, W., & Forest, M. (Eds.). (1989). *Educating all students in the mainstream of regular education*. Baltimore: Paul H. Brookes Publishing Co.

Strully, J., & Strully, C. (1985). Friendship and our children. *Journal of The Association for Persons with Severe Handicaps, 1*, 224–227.

Vaux, A. (1988). *Social support: Theory, research and intervention*. New York: Praeger.

25

Gaining and Utilizing Family and Community Support for Inclusive Schooling

Lynne C. Sommerstein and Marilyn R. Wessels

WHY, AFTER MANY years since the passage of the Education for All Handicapped Children Act of 1975 (PL 94-142), later reauthorized as the Individuals with Disabilities Education Act of 1990 (IDEA) (PL 101-476) and further amended in 1991 with PL 102-119, the Individuals with Disabilities Education Act Amendments of 1991, is it still necessary to write a chapter, "Gaining and Utilizing Family and Community Support for Inclusive Schooling?" Why, when the law should already be completely imlemented, are we not even close? We have analyzed, organized, scrutinized, and even successfully litigated, and yet we are still affecting children only on a case-by-case, limited basis. What else do we need to do? This chapter examines why PL 94-142 still has not been fully implemented (U.S. Department of Education, 1993), why our progress toward inclusion for people with disabilities has been so painfully slow, what parents of children with disabilities can do to gain and utilize family and community support, and what they need to *be aware of* and *beware of* to claim their children's rightful place in neighborhood classrooms and communities.

BE AWARE OF IRRELEVANT NEGATIVISM

After each examination, evaluation, diagnosis, prognosis, I'd escape with my daughter, Michelle, to our favorite bench in the mall. The nevers, can'ts and won'ts had kidnapped my confidence and captured my dreams. As I sat in front of Sears watching Michelle doing her two...three...five...seven-year-old thing, she ransomed my confidence and restored my dreams by reminding me that she was still the funny, silly, sweet, stubborn daughter she was when we awoke that morning. (Sommerstein, 1994)

Welcome to the world of disabilities where paper reigns and negativism, pessimism, and resistance to change ooze from every page. It does not have to be this way. The negativism is symptomatic of a competitive society that idolizes winners and shuns losers. This prejudice causes society and parents themselves to view a disability not as a neutral personal characteristic but as a defining negative quality requiring secrecy, defensiveness, and shame. The stigmatizing nature of this negativism has prevented children with disabilities from being welcomed into their neighborhood schools, thereby contributing to the denial of full citizenship in their communities for people with disabilities.

The negative perception of people with disabilities comes early in the evaluation process when professionals earnestly assure parents of the confidentiality of the information being discovered and shared. Although there are very good reasons to maintain confidentiality, the secrecy involved in the process and the reluctance to share full information even with the parents sends a negative message itself that something is "wrong" with the child. Parents need to understand that this message has nothing to do with their child's worth or abilities, but has to do with a process that is defined by societal attitudes.

Evaluations themselves are too often testimony to deficit documentation by well-intentioned statistical seers. Such descriptions "serve to emphasize a child's differences and create a negative, 'hopeless' picture" (Schaffner & Buswell, 1991, p. 16) of low expectations and self-fulfilling prophecies. Parents reel from shock and guilt, unaware that "when the oracle is loud and clear, it is often wrong. We have just been treated to...professional puffery, and it is very bitter medicine—all the more so for being almost totally ineffective" (Akerley, 1985, p. 24). What parents don't know *can* hurt their children. They *must* question, even challenge, evaluation results; they *can* refuse to sign release of information forms; they *can* demand independent evaluations by enlightened professionals who document strengths as well as needs; they *must* insist on a strengths-based emphasis in all aspects of their child's life.

> When I received Michelle's reports from her psychologist, speech therapist, physician, neurologist, or whomever, I always considered them a draft. The first thing I did was sit down with a yellow highlighter and highlight every positive comment about her. If the report was not at least 50% yellow, I made additions and asked for them to be inserted. Only once did I ever allow a report that I hadn't previewed to be shared with the school. I never, ever, did it again. (Sommerstein, 1994)

Parents must not accept the low ("realistic") expectations fostered by standardized tests whose predictions are too often as reliable as those in the *Farmer's Almanac*.

Plateaus Are for Maps

Parents must also be aware of some preconceived, old-fashioned, and even anachronistic notions held by some psychologists, educators, or administrators who too often recommend supports and services according to those beliefs. The idea of "plateauing" is one of those notions. When testing shows slowed or no progress, particularly in older children, services may be curtailed because the child has "plateaued." If we apply simple common sense, we then realize that learning is a lifelong activity and that the only thing that has "plateaued" is the instructional strategy or the expertise of those delivering the service. The expectation that students with disabilities need less support in high school reflects this thinking. Services instead should be person-centered and determined by the person's individual need rather than by what the system usually wishes to provide. Parents must guard against self-fulfilling prophecies by ensuring that expectations for their children remain optimistic and high. If we are to err in our expectations, let it be in favor of higher expectations rather than lower.

Share the Vision

Parents play a critical role in dispelling the pessimistic clouds surrounding their children, a role we have, perhaps, been reluctant to assume because we, too, have accepted society's negative perceptions. We need a call to arms to move beyond political correctness to educated enlightenment. We need to divest ourselves of guilt and fear and invest instead in our intuition and expertise as parents. We don't need to "fix" our children; we need, instead, to redefine "winner."

The most effective way parents can accomplish this is to use their own expertise in identifying the outcomes they value most for their children. They should begin with the expectations held for same-age children without disabilities as their guide instead of the expectations society has traditionally held for people with disabilities. They then can tailor those "normal" expectations to their child's wants and needs; this road map, or goals for the future, becomes the parent's vision and is the basis for all planning from which all decisions will come. In developing this vision, parents should use resources at hand for information about possibilities: the child him- or herself, family members and friends, other more experienced parents, people with disabilities whom they see as "success stories," and books and articles. "Think about those future years…jot down your ideas of what life for your son or daughter should be when the school years are over. From this time on, your vision must influence the development of…your child's future…" (Maryland Coalition, 1991, p. 6). The vision may need to be revised from time to time, but sharing the vision ensures that services are individualized and not predetermined by the system.

About dreaming—so much advice parents are given focuses on grieving the "death" of the perfect child. If parents of children with disabilities must grieve, so then must parents of children without disabilities, for there are no perfect children. Changing their expectations does not mean an end to dreaming—it just means that they are dreaming different dreams. In developing their vision, parents must not forget to dream.

BE AWARE OF THE MESSAGE OF SILENCE

In the brutal discovery process, parents tend to be reluctant to share information with even their closest confidants or the child him- or herself for fear they won't understand. Their secrecy reinforces the negative perceptions surrounding children with disabilities, unintentionally contributing to barriers to inclusion and acceptance. Parents can ease the way early in their child's life by replacing silence or defensiveness with openness, optimism, and celebration of personal best. A difficult trick, one might say, in light of the attitudinal negativism that exists among families, extended families, friends, or acquaintances.

EDUCATE THE WHOLE VILLAGE

We parents who cope by protecting our children from others through silence need to interrupt the cycle of society's ignorance by taking a risk and sharing our children with others, by allowing others access to the information and appreciation we already have so that they can feel some ownership of our children's gifts and achievements. For the vast majority of parents, having a child with disabilities does not have to be a tragedy. A challenge? Yes! An inconvenience? Often! Worrisome? Definitely! But not a tragedy. This is what we must tell a society that often feels sorry for a person with a disability, that thinks of the parent as a saint and wonders how they cope. If it is true, according to an African proverb, that "It takes a whole village to raise a child," parents have an obligation to share their child's gifts and needs with family members, friends, acquaintances, community members, employers, supervisors, grocery clerks, doctors, nurses, receptionists, bank tellers, bus drivers, and police officers, among others, in casual conversation, discussion, and even formal presentations. Don't expect people to recognize your child's accomplishments—tell them! Don't expect people to know what you or your child needs—tell them! Don't expect people to know who your child really is—tell them! Few parents keep their children's honors and achievements to themselves, and it is unnatural to do so. We need to develop our awareness so that the achievements of children with disabilities, no matter what the level, are valued, celebrated, and honored.

BE AWARE OF HOW TO SHARE

Sharing information about our children, which is sometimes called disability awareness, has been questioned by some respected advocates.

> Some practices commonly used in schools that are thought to help students develop relationships may actually divert friendship facilitation efforts. Although these activities may be useful for other reasons, they sometimes set students with disabilities apart by focusing on their "specialness" or differences. Facilitation is not...disability awareness activities…. (Schaffner & Buswell, 1992, p. 18)

We all, of course, hope that relationships will develop naturally, and they probably would in a better world in which people with disabilities and their parents did not have to struggle for acceptance. While the situation seems to be improving, friendships between people with disabilities and "nondisabled individuals still appear to be the exception rather than the rule" (Lutfiyya, 1990). Most people in our schools and communities have little meaningful contact with people with disabilities. Until all children are educated together in general education classes and schools, people with disabilities will be perceived as different. These perceptions are caused by an information gap.

Most people who do not understand differences will be superficially friendly or neutral at best, insensitive and cruel at worst. When that gap is filled with positive information, prejudice and discomfort decrease or disappear.

"We don't want to single out the student," or "The student with disabilities will be embarrassed," are concerns expressed by critics of disability awareness. Both reveal a negative attitude toward disabilities. Is it not true that we single out the valedictorian, the football hero, and the scholarship winner? Is it not true that students enjoy the positive attention of sharing information about themselves with their peers? Those who object on the grounds of singling out are denying that most students with disabilities are already singled out, already different, and that perhaps their reluctance to speak directly about a disability is a reflection of their own discomfort. Rather than setting the person apart, disability awareness when done correctly is an investment in removing the differentness; it is an essential piece in solving the friendship and employment puzzle.

"The children without disabilities will feel sorry for the child with disabilities" is another argument for silence. Unfortunately, most people already feel sorry for people with disabilities as demonstrated by the level of telethon giving. The task for parents of children with disabilities is to demonstrate their children's capacities and successes so that people do not have to feel sorry for them. If we perceive the disability as a neutral characteristic, then the information being shared is just information, not judgments, and no reason for pity, embarrassment, or shame.

What critics of disability awareness are really and rightly questioning is the manner of presentation and content of the awareness. The information too often is presented in a way that reinforces negative stereotypes of people with disabilities. The following guidelines identify strategies for sharing information through disability awareness:

Plan with Consent and Participation of the Person with Disabilities and Family

Some people may not be ready to share; others are afraid of what might be said. It would be wrong to share information without consent of the person and family, and it would be a violation of confidentiality. However, planning with them what will be said and demonstrating how it will be presented may address many of their concerns. At the very least, it will give them something to think about as an option for the future.

Use Person-Centered Information

Information being shared should be specific to the person being discussed. Information should present him or her as an individual and avoid generalizations that perpetuate stereotypes and misconceptions.

Maintain Dignity and Respect

Emphasizing sameness and showing appreciation for and pride in the person with disabilities goes a long way in creating positive attitudes. Using respectful language is essential. Avoid language which portrays the person as a victim or as suffering.

Use a Strength-Based Approach

It is important to show that a disability is only a small part of the total person. Showing capacity, ability, interests, and strengths instead of deficits contributes to positive perceptions: disABILITY instead of DISability, or better yet, ABILITY awareness.

Deemphasize Labels

Medical and technical (textbook) labels reinforce stereotypes and fears and create confusion. Labels give little information because they generalize and create barriers. Such labels should be avoided.

Be Prescriptive Instead of Descriptive

Information about a person's disability should focus on what that person needs to be successful instead of what is "wrong" with him or her. The majority of people who feel uncomfortable are really good, kind people who do not know what to do or how to help. When they feel uncertain or inadequate, they avoid the person or the situation. Prescriptive information must focus on why something might happen and what others might do to help appropriately.

Involve the Person as an Active Participant

The person with disabilities should be present when information is being given about him or her to avoid any perception of shame or of talking behind his or her back. If he or she chooses not to be present, the individual providing the information should make it clear that it was the person's choice not to attend, but that he or she knows and endorses what is being said. The person with disabilities should be encouraged to participate in whatever way he or she chooses. One particularly verbal person might make a presentation alone, another individual might use cards with icons, and another individual might distribute papers. Whatever the adaptation, being present and active in the sharing of information shows capacity and demands respect. It enables the person to accept more readily his or her disability by destigmatizing it.

Encourage Questions and Identify Sources of Support/Information

The tone of information sharing should be light; humor helps. People should be encouraged to ask questions so that they can progress to a level of comfort by which they forget about the disability. They should know to whom to go if questions arise, the first choice being the person with disabilities. Answering questions with back-up help and support encourages the development of self-advocacy skills; self-advocacy skills will assist the individual throughout his or her life to explain the disability, to identify needed supports, and to get them.

When children are young, the issue of disability awareness is not very significant to them and their peers. As they grow up and become aware of differences, acceptance of those differences can be difficult. In an essay, "Growing Up Together," the author described the changes in her son Billy's acceptance of his disability as he got older:

When Billy was small, we had no problem accepting his retardation; neither did he. He was happy, healthy, and confident of his place in the family. As he grew older and more integrated in school and social activities, his differences naturally became more apparent to us, to him, and to other people. We have always used the term *retarded* freely; and Billy himself, in helping me arrange my office, has said, "Reading books go here, 'tarded books go here," or "Come watch TV, Mom; its 'tarded children." As an adult, however, he does not use the term often and frequently attempts to deny his own retardation. (Schulz, 1985, p. 15)

From our experience, children under the age of 8 have no discomfort with disabilities and, in fact, seem not to notice. Their awareness of differences becomes apparent at about the age of 8 or 9, and a brief explanation in a naturally occurring situation will usually suffice, especially if it encourages questions. The next change seems to occur between sixth and seventh grades when children are going through dramatic social and physical changes. This is when parents and educators need to be proactive in sharing information in both structured and naturally occurring situations. Those who say the bridge between children with and without disabilities will develop naturally have not spoken to the many parents of isolated adolescent children with disabilities. All children have social problems at this age; children with and without disabilities need extra support during this critical period to bridge the emerging gap between them.

High school can be a time of great opportunity or great isolation, and this is when the payoff from sharing information comes. Although some children at any age can be very cruel, many can also be incredibly compassionate and helpful when given enough information through formal and informal ability awareness and support. In high school, parents and educators need to be creative and even direct in enlisting the assistance of peers to maximize contacts between students with disabilities and their classmates without disabilities. The more contact students have, coupled with information and support, the greater the probability that lasting relationships will develop.

BE AWARE OF ALLIES

In addition to sharing information, parents can assist in promoting disability awareness by opening their homes to neighborhood youngsters, by driving them to or from activities, by expecting the school to facilitate social relationships (even including this in the individualized education program [IEP]), by reading the school announcements and handbook to find out what is going on at school, by participating in such school activities as the PTA, booster club, shared decision-making committee, teacher recognition day, and post-prom party, among others. As they participate, parents can share, share, and share their vision, pride, and information in naturally occurring situations. The results will be allies in the community ranging from "cheerleaders" to active participants. These are the people who will reach out individually to students with disabilities and their parents by encouraging their own children to reach out, who will connect parents to a valuable word-of-mouth information network, who will assist parents in negotiating the special education maze by speaking up to school district administrators and boards of education to demand full participation for students with disabilities in their schools, and who will write letters to state and federal agencies supporting inclusive schools. These are also the people who will be the future neighbors, employers, co-workers, and friends of students with disabilities. Because parents shared their appreciation of and information about their sons and daughters with disabilities, these people will be more willing and able to include them in their communities. These educated allies are important in building the coalitions described later in this chapter.

Those parents who think this is exhausting are probably correct, but worry, isolation, and discrimination are worse. Our children with disabilities will have a better life because we expended our energies productively.

There are some parents and people with disabilities who cannot or do not want to share information because of culture, ability, or opportunity. So be it. The more invisible the disability, the greater the reluctance to share it. It is enough to change our own thinking, to know about different goals, and to work toward them. Those parents who can, should; those who cannot should support those who can. All of this awareness will become unnecessary when people with disabilities are no longer stigmatized. Destigmatization begins with the perceptions families and people with disabilities have of themselves.

BEWARE: NEGOTIATING THE MAZE IS NOT ALWAYS ENOUGH

When parents have done everything within their power and ability to enable their children to become an integral part of the entire community, why is it that children often continue to remain apart from it, especially from the school community? Parents often ask, "How is it that my child is accepted into scouts, into our church, into our community recreational activities, but yet is not allowed to be a part of our community school?"

"Building Community Support for Restructuring" (Wessels, 1992) identifies some of the reasons why we have not made more progress toward placing students into inclusionary settings despite the efforts of some very tenacious and dedicated parents. In this chapter, the question was raised, "How do we get administrators and school board members to sense parents' hurt, frustration, and indignation so that they become motivated to move with the utmost of speed to change an archaic school system?" (Wessels, 1992, p. 297)

With the acknowledgment that we have made much progress in organizing and in changing attitudes, placements in inclusive settings in far too many places are still made on a child-by-child basis instead of being based on systems change. Obviously, we have not gone far enough in exploring why, after so many years, we still have to wage such monumental battles in getting legislation implemented. We must look more closely at what circumstances still impede the full implementation of the Individuals with Disabilities Education Act of 1990 (IDEA). Are our school systems or the lack of appropriate monitoring by federal and state education departments to blame?

BEWARE OF THE LESSONS OF HISTORY

We know that in the 1940s there were few services for people with disabilities, adults or children. We know that technology that developed in World War II helped medical science successfully treat persons with disabilities, thereby increasing their lifespan and ability to function. We know that parents of those children began to challenge the system that said: Either keep your children at home hidden away or institutionalize them in a warehouse operated by the state or some private entity.

We know that out of that challenge, parent advocacy organizations began springing up in order to provide desperately needed support and services. By the mid-1960s, those organizations were beginning to have a real impact on state legislatures, which responded by allocating dollars for initially permissive and, later, mandated school programs. We know that as states and local school districts began to assume more and more responsibility for providing services for school-age youngsters with disabilities, some of those same advocacy organizations that had pioneered services realized that their role was changing—the children they had once served were becoming adults. They turned over the educational programs to local school districts and began to develop adult services. Regrettably, few of these services were in the community, and all were segregated.

Unfortunately, many of these once-visionary organizations that originally came into being out of the real need to provide educational services for children with disabilities failed to change their focus to adult services. These agencies continued to operate schools for children with disabilities despite the capability of local school districts to provide the same services. Although IDEA mandated that public schools provide services in the least restrictive setting, these agencies focused on their own desire to expand buildings and staffing—in other words, to perpetuate the status quo; they continued to provide segregated services despite the growing realization that they were more expensive, more restrictive, and less effective. Some agencies had found their niche, were content to keep things the way they were, and were able to convince others—parents, government officials, state and federal legislatures—that there continued to be a need to exist. In addition, they provided a ready excuse for school districts that did not want these children in their neighborhood schools and that were quite content to allow others to do the job of education. Segregated education provided by these private agencies was a handy alternative for dealing with certain students with disabilities, and the requirement in IDEA of a continuum of services allowed school districts to do it. Schools will maintain the status quo for their own purposes rather than change to benefit the individuals they profess to serve. This is the lesson of history that parents need to know. Parents must be aware of the self-serving nature of agencies and the conflict of interest which can negatively affect children's services.

BEWARE OF WELL-INTENTIONED LEGISLATORS

Reviewing the legislation enacted early in this century reveals that, for the most part, well-intentioned public officials passed legislation that incarcerated tens of thousands of individuals with disabilities in large institutions, putting them away "with their own kind," away from their families and communities. Such legislation deprived individuals with disabilities of their constitutional rights without benefit of due process of law (Cook, 1990). What this legislation really accomplished was to remove a source of discomfort from society. Most people with disabilities were forced to live in horrendous, subhuman conditions (Blatt & Kaplan, 1967).

While those inequities have, for the most part, been eliminated, it is important to revisit the political scene to find out why our legislators are not taking a more active role in ensuring that IDEA and its subsequent amendments are fully implemented. Could the answer still be, as it once was, that society in general wishes to segregate persons with disabilities, and, thus, many of our legislators, not willing to upset their constituents, are keeping a low profile about this or, even worse, are contributing to the problem? After all, legislators, for the most part, are really no different from any of us when it concerns their jobs. Once they have been elected, they want to keep the position by doing everything possible to avoid offending anyone so that they get reelected. In fact, if they end up offending people, it had better be a small minority of their constituency, such as people with disabilities, and not the majority.

Many of the same service providers that were so successful in the 1950s and 1960s in getting legislators to recognize the needs of persons with disabilities have longevity and credibility with their legislators despite their more recent poor track record of perpetuating segregation. It is not surprising that public and private providers of segregated services feel threatened by any attempt to enforce the provision of the law that requires children with disabilities be educated in the least restrictive environment: They fear that they may have to go out of business or at least reconfigure how they do business. Legislators are, perhaps, one of the first and most crucial contacts that they pursue to maintain their organizations despite the needs of the children and the requirements of the law.

Because of the providers' long association with legislators, it becomes very difficult for other more recent organizations to gain the influence necessary to have legislation enforced and amended. It, therefore, is necessary for parents attempting to make changes to be aware of the power of influential agencies and of the control they exert over well-intentioned legislators and their staffs. We cannot expect politicians to understand the conflicts of interest in agencies or the issues that generate them. Individual parents can have enormous credibility with their own legislators. Parents must take the time to educate their representatives about their children and the issues of inclusion, segregation, and least restrictive environment. They can do this by, again, sharing personal information about their children, including photographs, schoolwork, and, most important, their vision for an inclusive future for their children. They must point out the self-serving nature of some agencies' advocacy by putting together packets of information, including copies of the section on least restrictive environment (300.550) of IDEA (PL 101-476), articles, and essays available through parent training and advocacy centers.

Parents must amass at least the same degree of influence as have those who are striving to maintain the status quo. In other words, advocates for inclusion must become as strong in numbers and voice in order to counter the often misleading message delivered to legislators by the providers of segregated services. Although some legislators make informed decisions by evaluating the outcomes of children educated in inclusive settings, by looking at the research, or even visiting model programs, others determine their actions by sheer numbers of those who take the time to call, write, or visit. The highest number of advocates, whether pro or con, often determines the legislator's decision, especially in an election year.

Although pulling together the necessary supports to influence the legislative arena is not easy, it can be done by looking around in the community to see who will support the cause. Parents who have shared their children's achievements and needs with their family, friends, and community already have allies in their cause. Many of these allies will be willing to write letters or make phone calls. Some may be willing to enlist the support of groups to which they belong, but do not expect them to think of it—ask them! The ripple effect can generate surprising support. In addition, if need be, parents can organize individuals into an important and necessary support group. Organizing a support group does not have to be a complicated process; some of the most effective groups began with coffee at someone's house. Some of the most effective parents began with nothing more than a desire to improve the lives of their sons and daughters with disabilities.

> We grow in all parts of the country, we pushy ones who are never content, no matter how modern the separate schools you build and how up-to-date the equipment. We cannot be squelched. Therapy tanks no longer satisfy us.... We reject what you offer.... We muster the courage to insist that our children belong. (Moore, 1992)

BEWARE OF BEING MISUSED

One of the popular buzzwords of the 1990s has been parent choice. Many providers of segregated programs have often used that term to manipulate and confuse parents into advocating for the services that they, the providers, offer. However, parents have the legal right to be meaningfully involved in decision making on behalf of their youngsters. They have a right to seek an independent evaluation at district expense if they disagree with the district's evaluation. They have a right to provide information to the child's educational team about their child. They have a right to assist in developing their child's IEP. They have a right to prefer and to recommend options. They have a right to challenge decisions. However, they do not have a right to choose a placement for their child by themselves; they must do it in concert with the child's team. Parents also do not have a right to choose placements that do not provide the least restrictive environment. However, school districts often allow parents to make that choice rather than go through a costly due process hearing.

That is why it becomes so incredibly important that parents become educated consumers not only about their rights but also about various options so that they can argue intelligently and forcefully for what their children require and deserve. Only educated consumers can effectively evaluate the recommendations made for their child.

When parents first become aware of their child's disability, needless negativism causes them to feel shock and vulnerability. Often they are uninformed about what they should do, where they should go, with whom they should talk, and what they should believe. Too often they are unable to access the common sense of those closest to them because they have not yet become comfortable with sharing information about their child. They instead rely upon what is told to them by a professional who may be as concerned with filling quotas and receiving financial reimbursement as he or she is with the welfare of the child. The sad part about this is that the child and the parents get trapped in a service delivery system that is often not in the best interest of the child. In this situation, parents are unknowingly manipulated into defending these agencies against changes that probably will help their child.

Agencies whose main interest is to perpetuate themselves often tell parents that if certain changes occur, their children will lose services. Parents are persuaded that it is incumbent upon them to lobby their legislators on the agency's behalf. They are even coached as to what to write or say. Despite this shameful exploitation, the practice is almost impossible to stop because of the inability of advocates to access families who are so manipulated. Parents must be aware of their vulnerability to such practices and ask themselves if they are fully informed of many points of view. They can seek information through parent groups, parent training and information centers, and advocacy groups. They can also seek the counsel of family and community members who are knowledgeable about their children; these people often have valuable common sense insight.

BEWARE: RALPH NADER IS NOT WATCHING THE WATCHERS

The drafters of IDEA knew it would not be sufficient to draft legislation that included only programmatic and procedural requirements, such as all children, regardless of disability, have a right to a free appropriate public education; all children must have an individualized education program, and all children have the right to attend school in the least restrictive setting. They, the advocates who had struggled for years to gain the rights of students with disabilities, knew that other safeguards had to be put in place that would ensure that school districts did not violate those requirements. Thus, certain responsibilities were assigned to national and state governments that required monitoring of programs at state and local levels in order to ensure compliance with the law.

For example, at the national level, the U.S. Department of Education (DOE) is charged with ensuring that all states have a system of checks and balances that guarantees that all parts of IDEA are in place and fully implemented. Every state is required to submit to the DOE a state plan to document how IDEA is functioning in each state. The Office of Special Education Programs (OSEP) requires that states provide them with these plans every 3 years. In addition, OSEP is supposed to monitor each state every 3 years in order to validate the implementation documented in the state plan. During these monitoring visits, representatives of OSEP, in addition to reviewing state policies, visit local districts to review students' IEPs to ensure that what the state and districts say is happening really is happening.

To make what appears to be a foolproof oversight system even more effective, state departments of education, in turn, must monitor each public and private educational agency (school) every few years, by interviewing teachers and administrators, reviewing IEPs, ensuring that documents required by federal legislation are in place and being used appropriately. Given this multilevel monitoring system, it would seem that violations of the rights of students, in this case, inappropriate placements in other than inclusive settings, would be few and far between. According to The ARC Report Card (1992), we have failed miserably to educate students with more severe disabilities with children without disabilities. The *Thirteenth Annual Report to Congress on the Implementation of the Individuals with Disabilities Education Act* (1991)

> reveals nationwide violations of crucial statutory requirements. Nevertheless, in spite of DOE's clear obligation to correct such violations, the report also displays a federal compliance monitoring and enforcement process that is virtually nonfunctional in important respects. Hence, oversight of compliance issues is left to the very agencies for the compliance violations in the first place. Moreover, DOE has apparently abdicated its responsibilities for reporting to Congress these very same agencies, thus creating an institutional arrangement which amounts to a classic case of the fox guarding the henhouse; this arrangement ensures that violations will neither be corrected nor reported to Congress.... The IDEA requires that students with disabilities be educated in the least restrictive environment (LRE). The IDEA assigns the responsibility for ensuring that school districts comply with the LRE requirements to state educational agencies (SEAs); DOE is assigned the obligation of making certain that SEAs fulfill their oversight, compliance and enforcement responsibilities. It is clear from this structure of responsibilities that if DOE does not adequately fulfill its obligation, it is less likely that SEAs will fulfill theirs, and if SEAs do not live up to their responisbilities, it is less likely that school districts will be educating students in the LRE. (M. Mlawer, personal correspondence, 1992)

In the *Thirteenth Annual Report to Congress* (1991), the U.S. Department of Education, the guardians of the law, stated that

> The variation in state placement rates across the different educational environments may be due to several factors, including: the historic role of private schools in the state, the role of separate facilities in the state, the state's reporting practices and interpretation of the OSEP data collection forms, and actual differences in the populations and needs of students.

But as Mr. Mlawer pointed out,

> It is curious that an obvious possibility—that LRE violations are a major cause of the variation in placement rates across states—is not even mentioned as a possible explanation... This interesting omission is even more puzzling in light of the fact that the first three possible explanations advanced by DOE clearly violated the LRE requirements of the IDEA. Public agencies cannot segregate students due to the historic role of private schools in the state, the role of separate facilities in the state, or the state's special education funding formula.

OSEP has done much since the 1991 report to ensure compliance with IDEA by the states, yet 2 years later the *Fifteenth Annual Report to Congress on the Implementation of the Individuals with Disabilities Education Act* (1993), still cited a litany of problems that were identified as significant noncompliance issues.

> In all 14 of the States and Outlying Areas that received final monitoring reports in 1992, OSEP documented concerns about the SEAs monitoring procedures for identifying deficiencies and ensuring correction. Some of the findings found by OSEP regarding State monitoring include: 13 of 14 SEAs were found not to have State monitoring procedures to identify deficiencies regarding the provision of a free and appropriate public education; 8 of 14 SEAs were found not to have State monitoring procedures in place, or to have ineffective procedures for ensuring that IEPs were developed in meetings that were held at least once a year; 14 of 14 SEAs were found not to have State monitoring procedures in place, or to have ineffective procedures for ensuring that the IEP program for each child included the content required; 11 of 14 SEAs were found not to have State monitoring procedures in place, or to have ineffective procedures for ensuring that the notice under 34 CFR 300.504 included a full explanation of all of the procedural safeguards available to the parents under Subpart E and 9 of 14 SEAs were found not to have State monitoring procedures in place, or to have ineffective monitoring procedures for ensuring that the educational placement of each child with disabilities is based on his or her individualized education program. (U.S. Department of Education, 1993, p. 135)

Over and over again, the DOE has documented clear and significant violations of IDEA that only reinforce the image of the fox guarding the henhouse. The DOE is like a parent who continually threatens his or her child for serious misbehavior but never follows through with consequences. States know that, although they violate the law, the most they will receive is a slap on the wrist. No wonder the challenge appears so insurmountable—if the policies and procedures mandated by IDEA were conscientiously applied, the vast majority of children would now be educated in age-appropriate classrooms in their neighborhood schools.

If IDEA and the legislation it reauthorized were new, the level of noncompliance described above might be excusable. However, we are not really talking about new laws. Some of the more simple explanations for noncompliance could be that federal and state agencies do not have enough personnel to monitor implementation as frequently as they should, the monitoring instruments designed to identify noncompliance areas are not useful, the monitoring personnel are not as well trained as they need to be, those implementing IDEA at the district level have too many other assignments and are unable to ensure full compliance, and not enough money is set aside for staff training. These are some of the routine excuses we continue to hear year after year, and none of them are justifiable. There really is no acceptable excuse for continued ignorance of and noncompliance with these laws.

The real reason for noncompliance takes us back to the political winds that continue to swirl around children with disabilities and prevent compliance. The questions parents must ask themselves are: Who is watching the watchers? Why is the wonderful system of oversight that is in place and has been in place for all of this time not working? Making the system accountable is not as overwhelming as it sounds. Parents should not be reluctant to call the local, state, and federal departments of education and report violations. We cannot emphasize enough the importance of building strength in numbers and using that strength to send a loud message to Congress that we want IDEA and its subsequent amendments fully implemented. In the absence of adequate federal oversight, each and every parent must be vigilant in ensuring that his or her child is educated in the least restrictive environment. We must be resolute enough to take the next bold step of initiating a lawsuit against the U.S. Department of Education for failure to ensure implementation of IDEA and its amendments.

CONCLUSION

Changes for people with disabilities are taking place all over the country. Increasing numbers of parents, educators, and advocates are committed to full participation and citizenship for people with disabilities. This Pandora's Box was opened in 1975, and we will never go back. Parents can take heart from the progress—though slow, people with disabilities are moving ahead. The pace of progress will increase as parents become aware of the power they possess by connecting their sons and daughters to family and community and by becoming aware of the political pitfalls that can impede their progress. As Corey Moore (1992), a national leader and parent of a child with disabilities, observed,

> I see a bureaucracy as a sleeping elephant. You try pushing him from behind and he doesn't budge. You pull on his trunk and he stays asleep. But there is another way to wake the elephant and that is to be a buzzing mosquito, relentless in your direct attack. Sooner or later, that elephant of bureaucracy may just move.

Each parent can make a difference for his or her child. Our allies are everywhere. It is up to us to use them.

REFERENCES

Akerley, M.S. (1985). False gods and angry prophets. In H.R. Turnbull & A.P. Turnbull (Eds.), *Parents speak out then and now* (pp. 23–31). Columbus: Charles E. Merrill.

Blatt, B., & Kaplan, F. (1967). *Christmas in purgatory.* Boston: Allyn & Bacon.

Cook, T. (1990). The Americans with Disabilities Act: The move to integration. *Temple Law Review, 64,* pp. 393–469.

Education for All Handicapped Children Act of 1975, PL 94-142. (August 23, 1977). Title 20, U.S.C. 1401 et seq: *U.S. Statutes at Large, 100,* 1145–1177.

Individuals with Disabilities Education Act of 1990 (IDEA), PL 101-476. (October 30, 1990). Title 20, U.S.C. 1400 et seq: *U.S. Statutes at Large, 104,* 1103–1151.

Individuals with Disabilities Education Act Amendments of 1991, PL 102-119. (October 7, 1991). Title 20, U.S.C. 1400 et seq: *U.S. Statutes at Large, 105,* 587–608.

Lutfiyya, Z.M. (1990). *Affectionate bonds: What we can learn from listening to friends.* Syracuse, NY: Center on Human Policy, Syracuse University.

Maryland Coalition for Integrated Education. (1991). *Achieving inclusion through the IEP process.* Hanover, MD: Author.

Moore, C. (1992, February). *From a parent's point of view.* Address to U.S. Department of Education Office of Special Education Programs, Washington, DC.

Schaffner, C.B., & Buswell, B.E. (1991). *Opening doors: Strategies for including all students in regular education.* Colorado Springs, CO: PEAK Parent Center, Inc.

Schaffner, C.B., & Buswell, B.E. (1992). *Connecting students.* Colorado Springs, CO: PEAK Parent Center, Inc.

Schulz, J.B. (1985). Growing up together. In H.R. Turnbull & A.P. Turnbull (Eds.), *Parents speak out then and now* (pp. 11–20). Columbus: Charles E. Merrill.

Sommerstein, L.C. (1994, November). *Curriculum adaptations/classroom modifications.* Paper presented at The Launching The Dream Conference, Rochester, New York.

The ARC's Report Card on including children with mental retardation in regular education. (1992, October). *The Arc.*

U.S. Department of Education. (1991). *Thirteenth annual report to Congress on the implementation of the individuals with disabilities education act.* Washington, DC: Author.

U.S. Department of Education. (1993). *Fifteenth annual report to Congress on the implementation of the individuals with disabilities education act.* Washington, DC: Author.

Wessels, M.R. (1992). Building community support for restructuring. In R.A. Villa, J.S. Thousand, W. Stainback, & S. Stainback (Eds.), *Restructuring for caring and effective education: An administrative guide to creating heterogeneous schools* (pp. 285–297). Baltimore: Paul H. Brookes Publishing Co.

26

Concluding Remarks

Concerns About Inclusion

Susan Stainback and William Stainback

THE CONTRIBUTING AUTHORS to this volume have discussed theoretical arguments as well as practical strategies for restructuring schools so that the needs of all students can be met within a single inclusive system of education. The authors of each chapter have presented pieces of this vision. Together, they have identified specific ways in which school personnel can collaborate with each other, foster friendships among students, implement classroom instructional strategies that enhance the learning of all students, and address behavioral concerns.

However, in the professional literature there have been concerns and reservations expressed about inclusion and the restructuring of schools. In this final chapter, we address some of those major concerns.

IT SHOULD NOT BE DONE

When racial integration in the schools began in the 1950s, there were numerous rationales given as to why it was not a good idea or would not work: Black students will be rejected by white teachers and students; it's not in their best interest; the schools are not ready; we need more analysis and study; and it's a communist plot. The justifications that have been offered (e.g., Fuchs & Fuchs, 1994; Kauffman, 1989; Kauffman, Lloyd, Baker, & Riedel, 1995; Vergason & Anderegg, 1989) for continuing to place students with disabilities into segregated special classes and schools are also numerous. A few examples are the following: Regular education is not prepared; integration is a plot to reduce funds to students with disabilities; there is a need for further analysis and study; we need to maintain a continuum of services; students with disabilities need special treatments and interventions; and educational achievement is more important than placement.

But none of these arguments can really justify segregating students with disabilities or any other students from the mainstream of school and community life. An analogy may make this point clearer.

> At the time of the American Civil War, should Abraham Lincoln have asked to see the scientific evidence on the benefits of ending slavery? Should he have consulted with "the expert," perhaps a sociologist, an economist, a political scientist? Of course not. Slavery is not now, and was not then, an issue for science. It is a moral issue. But, just for a moment, suppose that an economist had been able to demonstrate that Blacks would suffer economically, as would the entire South, from emancipation. Would that justify keeping slavery? And suppose a political scientist had argued that Blacks had no experience with democracy, they were not ready for it. Would that have justified extending slavery? Or imagine that a sociologist could have advised Lincoln against abolishing slavery on the grounds that it would destroy the basic social structure of Southern plantations, towns, and cities. All of the arguments might have seemed "true." But could they really justify slavery? Of course not. Slavery has no justification. (Biklen, 1985, pp. 16–17)

Although arguments can be made about Lincoln's motivation and that the abolition of slavery did not actually occur until the 13th Amendment became law, the above analogy nevertheless points out that some things are simply morally and ethically wrong. Those parents, professionals, politicians, and community members who have entered the struggle for the inclusion of all students into the educational mainstream have made a value judgment that integrated education is the best and most humane way to proceed. From their perspective, the point just made about slavery also applies to current segregationist practices in schools throughout America. If we want an integrated society in which all persons are considered to be of equal worth and to have equal rights, segregation in the schools cannot be justified. No defensible excuses or rationales can be offered and no amount of scientific research can be conducted that can, in the final analysis, justify segregation. Segregation has no justification. As Gilhool (1976) noted: "Separation is repugnant to our constitutional tradition. Integration is a central constitutional value—not integration that denies difference, but, rather, integration that accommodates difference; appreciates it and celebrates it" (p. 8).

IT CANNOT BE DONE

Some educators believe that integration simply cannot be done (e.g., Lieberman, in press). However, growing numbers of people are convinced that it is possible to educate all students in the mainstream of America's schools, provided that the mainstream is sensitive to individual differences and teachers and students are provided adequate support and assistance. The reason is that integration is being successfully implemented in some schools in the United States, Canada, Italy, and a number of other countries (see Falvey, 1995; Thousand, Villa, & Nevin, 1994; York, Kronberg, & Doyle, 1995). Basically, these schools have identified appropriate but challenging goals in the mainstream for students with diverse needs rather then required them all to learn exactly the same things or always function at the same level of proficiency as their peers. These schools also have worked to provide teachers and students the support and assistance they need to make successful inclusion a reality. See the chapters in this book and Falvey (1995), Stainback and Stainback (1992), and York, Kronberg, and Doyle (1995) for a review of specific and practical procedures schools have used to make inclusive education a reality for all students.

It will, however, be difficult to achieve success on a widespread basis if, as a society, we are unwilling to 1) provide each student the support necessary for him or her to be educated in the mainstream; and 2) adapt and adjust, when necessary, the mainstream to accommodate all students. The key to successful inclusion is our willingness to visualize, work for, and achieve a mainstream that is adaptive to and supportive of everyone. Few people, including those labeled as having disabilities, want to be in a mainstream that does not meet their needs or make them feel welcome and secure. Thus, it is essential that we make the mainstream flexible and sensitive to the unique needs of each student and that we foster friendships for students who lack friends in the mainstream. This is why restructuring is so critical. Through restructuring, the literally billions of dollars now spent on segregated special education programs and the hundreds of thousands of educators now working in segregated special settings could be integrated into general education to help the mainstream become supportive, flexible, and adaptive to the individual needs of all students.

CONCLUSION

Finally, it should be emphasized that saying that restructuring can be done is not the same as saying it is easy to do. Segregation has been practiced for centuries, and there are entrenched attitudes, laws, policies, and educational structures that work against achieving inclusion of all students on a widespread basis. In addition, because a second system of education (i.e., "special" education) has operated for so long, many schools unfortunately do not know at the present time how to design and modify curricula and instructional programs to meet diverse student needs; deal with difficult behaviors; and provide the tools, techniques, and supports some students need to be successful in the mainstream. Thus, achieving the inclusion of all students is a very challenging undertaking. However, the goal of having inclusive schools where everyone belongs, has friends, and is provided appropriate educational programs and supports is far too important not to accept the challenge.

If inclusion is truly valued, "Does mainstreaming work? is a silly question... Where it is not working, we should be asking what is preventing it from working and what can be done about it" (Bogdan, 1983, p. 427).

REFERENCES

Biklen, D. (1985). *Achieving the complete school.* New York: Columbia University Press.
Bogdan, R. (1983). "Does mainstreaming work?" is a silly question. *Phi Delta Kappan, 64,* 427–428.

Falvey, M. (Ed.). (1995). *Inclusive and heterogeneous schooling: Assessment, curriculum and instruction.* Baltimore: Paul H. Brookes Publishing Co.

Fuchs, D., & Fuchs, L. (1994). Inclusive schools movement and the radicalization of special education reform. *Exceptional Children, 60*(4), 294–309.

Gilhool, M. (1976). Changing public policies. In M. Reynolds (Ed.), *Mainstreaming* (pp. 8–13). Reston, VA: Council for Exceptional Children.

Kauffman, J. (1989). The regular education initiative as Reagan-Bush education policy: A trickle down theory of the hard-to-teach. *Journal of Special Education, 23,* 256–279.

Kauffman, J., Lloyd, J., Baker, J., & Riedel, T. (1995). Inclusion of all students with emotional and behavioral disorders? Let's think again. *Phi Delta Kappan, 76*(7), 542–546.

Lieberman, L. (in press). Preserving special education...for those who need it. In W. Stainback & S. Stainback (Eds.), *Controversial issues confronting special education: Divergent perspectives* (2nd ed.). Boston: Allyn & Bacon.

Stainback, S., & Stainback, W. (Eds.). (1992). *Curriculum considerations in inclusive classrooms: Facilitating learning for all students.* Baltimore: Paul H. Brookes Publishing Co.

Thousand, J.S., Villa, R.A., & Nevin, A.I. (Eds.). (1994). *Creativity and collaborative learning: A practical guide to empowering students and teachers.* Baltimore: Paul H. Brookes Publishing Co.

Vergason, G., & Anderegg, M. (1989). Bah, humbug, an answer to Stainback & Stainback. *Journal of The Association for Persons with Severe Handicaps, 15*(11), 8–10.

York, J. Kronberg, R., & Doyle, M. (1995). *Creating inclusive school communities: A staff development series for general and special educators.* Baltimore: Paul H. Brookes Publishing Co.

Index

Page numbers followed by "f" or "t" indicate figures or tables, respectively.